Viewpoints

Seventh Edition

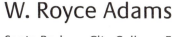

Readings Worth Thinking and Writing About

W. Royce Adams

Santa Barbara City College, Emeritus

WADSWORTH
CENGAGE Learning™

Australia • Brazil • Japan • Korea • Mexico • Singapore • Spain •
United Kingdom • United States

WADSWORTH
CENGAGE Learning™

Viewpoints: Readings Worth Thinking and Writing About, Seventh Edition
W. Royce Adams

Director Developmental English & College Success: Annie Todd

Assistant Editor: Janine Tangney

Assistant Editor: Daisuke Yasutake

Editorial Assistant: Melanie Opacki

Media Editor: Emily Ryan

Marketing Manager: Kirsten Stoller

Marketing Coordinator: Ryan Ahern

Marketing Communications Manager: Talia Wise

Content Project Manager: Corinna Dibble

Art Director: Marissa Falco

Print Buyer: Marcia Locke

Senior Rights Acquisition Account Manager Text: Katie Huha

Rights Acquisition Account Manager Image: Jennifer Meyer Dare

Image Researcher: Bruce Carson

Production Service: Carlisle Publishing Services

Text Designer: [TO COME]

Cover Designer: [TO COME]

Cover Image: [TO COME]

Compositor: Carlisle Publishing Services

For product information and technology assistance, contact us at
Cengage Learning Customer & Sales Support, 1-800-354-9706

For permission to use material from this text or product, submit all requests online at
www.cengage.com/permissions.
Further permissions questions can be emailed to
permissionrequest@cengage.com.

Library of Congress Control Number: 2008941344
ISBN-13: 978-0-547-18279-7
ISBN-10: 0-547-18279-1

Wadsworth
20 Channel Center Street
Boston, MA 02210
USA

Cengage Learning products are represented in Canada by Nelson Education, Ltd.

For your course and learning solutions, visit
www.cengage.com.

Purchase any of our products at your local college store or at our preferred online store
www.ichapters.com.

Printed in the U.S.A.
2 3 4 5 6 7 13 12 11 10

Contents

◩   Indicates pairs of essays with opposing viewpoints.

PART 2 Readings Worth Thinking and Writing About   79

CHAPTER 3 Viewpoints on Acquiring Knowledge   80

CHAPTER 7 Viewpoints on Family and Marital Relationships   272

Rhetorical Table of Contents

Since few, if any, essays serve as exact models for one particular rhetorical mode, reading selections containing paragraph examples of several modes appear under more than one category.

Description

Narration

Analysis

Illustration and Example

Division and Classification

Comparison and Contrast

Definition

Preface

This Seventh Edition of *Viewpoints: Readings Worth Thinking and Writing About* continues to provide a thematic collection of readings for students who have difficulty writing compositions. Designed to help students understand the relationship between reading and writing skills, the Seventh Edition explains what an essay is, how it is constructed, as well as what to look for when they read. The reading selections contain a variety of writing styles and ideas selected to provoke student thinking and emotion that we hope will lead to thoughtful student class discussions and essays.

Overview of the Readings and Writings

Chapters 1 and 2 make up **Part 1, Viewpoints on Reading and Writing Essays**, offering an overview of the skills required for thoughtful reading and writing. Chapter 1 covers the basic structure of an essay, its thesis, and various rhetorical modes of support. It also discusses how reading comprehension can be aided by separating main ideas from supporting points, distinguishing fact from opinion, and drawing inferences. Marking and note taking suggestions are offered along with advice for writing summaries of readings. Students are encouraged to keep a reading journal and to develop their vocabulary by learning unfamiliar words used in assigned essays. A major goal of this text is to show students how to approach and understand, rather than avoid, what may appear to be a difficult reading selection. Inexperienced readers, if taught well, can respond positively to the challenge of material often considered too difficult.

Chapter 2 draws on the information provided in Chapter 1, strengthening students' understanding of the connections between reading and writing by presenting three stages of writing: prewriting, drafting, and revising. Chapter 2 teaches students that writing is not a linear process but a recursive one in which prewriting, drafting, and revising recur throughout. Students are shown how to make a writing assignment their own; find and develop a working thesis; arrange supporting evidence; and revise, edit, and proofread their way to a final draft. To illustrate this, each stage of the writing process from brainstorming to final draft is presented visually. In addition, paragraph rhetorical patterns are explained as aids to both reading and writing. References and reviews of the contents of the first two chapters should be made throughout the course to remind students of the skills they should develop both in reading and writing.

The Readings

Part 2, Readings Worth Thinking and Writing About, Chapters 3–10, contains eight thematically organized reading chapters. Of the 65 reading selections in

Viewpoints, 35 of them are new to this edition. Each chapter is theme-based, covering viewpoints such as how we acquire knowledge; human behavior; cultural differences; social concerns; family and marital relationships; work; media and technology; and human rights. The reading selections come from a wide range of sources to provide a variety in style and thought and do not have to be assigned in any particular order. Each chapter contains readings with opposing views on the chapter's theme. Exposing students to viewpoints worth reading and thinking about takes precedence over organizing essays by rhetorical modes. A rhetorical table of contents is provided for instructors who prefer to approach the readings in that order. Except for Chapter 10, a student essay is provided in each chapter to illustrate the way some students make an essay their own. Both early drafts and finished student essays are used to help the instructor illustrate specific writing problems and effective revision approaches.

Apparatus

Each chapter in Part 2 opens with suggestions for a prewriting assignment that asks students to focus on the theme of the chapter, along with a brief introduction to the chapter's theme. Prior to each reading, and reinforcing information from Chapter 1, students are asked to take a minute or two to look over the essay and answer a few pre-reading questions, as well as look over the vocabulary list taken from the reading selection to help focus their attention on the topic. Following each reading selection are four sets of questions: "Understanding the Content," "Looking at Structure and Style," "Evaluating the Author's Viewpoints," and "Pursuing Possible Essay Topics." To answer the questions in the exercises, students must draw upon the information they have learned in Part 1 about reading and writing.

Chapters 3–10 each end with a section "Viewpoints on Images" featuring a photo and a question that asks students to write a response after viewing the photo carefully. These exercises are designed to help students see how concepts and ideas can be presented visually. Also ending each of these chapters is an "On the Net" section which asks students to explore and do research on the Internet. Doing so can provide students with further and more current information about the subject or theme they plan to use for an essay of their own.

In addition to the 35 new reading selections, all the photos used are new. Also new to this edition is the inclusion of short biographical information about the authors along with the source of the reading selection. Some of the citations in the Appendix have been updated as appropriate.

The accompanying Instructor's Manual (IM) offers suggestions for using the readings. The IM, which is available only online, calls attention to readings that work well in pairs and commentaries on each of the chapters and individual reading selections that may help the instructor decide which selections to assign and in which order.

More than 2,000 self-paced exercises in grammar, punctuation, and mechanics, as well as diagnostic tests with helpful assessment tools, are available through the WriteSpace Online Writing Program. More than 75 guided writing modules (tutorials) can be used for homework or independent review to meet individual student needs.

Acknowledgments

The Seventh Edition owes a great deal to the following reviewers:

Alette W. Corley of Bethune-Cookman University

Jessica Datema of Bergen Community College

Robin Griffin of Truckee Meadows Community College

Catherine S. Hewlette of Craven Community College

Caroline Mains of Palo Alto College

Pat McCurdy of Cayuga Community College

Kathryn McGrath of Bergen Community College

J. Michael Moran of St. Philip's College

Karen D. Nelson of Craven Community College

Andi Penner of San Juan College

Jenia Walter of San Juan College

It is always gratifying when a text is considered worthy of another edition. Thanks must go to users of the previous editions. For this Seventh Edition, acknowledgment and appreciation is given to Maggie Barbieri for her work on the apparatus. Special thanks are also extended to the Cengage Learning editorial, production, and marketing team: Annie Todd, Kirsten Stoller, Corinna Dibble, Janine Tangney, and Daisuke Yasutake.

W. Royce Adams
Santa Barbara, California

PART 1

Viewpoints on Reading and Writing Essays

CHAPTER 1

Viewpoints on Reading Essays

Topics in This Chapter

Research shows that unless we keep notes and regularly review them, we will forget over 80 percent of what we learn within two weeks. Considering the time, energy, and money you put into learning, that's a big waste. For this class, a good way to make certain that you don't lose what you have read and studied is to keep some type of reading journal. To help you get into the "journal habit," this book periodically directs you to stop reading and to make various types of journal entries. The following are some suggestions for keeping a reading journal.

Keeping a Reading Journal

As a companion to your textbook, buy an 8½-by-11 spiral notebook to use only for this class. It should be used for three basic purposes: (1) keeping **notes** of the key points made in Part 1; (2) recording any **reactions, reflections,** or **questions** you may have regarding what you read; and (3) writing **summaries** of the essays you read in Part 2. Later in this chapter you will learn how to write summaries. Of course, anything else you want to keep in your journal, such as vocabulary words you want to learn or ideas for possible essays, is up to you. Keeping a journal for this class is not "busy work." It's a vital part of the learning process, and you'll find that you get much more from this class by keeping a journal than you might think.

Reading Essays

Take a minute to look at the table of contents in this book. Notice that the reading selections in Part 2 are grouped into chapters based on themes such as learning, human behavior, cultural heritage, family, and so on. Each chapter contains several readings expressing various viewpoints on that theme. The readings will provide you with (1) information on the theme, (2) ideas for possible essays of your own, (3) examples of ways to write essays, and (4) practice in developing your reading versatility.

In most chapters, you will find that authors' viewpoints on certain themes are different and frequently conflict with each other. Some essays are longer than others, some better written than others, some more interesting to you than others. You will also discover as you read that there are many different styles of writing. But despite these differences, all essays share three particular features: a thesis or point the author wants to make about a subject, support for that thesis, and a logical arrangement of that support. This section shows you what to look for when you read essays; how to look more closely at the methods writers use to express their opinions, feelings, and experiences; and more detailed information on keeping a reading journal.

The Structure of an Essay

Not all essays are structured the same way. Some essays use what might be called the traditional form: the thesis or point the author wants to make appears in the first paragraph (the beginning), several paragraphs are used to develop or support that point (the middle), and the last paragraph draws a conclusion or summarizes the support used (the end). Many instructors use this basic form to teach beginning writers the essay structure.

In reality, essays don't always follow that form. Some writers may choose to withhold their main idea until the last paragraph, building up to the point they want to make. Some essays may begin with an anecdote or a story that consumes several paragraphs before the point is made. In some cases, the point is never stated directly in words, but instead is implied through what the writer says. As a reader, you will see the variety of forms used when you read the essays in Part 2. As a beginning writer, you may be asked to work on developing essays using the more traditional approach until you are able to break away from the mold.

Regardless of its form or style, an essay contains the three basic ingredients mentioned earlier: a thesis, either stated or implied; sufficient support for that thesis; and a logic behind the arrangement of that support. As a good reader, you need to identify these ingredients and understand how they function as a whole, no matter what the structure of the essay might be.

Thesis

Every good essay has a **thesis,** which is the main idea or point an author wants to make about a topic. The **topic** of an essay is a broad or general subject, such as smoking among teenagers. A thesis, on the other hand, is the point the author wants to make about the subject. On the subject of smoking among teenagers, a thesis might be, "The increase in teenage smoking, despite the evidence that smoking causes cancer, is due to advertising directed at teenagers," or "The claim that teenage smoking is on the rise is exaggerated." In other words, a thesis is what the author thinks or feels about the subject of the essay. It's the purpose for writing, the main point around which everything else is written. If you fail to recognize an author's thesis, you may miss the whole point of the essay.

To help clarify the difference between a topic and a thesis, look at the examples below. Notice that topics are broad, general categories, whereas thesis statements are more specific.

Topic	Possible Thesis Statements
religion	The use of the Bible to swear in a witness at court trials actually establishes religion and is therefore unconstitutional.
	Recent biblical research, such as the translation of the Book of Q, suggests that Jesus was not the Messiah, but rather a roving sage who preached acceptance of one's fellow human beings.
marriage and family	Gay marriages should be legally recognized as long as the couple abides by the rules of love, to honor

and cherish, through sickness and in health, for better or for worse.

Evidence suggests that one of the important causes of social problems today is the absence of fathers from the lives of many children.

animal rights   Animal rights should not take priority over research experiments that fulfill human needs.

When millions of animals die for such frivolous reasons as the testing of new cosmetics, shampoos, household cleaners, and radiator fluids when safe products already exist, we've gone too far.

Notice that in each case the thesis statement is a viewpoint about the subject or topic. The thesis deals with a narrower view of the broader subject and makes the author's position clear. You may not agree with the viewpoint, but if the essay is well written, it will support the author's opinion and cause you to evaluate your own viewpoint. A key element in reading, then, is to make certain that you understand an author's thesis or viewpoint on the subject of the essay.

Below are some thesis statements. Separate the topic from the writer's viewpoint. In the space provided, write two phrases, one explaining the topic and the other explaining the point being made about the topic.

1. A college education may be important, but its value is overemphasized by many employers.

    topic: _____

    viewpoint: _____

2. A good divorce is better for children than a bad marriage.

    topic: _____

    viewpoint: _____

3. Our society seems afraid or ashamed of growing old and places too much emphasis on youth.

    topic: _____

    viewpoint: _____

4. Most of the suggestive visuals shown on MTV distract from the music and subliminally brainwash the viewer.

    topic: _____

    viewpoint: _____

Compare the content of your phrases with the following chart:

Topic	Viewpoint Expressed
1. college education	value overemphasized by employers
2. divorce	children better off than in a bad marriage
3. aging	ashamed/afraid of aging, too much value placed on youth
4. MTV visuals	distract from music and subliminally brainwash

Thesis statements are usually clearly stated within the essay; often you can find a sentence or two that directly states the author's views. At other times, no one sentence states the thesis, but instead the author's viewpoint becomes clear once you have read the supporting evidence. In those cases, it's necessary to form the author's thesis in your own words.

Writing Exercise

In your reading journal or on a separate sheet of paper, write today's date and the page numbers you just read. In a paragraph, explain the difference between an essay thesis and a topic. Provide two examples of each.

Supporting Evidence

Once a writer has a thesis in mind, the next step is to provide **supporting evidence.** If a thesis is controversial, such as whether or not abortion should be legal, then the writer must provide evidence that will at least cause someone who disagrees to look at abortion from a new angle. As a reader, you need to look for the reasons given to support the thesis. You may still disagree with the author when you have finished reading, but you will understand why the author feels as he or she does.

Of course, you have to be careful that your own feelings or bias on the subject don't cause you to reject or accept the author's viewpoints without thinking carefully about the evidence presented. Let's say you or your family members have participated in antiabortion protests. Because of your close involvement, you immediately resent or reject the thesis that abortion should be legal. Your own bias or prejudice (feelings that keep you from seeing another view) could cause you to miss some valid points that you had not considered before, points that might help you understand another person's viewpoint. You still might not change your mind, but it's important to keep an open mind as you read supporting evidence.

In essays, support is given in the form of paragraphs. A paragraph is in some ways similar to a mini-essay. Just as every essay has an implied or stated thesis, a well-written paragraph has an implied or stated **topic sentence.** A topic sentence states the key point or idea of the paragraph. The rest of the sentences support it, just as paragraphs support a thesis.

Good writers use a variety of paragraph types to support their thesis statements. These types are sometimes called **rhetorical modes or patterns.** Because humans think in certain basic ways, we can sometimes communicate better with one another if we use these thinking patterns in our writing. Eight common patterns are presented here.

Description: When authors want to reach one or all of our five senses—sight, sound, smell, touch, and taste—they use description. See if you can visualize what's being described in this paragraph:

> Unable to pay city taxes or incapable of influencing the city to live up to its duty to serve all citizens, the poorer barrio families remain trapped in the nineteenth century and survive the best they can. The backyards have well-worn paths to the outhouses, which sit near the alley. Running water is considered a luxury in some parts of the barrio. Decent drainage is usually unknown, and when it rains, the water stands for days, an incubator of health hazards and an avoidable nuisance. Streets, costly to pave, remain rocky trails. Tires do not last long, and the constant rattling and shaking grind away a car's life and spread dust through screen windows.
>
> —Robert Ramirez, "The Barrio"

Even though there is no stated topic sentence in the paragraph, it is not difficult for us to understand the point the author wants to make about the poorer barrio communities. The city does not live up to its duty to all citizens in the barrio, resulting, we are shown, in "trapped" families using "well-worn paths to the outhouses" where "running water is a luxury." Standing rainwater becomes an "incubator of health hazards." Cars wear out fast because of the unpaved, rocky roads. The author relies on our reactions to his description to imply (suggest or hint at) his message.

Narration: Authors often use narration when they want to tell a story or relate an anecdote about something that has happened in their lives. A paragraph using narration moves from one occurrence to another, generally in chronological order and often in the first person. Here's an example of first-person narration:

> In 1985, I gave up my performing artist aspiration, bet it all on my song writing and moved cold to music row, Nashville. After four years as a

$150-to-$200-a-week staff writer for a large publishing company and (still) a club and studio musician, I got the validation I had been working and praying for—a hit single. The week it made the top 10, my wife of 14 years asked for a divorce. We split the 40K (before taxes) that the song had earned, and I pressed on, now 41 years old. I kept my kids half the time, got a gig on the Grand Ole Opry, played guitar on recording sessions and kept trying to become a better writer.

—Bob Regan, "Freeloaders"

Here the author uses first-person narration, which means that he tells us his story from his own point of view. He takes us chronologically from the time he gave up being a performing artist and moved to Nashville. Then he takes us through the major events of his life from that point on. As readers, we can expect that the writer will continue in a chronological fashion, moving from one incident to the next, until he gets to the major point of his essay. No one sentence in the paragraph can be called the topic sentence, but we can infer from what he says that making a living in the music world is not always easy.

Analysis: An author may wish to take a subject and examine its parts. For example, a writer could analyze a poem by looking at the way it is structured, examining the number of lines and stanzas, identifying the rhyme scheme, or weighing the reasons behind the use of certain words. Another author may wish to show how a rotary engine works, which would be called a **process analysis,** a step-by-step explanation of the way the engine works. A paragraph based on an analysis pattern reads like this:

An algorithm is a step-by-step procedure for solving a problem in a finite amount of time. When you start your car, you go through a step-by-step procedure. First, you insert the key. Second, you make sure the transmission is in neutral or park. Third, you depress the gas pedal. Fourth, you turn the key to the start position. If the engine starts within a few seconds, you then release the key to the ignition position. If the engine doesn't start, you wait ten seconds and repeat steps three through six. Finally, if the car doesn't start, you call the garage.

—Nell Dale, *Programming in Pascal*

The paragraph begins analyzing or explaining the process in chronological order. As a reader, we can follow each of the steps. In this case, the process can be told in one paragraph. If the process were more complex, each step in the process might require a paragraph or more to elaborate.

Illustration and example: If you are explaining something to someone who doesn't quite understand, you might say, "For example", and then proceed to give an example or two to clarify what you mean. The same technique is used in writing. Notice how "example" is used here to help define critical thinking:

In the broadest terms, critical thinking refers to an ability to evaluate, compare, analyze, critique, and synthesize information. Critical thinkers are willing to ask hard questions and challenge conventional wisdom.

For example, many people believe that punishment (spanking) is a good way to reinforce learning in children. A critical thinker would immediately ask: "Does punishment work? If so, when? Under what conditions does it not work? What are the drawbacks? Are there better ways to guide learning?"
    —Dennis Coon, *Introduction to Psychology: Gateways to Mind and Behavior*

The first sentence is the topic sentence, defining critical thinking in the broadest terms. In order to explain what one must do to think critically and ask hard questions, the author gives examples of the type of questions a critical reader would ask if he or she were told that spanking is a good way to reinforce learning.

Notice that the **transitional phrase** "for example" alerts us to what is coming. Transitional expressions such as *for instance, also, likewise, in addition, furthermore,* and *more than that* alert us that more examples of the same idea are about to be presented. Words such as *but, however, although,* and *rather* should make us aware that a point is about to be modified or contrasted. When we read *consequently, so, therefore, in conclusion, thus,* or *as a result,* we know that we are about to get a summary or the conclusion of a point. An author's use of transitional words is of great help when we read. Remember to use them in your own writing.

Before learning about more paragraph patterns, read the paragraphs below. Underline the topic sentence of each paragraph, and then in the spaces provided, write the paragraph pattern being used and its purpose. Some paragraphs may use more than one pattern.

1. My rented H2 [Hummer] was a subtle gray, unobtrusive in the way Orsen Welles would be unobtrusive in a charcoal pinstriped suit. It was one obnoxious hunk of steel, plastic and wishful thinking. It was so big that you could measure it in hands, like a horse. I sat so high I was eye to eye with the driver of a cement-mixing truck. It was so tall that the antenna twanged like a guitar string against every beam in my underground garage. It had all the nimbleness of the Nimitz. It was so wide that I gave up trying to get a veggie burger at the Burger King drive-thru because I concluded "drive-thru" would mean "drive thru the back wall."
                                    —Pat Morrison, "It's Big, It's Thirsty,
                                    It's the Hummer—An American Excess Story"

pattern used: _____

purpose: _____

2. Americans, unlike people almost everywhere else in the world, tend to define and judge everybody in terms of the work they do, especially work performed for pay. Charlie is a doctor; Sam is a carpenter; Mary Ellen is a copywriter at a small ad agency.
                                    —Nickie McWhirter, "What You Do Is What You Are"

pattern used: _____

purpose: _____

3. Here is a four-step method to prevent your mind from wandering while reading. First, before you attempt to read anything, look over the length of the material to see whether or not you have the time to read it all; if not, mark a spot where you intend to stop. Second, read the title and the first paragraph, looking for the main idea of the content. Next, read the boldface headings, if there are any, and the first sentence of each paragraph. Finally, read the last paragraph, which probably contains a summary of the material. These steps condition your mind to accept the material you want to read and keep it from wandering.

—W. Royce Adams and Becky Patterson,
Developing Reading Versatility

pattern used: _____

purpose: _____

4. Grasp the cone with the right hand firmly but gently between the thumb and at least one but not more than three fingers, two-thirds of the way up the cone. Then dart swiftly away to an open area, away from the jostling crowd at the stand. Now take up the classic ice-cream-cone-eating stance: feet from one to two feet apart, body bent forward from the waist at a twenty-five-degree angle, right elbow well up, right forearm horizontal, at a level with your collarbone and about twelve inches from it. But don't start eating yet! Check first to see what emergency repairs may be necessary. Sometimes a sugar cone will be so crushed or broken or cracked that all one can do is gulp at the thing like a savage, getting what he can of it and letting the rest drop to the ground, and then evacuating the area of catastrophe as quickly as possible.

—L. Rust Hills, "How to Eat an Ice Cream Cone"

pattern used: _____

purpose: _____

Paragraph 1 uses description, told through first-person narration, to let us know that the author believes that the Hummer is "one obnoxious hunk of steel, plastic and wishful thinking." Paragraph 2 uses examples to support the topic sentence, which is the first one. The purpose is to show that Americans judge people by the work they do. Paragraph 3 uses process analysis. Its purpose is to show the four steps it takes to prepare yourself to read so that your mind won't wander while you are reading. Paragraph 4 also uses analysis. But unlike Paragraph 3, this paragraph does not give the number of steps, and there is no stated topic sentence.

Writing Exercise

In your reading journal or on a separate sheet of paper, write today's date and the page numbers you just read. Define "topic sentence." Then differentiate the four rhetorical modes or patterns you just read about and explain why understanding them can help you read or write better.

Division and/or classification: In order to make it easy for readers to understand information, writers can divide their topic into segments or they can use classification. Notice how the division and classification pattern is used in the opening paragraph below to discuss the topic of lying:

> St. Augustine identified eight kinds of lies, not all of them equally serious but all sins nonetheless. The number Mark Twain came up with, not too seriously, was 869. In practice, there are probably as many lies as there are liars, but lying can be roughly classified according to motive and context. No hard boundaries exist between these categories, since some lies are told for more than one purpose. Most lies fall within a spectrum of three broad categories.
>
> —Paul Gray, "Lies, Lies, Lies"

Notice that the author, after mentioning St. Augustine's and Mark Twain's number counts of the kinds of lies, states the belief that there are three categories of lies. We can assume that from this point on, the author will categorize the various types of lies into three divisions or classifications.

Comparison and contrast: An author uses this pattern to show similarities (comparisons) and differences (contrasts) in the subjects under discussion. Notice how comparison and contrast is used in the following paragraph:

> Television is very different now from what it was thirty years ago. It's *harder.* A typical episode of *Starsky and Hutch*, in the nineteen-seventies, followed an essentially linear path: two characters, engaged in a single story line, moving toward a decisive conclusion. To watch an episode of *Dallas* today is to be stunned by its glacial pace—by the arduous attempts to establish social relationships, by the excruciating simplicity of the plotline, by how *obvious* it was. A single episode of *The Sopranos*, by contrast, might follow five narrative threads, involving a dozen characters who weave in and out of the plot. Modern television also requires the viewer to do a lot of "filling in," as in a *Seinfeld* episode that subtly parodies the Kennedy assassination conspiracists, or a typical *Simpsons* episode, which may contain numerous allusions to politics or cinema or pop culture.
>
> —Malcolm Gladwell, "Brain Candy"

Here the author's topic sentence is the first sentence. To show the difference, he contrasts the popular television shows of the 1970s (*Starsky and Hutch* and *Dallas*) with the popular programs of today (*The Sopranos, Seinfeld,* and *Simpsons*). Notice that the author uses the phrase *by contrast.* Other key transitional words often used to show contrasts are *although, however, but, on the other hand, instead of, different from,* and *as opposed to.* Words often used to show comparison are *likewise, similarly, compared with, both/and,* and *in the same way.*

Definition: In order to clarify words and terms by providing more explanation than a dictionary, or to explain the writer's interpretation of something, a longer definition is sometimes needed. Frequently, examples and comparison or contrast are used to help define. Notice in the following example how the author defines the term *American dream:*

> First, let us get this [American] dream business—and business it now seems to be—straight. The word *dream* is not a synonym for *reality* or *promise.* It is closer to *hope* or *possibility* or even *vision.* The original American dream had only a little to do with material possessions and a lot to do with choices, beginnings and opportunity.
> —Betty Anne Younglove, "The American Dream"

Here the author is defining the term *American dream* as she sees it. By comparing and contrasting, she defines what it is and is not, implying that there is a new, incorrect definition that has more to do with materialism than its original, true meaning.

Cause and effect: Another writing pattern often used is cause and effect. This pattern is used when an author wants to show how one action or a series of actions causes something to happen or brings about results. For example, a bad cold (cause) can bring about a cough, a runny nose, and sneezing (effects). See if you can identify causes and effects in the following example.

> Our preference for our own thinking can prevent us from identifying flaws in our own ideas, as well as from seeing and building upon other people's insights. Similarly, our pride in our own religion can lead us to dismiss too quickly the beliefs and practices of other religions and ignore mistakes in our religious history. Our preference for our own political party can make us support inferior candidates and programs. Furthermore, our readiness to accept uncritically those who appeal to our preconceived notions leaves us vulnerable to those who manipulate us for their own purposes. Historians tell us that is precisely why Hitler succeeded in winning control of Germany and nearly conquering the world.
> —Vincent Ryan Ruggiero, *Beyond Feelings*

The author points out some causes and effects of being closed-minded in our thinking. A preference for our own thinking (cause) can keep us from profiting from other people's insights (effect). Pride in our religion (cause) can lead us to dismiss other beliefs and practices, and to ignore mistakes in our religious history (effect). Our preference for a political party (cause) can make us support inferior candidates and programs (effect). A readiness to accept uncritically those who appeal to our preconceived notions (cause) leaves us vulnerable to those who would manipulate us (effect). The first sentence is broad enough to serve as the topic sentence for the paragraph.

Some keywords that serve as clues to paragraphs using cause and effect are *because, because of this, for this reason, as a result,* and *resulting in.*

To make certain you can recognize the writing patterns you just learned about, read the following numbered paragraphs. Underline the topic sentence of each, and then in the spaces provided, write the paragraph pattern being used and its purpose. Some paragraphs may use more than one pattern.

1. If you're within a few miles of a nuclear detonation, you'll be incinerated on the spot! And if you survive the blast, what does the future promise? The silent but deadly radiation, either directly or from fallout, in a dose of 400 rems could kill you within two weeks. Your hair would fall out, your skin would be covered with large ulcers, you would vomit and experience diarrhea and you would die from infection or massive bleeding as your white blood cells and platelets stopped working.

—Ken Keyes, Jr., *The Hundredth Monkey*

pattern used: _____

purpose: _____

2. An inference is a statement *about* the unknown made on the basis of what *is* known. In other words, an inference is an educated guess. If a woman smiles when a man tells her she is attractive, he can infer she is pleased. If she frowns and slaps him, he can guess she is not pleased. His inferences are based on what is known: people generally smile when they are pleased and frown when displeased. However, to know for certain why she slapped him, we would have to ask her.

pattern used: _____

purpose: _____

3. What do L.A. [Los Angeles] women want? According to the poll, their top two goals in life are having a happy marriage, named by 37%, and helping others, 21%. Those are followed by career and a desire to be creative. Power and fame rank low on the list, with 1% each. But among women who've never been married, career takes top priority, followed by marriage and helping others. Four percent chose fame. A happy marriage appears to be the most popular goal in the Valley and Southeast areas, where it was chosen by 46% of the women—about double the number on the Westside.

—Cathleen Decker, "The L.A. Woman"

pattern used: _____

purpose: _____

4. Every paragraph you write should include one sentence that's supported by everything else in that paragraph. That is the topic sentence. It can be the first sentence, the last sentence, the sixth sentence, or even a sentence that exists only in your mind. When testing your article for topic sentences, you should be able to look at each paragraph and say what the topic sentence is. Having said it, look at all the other sentences in the paragraph and test them to make sure they support it.

—Gary Provost, "The 8 Essentials of Nonfiction That Sells"

pattern used: _____

purpose: _____

5. Even Pentagon planners are concerned that global climate change may reach a "tipping point," after which widespread drought would turn farmland into dust and forests to ash. Even without accelerated weather change, parts of the Great Plains and Midwest will become desert as the Ogallala aquifer further shrinks. In Appalachia, more mine waste will choke rivers below more decapitated mountaintops. The soil of California's San Joaquin Valley will be too polluted to grow food. There will be fewer wetlands and forests to sustain fewer species of birds, fish and mammals. By 2050, our children will pay dearly for scarce water as well as energy and food. Ditto for national security, because large parts of Africa and Asia will suffer great harm induced by global warming before we do.

—Yvon Chouinard, "Time's Up"

pattern used: _____

purpose: _____

6. "Not Invented Here" is an old problem at Sony. The Betamax videotape recorder failed in part because the company refused to cooperate with other companies. But in recent years the problem got worse. Sony was late in making flat-screen TVs and DVD recorders, because its engineers believed that, even though customers loved these devices, the available technologies were not up to Sony's standards. Sony's cameras and computers weren't compatible with the most popular form of memory, because Sony wanted people to use its overpriced Memory Sticks. Sony's online music service sold files in a Sony format. And Sony's digital music players didn't play MP3s, which is a big reason the iPod became the Walkman's true successor. Again and again, Sony's desire to control everything kept it from controlling anything.

—James Surowiecki, "All Together Now"

pattern used: _____

purpose: _____

Compare your responses to the paragraphs with these:

1. The topic sentence is the third one. The basic pattern is cause and effect, with description of the effects of the blast provided. The cause is the nuclear bomb, and the effect is death. The purpose is to show that you will die from radiation even if the initial blast doesn't kill you.

2. The first sentence is the topic sentence. The pattern is definition, with the example of the man and woman used to clarify the definition. The purpose is to define *inference*.

3. There really isn't a topic sentence. The implied topic sentence is an answer to the question that begins the paragraph, such as "Here is the result of the polls showing what L.A. women want." To show us what they want, the author uses the classification "L.A. women" and divides or groups them according to poll percentages. She further groups the women by areas: the Valley, the Southeast, and the Westside. The purpose is to reveal what L.A. women want, according to the polls.

4. The first sentence is the topic sentence. The author uses both definition and process analysis. He defines what a topic sentence is and its position in the paragraph. Then he shows how to test for an implied or directly stated topic sentence in each paragraph. The purpose is to stress the importance of the topic sentence in writing.

5. The topic sentence is the first one, setting the stage for what the future environment will be like if global warming continues. The paragraph then gives examples of the changes that global warming will lead to in the United States. In a sense, all of the examples show cause and effect. Global warming (cause) will have disastrous effects on our future.

6. The topic sentence is the last one. The paragraph contains examples, each one showing a cause and effect. For instance, the Betamax videotape recorder failed (effect) because the company refused to cooperate with other companies (cause). Sony was late in making flat-screen TVs and DVD recorders (effect) because its engineers thought the technologies were not up to Sony standards (cause). This serves as a good example of the use of a combination of patterns to help make a point.

Make certain that you understand what a topic sentence is and that you can recognize all eight paragraph patterns before reading on.

Writing Exercise

In your reading journal or on a separate sheet of paper, write today's date and the page numbers you just read. Define the four rhetorical modes or patterns you just read about, and explain why understanding them can help you read or write better.

Order of Support

The third ingredient of a well-structured essay, in addition to thesis and supporting evidence, is the **order or arrangement of the thesis and its supporting evidence.** A good writer will arrange the supporting points for the thesis in a logical, progressive order. What we see when we read an essay is the final product. What we *don't* see are the many different drafts that the writer wrote before deciding which supporting point should go where or which paragraph pattern of development worked best. As a writer, you will need to go through the same process of writing several drafts before deciding which one works best for your audience.

It would be convenient if all essays followed the same writing pattern, but it would also be boring. Part of the pleasure of reading is experiencing the various ways writers work with words and ideas. Still, many essays do follow the traditional form, shown in the diagram on the next page. Keep in mind, however, that longer essays may take two or three paragraphs rather than one to introduce their topic and thesis. Most of your student essay writing assignments will probably be short enough to allow you to follow this model.

The diagram on page 17 represents the basic structure of an essay. Longer essays will, of course, contain more paragraphs. Sometimes an author writes two or three paragraphs of introduction. There may be a dozen supporting paragraphs, and the conclusion may well take more than one paragraph. Sometimes an author's thesis may not be clear until the last paragraph. The typical essay form, however, is much the way it is outlined here, and the diagram probably represents the way your instructor wants you to construct essays in this course.

Before Going On

You have learned that three basic ingredients make up a good essay: a thesis, sufficient support of the thesis, and a logical order or arrangement of the supporting material. Good reading comprehension depends upon being able to identify an author's thesis based on the support that is provided. You have also learned eight different paragraph patterns or rhetorical modes that writers use to express their views: description, narration, analysis, illustration and example, definition, division and/or classification, comparison and contrast, and cause—effect relationships. Topic sentences are supported through the use of these patterns. In addition, you have learned the basic structure most essays follow to support the thesis. Applying this knowledge can enhance both your reading and your writing skills.

Introductory Paragraph

- attempts to draw the reader's interest.
- usually states or hints at the subject.
- sometimes states or hints at the thesis.

Paragraph 2

- usually builds on or continues what was said in the introductory paragraph.
- sometimes contains the thesis if it's not in the introductory paragraph.
- uses varying methods of development depending on what point is being made.

Paragraph 3

- is connected to paragraph 2 by a transition.
- provides more support of the thesis.
- uses varying methods of development depending on what works best to clarify the supporting point.

Paragraph 4 (plus more paragraphs if needed)

- starts with a transition from paragraph 3.
- provides more support of the thesis.
- uses varying methods of development depending on what best clarifies the point.

Concluding Paragraph

- summarizes the points made or draws a conclusion based on the points provided.
- leaves the reader thinking about or reacting to the thesis.

Writing Exercise

In your journal or on a separate sheet of paper, write a paragraph that defines the three basic elements that constitute a well-structured essay. Make certain that your paragraph has a topic sentence to support. Your instructor may want to see it.

Understanding the Content

Let's look now at the skills you need to better understand what you read. To get the most from your reading, you need to be able to separate main ideas from supporting details, to distinguish fact from opinion and bias, and to draw inferences from implied statements. As you read, all of these skills work together, but for clarification purposes we'll look at each skill separately.

Separating Main Ideas from Supporting Details

The main idea in an essay is the thesis, which we've already discussed on pages 4–6. As you've seen, each paragraph in an essay supports that main idea. You've also learned that each paragraph is, in a way, a mini-essay. Paragraphs, too, have a main idea, which is expressed through the topic sentence and supported by the rest of the sentences.

Read the following paragraph and underline what you think is the main idea. Determine what paragraph pattern is used.

> There are almost as many definitions of meditation as there are people meditating. It has been described as a fourth state of consciousness (neither waking, sleeping, nor dreaming); as a way to recharge one's inner batteries; as a state of passive awareness, of "no mind." Some teachers regard meditation as the complement to prayer: "Prayer is when you talk to God; meditation is when you listen to God." Some say meditation teaches the conscious mind to be still.
>
> —Diana Robinson, "Recharging Yourself Through Meditation"

The point of the paragraph is to show that there are many definitions of meditation. Each of the supporting sentences provides an example of a different definition of meditation to show just how varied they are. An outline of the paragraph might look like this:

Main idea:	"There are almost as many definitions of meditation as there are people meditating."
Support:	one definition: fourth state of consciousness (neither waking, sleeping, nor dreaming)
Support:	second definition: recharging one's batteries
Support:	third definition: state of passive awareness, no mind

Support:	fourth definition: complement to prayer
Support:	fifth definition: teaches mind to be still

What we see are five different definitions that support the statement made in the first sentence. The first sentence, then, is the topic sentence.

Looking for the main idea in the first sentence of a paragraph is a good place to begin, but as you've already seen, it doesn't always appear there. Read the following paragraph and then underline the main idea:

> In one year, about $3.5 billion is spent for television commercial time. Where does all this money come from, and where does it go? Suppose Ford Motor Company buys $1 million worth of air time from NBC to introduce its new models in the fall. First it hires an advertising agency to actually produce the commercials. Of the $1 million, 15% goes to the agency for its services, and 85% goes to the network. The network in turn uses some of its 85% to pay program costs and some to pay the local stations that broadcast the shows on which Ford commercials are carried. This latter payment usually equals about one-third of the local station's base rate (the amount a station would receive for commercial time bought by a local advertiser).

In the above paragraph, the first sentence does *not* state the main idea. Most of the paragraph provides an example of what would happen to one million dollars spent by the Ford Motor Company on television advertising. The example is used to provide a breakdown of where the money spent on television advertising comes from and where it goes, providing an answer to the question in the second sentence of the paragraph: "Where does all this money [$3.5 billion spent on TV advertising] come from, and where does it go?" In a way, then, the main idea is really a combination of the first two sentences of the paragraph. An outline of the paragraph might look something like this:

Main idea:	Here's an example of where the $3.5 billion a year spent on advertising comes from and where it goes.
Support:	If Ford Motor Company spent $1 million on TV ads:

1. 15% would go to an advertising agency
2. 85% would go to the network, which would pay
   a. program costs
   b. local stations that broadcast the shows on which ads appear (about one-third of the local station's base advertising rate)

In this paragraph, then, there is no one topic sentence expressing the main idea, but by combining the first two sentences, we can form a topic sentence of our own.

Here is another paragraph. Underline what you think is the main idea.

> The Upjohn Company is studying anti-cholesterol therapy that would actually reverse some coronary artery injury. It is also doing some exciting

research in combating hypertension. In addition, it is working on important advances against deadly heart arrhythmias, or irregular heartbeat rhythms, plus a new way to zero in on blood clots with fewer side effects. These are just a few of the research projects against heart disease that Upjohn is working on.

The main idea in the paragraph appears in the last sentence. It sums up the purpose of each of the other sentences—to provide examples of the research projects Upjohn is working on in the area of heart disease. An outline of the paragraph might look like this:

Main idea:	Here are a few examples of Upjohn's research projects against heart disease.
Support:	anti-cholesterol therapy to reverse coronary artery injury
Support:	ways to combat hypertension
Support:	advances against heartbeat irregularities (arrhythmias)
Support:	ways to treat blood clots with fewer side effects

Thus, we see that it doesn't matter where a topic sentence is placed; first, last, or somewhere in between, it will always contain the main idea of the paragraph.

When you have difficulty separating main ideas from the details of a paragraph, you may need to stop and outline the passage that is giving you trouble. Remember that reading entails a combination of skills, only one of which is separating main ideas from supporting details. But identifying the main idea, whether in a paragraph or an essay, is crucial to good comprehension.

Separating Fact from Opinion

Once you have identified the main ideas and the supporting details, you need to separate facts from opinions. A **fact** is usually defined as something that can be proven. We accept something as a fact only when many different people come to the same conclusion after years of observation, research, and experimentation. Evidence that supports a fact is generally arrived at objectively. An **opinion,** on the other hand, is a belief, feeling, or judgment made about something or someone that a person may hold as fact but that he or she cannot prove. Evidence that supports an opinion is usually subjective. *Beautiful/ugly, wonderful/terrible, nice/disgusting,* and *greatest/worst* are examples of subjective words that writers often use to express their views. When you see them, you're reading opinions, even if you agree with the author.

But separating facts from opinions is not always easy. One reason is that facts change. At one time in history, it was a "fact" that the earth was flat (members of the Flat Earth Society still believe it); it was a "fact" that the sun revolved around the earth; it was a "fact" that the atom couldn't be split; it was a "fact" that no one would ever walk on the moon. Today, enough evidence has been gathered to prove that these and many other "facts" are wrong. Who knows what "facts" of today may be laughed at by future generations?

Another reason that separating fact from opinion is difficult is that opinion statements can be made to sound factual. We might read in one anthropology book that the first inhabitants of North America arrived "around 25,000 years ago." Another book might say North America was first inhabited "over 35,000 years ago." Which is the correct figure? Since no one who lived back then kept records, and since anthropologists disagree on the exact date the first Native Americans came, we have to be careful that we don't accept such information as actual fact. We could take the trouble to read several anthropology journals and textbooks to get an overview of what various anthropologists believe, but until there is more factual evidence, we can't accept either date as fact. In the future, there may be enough evidence gathered to prove a particular date.

Another reason for the difficulty in separating fact from opinion is our personal bias or prejudice. Frequently, we allow our feelings and beliefs to interfere with our acceptance of facts. Certain ideas and thoughts are instilled in us as we grow up. Family, friends, and people we admire all influence our thinking. Sometimes we unknowingly accept someone's opinion as fact simply because of our faith in that person.

Let's look now at some statements of fact and opinion. In the following paragraph, underline any verifiable facts (those statements that can be supported with objective evidence).

> In the U.S., 1 in 6 couples has difficulty conceiving or bearing a child. About 27 percent of women between ages 15 and 44 can't have children because of physical problems. The sperm count of U.S. males has fallen more than 30 percent in 50 years. Some 25 percent of men are considered functionally sterile. Experts suspect that environmental pollution is a cause.
> —Stanley N. Wellborn, "Birth"

In this case, the entire paragraph should have been underlined. You may have hesitated to mark the last sentence as fact. But the sentence doesn't say that environmental pollution *is* a cause; it merely says that experts suspect it is, and it can be verified that experts do suspect it is a cause. All of the paragraph can be accepted as factual. The author of the paragraph does not offer his opinion; he merely presents objective, statistical data.

Read the following paragraph and underline any statements in it that seem to be factual or that could be verified as fact:

> It's hard to believe, but in the ninth decade of the 20th Century, *The Catcher in the Rye, Of Mice and Men, Huckleberry Finn,* and *The Diary of Anne Frank,* among other books, are still the objects of censorship in the nation's public schools. And the incidence of book bannings is going up, according to a report by People for the American Way, the liberal watchdog group. In the

last year, the study found, there were efforts to ban books in schools in 46 of the 50 states, including California. Many of them succeeded.

—Editorial, *Los Angeles Times*

The opening four words, "It's hard to believe," constitute a statement of opinion, but the majority of the paragraph can be verified as fact. We could do research on censorship to see if the books mentioned are "still the objects of censorship in the nation's public schools." We could read the study by People for the American Way to see if the numbers quoted are correct. We could investigate the group that did the study to see if it is reliable. If we disagree with the statement because we don't want to believe it, that's because of personal bias; basically, there's no reason we shouldn't accept the statement as verifiable.

Now read the paragraph below and underline any statements that appear to be facts:

The purpose of education is to teach students to think, not to instill dogma or to train them to respond in predictable ways. Far from being banned, controversial material should be welcomed in schools. Students should be taught the critical ability to evaluate different ideas and to come to their own conclusions. It is a disservice to them and to society to restrict instructional material to a single viewpoint.

—Editorial, *Los Angeles Times*

If you underlined in the above paragraph, you didn't underline any facts. Regardless of how true or false you think the ideas in the paragraph are, they are all opinions. On a personal level, we may agree with the statements made, but that doesn't make them facts. Not everyone agrees with the purpose of education as stated above; many people do not want controversial materials presented to their children. In fact, some parents select certain schools for their children *because* only one viewpoint is taught.

Here's one more statement on censorship. Again, read it and underline any statements that seem to be factual.

Everyone older than 50 grew up in a time when Hollywood films were strictly censored by the industry itself to exclude explicit sexual scenes, gruesome violence, and vulgar language. The Supreme Court in the 1950s struck down movie censorship. It extended to film makers the First Amendment protection traditionally enjoyed by newspapers and book publishers. The court also redefined the anti-pornography and anti-obscenity statutes into meaninglessness.

Those decisions were praised as liberal advances, but their consequences were unforeseen and disastrous. . . . Unless they are reversed, the coarsening and corrupting of the nation's youth will continue.

—William Shannon, "Shield Our Youth with Censorship"

A mixture of fact and opinion appears here. At one time, the film industry *did* censor itself; in the 1950s, the Supreme Court *did* rule against movie censorship by expanding the interpretation of the First Amendment; some people *did* praise this as a liberal advance. This can all be verified. The last sentence, however, is opinion. There is no verifiable proof that the lack of censorship in the movies is the cause for the "coarsening and corrupting of the nation's youth," nor is there verifiable proof that unless the decisions the author cites are reversed, the corruption of youth will continue. He uses facts to make his opinions appear true.

As a careful reader, you will want to use the essays in Part 2 as a means of practicing the separation of facts from opinions.

Drawing Inferences

Another reading skill that is essential to effective reading is **drawing inferences.** Sometimes writers don't state directly what they mean; they imply or suggest their meaning. When that happens, we have to draw inferences from what they do say.

Drawing an inference is sometimes called "making an educated guess." Based on what an author tells us, we can often guess what other thoughts, feelings, and ideas the author may have that are not stated directly. For instance, what are some things you can tell about the writer of the following paragraph that are not directly stated?

> In 1997, we commemorated the 110th anniversary of Sherlock Holmes's "birth." The great sleuth made his first appearance in 1887, and right from the start was so popular that when his creator killed him off after twenty-four adventures, followers eventually forced Conan Doyle to bring him back to life. Even today, the intrepid duo of Holmes and his stalwart companion Dr. Watson continue to delight each new generation of readers.

The author doesn't say it directly, but we can infer from what is said that the writer is very knowledgeable about the Sherlock Holmes stories because of the facts presented. We also suspect that the author has probably read most or all of the stories and likes them very much; notice the use of such phrases as "great sleuth," "intrepid duo," and "continue to delight." Finally, based on the vocabulary and structural organization used, we can infer that the writer is fairly literate. These inferences help us get a sense of the person writing, a sense that goes beyond what is actually written. We may not always be right, but the more we practice, the more our inferences will be good educated guesses.

Read the following paragraph and see what inferences you can draw about the author.

> We say that it is our right to control our bodies, and this is true. But there is a distinction that needs to be made, and that distinction is this: Preventing a pregnancy is controlling a body—controlling your body. But preventing the continuance of a human life that is not your own is murder. If you attempt to control the body of another in that fashion, you become as a slave master was—controlling the lives and bodies of his slave, chopping off their feet when they ran away, or murdering them if it pleased him.
>
> —Ken Lonnquist, "Ghosts"

You probably can infer that the author of the paragraph is against abortion. While he agrees with pro-abortionists that we have a right to control our bodies, he draws the line after conception. We can infer, then, that he defines human life as beginning at the moment sperm and egg fuse. We can also infer that he is opposed to slavery. We might even suspect that his use of the unpleasant image of slave masters cutting off the feet of runaways in connection with abortion is done deliberately to win readers to his way of thinking. If we are pro-abortionists, we might still disagree with him, but we will better understand the reasons for his views.

Now let's put together all of this section on understanding content. Read the next paragraph, underline what you think the main idea is, and see what you can infer about the author:

> Controversy—the heart of politics—has gotten a bad name in the textbook business, and publishers have advised their writers to avoid it. This fear of controversy is distorting our children's education, leaving us with biology texts that neglect evolution history and texts that omit the important influence of religion. Similarly, in civics and government texts, it is treatment of such volatile events as the Vietnam war, the Watergate scandal, the civil rights movement, and the school prayer debate that is "dulled down" to the point of tedium, or minimized to the point of evasion.
> —Arthur J. Kropp, "Let's Put an End to Mediocre Textbooks"

If you underlined the first sentence as the main idea, you are partly right. But there are parts of the second sentence that also apply. One paragraph method used here is cause and effect: the cause, the fear of publishers to deal with controversial issues in textbooks; the effect, a distortion of children's education. Although the author mentions that publishers have advised their writers to avoid certain issues in textbooks, the paragraph does not support that point. The support statements that are provided are instead examples of issues that are either left out or watered down in textbooks, which the author believes then distort children's education. Thus, the paragraph uses a combination of cause and effect and illustration-example. Here is a possible outline of the paragraph:

Main idea:	Fear among publishers to deal with controversial issues has resulted in a distortion of children's education. (cause and effect)
Support:	biology texts that neglect evolution history
Support:	omission of the important influence of religion
Support:	civics and government texts that "dull down" or minimize
	a. Vietnam war
	b. Watergate scandal
	c. civil rights movement
	d. school prayer debate

Though he does not directly state it, we can infer that the author is against censorship and that he believes children should be exposed to controversy. We can infer that he does not want everything in textbooks to be watered down to show only the "smooth" side of life. We can also infer that the author believes publishers are responsible for producing books that do not challenge students. This, we might guess, is from the fear that controversial subjects in textbooks might offend some people, who would then put pressure on the schools not to buy those books.

As written, most of what is stated is opinion. To prove or disprove what the author says and implies, we would need to examine textbooks in many of the areas he mentions, or do further research on the subject of textbook censorship.

Use the following passage to practice the reading skills you have learned.

Adaptability and lifelong learning are now the cornerstones of success. What direction does a person take to prepare for a lifetime of change? The one degree which provides training which never becomes obsolete is the liberal arts degree; it teaches you how to think. It also teaches you how to read, write and speak intelligently, get along with others, and conceptualize problems. For the first time in several decades, the liberal arts degree is coming to the forefront of the employment field.

Growing ranks of corporate executives are lamenting that college students are specializing too much and too early. What corporate America really needs, according to chief executive officers of major corporations, is students soundly grounded in the liberal arts—English, especially—who then can pick up more specific business or technical skills on the job. Few students, however, seem to be listening to this message. Today's best selling courses offer evidence that students want to take the courses that provide direct job related skills rather than the most basic survival skills in the workplace: communication and thinking skills. They want courses they can parlay into jobs—and high paying ones at that.

—Debra Sikes and Barbara Murray,
"The Practicality of the Liberal Arts Major"

Writing Exercise

In your journal or on a separate sheet of paper, answer the following questions about the two paragraphs you just read. You may look back at the essay paragraphs if you need to do so.

1. What writing pattern is used in the first paragraph?

2. In your own words, write a one-sentence statement of the main idea of the first paragraph.

3. List the support provided for the main idea of the first paragraph.

4. In your own words, write a topic sentence for the second paragraph.

5. What inference can you draw regarding the authors' attitude toward a liberal arts degree?

6. Is the passage mostly fact or opinion? Explain.

7. What does the passage imply about most of today's college students?

The wording will be different, of course, but compare your answers with these:

1. Examples of the benefits of a liberal arts education make up the bulk of the paragraph; thus the illustration and example pattern is used.

2. A combination of the first three sentences is needed to cover the major point of the paragraph, so the main idea is "The one degree that provides adaptability and lifelong learning skills is the liberal arts degree."

3. The liberal arts degree (1) teaches you how to (a) think, (b) read, write, and speak intelligently, (c) get along with others, and (d) conceptualize problems; and (2) it is coming to the forefront of the employment field.

4. The basic idea is, "Corporate executives feel that college students are coming into business too specialized, but students don't seem to be listening."

5. The authors seem to be in favor of the degree.

6. The passage is mostly opinion. (However, you should be aware that the passage is taken from an article that is based on the findings of research conducted with corporate executives.)

7. The last two sentences imply that most of today's college students are more interested in obtaining job skills that they think will land them high-paying jobs. They are more interested in making money than in preparing for lifelong change and adaptability.

Make your goal the ability to read well enough to answer these types of questions correctly when you read. Part 2 will provide ample practice.

Before Going On

You have learned that reading critically requires the ability to distinguish main ideas from supporting details, to separate fact from opinion, and to draw inferences from authors' direct statements.

Writing Exercise

In your journal or on a separate sheet of paper, write a paragraph explaining what major field of study you have selected, why you selected it, and what you hope to learn. If you have not yet selected a major, write a paragraph that discusses areas of study you are considering and why. Make certain that you have a clearly stated topic sentence and adequate support. Your instructor may want to see this exercise.

Marking as You Read

To improve your comprehension and concentration, read the essays in Part 2 with a pen or pencil in hand, making notations in the margins. Marking as you read slows you down; it helps you to get engaged with the author, to catch your thoughts and put them in writing before you forget them. How you mark or take notes as you read is up to you, but you might want to consider doing all or some of the following:

1. Underline only major points or statements. Don't underline almost everything, as some students do. Force yourself to read so carefully that you are sure that a statement or phrase is important before you mark it. Identifying the paragraph method used may help you see the difference between main ideas and supporting points.

2. Use numbers in the margins when a series of points is listed or discussed. This practice will help you distinguish the main ideas from supporting points.

3. Think about and react to what you are reading. In the margins, write your reactions, such as "Good point!" or "Never thought of that" or "Where's the proof?" if you don't believe a statement.

4. If there's not much room in the margins, create your own kind of shorthand: Use an exclamation mark (!) when a statement surprises you, a question mark (?) when you don't understand a point, or abbreviations, such as "ex" for example or "prf" for proof—anything that will remind you of your reaction.

5. Write a paragraph summarizing the reading selection. If you can't, then you may need to read it again.

6. If the publication from which the reading comes cannot be written on, such as a borrowed or library book, you may need to use Post-It notes or sticky flag markers of some kind with your notes on them. If you are assigned a reading from the Internet, print it out so that you can write your notes on it.

These are just suggestions. You or your instructor may have other methods for marking. Feel free to mark your books in any way that will help your reading concentration. Whatever the method, the reasons for marking are to gain control of concentration and to develop close, analytical reading.

Try to cultivate an interest in the assigned readings. If you don't know anything about the subject of a reading selection, keep asking questions as you read, such as "What does the author mean by this statement?" and "How do I know if this is true?" and "What's the point of this comment?" Asking questions about what you are reading will keep you involved. Don't try to read for long periods of time. And don't try to read assignments when you are tired; you won't concentrate very well. Good reading requires a fresh mind.

Here's a reading selection typical of the kind in Part 2 of this book. Read it once, then read it a second time, marking it up as suggested above or using your own marking techniques.

The Wet Drug

PETE HAMILL

1   Among the worst bores in the Western world are religious converts and reformed drunks. I have never been knocked off a horse on the way to Damascus, but I did give up drinking more than a dozen years ago. This didn't make me feel morally superior to anyone. If asked, I would talk about going dry but, from the first, I was determined to preach no sermons and stand in judgment of no human being who took pleasure in the sauce. Booze? Ah, the wet drug!

2   But I must confess that lately my feelings have begun to change. Drinking and drunks now fill me with loathing. Increasingly, I see close friends—human beings of intelligence, wit and style—reduced to slobbering fools by liquor. I've seen other friends ruin their marriages, brutalize their children, destroy their careers. I've also reached the age when I've had to help bury a few people who allowed booze to take them into eternity.

3   In the past few weeks, two ghastly episodes have underlined for me the horror that goes with alcohol. In New Bedford, Mass., a 21-year-old woman was beaten and repeatedly raped by a gang of drunks in a bar called Big Dan's. There were at least 15 onlookers to her violation; they did nothing to prevent it. All of them were drunk or drinking.

4   In New York, four teenage boys were killed when a car driven by a fifth kid smashed into a concrete wall at 90 mph. They were all under the legal drinking age of 19; nevertheless, they had managed to spend

a long night drinking in a public bar, and got drunk enough to die. When it was over, and they had pried the human pieces out of the torn rubber and steel, the driver was charged with four counts of manslaughter. His worst punishment may be that he lived.

5   These are not isolated cases. This year more than 25,000 Americans will die in auto accidents caused by alcohol. And the roads are not the only site of the horror. Studies indicate that alcohol is a factor in 86 percent of our homicides, 83 percent of our fatal fires, 72 percent of robberies, 52 percent of wife-beatings, 38 percent of cases of child abuse. We can never be certain how many on-the-job accidents are caused by drinking, how many drownings, how many suicides.

6   All of this is bizarre. We live in a culture that certifies alcohol as an acceptable drug and places marijuana smokers or coke dealers in jail. Presidents and statesmen toast each other with the wet drug. It's advertised on radio and TV. Popular music is full of references to it. But when the mellow moments, the elegant evenings are over, there are our kids, smashing themselves into eternity with the same drug.

7   I'm not suggesting here any bluenose return to Prohibition. But I wish we would begin to make it more and more clear that drinking to drunkenness is one of the more disgusting occupations of human beings.

8   For every beer commercial showing all those he-men getting ready to drink, we should show footage of destroyed teenagers, their bodies broken and bleeding, beer cans filling what's left of the back seat. For every high fashion couple toasting each other with wine, show men and women puking on their shoes, falling over tables, sliding away into violence.

9   If cigarette advertising could be banned from TV, so should commercials for the drug called alcohol. Cigarette smokers, after all, usually kill only themselves with their habit. Drunks get behind the wheels of their cars and kill strangers.

10   At night now, driving along any American road, you come across these vomiting slaughterers, slowly weaving from lane to lane, or racing in confused fury to the grave at 90 mph. They don't know the rest of us exist and, what's more, they don't care. They are criminal narcissists, careening around until they kill others and themselves.

11   We Americans should begin immediately to remind ourselves that when we drink we are entering the company of killers and fools.

Here again is the essay you just read. Compare your markings with those below. Your markings will be different, but compare what you underlined as main ideas and what you marked as supporting points with those marked in the model. They should be similar.

The Wet Drug

what's a wet drug?

PETE HAMILL

Among the worst bores in the Western world are religious converts and reformed drunks. <u>I have never been knocked off a horse on the way to Damascus</u>, but I did give up drinking more than a dozen years ago. This didn't make me feel morally superior to anyone. If asked, I would talk about going dry but, from the first, I was determined to preach no sermons and stand in judgment of no human being who took pleasure in the sauce. *Booze? Ah, the wet drug!*

ask instruc what means

transiti

changed his mind why?
1. foolish acting
2. ruined marriages
3. child beating
4. ruined careers
5. death

But I must confess that lately my feelings have begun to change. <u>Drinking and drunks</u> now <u>fill me with loathing</u>. Increasingly, I see close friends—human beings of intelligence, wit and style—reduced to slobbering fools by liquor. I've seen other friends <u>ruin their marriages, brutalize their children, destroy their careers</u>. I've also reached the age when I've had to help <u>bury a few people</u> who allowed booze to take them into eternity.

In the past few weeks, <u>two ghastly episodes</u> have underlined for me the horror that goes with alcohol. In New Bedford, Mass., a 21-year-old woman was beaten and repeatedly raped by a gang of drunks in a bar called Big Dan's. There were at least 15 onlookers to her violation; they did nothing to prevent it. <u>All</u> of them were <u>drunk or drinking</u>.

example of drunks in bar—beating/raping woman

example of 4 teenage deaths from drunk driving
Yuk!
(Descriptive)

In New York, <u>four teen-age boys</u> were <u>killed</u> when a car driven by a fifth kid smashed into a concrete wall at 90 mph. They were all under the legal drinking age of 19; nevertheless, they had managed to spend a long night drinking in a public bar, and got drunk enough to die. When it was over, and they had <u>pried the human pieces</u> out of the <u>torn rubber and steel</u>, the driver was charged with four counts of manslaughter. His worst punishment may be that he lived.

statistics on damage from drink-ing problems
1. auto accidents
2. homicides
3. fires
4. robberies
5. wife beating
6. child abuse

These are not isolated cases. This year more than 25,000 Americans will die in <u>auto accidents</u> caused by alcohol. And the roads are not the only site of the horror. Studies indicate that alcohol is a factor in 86 percent of our <u>homicides</u>, 83 percent of our <u>fatal fires</u>, 72 percent of <u>robberies</u>, 52 percent of <u>wife-beatings</u>, 38 percent of cases of <u>child abuse</u>. We can never be certain <u>how many on-the-job accidents</u> are caused by drinking, <u>how many drownings, how many suicides</u>.

good point if alcohol is so damaging why legal?

examples of accept-ability contrasted with problem

<u>All of this is bizarre. We live in a culture that certifies alcohol as an acceptable drug</u> and places marijuana smokers or coke dealers in jail. Presidents and statesmen toast each other with the wet drug. It's advertised on radio and TV. Popular music is full of references to it. But when the <u>mellow moments, the elegant evenings</u> are over, there are our kids, smashing themselves into eternity with the same drug.

I'm not suggesting here any bluenose return to Prohibition. <u>But</u> I wish we would begin to make it more and more clear that drinking to drunkenness is one of the more disgusting occupations of human beings.

For every beer commercial showing all those he-men getting ready to drink, we should show footage of destroyed teenagers, their <u>bodies broken and bleeding</u>, beer cans filling what's left of the back seat. For every high fashion couple toasting each other with wine, show men and women <u>puking on their shoes, falling over tables</u>, sliding away into violence.

If cigarette advertising could be banned from TV, so should commercials for the drug called alcohol. Cigarette smokers, after all, usually kill only themselves with their habit. Drunks get behind the wheels of their cars and kill strangers.

At night now, driving along any American road, you come across these <u>vomiting slaughterers</u>, slowly weaving from lane to lane, or racing in confused fury to the grave at 90 mph. They don't know the rest of us exist and, what's more, they don't care. They are criminal <u>narcissists</u>, careening around until they kill others and themselves.

We Americans should begin immediately to remind ourselves that when we drink we are entering the company of killers and fools.

Handwritten margin notes (left):
wants to counter all "acceptable" drinking images in media with negative, "realistic" ones

wants to ban alcohol ads

Handwritten margin notes (right):
compare contrast

strong images

strong image

? forceful ending! Sounds fed up.

Handwritten notes below:
—ask teacher about "... way to Damascus" in first ¶
—look up narcissist
—strong argument—uses personal appeal, emotional appeal, facts & figures
—guess booze is a wet drug—never thought about it before

If you aren't used to this type of reading, it may take one or two practices before you feel confident about what you are doing. But it's practice worth your time.

Writing Summaries

Another habit worth developing is to write in your journal a one-paragraph summary of each essay you are assigned to read. Doing so requires that you put to use all the reading skills discussed earlier. To write an accurate summary, you need to recognize the main idea of the essay (the thesis), identify its supporting points, separate fact from opinion, and draw inferences. You then use this information to write an objective summary, including only what the author says, not your opinions. When you write a summary in your journal, follow these steps:

1. First, think about what you want to say. Think about what you want to say first. Try writing down the author's thesis in your own words and then listing the supporting points. Use this as an outline for your summary.

2. Don't write too much, about two hundred words or less. One paragraph is usually enough, although there may be times when two paragraphs are needed. The idea of a summary is to present only the main idea and supporting points.

3. Be objective; that is, don't give your own opinions or value judgments.

4. In your first sentence, provide the author's name, the title of the work, and an indication of what the essay is about. Once you have stated the author's name, you don't need to repeat it in your summary.

5. Use your own words, except for phrases you feel are important to include for clarity of a point. These phrases should have quotation marks around them.

6. Avoid using phrases such as "the author believes" or "another interesting point is." Just state what the author says.

Writing Exercise

As practice, write a one-paragraph summary in your journal or on a separate sheet of paper of the essay you just read, Pete Hamill's "The Wet Drug." You will probably want to look over your markings or reread the essay before you begin.

Naturally, your wording will be different, but see if your summary contains the same basic points as this one:

> Excessive drinking is disgusting and harmful, says Pete Hamill in his essay, "The Wet Drug." Although he had vowed not to moralize or pass judgment on those who still drank after he quit, Hamill has changed his mind after witnessing the harm he has seen from the "drinking to drunkenness" of friends and others. As support, Hamill provides examples of what excessive drinking has done to some of his friends, such as acting foolish, ruined marriages and careers, child beating, and even death. He then cites two recent news accounts of harm from excessive drinking, one regarding a woman who was beaten and raped by a gang in a bar, another of four teens killed in an auto accident. Finally, the author presents some national statistics on the effects drinking has on auto accidents, homicides, fatal fires, wife beatings, child abuse, and on-the-job accidents. Because we live in a society that "certifies alcohol as an acceptable drug," we should counter all acceptable images of drinking with more realistic images of the results of drunkenness. Commercials for alcohol, like those for cigarettes, should be banned from TV.

Notice that the summary's first sentence includes the author, title, and thesis of the essay. The summary then presents the evidence Hamill uses to support his thesis: examples of the effects drinking has had on Hamill's friends, recent "horror stories" in the news about crime and violence related to drinking, and statistics on the harm caused by drinking. The summary concludes with Hamill's suggestion for countering the "acceptable" media images of drinking with more realistic ones.

The summary is objective; the only opinions used are those of Hamill, the author of the essay. Notice, too, that when the summary uses words from the essay, those words are identified with quotation marks.

You can write a good summary only when you truly understand what you have read. Writing good summaries in your journal ensures that you have read carefully. In addition, the summaries serve as good resources if you ever need to go back to review what you've read.

Writing Reflections

Writing your reflections on what you read is another useful type of journal entry to consider. Writing summaries requires objectivity; but you also need to capture on paper your subjective reactions, ideas, and questions that arise from the assigned reading selections. For instance, the following are some examples of subjective responses to Pete Hamill's thesis that commercials for alcoholic beverages should be banned. You may have had one or more of these reactions after you read it.

- I disagree with Hamill's thesis; ads don't cause drunken behavior.

- Why is alcohol legal when other drugs, such as marijuana, are not?

- Hamill's essay reminds me of my Uncle Al, killed by a drunk driver.

- I never thought of alcohol as a "wet drug," but I see it is.

- A recent beer commercial did make drinking beer look like fun. Could such ads get people to start drinking?

- I never realized that alcohol was such a contributing factor to so much destruction.

- I doubt if Hamill's essay will stop anyone from drinking, especially college students.

None of the examples are "right" or "wrong." They are subjective responses to Hamill's thesis. Such reactions should be written down, even if they don't directly relate to the essay. They could become useful seeds for writing an essay of your own at some later date.

Reflection entries are also a good place to write down some examples of the way a writer works. For instance, you may have been struck by Hamill's use of language to reveal his disgust. You might want to write down some of the passages that struck you the most, such as:

- "I've had to help bury a few people who allowed booze to take them into eternity."

- "... these vomiting slaughterers, slowly weaving from lane to lane..."

- "... when we drink we are entering the company of killers and fools."

Or you may have found the language too dramatic. State how you feel. Such entries help you pay more attention to a writer's style and use of language. In turn, you will become more conscious of your own word choices.

Reflection entries are also a good place for questions you might want to pursue later or ask your instructor. Here are some possible questions that might come up during or after reading Hamill's essay:

- To what does "knocked off a horse on the way to Damascus" refer?

- What does the word "bluenose" in paragraph 7 mean?

- When did Prohibition occur? Why didn't it work?

- What does he mean by "criminal narcissists"?

Some of your questions can be answered by looking in a dictionary, others by asking your instructor.

Capturing your thoughts, ideas, and questions in writing while actually thinking about them helps you remember them and can be referred to later for review.

Collecting Words to Learn

It is a good idea to set aside a section in your journal where you keep a list of the words you want to learn and add to your vocabulary. The best way to enlarge your vocabulary is to take the time to expand it. You need a strong vocabulary not only to handle sophisticated reading but also to express yourself in your own writing.

How you can best develop your vocabulary is something only you know, but just collecting a list of words is not going to help you learn them. You need to do something with the list.

As you know, words often have more than one meaning; their definitions depend on their contextual usage—that is, how they are used in a given sentence. So don't merely accumulate unknown words from the reading selections. Write down the entire sentence or at least the phrase in which the word appears. That way, when you look up the word in a dictionary, you can pick from among the various meanings the definition that fits. Once you have looked up the word you want to learn, write a sentence of your own using it in the proper context. To make certain you are using the words correctly, show your sentences to your instructor. Then use as many of your newly learned words as possible in your own writing until they become as familiar to you as the words you already use. Yes, this takes time, but how else are you going to develop your vocabulary?

Before Going On

In order to better understand what you read, and in order to remember it longer, be an active reader by carrying on a dialogue with the author. Make brief notations and marks in your books as you read. In addition, keep a reading journal where you can write objective summaries of the readings. Also use the journal as a place to record your reactions, ideas, and questions prompted by the reading selections. Finally, in order to enlarge your vocabulary, keep a list of new words from the readings and learn as many as you can.

Writing Exercise

In your reading journal or on a separate sheet of paper, write today's date and the page numbers you just read. Summarize the important points in Chapter 1. Use your previous journal entries as a guide.

Topics in This Chapter

I n Chapter 1, "Viewpoints on Reading Essays," you looked at some methods and qualities of a good essay reader. Now you'll learn what it takes to be a good essay writer. What you learned in the previous chapter about an essay's thesis, supporting paragraphs, and organization you will find useful in writing essays. In fact, much of that information will sound familiar. The difference is that you will now look at the essay from a writer's point of view rather than a reader's. As a reader, you see only the final efforts of a writer; in this chapter, you'll see each of the various writing stages that lead to the finished product.

Three basic writing steps are presented here: how to get started, how to get your ideas in writing, and how to rewrite or polish what you write. But good writing is seldom a quick one-two-three process. It involves starting and stopping, eagerly writing away and angrily throwing away, moving along and stalling, feeling pleased and feeling frustrated, thinking you're finished and then realizing you need to start again. Sometimes completing a writing assignment may seem effortless; more often than not you will have to work very hard at it.

Writers approach writing in various ways. Hundreds of books exist on how to write, each one offering "the right way." But regardless of their differences, most of these books cover at least three basic stages of writing: methods for getting started, methods for writing a first draft, and methods for revising and editing. This section presents these three stages in that order, but the order in which you follow them may vary with each essay you write. Once you increase your knowledge of what goes into writing an essay, you may modify the stages to suit yourself.

This basic three-step approach should make writing easier for you. It will give you a sense of direction and an understanding of what is expected of you as a writer. Let's look at each of these steps more closely.

Getting Started: Finding a Working Thesis (Stage 1)

As you learned in the section on reading, essays are structured around a thesis, the main idea an author wants to develop. The thesis is what the author wants to say about the topic or subject of the essay. Sometimes an instructor gives you a topic for an essay. In that case, you have to decide what you want to say about it and what thesis will guide what you want to say. Sometimes you are left on your own and must come up with both an essay topic and a thesis.

Once you've been given a writing assignment, make the topic interesting for yourself. Finding an approach to the subject that interests you will make it easier to write about the subject assigned. Also, unless the assignment requires research, think about the assignment in terms of what you already know. Depending upon the topic, that's not always easy, but here are some methods for selecting and making a topic your own.

Discovering Ideas in Your Reading Journal

Your reading journal is one of the best places to start searching for a topic and thesis. If your instructor asks you to write an essay dealing with the general topic of an assigned reading selection, you may have already written down some reactions, ideas, or questions that you can use as a starting point. So look over your journal entries. Also, look over any textbook markings you made when you read the assignment. Just by keeping in mind that you have to write about something from that particular reading selection, you might see other essay possibilities in your markings that didn't occur to you before. By using your reflections on what you read, you will have not only a possible topic and working thesis, but you will also have an essay that is based on your feelings and opinions.

Let's say you are assigned to read Pete Hamill's "The Wet Drug" from Chapter 1. The writing assignment is to agree or disagree with the author's opinion that advertisements for alcoholic beverages should be banned from television. In this case, both your topic and your thesis have been given to you. By checking your journal entry for the essay, you discover that you wrote down your reaction, a notation that you agree (or disagree) with the author. You might begin by writing down a working thesis: "I agree (or disagree) with Pete Hamill in his essay, 'The Wet Drug' when he says advertisements for alcoholic beverages should be banned from television." Then look again at each of Hamill's supporting points and show why you agree or disagree with his points. Such an approach at least gets you started. You may even change your mind once you begin. That's why the term *working thesis* is used at this stage. It's quite normal to discover that you want to go in a different direction after writing several hundred words. Just accept that forced flexibility as part of the writing process.

At other times you may be assigned a broader topic that you must write about. Let's say that an instructor wants you to write a 500-word essay on some aspect of television commercials. A review of your journal entry on Hamill's essay shows that you wrote some questions: "Where did Hamill get his statistics?" "Doesn't Hamill know that hard liquor ads are already banned on TV?" "How much of an effect do beer and wine ads on TV have on teens? adults?" "Why should such ads be banned from TV but allowed in magazines?" Looking for answers to your own questions is also a good place to find a topic and a thesis. You can see how thoughtful journal entries can stimulate your own writing.

Brainstorming

When the topic is too broad for a short essay, you have to narrow it down. How do you reduce a topic to something smaller if you can't even think of something to write about? **Brainstorm.** There are at least two ways to brainstorm for ideas: One way is to create a list of your ideas, and another is to cluster them. Let's look at **creating a list** first.

You've probably participated in brainstorming sessions at one time or another. If so, you know it is important to follow the rules. Done correctly, brainstorming can be used to help you select a topic. For instance, if the general writing assignment is to write about television commercials, then take a sheet of paper and start writing down whatever ideas about the topic pop into your head. The trick here is not to be critical as you jot down your thoughts; just put your ideas on paper even if you don't like them at the time. It's important not to interrupt the flow of thoughts by stopping to ask yourself if what you've written is a good idea or not; you can decide that later. Just let your brain "storm." Once you have exhausted all your thoughts about the topic, then look at your list and see which ones are useful.

Sometimes it's helpful (and fun) to work with other classmates as a team. Getting together with two or three others to brainstorm brings out ideas for the assigned topic that you might not have thought about on your own.

Here is an example of a brainstorming list a student wrote on television commercials:

TV Commercials

too many at once
seem louder than program
being watched
mixture/dumb to serious
trucks splashing through
rivers and mud
Bud Lite chimp steals
beer bottle
obnoxious but memorable
mood music
pharmaceutical ads – ask
your doctor
causes dissatisfaction with
what you don't have
beer ads usually in a bar
are they convincing?
use of celebrities

must cost a lot to make
seems to be an ad for
everything
bodybuilding
phony, long infomercials
food/BBQ sauce to
Ronald McDonald
Match.com "How to find
the right person in
90 days"
slogans like "Powered
by Tyson"
credit/debt ads

As you can see, some of these entries provide a sense of direction for an essay on television commercials. Some are slogans and scenes from TV commercials that she remembers. Others are her opinions about commercials. A closer look at the list may reveal that some items are dated or unusable. It doesn't matter. Making the list prompted her to think about the assigned subject.

Or, you might decide upon a topic and you may need to do more brainstorming. Another brainstorming session dealing with the chosen topic should provide more specific ideas on it. If few ideas come, you might want to consider selecting another topic. Making a brainstorming list is useful because it helps prevent writer's block and gets ideas flowing. Discovering and narrowing down a possible topic through brainstorming saves you from false starts.

Try a little brainstorming. In the space provided, brainstorm for three minutes on the topic "sports." Remember to write down everything that comes into your mind, even if it doesn't seem related. Don't be critical of any ideas; just list as many as you can in the time your instructor allows.

SPORTS

Now look over your brainstorming list. Sports is obviously a broad subject, too broad to write about in an essay. Circle any items on your list that could serve as a narrower topic for an essay dealing with some aspect of sports. For instance, you might have listed the name of your favorite athlete, or the disappointing basketball game you attended last night, or a memorable moment in a game you might have played in high school, or your favorite sport.

Once you have decided on a narrower topic in your brainstorming list, place a check mark beside any other items that might help support your topic. If you can't find many, brainstorm again on the new topic you've chosen. Gradually, you will begin to narrow a topic down to a size you can handle with ideas for supporting points.

In following spaces, list two topics from your final brainstorming session that you might use for an essay topic, and then create a working thesis statement for each.

topic: _____

working thesis statement: _____

_____

topic: _____

working thesis statement: _____

_____

Another method is **clustering.** In *Writing the Natural Way,* Gabriele Rico claims that we have two minds, our "Design mind" and our "Sign mind." Most of us have learned to write through our Sign mind, the part of the brain that deals with rules and logic. Our Sign mind criticizes, censors, and corrects errors. Because most of our training in writing deals with the Sign mind, our Design mind—the creative, less critical side of our brain—doesn't get developed much. This often leaves our creative side blocked and unused. A good piece of writing requires that both minds work together. Using an analogy with music, Rico says that our Sign mind "attends to the notes," whereas our Design mind "attends to the melodies."

Clustering is a way to tap into the Design mind, the part of the brain that doesn't care about rules. It helps bring out our more creative side. A type of brainstorming, clustering brings our hidden thoughts to the surface. Rather than merely making a list of ideas, clustering creates a design, a pattern of thought.

Here's how clustering works. Write down a word or phrase in the center of a page (the **nucleus thought**), and then allow your mind to flow out from the center, like ripples created by a stone thrown into water. Quickly write down and circle whatever comes to mind, connecting each new word or phrase with a line to the previous circle. When a new thought occurs, begin a new "ripple," or branch.

An example of clustering on the topic "TV commercials" appears on page 42. Notice there are four branches stemming from the nucleus thought: "costly," "dumb," "harmful," and "serious ones." Each one of these leads the writer closer to a possible subject. If one of these branches seems interesting enough to write about, that branch can become the nucleus for a new clustering group adding more specific details. A few minutes of clustering on an assigned topic frequently provides a sense of direction toward a usable essay. Chances are that your essay will be different from the norm because clustering has brought forth ideas in your mind that your usual approach to writing would not have touched.

Give clustering a try. In your journal or on a separate sheet of paper, use the clustering technique for three minutes on the topic "social problems." Write the nucleus thought "social problems" in the middle of the page and circle it. Then begin branching and clustering your ideas on the subject.

Look over your clustering. Pick two of the branches from the cluster that could serve as a narrower essay topic than "social problems." For instance, you might have a cluster branch on AIDS education, rising unemployment, inner-city gangs, racial bigotry, or police brutality. Make certain your branch contains some support for that issue. If not, you may need to take one of your branches and do some more clustering on that branch.

In the following spaces, write two possible topics from your clustering that you could use for an essay and create a working thesis statement for each.

topic: _____

working thesis statement: _____

_____

topic: _____

working thesis statement: _____

_____

Writing Exercise

In your journal or on a separate sheet of paper, write a summary of what you just read about brainstorming and its usefulness in finding a suitable topic for an essay.

Freewriting

In his book *Writing with Power,* Peter Elbow recommends freewriting as still another way to focus on a writing topic or to break writer's block. Elbow claims that practicing freewriting for ten minutes a day increases writing skills within a few weeks. Freewriting isn't polished writing, but it helps open you up to the thinking–writing process without the worrying about mechanical errors that often blocks thinking. As Elbow states in his book, what's important about freewriting is not the end product, but the process.

To freewrite, simply start writing words on a page and see what comes out. There are only two rules: don't stop to think about what you are writing, and don't stop to worry about errors in writing. Just try to write down as fast as you can exactly what's going through your mind. If you can't think of anything, write, "I can't think of anything." Repeat the phrase until you do think of something. It won't take long. You'll be surprised to see how many useful ideas for topics often emerge as you read what you've freewritten.

On page 44 there is an example of freewriting done by a student who was asked to freewrite for a few minutes about television commercials. The errors aren't important here; the ideas are.

Notice that the student didn't stop to fix spelling or grammatical mistakes made during the freewriting. Such mistakes in freewriting don't matter. What matters in freewriting is what thoughts you capture.

If you look carefully at the sample, you'll notice that after expressing resentment toward the freewriting idea and some spinning around, the student begins to form thoughts about television commercials. He touches on possible ideas to pursue: why he hates commercials but watches them; the need for advertisements so that programs can exist; the purpose of television; the success of television advertising; the costs of advertising. In the end, the student realizes he may need to carefully examine some television advertisements before writing about any specific commercial. All these possibilities came from a few minutes of freewriting.

TV commercials? I don't know anything about TV Commercials. This is stupid. Don't see how writing without stopping is going to help get a topic. Any way I can't think of anything to say - can't think of anything to say - can't think - okay, enough! Maybe I could write about how much I hate commercials. I guess I do watch them cause I'm too lazy to get up and turn them off or down. Need a remote control. Even PBS stations have commercials now I've noticed. "This program brought to you buy... blah, blah, blah." Guess there'd be no TV programs without commercials, a necessary nuisance. Really the purpose of television is to sell things. We get so caught up in certain programs we forget why they are there - to sell. I guess people - me - buy the stuff they sell or they wouldn't put so much money into advertising. Super Bowl ads run into the millions just for 30 seconds. But we buy, buy, buy. I need to watch some commercials and relly look at them.

A ten-minute freewriting session is also useful before you begin to write an essay. It can get you warmed up to write, discipline you to write when you don't feel like it, and help you put ideas into words without worrying about the writing process itself. Once the words begin to flow, so do the ideas buried in your subconscious.

Some students like to freewrite for a few minutes in their journals after completing a reading assignment. It helps them capture ideas, experiences, feelings, and reactions prompted by the reading assignment and exercises. You might want to make this a part of your assignments, too.

Freewriting is an especially good technique to use if you work with a word processor. You can turn off the monitor light, and since you won't see anything on the screen, you can concern yourself only with writing your thoughts. When you're finished, turn on the monitor light and read what you have written. Chances are that you will find a topic you can handle.

Use a page in your journal to see how freewriting works. Write for just five minutes on the topic "family." Remember, keep writing the whole time. Don't stop to think about what you are saying; just write whatever comes to your mind, even if it's not about family. Don't worry about mistakes in spelling or grammar. When you have finished, return to this point in the chapter to continue.

Now look over your freewriting. In your journal, write down all possible essay topics that you see in it. Pick two topics from the list and in the following spaces, write each topic and a working thesis statement for each topic.

topic: _____

working thesis statement: _____

_____

topic: _____

working thesis statement: _____

_____

Before Going On

You now know some approaches for finding an essay topic on your own. One way is to look over your journal entries for possible topics. Another is to brainstorm for topics, either by making a list or by clustering. Still another is to freewrite. If you experience difficulty selecting a topic for an essay, try one or all of these approaches. Feel free to modify them to fit your style of thinking and writing.

Writing Exercise

In your journal or on a separate sheet of paper, write a paragraph that explains and describes one of the four methods for finding an essay topic: using journal entries, listing, clustering, or freewriting. In a second paragraph, tell which one you prefer and why. Your instructor may want you to turn in this exercise.

Getting It on Paper: Supporting Your Thesis (Stage 2)

Refining Your Thesis

Sometimes it's possible to sit down and write an essay from beginning to end. But more often than not, you'll find yourself surrounded by crumpled sheets of paper containing false starts, because you tried to write before you and your thesis were ready.

Here's a more practical and productive way to get your ideas on paper. Let's say that after clustering for ideas on the broad topic of television commercials, you narrow your subject to harmful television commercials. That branch of your cluster contains four reasons you think they are harmful: "create false needs," "poor role models," "numb the mind: no imagination needed," and "charge it today." You realize now that when you wrote "numb the mind" you were really thinking about television in general, not just commercials. So that leaves only three points.

Now you are wondering exactly what you meant about "role models" and "charge it today." You decide they are not something you could easily write about. That leaves only one point: "create false needs." You consider forgetting the whole idea, but you scribble down a possible working thesis: "Television advertisements create false needs for things we don't need and often can't pay for." That, you think, is something you can write about because you have experienced those false needs or desires.

Had you gone ahead and started writing a draft on the three items of the cluster "leg," you would have eventually realized you couldn't do it, but not before you wasted a lot of time, effort, and paper. In most cases, it pays to think before you write.

Even now, with a working thesis, you still aren't ready to write a first draft. To defend your thesis as stated, you'd have to show that TV ads create a desire for things we don't need and sometimes can't pay for. Do all television ads do this? No, so you change your thesis: "*Some* television advertisements create desires for things we don't need and often can't pay for." Now, which ones do that? You remember a television advertisement you saw for a truck. The ad made the truck look so appealing that you bought one, even though you really couldn't afford it. In fact, you had to get your parents to cosign on the loan. Also, you bought new speakers for the truck's stereo, which you didn't really need either.

As you think about your working thesis, it dawns on you: you use a brand of toothpaste and after-shave lotion because you've been influenced by commercials on television! You never used any after-shave lotion until that ad appeared. Even last night, you called an 800 number to order a collection of rock-and-roll oldies CDs advertised on television.

Suddenly, you realize that your thesis really applies to you! So you change your working thesis again: "Some television advertisements create desires *in me* for things *I* don't really need and often can't pay for." But the thesis sounds awkward, so you refine it: "Sometimes I am influenced by television advertisements and buy things I don't need and often can't afford."

Now you can see why the term *working thesis* is used at this stage of essay writing.

In the process of developing a thesis, the ideas used to form it often become part of the support, as in the previous example.

Working thesis: Sometimes I am influenced by television advertisements and buy things I don't need and often can't afford.

Support: the truck I bought

Support: the toothpaste I use

Support: the after-shave lotion I started using

Support: the CDs I ordered

Rather than writing a draft at this point, it would be better to brainstorm a bit more. What other ads have given you the "wants"? You soon come up with these:

Support: subscription to *TIME* magazine (a free watch came with it)

Support: subscription to *Sports Illustrated* (a free videotape came with it)

Support: a GPS system

Support: Nike tennis shoes (they had to be that brand)

Support: a survival knife I didn't need

By now, you are embarrassed by the growing list; that's enough support to prove your point.

Before going on, make certain you understand what is meant by a working thesis and support. In the following list of statements, circle only those statements that are valid working thesis statements. Then for those statements only, list in the space provided the topic and the supported needed.

1. First impressions of people can be misleading.

   _____

   _____

2. The salaries of major league sports players compared with those of teachers reflect the real attitude people have toward education.

   _____

   _____

3. The value of pets

   _____

   _____

4. Marriage, an outdated institution, is kept alive by religious advocates and lawyers who make money from divorces.

_____

_____

5. The problems of today's students

_____

_____

6. Affirmative action in the workplace is no longer needed.

_____

_____

Compare your answers with these. Item 1 could be used as a working thesis. The essay topic is first impressions of people. The keyword requiring support is "misleading." Examples are needed to support how first impressions can be misleading. Item 2 is also a possible working thesis. The topic is inequities in the salaries of teachers and major sports figures. The implied thesis is that people don't really care about education as much as they care about sports. Item 3 should not have been circled. The value of pets is a topic, but there is no statement about the value of pets. Item 4 contains the thesis that marriage is an outdated institution. Support would attempt to show that religious advocates and lawyers are responsible for keeping marriage a legal institution because of their own gain. Item 5 is only a topic, not a thesis statement. What about the problems of today's students? Are there any? If so, what are they? Item 6 should have been circled. The subject or topic is affirmative action; the support must show that there is no need for it in the workplace.

Grouping Your Ideas

Even after deciding on a working thesis, you're not quite ready to begin your first draft. You can't simply go down the list of supporting ideas, write a sentence about each one, and connect the sentences into an "essay." You need to organize the list in some way. Here's one way:

Group 1	Group 2	Group 3	Group 4
truck	toothpaste	*Time* subscription	records
truck's speakers	after-shave	*Sports Illustrated* subscription	knife
GPS system	tennis shoes		

Group 1 deals with the truck; Group 2, personal items; Group 3, magazine subscriptions; and Group 4, miscellaneous items.

Outlining Your Support

Using the reasoning behind your grouping, write an **informal outline** to follow when you begin your first draft.

Thesis:	Sometimes I am influenced by television advertisements and buy things I don't need and often can't afford.
Major support:	unnecessary truck purchase
	—didn't need it; old car OK
	—parents had to cosign
	—didn't need new speakers
	—didn't need a GPS system
Major support:	unnecessary personal items
	—changed toothpaste
	—started using after-shave
	—bought Nike tennis shoes; already had new Pumas
Major support:	unnecessary magazine subscriptions
	—subscribed to *Time* for the free watch; already have one
	—subscribed to *Sports Illustrated* for the free videotape of sports events
Major support:	unnecessary miscellaneous purchases
	—could have borrowed CDs from friends and made copies
	—survival knife, for what?

This informal outline provides a structure for getting your ideas on paper. Following it ensures organized support of the thesis.

There may be times when an instructor requires you to attach a more **formal outline** to your essay. In that case, you should submit something along these lines:

Main idea:	Sometimes I am influenced by television advertisements and buy things I don't need and often can't afford.

I.   Unnecessary truck purchase

   A. didn't need it; old car fine

   B. couldn't afford it

      1. parents had to cosign

      2. stuck with payments

    C. spent even more on unnecessary new speakers

    D. don't travel where I would need a GPS

II. Unnecessary changes in personal items

    A. switched brand of toothpaste

    B. started using after-shave lotion

    C. bought Nike tennis shoes because of ad

III. Unnecessary magazine subscriptions

    A. subscribed to *Time* for the free watch

    B. subscribed to *Sports Illustrated* for the free videotape

IV. Unnecessary miscellaneous purchases

    A. CDs

    B. survival knife

Regardless of what form an outline takes, it is, like a working thesis, usually a working outline. Once you start writing, new ideas may surface and you may add, delete, or change what you have in your outline. Until the final essay draft, nothing written should be considered permanent.

For practice, pick one of the topics you got from brainstorming or clustering on pages 42–45. In the space provided, write a topic, a working thesis, and a list of supporting points. If you don't have at least eight supporting points, do more brainstorming or clustering on your topic.

topic: _____

working thesis: _____

_____

support: _____

support: _____

support: _____

support: _____

support: _____

support: _____

support: _____

support: _____

_____

_____

Writing Exercise

In your journal or on a separate sheet of paper, group your support in the preceding activity into an organizational pattern you could follow to write your first draft.

Writing an Argumentative Essay

An argumentative essay contains a thesis that is debatable. Good topics for argumentative essays are controversial and can be disputed. The working thesis for the outline on pages 48–50, "Sometimes I am influenced by television advertisements and buy things I don't need and often can't afford," is not argumentative. A thesis that states, "Television advertisements use subliminal techniques to force viewers to buy goods they don't need or want" is argumentative.

Which of the following statements do you think would make a good argumentative thesis?

1. Atheists should not be allowed to teach elementary-school children.

2. We would all be healthier if we became vegetarians.

3. A healthy liver is vital to our bodily functions.

4. Campus parking fees should be reduced, since there is currently inadequate parking space for students.

5. Many college English departments no longer require students to read Shakespeare in order to graduate.

6. For population control, the United States should establish an immigration quota allowing only 50,000 entrants a year for the next five years.

As stated, items 3 and 5 are not argumentative. They are both factual statements, and while essays could be written based on the statements, there is nothing to argue. The rest of the statements can be debated because counterarguments can be made against them. Notice that all the thesis statements are conclusions and must be supported with evidence or critical reasoning. Such support must be supplied to argue for or against each of the thesis statements.

Purpose and audience: In writing an argumentative essay, your basic purpose is to convince readers that your viewpoint or position is better than an opposing one. Depending on your subject, you need to consider your audience. Do you want to give more support to an audience that already agrees with you? Do you want to win over those opposed to your views? Do you want to inspire readers to some action? Do you want to stop your audience from acting upon some issue? These are questions you must think about before developing your thesis, since your support must reach the audience you want to convince.

Rational and emotional support: Good arguments usually combine rational appeals involving logical evidence that supports the thesis with emotional appeals to the reader's feelings and beliefs. An argument that appeals only to the reader's rational side could fail to reach a common ground between the writer and the audience. However, emotional appeal should not be used alone and should not be used at all when the emotional issues raised do not relate to the thesis.

A reasonable argument depends on the evidence you use. Facts, statistics, specific examples, and opinions of experts are all useful in supporting your argument. Don't distort, exaggerate, oversimplify, or misquote your evidence to fit your argument. You will probably need to do some research on your topic in order to gather the evidence you need.

Consider your opposition's viewpoints. A good argument will take on the opposing views and show why they are not as reasonable or as true as yours. Be willing to recognize the merits of your opposition, but try to show why your viewpoint and evidence is more reasonable to consider.

Logical fallacies: Logical fallacies are errors in reasoning. You need to be able to spot them in the arguments of your opposition as well as to avoid making them yourself in any essay you write. Here is a list of some of the more common ones you should know and their definitions:

1. **Hasty generalization:** a conclusion or an opinion based on too little evidence.

2. **Either/or fallacy:** an implication that something must be either one thing or another; giving a complicated problem only two alternatives.

3. **False analogy:** a refusal to consider key differences or overreliance on the similarities in an analogy.

4. **Bandwagon fallacy:** an appeal to the audience's desire to be part of the in-group.

5. *Non sequitur:* a false conclusion drawn from irrelevant data.

6. **Begging the question:** accepting an opinion that is open to question as if it were already proved or disproved.

7. **Argument *ad hominem*** (Latin for "to the man"): an attack on the opponent rather than on the opponent's thesis.

8. **Argument *ad populum*** (Latin for "to the people"): an argument for a conclusion that is based on shared prejudices and values.

When reading or writing an argumentative essay, be aware of these common fallacies. They weaken any argument.

Checking your argument: If you write an argumentative essay, check for the following points:

1. Make certain that your thesis is arguable and can be developed through rational and emotional support.

2. Consider the members of your audience and the type of information they need.

3. Make certain your evidence is accurate, relevant, and adequate.

4. Consider the opposition's viewpoint and provide logical rebuttal if needed.

5. Check for logical fallacies in your own argument.

Of course, the three organizational writing stages discussed in this chapter apply to argumentative essays as well.

Writing Exercise

In your journal or on a separate sheet of paper, write down three topics that lend themselves to an argumentative essay. Write a possible thesis statement for each one that you feel you could develop in an essay. Then write another thesis statement for each topic that reflects an opposing viewpoint.

Nutshell Statements

You could begin writing your first draft at this point, but first you might want to write a nutshell statement. A nutshell statement is a one-paragraph statement of the **purpose** of your essay, the **support** you will use, and the **audience** for whom you are writing. *It is not, nor should it be considered, the opening paragraph of your essay.* It is a way for you to make certain that your purpose, support, and intended audience align well with each other.

A nutshell statement for an essay based on the outline on pages 49–50 might read:

> The purpose of my essay is to show how I am influenced by television commercials to buy things I don't need and often can't pay for. As support, I will reveal some of the items I have purchased recently because of ads I have

seen, such as my new truck, personal items, magazine subscriptions, and other miscellaneous things. My intended audience will be other buyers like myself, who have yet to realize the persuasive power television ads have on us.

Notice that the statement of purpose contains the thesis. The statement regarding support summarizes the major groups or categories of evidence to be discussed. The statement about audience provides a picture of the real or imaginary people interested in the subject or those you want to make more aware of your subject.

Whenever you write your audience is an important factor. A quick note containing sentence fragments and no punctuation that informs your roommate on your whereabouts may be acceptable, but it is certainly not appropriate for your boss. When planning an essay, then, you need to give thought to its purpose and the audience. Suppose, for instance, your audience is not other buyers like yourself, but parents of young children. Your revised nutshell statement might read like this:

> The purpose of my essay is to show the negative influence of television commercials aimed at young children. As support, I will describe some of the advertisements that appear on children's early-morning and Saturday programming that brainwash children and turn them into would-be consumers. My intended audience will be parents who allow their children to watch television unsupervised.

Notice the changes that need to be made as a result of your new audience. Now the thesis goes beyond the personal influence of television advertising to its influence on younger children. A different set of advertisements will be necessary for support of the thesis. Since the intended audience is now parents, even the language of the essay will need to be more formal and, given your purpose, more convincing.

Here is still another nutshell statement dealing with television commercials:

> The purpose of my essay is to write an argument in rebuttal to an article that appeared in the *Boston Globe*'s editorial pages today that claims that television commercials do not influence us. As support, I will use my own experiences, as well as factual information taken from my library research. My intended audience is the author of the article with whom I disagree and other *Globe* newspaper readers.

In this case, the final piece will be an argumentative essay that explains what the article in the *Globe* says and then provides proof that those comments about television commercials are wrong. Since the audience interested in the topic will be a fairly literate group of newspaper readers, the language selected must be appropriate, the arguments persuasive, and the other author must be shown to be wrong.

Even though your ultimate "audience" is your instructor, who will read and grade your essay, you should write for an audience that is either interested in your thesis or that needs to be made aware of it. Thinking about your audience before you write can help you determine the type of vocabulary to use, what arguments to present, and what to assume your audience may know about the subject. For instance, if your intended audience is fifth-grade students, you will have to write at a level they can understand. The words you use, your sentence structure, and the content will have to be geared to that group. On the other hand, if you are writing to convince antiabortionists to change their minds, you will need to understand their reasoning and provide counterarguments. You will have to imagine what they might say in reaction to what you say. You will have to decide what approach will get them to even listen to your views. Should you use sarcasm? Sympathy? Medical terms?

A nutshell statement requires that you have your purpose, support, and audience in mind before you begin writing. If you can complete a nutshell statement, then you are ready to begin your first draft. But keep in mind that the nutshell statement is *not* your opening paragraph.

Once you have your thesis, support, and audience in mind, you're ready to start your first draft.

Writing Exercise

In your journal or on a separate sheet of paper, write a one-paragraph nutshell statement for an essay based on the outline you completed on pages 50–51.

Patterning Your Paragraphs: The Beginning

As readers, we see only the finished product of a writer, not all the changes that went into creating it. What finally appears as a beginning or introductory paragraph may actually be the last paragraph an author writes. In other words, it is not infrequent that the opening paragraph you write in a first draft is *not* the opening paragraph in the final draft. In fact, that first paragraph may not even be used in the final draft, or it could be changed so much that it no longer resembles what you started with. By the time revisions are made and the support has been established, the original draft of your introductory paragraph may be obsolete.

Most of us, however, begin writing our first drafts with what we think will be our introduction. It helps us formulate and state our thesis. Such a paragraph may help *us* get started, but it may not get our readers interested in what we have to say. What, then, are some effective ways to begin an essay?

Here are some suggestions that may work for you, depending on your essay audience and purpose. Many of the essays in this book use these methods. Read the essays mentioned to see each strategy at work.

1. Get right to the point, stating your thesis and your general reasons for feeling or believing as you do. One drawback to this approach is that unless your thesis is stated in such a way that your audience will be interested in reading on, it could be a boring opening. See how this method is used in the essay on outsourcing work (page 399).

2. Use a quotation or reference to other writings that relate to your thesis, one by someone respected by almost everyone, one that supports your point of view, or one with which you disagree and want to disprove in your essay. Jeff Yeager does this in his essay "Less Is More" (page 323).

3. Tell a brief anecdote or story that relates in some way to or introduces the point of your thesis. For examples, look at the introductory paragraphs in Roger von Oech's "To Err Is Wrong" (p. 88) or Brent Staples's "Night Walker" (p. 139).

4. Use one or more questions that cause the reader to think about your topic, questions that you intend to answer in the body of your essay. Notice how both the title and the opening paragraph use a question to draw your interest (p. 133).

5. Provide some startling statistics or information that will get the reader's attention and that will appeal to the reader's good sense. Notice how this is done in Mary Sherry's "In Praise of the F Word" (p. 97).

6. Describe a scene that gets attention and pulls your reader into the subject. Francis Flaherty describes a troubling scene in "'The Ghetto Made Me Do It'" (p. 163) that sets the stage for the selection.

7. Be creative and use a combination of the above strategies.

The introductory paragraph is an important one. Make certain that whatever method you use, that your opening draws your reader's interest, fits into the point of your essay, and gets the reader involved in your subject. As a reminder, don't use your nutshell statement as an introductory paragraph.

Patterning Your Paragraphs: The Middle

As a means for better reading comprehension, Chapter 1 presented some paragraph methods that writers use. Now let's look at those same paragraph patterns from the writer's angle.

Recall that the **topic sentence** in a paragraph serves the same function as the thesis statement in an essay. Just as what you say in your essay depends on the point of your thesis, what you say and how you say it depend on the topic sentence of your paragraph. Here are some possible topic sentences for paragraphs. Notice that the way they are written pretty much determines the paragraph pattern.

Topic Sentence	*Best Pattern*
The Chevy Blazer commercial was very appealing.	**description** Descriptive details should be provided to create an image in the reader's mind of the commercial's appeal.
Yesterday I went from one truck dealership to the next looking for the best deal.	**narration** A narrative would take the reader from one dealership experience to the next, relating what happened at each.
I now recognize three reasons why I buy many things I don't really need.	**analysis** Each of the three reasons for the buying problem needs to be examined.
I recently bought several things I don't need.	**illustration-example** Evidence needs to be provided to illustrate the unnecessary items purchased. Examples of the things not needed or a narrative about the buying of unnecessary items is required.
Pat's mother says he is the perfect example of an impulsive buyer.	**definition** The term *impulsive buyer* needs to be defined so that readers understand what Pat is an example of.
The commercial showed the four basic types of auto stereo speakers.	**division-classification** The topic sentence divides the speakers into four basic types, each of which needs to be named and discussed.
The Dodge truck commercial appealed to Jim more than the one for Chevrolets.	**comparison-contrast** Although some description of the two truck ads may be needed, the topic sentence calls for a comparison of the two ads to show why Jim preferred one over the other.
Because the Ford commercial was so well done, I bought one of Ford's trucks.	**cause-effect** The cause here is the ad, and the effect is the purchase; description of the well-done ad may be needed to help explain the cause.

It is important to see here that the way you state a topic sentence requires that you structure your paragraph with a pattern that supports it. Of course, all the examples above are "working" topic sentences. After you have developed your support, you may need to change the wording of the topic sentence to fit what you wrote. You may decide that the topic sentence is best placed at the end of the paragraph or in the middle, or that it should be implied rather than stated. Remember, revision is not limited to any one particular stage. It occurs at all points during the writing process. But if writing does not come easily for you, try writing a topic sentence that you can use as the first sentence in the paragraph and work from there.

Read the following topic sentences. In the space provided below each sentence, write a one-sentence statement that tells what pattern or method should be used to develop the paragraph and why.

1. "Compared to the animals around us, there's no doubt we are a remarkable phenomenon."

   _____

   _____

2. "I will never forget that Sunday as long as I live."

   _____

   _____

3. "I remember going out to play tennis one day about 20 years ago and having my wife stop me in the doorway with a piece of friendly advice."

   _____

   _____

4. "There are four reasons for practicing freewriting."

   _____

   _____

5. "After the dishes have soaked in water hot enough to deform small plastic implements, I begin my attack."

   _____

   _____

6. "We humans live with contradictions in our behavior."

_____

_____

7. "Irony is not easy to explain."

_____

_____

8. "Television journalism has recently stimulated political conservatism."

_____

_____

Compare your statements with the following. The wording may be different, but the explanations should contain the same ideas.

1. The **comparison-contrast** method will show why humans are a phenomenon compared with other animals.

2. A **narration** will tell us about that unforgettable Sunday.

3. The rest of the paragraph is an example of **description**—the author describes his wife's advice.

4. **Division-classification** is required to show each of the four reasons for practicing freewriting.

5. The "attack" on the dishes is a process calling for a **step-by-step analysis.**

6. **Examples and illustrations** of contradictory behavior are needed for support.

7. An extended **definition** of irony should show why it isn't easy to define.

8. If television journalism has stimulated political conservatism, some proof or support of this **cause-effect** relationship is required.

If you had trouble with these, you may want to review the section on paragraph patterns in Chapter 1.

Patterning Your Paragraphs: The Ending

As with essay introductions, there is no one way to conclude an essay. Many students tend to repeat almost verbatim in their closing paragraph what they said in their opening one. However, the concluding paragraph of an essay should not simply duplicate what has already been written. Instead, you will usually want to do one of these three things in your last paragraph, depending on your thesis:

1. Summarize the major points of the essay. This can be tricky. Try to summarize by using different wording to restate the points you've made in a fresh but familiar way. Don't use this method in a short essay with only three or four supporting paragraphs. This approach works best when you have written a longer piece with many points. Your summary will help your reader pull together all the points.

2. Draw a conclusion based on the information you presented. This method works best when you have argued for a particular viewpoint and you have presented evidence that must be highlighted so the reader can draw a conclusion. Usually, you begin your closing paragraph with words such as "From these facts we can see that. . .," or "For these reasons we must conclude that. . .," and then you state your conclusion. Note that you should not confuse the word *conclusion,* meaning "the end," with "drawing a conclusion," or making a judgment based on information provided.

3. Emphasize the need for change or more attention on the subject. Make a pitch for what needs to be done, based on the information you have presented in your essay. Call upon your readers to think more, care more, or act more on the subject of your essay now that you have successfully made your case.

Many of the paragraph patterns already discussed can be used effectively in concluding paragraphs.

 ## Writing Exercise

In your journal or on a separate sheet of paper, summarize the information on writing beginning, middle, and ending paragraphs. Make certain you understand pages 55–60 before going on.

First Draft

Let's say that you decide to follow the formal outline on pages 49–50 about the effect of television commercials. The first draft might look something like this:

```
                         First Draft
    1       I have a tendency to buy things I see on television com-
         mercials even though I don't need them and often can't pay
```

for them. The other night I was putting myself to sleep by watching a late movie on TV when an ad with a fast-talking announcer began describing a new collection of rock-and-roll oldies CDs. You've probably seen the kind I mean. You get to hear little pieces of music with famous singers singing one or two lines sung then they cut to the next song. Anyway, I like all of the songs they played, and when the announcer said, "Call this 800 number now and get these fabulous songs not sold in any record store," I called and ordered the record set. This is not unusual behavior for me.

2　　I bought my truck because of a TV commercial. It seemed like every time I watched TV I'd see the same ad for the truck. It showed the truck going through mud, climbing hills, and carrying heavy loads. Then it showed a guy and his girl-friend all dressed up pulling up in front of some fancy res-taurant in the truck all shined up. The girl was something else and every time the ad came on I caught myself looking at her and not the truck. Anyway, the next thing I knew I had talked my folks into cosigning the loan for me even though they tried to talk me out of it. Banks don't loan money to college students to buy trucks. There wasn't anything wrong with my old car. But I came up with this crazy idea I could get some part-time work hauling or something to help make the payments. I think that's what convinced them to help out. Any-way, now I can't afford to take a girl out because I'm too busy with classes, homework, and an evening job I have to keep to make my truck payments.

3　　I also have two magazine subscriptions that I don't even have time to read. When TIME showed an ad on TV for a good deal on a subscription, plus a free watch, I called their toll-free number. Then Sports Illustrated ran an ad for their magazine offering a free videocassette of famous sports plays if you subscribed to them. Of course, I called their toll-free number. Now unread magazines are stacking up around my room. Not only that, they sent me a Beta videocassette and we've got VHS.

4   I realize now that I have even been persuaded by TV ads to
buy items I never used before. My family has always used Crest.
After seeing all those ads for Closeup and having kissable
breath, I got my mom to buy some for me. I even use an after-
shave lotion now because of ads. I use to do like my dad and
just put on a little of mom's skin cream after I shaved. And
even though I didn't need them, I bought a new pair of Nike
tennis shoes because a TV commercial for a local shoe store had
them on sale.

5   Last night there was a commercial on TV for a good deal on a
neat looking survival knife. It looked like something the commandos use. It had a big blade, a compass in the handle, with a
fish hook and line, matches and the sheath had a little pocket
with a sharpening stone in it. Naturally, I ordered one.

6   When my mom heard about this she called me an "impulsive
compulsive buyer." When I asked her what she meant, she just
yelled look it up. After looking it up, I realize she's right.
I need to belong to a "buyers anonymous" group or something.

Even though the outline wasn't followed exactly, it served to get the ideas into a rough draft in essay form. Of course, this is just the first draft. There's more to be done.

This is a good place to make another pitch for using a word processor. If you don't know how already, you should learn to write using word processing soft-ware. Making changes, doing revisions, and producing neat essays is so much easier once you learn word processing software. A recent study done by a profes-sional organization of English teachers revealed that students who submitted typed papers usually got a letter grade higher than those who submitted hand-written papers. But more importantly, word processing software lets you make changes without having to retype your entire essay.

Whatever you use for your first drafts-pencil, pen, typewriter, or word processing software—don't worry about mistakes in punctuation, word choice, spelling, and the like. At this point, you just want to get your essay ideas into words on paper. If you stop to make too many corrections as you write, you may lose your train of thought. Worry about the "details of correct English later. If there's an error you can quickly fix, go ahead and do it, but never do it at the expense of thoughtful content.

Before Going On

Remember that a working thesis statement is open to changes based on your sup-porting ideas. Before writing a first draft, make certain that you have sufficient support to develop your thesis. Once you are satisfied that you do, organize or outline the support as a writing guide. Writing a nutshell statement before you begin your draft helps you focus on your thesis, support, and audience. As you write your draft, be aware that all paragraphs should have an implied or directly stated topic sentence. The wording of your topic sentence often can provide a clue as to the best paragraph pattern to use. However, don't let concern over paragraph patterns or mechanical errors get in the way of getting your ideas on paper. Changes and corrections can be made during the revision and editing process.

Writing Exercise

Look again at the draft of the student essay on television commercials. Apply the information on reading essays from Chapter 1. Mark and take notes as you read. Then, in your journal or on a separate sheet of paper, write what you would tell the student about the essay, offering your suggestions for improvement and indicating errors that should be corrected. Your instructor may want to see your paper.

Getting It Right: Revising and Editing (Stage 3)

It can't be said too often that good writing frequently requires many rewrites. Don't be impatient. Revision is necessary, expected, and part of the writing process. A final draft may look nothing like the first one. There's much to do before turning in your masterpiece.

Revising

Here's a checklist to guide your revision of your first draft:

1. *Have you made your point?*
   Make sure your thesis is clear. Stated or implied, your purpose should be clear to the reader. Have someone read your draft; if he or she doesn't understand the point you're trying to make, rewrite until it becomes clear. It's even possible that you will need to change your entire thesis once a first draft is completed.

2. *Does your support move smoothly from one point to the next?*
   Rearrange what you have written so that the ideas flow easily from one to the next. You may need to "cut and paste," or move a sentence or paragraph from one place to another. Use scissors and literally cut up your draft, moving parts around where you want them. (Here again, word processing helps. With word processing software you can easily move entire paragraphs without having to

cut or retype.) To move smoothly and logically from one point to the next, use transitional words and phrases such as these:

however	thus	in addition
although	on the other hand	first
therefore	in conclusion	next
furthermore	in other words	finally
moreover	for instance	as a result
consequently	for example	also

3. *Have you developed each paragraph fully?*
   Look closely at the topic sentence of each paragraph. Do you provide enough support to fully develop the topic sentence? You may need to add more information or take out information that does not relate to the topic sentence. You may need to rewrite your topic sentence to fit the content of the paragraph.

4. *Will your essay interest your audience?*
   Try to make your essay interesting for your audience. Your opening paragraph should grab the readers' attention and make them want to read on. Try to get a picture in your mind of your audience and talk to them in writing. Sometimes the opening paragraph doesn't take shape until several drafts have been completed.

5. *Is the tone of your essay consistent?*
   Use the same **tone of voice** throughout your essay. For instance, the tone of the student's rough draft on television commercials is personable and friendly. Using contractions (such as **don't** instead of **do not**) is acceptable in informal writing. The essay is not written for the audience of a scholarly or professional journal. If it were, it would need more formal language, less personal narrative, and a thesis that deals more broadly with television commercials and that cites sources other than personal experience.

6. *Have you said everything you want and need to say and nothing else?*
   Make certain you have said everything necessary to support your thesis. On the other hand, you may need to cut out passages that aren't relevant or that repeat what you've already said.

7. *Have you thought of a title that reflects your thesis?*
   Sometimes a title for an essay immediately comes to mind, even before it is written. But generally it's best to hold off on coming up with a title until you have at least written your first draft. A title, like a thesis, should not be too general. It should reflect the purpose, the content, and the tone of your essay.

Let's apply the above checklist to the rough draft on television commercials. Here's what it might look like:

1 I have a tendency to buy things I see on television commercials even though I don't need them and often can't pay for them. [place at end of essay] The other night I was putting myself to sleep by watching a late movie on ~~my~~ [television] when a~~n~~ ~~ad~~ [commercial] with a fast-talking announcer began describing a new collection of old rock-and-roll CDs. You've probably seen the kind I mean. ~~You get to hear~~ [They play] little ~~pieces~~ [snippets] of ~~music~~ one or two lines ~~song~~ [of a song] then they cut to the next ~~song~~ [one]. ~~Anyway,~~ I like all of the songs they played, ~~and~~ [so] when the announcer said, "[Operators on duty.] Call this 800 number now and ~~get these~~ [order this] fabulous ~~songs~~ [CD set] not sold in any ~~record~~ store," I ~~called and ordered the record set~~ [did.] [new ¶] This is not unusual behavior for me.

2 I bought my truck because of a TV commercial. It seemed like every time I watched TV I'd see the same ad for the truck. It showed the ~~truck~~ [truck at work during the day] going through mud, climbing hills, and carrying heavy loads. Then it showed ~~a guy and his girlfriend all dressed up~~ [the truck at night, cleaned and polished] pulling up in front of ~~some fancy~~ [a posh] restaurant ~~in the truck all shined up. The girl was something else and~~ [As the driver got out, a doorman helped the woman out. Both looked elegant, but she really got to me.] Every time the ad came on I caught myself looking at her and not the truck. [new ¶] [I realize now it wasn't the truck I wanted.] Anyway, the next thing I knew I had talked my folks into cosigning ~~the~~ [a] loan for ~~me even though~~ [a new truck since] They tried to talk me out of it. Banks don't loan money to college students to buy trucks [because] There wasn't anything wrong with my old car. But I came up with this crazy idea I could get some part-time work hauling or ~~something~~ [delivering] to help make the payments. I think that's what convinced them to help out. ~~Anyway,~~ Now [I wish I hadn't been so convincing.] I can't afford to take a girl out because I'm too busy with classes, homework, and an evening job I have to keep to make my truck payments.

3 [Thanks to television commercials] I also have two magazine subscriptions that I don't even have time to read. When ~~Time showed an ad on TV~~ [I saw a commercial] for a ~~good deal~~ [reduced price] on a subscription [for Time] plus a free watch, I called their toll-free number. Then *Sports Illustrated* ~~ran an ad for their magazine offering~~ [offered a low-priced subscription and] a free videocassette of famous sports plays. ~~if you subscribed to them.~~ Of course, I called their toll-free number. Now unread magazines are stacking up around my room.

4   I realize now that I have even been persuaded by TV ads to
buy items I never used before. My family has always used Crest.
After seeing all those ads for Closeup and ~~having~~ kissable
the need for
breath, I got my mom to buy some for me. I even ~~use~~ an after-
began using
shave lotion now because of ~~ads~~. I use to do like my dad and
the influence of commercials
just put on a little of mom's skin cream after I shaved. And
even though I didn't need them, I bought a new pair of Nike
tennis shoes because a TV commercial for a local shoe store had
them on sale.

5   Last night there was a commercial on TV for a good deal on
interesting   *similar to the ones*
an ~~neat~~ looking survival knife. ~~It looked like something the~~
s
commandos use. It had a big blade, a compass in the handle,
with a fish hook and line, matches and the sheath had a little
pocket with a sharpening stone in it. Naturally, I ordered
one. *end here*

When my mom heard about this she called me an "impulsive compulsive buyer." When I asked her what she meant, she just
yelled look it up. After looking it up, I realize she's right.
I need to belong to a "buyers anonymous" group or something.

Look more closely at some of the changes being considered for the next draft.
Sentences are to be moved or removed. Wording has been changed, in some cases
to keep from repeating words, in others to be more descriptive or clear. New
paragraphs have been started in different places, and the last paragraph has been
moved. While none of the support has changed, more attention has been paid to
the flow of support, with smoother transitions from one idea to the next. Attention to such details is the basis for the second draft. And even after that draft is
completed, it may be necessary to write still another.

After applying the revision checklist to several different drafts, you might have
a paper resembling this one. Look carefully at the changes made.

About to doze off while watching an old movie on television
the other night, a commercial caught my eye. The sound came up
as a fast-talking announcer began describing a new CD
collection of old rock-and-roll music. You've probably seen the
kind I mean. They play little snippets of singers singing one
or two seconds of a song that made them famous, cutting quickly
from one to the next. I like all the tunes they played, so when
the announcer urged, "Call this toll-free number now . . .

operators are standing by . . . order this fabulous set of
records not available in any store," I did.

    This, I'm sorry to say, is not unusual behavior for me. For in-
stance, when I saw a television commercial offering a free digital
watch along with a reduced price on a subscription to TIME, I
called its toll-free number. Then Sports Illustrated offered a low
price subscription along with a free videocassette of some famous
sports plays. Of course, I had to call its toll-free number too.
Now I have unread magazines stacking up around my room.

    TV commercials have influenced me so much that I even use
personal items I have never used before, my family has used
Crest toothpaste ever since I can remember. But after all those
ads for Close-up (I think its the kissable breath idea) I had
my mom buy some just for me. And, like my dad, I used to just
apply a little of moms skin cream on my face after I shaved.
But now, thanks to the influence of television commercials,
I have tried several bands of after-shave lotion.

    The biggest purchase I ever made because of a TV commercial is
my truck. It seemed like every time I watched TV I'd see the same
ad for a pickup truck. It showed the truck at work during the day
going through mud, climbing hills, and carrying heavy loads. Then
it showed the truck at night, cleaned and polished, pulling up in
front of a plush restaurant. As the driver got out, a doorman
helped his date step out. Both of them looked elegant. But it was
the woman that got me. Every time the commercial comes on,
I caught myself looking at her, not the truck. Anyway, the next
thing I knew I had talked my folks into cosigning a loan for a
new truck, since banks don't loan money to unemployed college
students to buy new trucks. They tried to talk me out of it
because there wasn't anything wrong with my old one. But you know
how it is when you think you really want something. I rationalized that I could get part-time work hauling or delivering to
help make payments. I think that's what convinced my mom and dad
to help out.

    Now I wish I hadn't been so convincing. I can't afford to go
out on a date because I'm too busy with classes, homework, and

an evening job. If I don't make my truck payments, my parents
said they will sell my truck. They don't want to be stuck with
the payments. I can't blame them. Recently a local shoe store
announced on television that Nike tennis shoes were on sale. The
next day, I bought a pair, even though I had just bought a pair
of Pumas a week before. When my mom heard, she called me an "impulsive compulsive buyer". When I asked her what she meant, she
yelled, "Look it up!" and mumbled something about my need to
join a "buyers anonymous" group or quit watching so much TV.

   She's right I have a tendency to buy things I see on television even though I don't need them or can't really afford them.
Even last night, there was a commercial for a survival knife
similar to the type commandos use. The knife has a big blade, a
hollow handle with a fish hook, some line, a few matches, a
compass that screws on top of the knife handle, and the sheath
has a little pocket on the side with a sharpening stone, I just
couldn't resist calling there toll-free number.

This draft still retains the same thesis and support, but it is structured differently. The position of the thesis has been moved from the opening paragraph to the end. The first draft opened with the thesis statement and then provided examples of "impulsive compulsive" buying. This draft opens with a narrative anecdote that reflects the subject and thesis of the essay, rather than directly stating it. The narrative now builds on one purchase after another and ends with the thesis statement. This seems to work better because the thesis itself doesn't deal with any resolution of the problem, only an awareness of the influence of television commercials on the author.

Other changes in the position of the supporting materials have been made. The largest purchase, the truck, has been moved toward the end of the essay, with smaller purchases leading up to it. The placement of the Nike purchase after the truck purchase works well because it reflects the mother's exasperation with her son's buying habits. It also serves as a transition to the last paragraph, which now contains the thesis and an acknowledgment that the author's mother is right: Another needless purchase, the survival knife, is made. The essay ends with a touch of humor, yet it leaves the reader with a feeling of pity for the author.

While the student essay is not perfect, it is an honest essay based on personal experience, and it fits the assignment given: to write an essay on some aspect of television. Had the assignment been more specific, such as one requiring research on the effects of television advertising, then this first-person essay would not do.

As improved as this draft is over the first, there is still more to do before the student can turn it in. The essay needs editing.

Editing

Once you are satisfied that your essay's organizational structure and thesis are clear and fully developed, you need to edit your essay for errors in punctuation and mechanics. Of course, as you do this, you may also see other problems or errors that need revision. Revision is a continual process, even though you may be focusing on making specific corrections.

Here is a list of questions to ask yourself when you edit your latest draft:

1. *Have you given yourself some time off between drafts?*
   Put your essay aside for at least a couple of hours before editing. In fact, it's a good idea to do this after each draft. You need to get away from what you've written so that you can come back to it with "fresh eyes."

2. *Have you read each sentence aloud to hear how it sounds?*
   Begin editing by reading aloud the *last* sentence of your essay. Once you're satisfied that it is the best you can do, read aloud the next-to-last sentence and evaluate it the same way. Sentence by sentence, gradually work your way to the beginning of the essay sentence by sentence. It sounds odd, but doing this forces you to look at each sentence out of context, as a separate piece of writing. Listen to the way each sentence sounds. If it is difficult to read or if it sounds awkward, rewrite it. Make certain each sentence is complete, not a fragment, not a piece of a sentence.

3. *Have you used proper punctuation?*
   Don't form a comma splice by putting a comma (,) between two sentences. If you aren't sure where a comma belongs, it's probably best to leave it out. Place periods (.) at the ends of sentences, not at the ends of phrases or introductory clauses. Use apostrophes (') to show possession (Tom's house, the grandparents' house). Watch for *you're* (you are) as opposed to *your* (belonging to you), and *it's* (it is) as opposed to *its* (belonging to it). Use the serial comma (x, y, and z).

4. *Do your verbs agree with their subjects?*
   Watch for sentences that contain singular subjects and plural verbs. For instance, in the following sentence, the subject is singular, but a plural verb is used:

   A set of books are missing.

   Because *set* is the subject, not *books,* the verb *is* should be used. Also look for sentences that contain plural subjects but singular verbs, such as:

   Boxes of computer software was everywhere.

   The sentence should use the verb *were* to agree with the subject *boxes.* Such mistakes are easy to make.

5. *Are your pronoun references correct?*
Look at each pronoun (*his, her, their, its,* etc.) and make sure it agrees with the noun to which it refers to. For instance, it's incorrect to write:

> Everyone in the group must buy their own lunch.

Since *everyone* is singular, the plural pronoun *their* can't be used. It should read:

> Everyone in the group must buy his or her own lunch.

[Note: Avoid sexist usage. Don't use *his* when the reference being made is to a group containing both men and women.] Don't confuse *there* (not here), *they're* (they are), and *their* (belonging to them).

6. *Have you repeated the same word too often?*
If you don't own a thesaurus, a dictionary of synonyms (words that mean the same thing), you should buy one. Several are published in paperback editions. A good thesaurus will not only define words for you but also provide synonyms and antonyms (words that are opposite in meaning). When you notice that you are repeating a word, look it up and use a synonym. There are also many good free online thesauruses.

7. *Do you have a title that reflects your thesis?*
A title, like a thesis, should not be too general. It should reflect the purpose and the content of your paper. Your title should also fit the tone of your essay. If your essay is serious in tone, it's probably best to have a title that is direct; if your essay is light or humorous, try a catchy title.

For practice in editing, apply the steps of the preceding editing checklist to the last draft of the student essay on pages 63–70. Change any errors you find and give the essay an appropriate title.

Writing Exercise

In your journal or on a separate sheet of paper, write a one-paragraph summary of the editing checklist. Make certain you have a topic sentence that allows you to discuss all the steps. Your instructor may want to see your summary.

Here is what the next draft of the essay might look like after editing and minor revisions. Compare your markings with those below.

Trouble with Toll-Free Numbers

About to doze off while watching an old movie on television

awkward opening [the other night, ~a commercial caught my ~eye~. The sound came up
change opening

as a fast-talking announcer began describing a new CD

the sound of (inserted above "a commercial")

attention (inserted above "eye")

collection of old rock-and-roll music. You've probably seen the kind I mean. They play little snippets of singers singing one or two seconds of a song that made them famous, cutting quickly from one to the next. I like all the tunes they played, so when the announcer urged, "Call this toll-free number now . . . operators are standing by . . . order this fabulous set of records not available in any store," I did.

This, I'm sorry to say, is not unusual behavior for me. For instance, when I saw a television commercial offering a free digital watch along with a reduced price on a subscription to *Time*, I called their toll-free number. Then *Sports Illustrated* offered a low price subscription along with a free videocassette of some famous sports plays. Of course, I had to call their toll-free number, too. Now I have unread magazines stacking up around my room.

italicize magazine titles

TV commercials have influenced me so much that I even use personal items I have never used before. my family has used Crest toothpaste ever since I can remember. But after all those ads for Close-up (I think it's the kissable breath idea), I had my mom buy some just for me. And, like my dad, I used to just apply a little of mom's skin cream on my face after I shaved. But now, thanks to the influence of television commercials, I have tried several bands of after-shave lotion.

cap m

it's=it is

possessive

Comma splice replace with period

Comma after intro phrase

The biggest purchase I ever made because of a TV commercial is my truck. It seemed like every time I watched TV I'd see the same ad for a pickup truck. It showed the truck at work during the day going through mud, climbing hills, and carrying heavy loads. Then it showed the truck at night, cleaned and polished, pulling up in front of a plush restaurant. As the driver got out, a doorman helped his date step out. Both of them looked elegant. But it was the woman that got me. Every time the commercial comes on, I caught myself looking at her, not the truck. Anyway, the next thing I knew I had talked my folks into cosigning a loan for a new truck, since banks don't loan money to unemployed college students to buy new trucks. They tried to talk me out of it because there wasn't anything wrong with my

that

-looking

the doorman's date?

use who to refer to people

who

came

Past tense

parents

old one. But you know how it is when you really want something. I rationalized that I could get part-time work hauling or delivering to help make payments. I think that's what convinced my mom and dad to help out.

Now I wish I hadn't been so convincing. I can't afford to go out on a date because I'm too busy with classes, homework, and an evening job. If I don't make my truck payments, my parents said they would sell my truck. They don't want to be stuck with the payments. I can't blame them. [new ¶] Recently a local shoe store announced on television that Nike tennis shoes were on sale. The next day, I bought a pair [*them*], even though I had just bought a pair [*pair used twice*] of Pumas a week before. When my mom heard she called me an "impulsive compulsive buyer". When I asked her what she meant, [*period goes inside*] she yelled, "Look it up!" and mumbled something about my need to join a "buyers anonymous" group or quit watching so much TV.

She's right, I have a tendency to buy things I see on television even though I don't need them or can't really afford them. [*run-on sentence needs ;*] Even last night, there was a commercial for a survival knife similar to the type commandos use. The knife has a big blade, a hollow handle with a fish hook, some line, a few matches, a compass that screws on top of the knife handle, and the sheath has a little pocket on the side with a sharpening stone, I just couldn't resist calling there [*their*] toll-free number. [*ww wrong word*]

You are now ready to type up the final draft to submit to your instructor.

Proofreading

Once you write, type, or print out your final draft, you should proofread your paper for typing and spelling mistakes. It's possible that even then you might notice changes that have to be made. Remember that revising and editing, even though presented here as Stage 3, can happen at any stage of the writing process.

If the final copy of your essay has many mistakes, you may need to recopy or retype it. However, if it has only a few minor errors, use standard proofreading symbols to make your corrections.

Your final copy might be marked like this after proofreading:

Trouble with Toll-Free Numbers

The other night I was about to doze off while watching an old movie on television when the sounds of a commercial caught my

attention. A fast-talking an*o*nuncer began describing a new compact disk collection of old rock-and-roll music. You've probably seen the kind I mean. They play little snippets of singers
singing one or two seconds of a song that ma*d*ke them famous,
cutting quickly from one to the next. I like all the tunes they
played, so when the announcer urged, "Call this toll-free
number now...operators are standing by...order this
fabul*í*ous set of CDs not available in any store," I did.

This, I'm sorry to say, is not unusual behavior for me. For
instance, when I saw a television commercial offering a free
digital watch along with a reduced price on a subscription to
Time, I called ~~their~~ *its* toll-free number. Then *Sports Illustrated*
offered a low-priced subscription along with a free videocassette of famous sports plays. Of course, I had to call ~~their~~ *its*
toll-free number, too. Now I have stacks of unread magazines
around my room.

TV commercials have influenced me so much that I even use
personal items I never used before. My family has brushed with
Crest toothpaste ever since I can remember. But after all those
ads for Close-up (I think it's the kissable breath idea), I had
*M*mom buy some just for me. And, like my dad, I used to just
apply a little of *M*moms skin cream on my face after I shaved.
But now, thanks to the influence of television commercials, I
have tried several b*r*ands of after-shave lotion.

The biggest purchase I ever made because of a TV commercial
was my truck. Almost every time I watched TV, I would see the
same ad for a pickup truck. It showed the truck at work during
the day going through mud, climbing, ~~rails~~ *trails*, and carrying heavy
loads. Then it showed the truck at night, cleaned and polished.
Neon signs reflected off the truck as it pulled in front of a
plush-looking restaurant. As the driver, now dressed in his
finest, got out, a doorman helped ~~his~~ *the driver's* elegant-looking date step
from the truck. But it was the woman who got me. Every time the
commercial came on, I caught myself looking at her, not the truck.

Anyway, the next thing I knew I had talked my parents into
cosigning a loan for a new truck, since banks don't loan money
to unemployed college students to buy new trucks. They tried to

discourage me because there wasn't anything wrong with my old
one. But you know how it is when you really want something. I
^think you^
rationalized that I could get part-time work hauling or delivering to help make payments. I think that's what convinced my
mom and dad to help out.

Now I wish I hadn't been so convincing. I can't afford to go
out on a date because of my truck payments. After attending
classes, doing my homework, and working an evening job, I'm too
tired to do anything b~~y~~t watch TV. If I don't make my truck
payments, my parents said they ~~would~~ sell my truck. They don't
^will^
want to be stuck with the bill. I can't blame them.

But my buying hasn't stopped there. Recently a local shoe
store announced on television that Nike tennis shoes were on
sale. The next day, I bought them, even though I had just
bought a pair of Pumas a week before. When my mom heard, she
called me an "impulsive compulsive buyer." When I asked her
what she meant, she yelled, "Look it up!" and mumbled something
about my need to join a "buyers anonymous" group or quit watching so much TV.

She's right; I have a tendency to buy things I see on television even though I don't need them or can't really affrod them.
Even last night, there was a commercial for a survival knife
similar to the type commandos use. It has a big blade, a hollow
handle with a fish hook, some line, a few matches, a compass
that screws on top of the handle, and the sheath has a little
pocket on the side with a sharpening stone. When the~~ir~~ toll-
free number was announced, I just couldn't resist calling.

Using the proper proofreading marks relieves you of retyping or recopying
your entire essay. One of the reasons for double-spacing each page is to leave
room to make corrections neatly. Of course, if there are so many corrections that
the paper is too messy to read, you will have to redo it.

To practice your proof-marking skills, use these standard proofreading symbols to correct the paragraph below the list.

to remove a letter   reaĺlly

to insert a word or letter   lib^á^ry

to insert punctuation	professor's book
to insert a space	the model essay
to reverse letters	revrese
to change a word	a little ~~larger~~ smaller
to close up a space	re verse

> Lets say you are assigned to do research on what critics have said abuot John Updikes novel *The Witches of Eastwick*. In such a case secondary sources will be called for in your pa per. If, on the other hand the assignment calls for your own analysis of the novel, you will neeed to stick to the primary source, the novel Reading secondarysources on the novel, however, may provide you with ideas arguments that could be useful in supporting your own analysis of the book.

Compare your markings with the following to see how well you did.

> Let's say you are assigned to do research on what critics have said abuot John Updikes novel *The Witches of Eastwick*. In such a case, secondary sources will be called for in your paper. If, on the other hand, the assignment calls for your own analysis of the novel, you will neeed to stick to the primary source, the novel. Reading secondary sources on the novel, however, may provide you with ideas and arguments that could be useful in supporting your own analysis of the book.

Before submitting an essay that has this many corrections in one paragraph, you should retype it. The corrections get in the way of the content.

Your instructor may require that you follow a particular format regarding size of margins; position of name, title, and page numbers; and so on. Check with your instructor on the desired format.

Before Going On

Remember that revising and editing are necessary and vital to good writing. Use the revision stage to make certain that your essay makes its point, that the point is supported adequately, that each paragraph is developed fully, that your tone is consistent, and that you have done your best to make the essay interesting to your audience. When editing, look at each sentence separately. Make certain that each sentence is complete and that it sounds correct. Check for correct punctuation, subject-verb agreement, pronoun agreement, and overuse of certain words.

Writing Exercise

In your journal or on a separate sheet of paper, write three paragraphs summarizing the major points of each of the three stages of writing presented in this chapter. Make certain each paragraph has a topic sentence and that each paragraph is developed fully. Apply the three writing stages to this writing exercise. Your instructor may want you to turn in this exercise.

Revising and Editing Checklists: Brief Versions

Before turning in a completed essay to your instructor, use the following check-lists to make certain you have applied the steps in the three writing stages presented in this chapter.

   Revision checklist (pages 63–64):   When you revise the various drafts of an essay, ask yourself the following questions:

_____   1. Have I made my point? Is my thesis clear?

_____   2. Does my support move smoothly from one point to the next? Is my support logically arranged? Do I use transitional words and phrases to aid the reader?

_____   3. Have I fully developed each paragraph? Does each paragraph have a topic sentence? Have I added or cut information if necessary?

_____   4. Will my essay interest my audience? Does my opening paragraph grab the reader's attention?

_____   5. Is the tone of my essay consistent? Do I use the same tone through-out? Is the language appropriate for my audience?

_____   6. Have I said everything I want and need to say? Is my thesis fully developed? Does everything relate to the thesis?

   Editing checklist (pages 69–70):   When you edit the various drafts of an essay, ask yourself the following questions:

_____   1. Have I given myself some time off between drafts? Have I put aside my essay for at least two hours?

_____   2. Have I read each sentence aloud to hear how it sounds? Did I read each sentence from last to first?

_____   3. Have I used proper punctuation?

_____   4. Do my subjects and verbs agree in tense and number?

_____   5. Are my pronoun references correct?

_____ 6. Have I avoided repeating the same word too often?

_____ 7. Do I have a title that reflects my thesis or subject?

On the Net

There are many places on the Internet to go for help with your writing. If you need assistance, the sites may be able to help you:

1. The On-Line Writing Lab (OWL) at Purdue University offers assistance with writing projects, help with grammar, referrals to other sources, downloadable handouts, and Internet search tools. There is a comprehensive list of other OWL sites, so you can be sure to get whatever you need, whenever you need it. Online tutors will answer your questions and provide assistance. To access the site, go to *owl.english.purdue.edu* and follow the instructions to get the help you need.

2. The University of Maine Writing Center can be found at *www.ume.maine. edu/wcenter/*. This site provides a comprehensive online list of other online writing labs for you to visit. Visit a few and see if one is more appropriate for your writing research needs.

Visit either of these sites or browse the Internet to find a new site using the keyword "writing."

PART **2**

Readings Worth Thinking and Writing About

CHAPTER

3 Viewpoints on Acquiring Knowledge

Focus on Ways We Learn

To help you focus on the subject of this chapter, take a few minutes to prepare for the topic by prewriting on one or more of the following prompts:

1. learning from mistakes
2. different types of knowledge
3. sex education in public schools
4. cutting classes
5. home schooling versus public education
6. street "smarts"

magine what your life would be like if you woke up one morning and everything you had ever learned was gone from your head. You wouldn't be able to
get out of bed, dress yourself, feed yourself, or find the bathroom, much less
know how to use it. You wouldn't be able to talk, read, or write. You wouldn't know
what a television was, how to drive a car, or how to use a cellphone. In other words,
you'd be helpless.

We all know that learning is important. But what exactly is it? A dictionary
might tell you that learning is acquiring knowledge through experience or study
(sounds all right); a teacher might tell you that it's memorizing what you need to
know for a test (we could argue that one); your boss might tell you that it's mastery
of the task you're hired to do (OK, if the pay's good); a psychology book might tell
you that learning is a relatively permanent change in behavior due to past experience (that one could use some examples); your parents may tell you that learning
is achieved by a "Do as I say, not as I do" approach (no comment).

Obviously, learning takes place in many ways and forms. Hardly a day goes by
that we don't learn something, either directly or indirectly. For instance, from
television you will "learn" that minorities are generally criminals, victims, service
workers, or students (come on, now!), and you might "learn" from a friend that
smoking is "cool" (but what about the Surgeon General?). The tendency, however,
is to link learning with school. Then, of course, we can think about the definition
of school. Is it a building labeled elementary, junior high, or senior high school?
Is it the ivy-walled institution called college or university? Is it the warehouse
converted into an adult education center? Is it Sunday school, the synagogue, or
church? Is it the media—from television to the *National Enquirer?* Is it the city
streets? Some type of schooling certainly occurs in all these places.

This chapter does not provide any answers to clearly define the concepts of
learning and schooling. Instead, this chapter offers reading selections with various
viewpoints on the ways we learn. As you practice your reading skills, let your reactions to the ideas and the exercises provide some ideas for essays of your own.

Preparing to Read

Take a minute or two to look over the following reading selection. Note the title and author, read the opening paragraph, and check the essay's length. Make certain you have the time now to read it carefully and to do the exercises that follow it. Then, in the spaces provided, answer the following questions.

1. From the title and the opening paragraph, what do you think the essay will be about? _____

_____

2. What do you learn about the author from the opening paragraph? Is this information important, do you think, to your understanding of the essay to follow?

_____

_____

Vocabulary

Good comprehension of what you are about to read depends upon your understanding of the words below. The number following each word refers to the paragraph where it is used.

surplus (1) an amount that is more than what is needed or required

narrative (4) a story

prodigy (5) an exceptionally-talented person

oddity (5) strangeness; a person or thing that is odd

subverted (6) destroyed or ruined completely

monosyllabic (6) having only one syllable

sullen (8) dour or morose; resentfully silent

Superman and Me

Sherman Alexie

Sherman Alexie is a Spokane/Coeur d'Alene Native American, raised on the Spokane Indian Reservation in Washington State. He has published more than two hundred poems, stories, and articles. His books include The Lone Ranger and Tonto Fistfight in Heaven, Reservation Blues, *and* The Absolutely True Story of a Part-time Indian.

1   I LEARNED TO READ with a *Superman* comic book. Simple enough, I suppose. I cannot recall which particular *Superman* comic book I read, nor can I remember which villain he fought in that issue. I cannot remember the plot, nor the means by which I obtained the comic book. What I can remember is this: I was three years old, a Spokane Indian boy living with his family on the Spokane Indian Reservation in eastern Washington state. We were poor by most standards, but one of my parents usually managed to find some minimum-wage job or another, which made us middle class by reservation standards. I had a brother and three sisters. We lived on a combination of irregular paychecks, hope, fear, and government-surplus food.

2   My father, who is one of the few Indians who went to Catholic school on purpose, was an avid reader of westerns, spy thrillers, murder mysteries, gangster epics, basketball-player biographies, and anything else he could find. He bought his books by the pound at Dutch's Pawn Shop, Goodwill, Salvation Army, and Value Village. When he had extra money, he bought new novels at supermarkets, convenience stores, and hospital gift shops. Our house was filled with books. They were stacked in crazy piles in the bathroom, bedrooms, and living room. In a fit of unemployment-inspired creative energy, my father built a set of bookshelves and soon filled them with a random assortment of books about the Kennedy assassination, Watergate, the Vietnam War, and the entire twenty-three-book series of the Apache westerns. My father loved books, and since I loved my father with an aching devotion, I decided to love books as well.

3   I can remember picking up my father's books before I could read. The words themselves were mostly foreign, but I still remember the exact moment when I first understood, with a sudden clarity, the purpose of a paragraph. I didn't have the vocabulary to say "paragraph," but I realized that a paragraph was a fence that held words. The words inside a paragraph worked together for a common purpose. They had some specific reason for being inside the same fence. This knowledge delighted me. I began to think of everything in terms of paragraphs. Our reservation was a small paragraph within the United States. My family's house was a paragraph, distinct from the other paragraphs of the LeBrets to the north, the Fords to our south, and the Tribal School to the west. Inside our house, each family member existed as a separate paragraph, but still had genetics and common experiences to link us. Now, using this logic, I can see my changed family as an essay of seven paragraphs: mother, father, older brother, the deceased sister, my younger twin sisters, and our adopted little brother.

4   At the same time I was seeing the world in paragraphs, I also picked up that *Superman* comic book. Each panel, complete with picture, dialogue, and narrative, was a three-dimensional paragraph. In one panel, Superman breaks through a door. His suit is red, blue,

and yellow. The brown door shatters into many pieces. I look at the narrative above the picture. I cannot read the words, but I assume it tells me that Superman is breaking down the door. Aloud, I pretend to read the words and say "Superman is breaking down the door." Words, dialogue, also float out of Superman's mouth. Because he is breaking down the door, I assume he says, "I am breaking down the door." Once again, I pretend to read the words and say aloud, "I am breaking down the door." In this way, I learned to read.

5   This might be an interesting story all by itself. A little Indian boy teaches himself to read at an early age and advances quickly. He reads *Grapes of Wrath* in kindergarten when other children are struggling through Dick and Jane. If he'd been anything but an Indian boy living on the reservation, he might have been called a prodigy. But he is an Indian boy living on the reservation, and is simply an oddity. He grows into a man who often speaks of his childhood in the third-person, as if it will somehow dull the pain and make him sound more modest about his talents.

6   A smart Indian is a dangerous person, widely feared and ridiculed by Indians and non-Indians alike. I fought with my classmates on a daily basis. They wanted me to stay quiet when the non-Indian teacher asked for answers, for volunteers, for help. We were Indian children who were expected to be stupid. Most lived up to those expectations inside the classroom, but subverted them on the outside. They struggled with basic reading in school, but could remember how to sing a few dozen powwow songs. They were monosyllabic in front of their non-Indian teachers, but could tell complicated stories and jokes at the dinner table. They submissively ducked their heads when confronted by a non-Indian adult, but would slug it out with the Indian bully who was ten years older. As Indian children, we were expected to fail in the non-Indian world. Those who failed were ceremonially accepted by other Indians and appropriately pitied by non-Indians.

7   I refused to fail. I was smart. I was arrogant. I was lucky. I read books late into the night, until I could barely keep my eyes open. I read books at recess, then during lunch, and in the few minutes left after I had finished my classroom assignments. I read books in the car when my family traveled to powwows or basketball games. In shopping malls, I ran to the bookstores and read bits and pieces of as many books as I could. I read the books my father brought home from the pawnshops and secondhand stores. I read the books I borrowed from the library. I read the backs of cereal boxes. I read the newspaper. I read the bulletins posted on the walls of the school, the clinic, the tribal offices, the post office. I read junk mail. I read auto-repair manuals. I read magazines. I read anything that had words and paragraphs. I read with equal parts joy and desperation. I loved those books, but I also knew that love had only one purpose. I was trying to save my life.

8   Despite all the books I read, I am still surprised I became a writer. I was going to be a pediatrician. These days, I write novels, short stories, and poems. I visit schools and teach creative writing to Indian kids. In all my years in the reservation school system, I was never taught how to write poetry, short stories, or novels. I was certainly never taught that Indians wrote poetry, short stories, and novels. Writing was something beyond Indians. I cannot recall a single time that a guest teacher visited the reservation. There must have been visiting teachers. Who were they? Where are they now? Do they exist? I visit the schools as often as possible. The Indian kids crowd the classroom. Many are writing their own poems, short stories, and novels. They have read my books. They have read many other books. They look at me with bright eyes and arrogant wonder. They are trying to save their lives. Then there are the sullen and already defeated Indian kids who sit in the back rows and ignore me with theatrical precision. The pages of their notebooks are empty. They carry neither pencil nor pen. They stare out the window. They refuse and resist. "Books," I say to them. "Books." I say. I throw my weight against their locked doors. The door holds. I am smart. I am arrogant. I am lucky. I am trying to save our lives.

Understanding the Content

Feel free to reread all or parts of the selection to answer the following questions.

1. How did Sherman Alexie learn to read? What was the first thing he read?

2. What was Alexie's background and family situation?

3. What influence did Alexie's father have on him in terms of learning to read?

4. According to Alexie, why is a "smart Indian" a "dangerous person"?

5. What is Alexie's current career and how does he give back to the reservation community where he grew up?

Looking at Structure and Style

1. What is the purpose of paragraph 3? Why do you think Alexie includes his thoughts on the purpose of the paragraph in this essay?

2. How does Alexie juxtapose his descriptions of the child he was with the adult he has become?

3. How does Alexie describe the two groups of Indian children in the last paragraph? Which group do you think he identifies with most closely?

4. Read the first few sentences of paragraph 7 and the last few sentences of paragraph 8. What is the purpose of this repetition of sentences? Is it effective?

5. Why is it important to understand what life was like on the reservation for Alexie? Why does he include descriptions of his family and his reservation life in this essay?

Evaluating the Author's Viewpoints

1. How do you think Alexie's childhood influenced the man he is today? How can you tell?

2. What do you think Sherman Alexie means when he describes his father as "one of the few Indians who went to Catholic school on purpose"?

3. Why do you think that smart Indians are considered dangerous?

4. Why do you think understanding the purpose of a paragraph was so important to Alexie? What implications did it have beyond his developing his ability to read?

5. When Alexie writes that he was "trying to save my life" by reading everything he could get his hands on, what does he mean?

6. What is Alexie's attitude toward the "sullen and already defeated Indian kids" he sees when he goes back to the reservation as a guest teacher?

7. Why do you think Alexie describes himself as someone who often speaks of his childhood in the third person?

Pursuing Possible Essay Topics

1. Have you had a passion for something and as a result, taught yourself to do it? What was it? Write an essay about your experience, describing the process of how you taught yourself to do something.

2. Are you an avid reader? If so, describe the last book you read and write a short review of it, whether it be positive or negative.

3. What role has reading played in your life? Write an essay describing how learning to read has affected you as a person and now as a student.

4. If you could read only one section of the newspaper daily, which one would it be and why? Write an essay discussing your preference.

5. Brainstorm or freewrite on one or more of the following:

   a. reading   c. education   e. poverty
   b. lifelong learning   d. Native Americans

6. If you don't like any of these topics and have one that you want to write about it, go ahead!

Preparing to Read

Take a minute or two to look over the following reading selection. Note the title and author, read the opening paragraph, and check the essay's length. Make certain you have the time now to read it carefully and to do the exercises that follow it. Then, in the spaces provided, answer the following questions.

1. What does the title mean to you? _____

_____

_____

2. What do you think this selection will have to say about making mistakes?

_____

_____

3. How do you feel about making mistakes? _____

_____

_____

Vocabulary

Good comprehension of what you are about to read depends upon your understanding of the words below. The number following each word refers to the paragraph where it is used.

plateau (1) an elevated, stable state

garners (4) acquires, gains

stigma (4) mark of shame or disgrace

adherence (8) faithful attachment, devotion

germinal phase (8) beginning or earliest stage

erroneous (9) mistaken, based on error

exemplifies (10) serves as an example

phenomenon (10) a perceivable occurrence or fact

combust (11) burn

analogous (11) alike in certain ways

Brittany (16) an area on the northern coast of France across the English Channel from England

precedence (18) the state of having prior existence, priority

innovators (18) creators or introducers of something new

diverging (24) branching out, departing from the norm

deleterious (25) damaging, harmful

amoeba (25) shapeless, microscopic, one-celled organism

atrophy (26) waste away

To Err Is Wrong

ROGER VON OECH

Roger von Oech is the author of A Whack on the Side of the Head—*a creative thinking classic—from which this excerpt is taken. He has written other books on creative thinking, and his latest work is the* Ball of Whacks, *a set of magnetic design blocks that acts as "a creativity tool for innovators."*

Hits and Misses

1   In the summer of 1979, Boston Red Sox first baseman Carl Yastrzemski became the fifteenth player in baseball history to reach the three thousand hit plateau. This event drew a lot of media attention, and for about a week prior to the attainment of this goal, hundreds of reporters covered Yaz's every move. Finally, one reporter asked, "Hey Yaz, aren't you afraid all of this attention will go to your head?" Yastrzemski replied, "I look at it this way: in my career I've been up to bat over ten thousand times. That means I've been unsuccessful at the plate over seven thousand times. That fact alone keeps me from getting a swollen head."

2   Most people consider success and failure as opposites, but they are actually both products of the same process. As Yaz suggests, an activity which produces a hit may also produce a miss. It is the same with creative thinking; the same energy which generates good creative ideas also produces errors.

3   Many people, however, are not comfortable with errors. Our educational system, based on "the right answer" belief, cultivates our thinking in another, more conservative way. From an early age, we are taught that right answers are good and incorrect answers are bad. This value is deeply embedded in the incentive system used in most schools:

Right over 90% of the time = "A"

Right over 80% of the time = "B"

Right over 70% of the time = "C"

Right over 60% of the time = "D"

Less than 60% correct, you fail.

From this we learn to be right as often as possible and to keep our mistakes to a minimum. We learn, in other words, that "to err is wrong."

Playing It Safe

4   With this kind of attitude, you aren't going to be taking too many chances. If you learn that failing even a little penalizes you (e.g., being wrong only 15% of the time garners you only a "B" performance), you learn not to make mistakes. And more important, you learn not to put yourself in situations where you might fail. This leads to conservative thought patterns designed to avoid the stigma our society puts on "failure."

5   I have a friend who recently graduated from college with a Master's degree in Journalism. For the last six months, she has been trying to find a job, but to no avail. I talked with her about her situation, and realized that her problem is that she doesn't know how to fail. She went through eighteen years of schooling without ever failing an examination, a paper, a midterm, a pop-quiz, or a final. Now, she is reluctant to try any approaches where she might fail. She has been conditioned to believe that failure is bad in and of itself, rather than a potential stepping stone to new ideas.

6   Look around. How many middle managers, housewives, administrators, teachers, and other people do you see who are afraid to try anything new because of this fear of failure? Most of us have learned not to make mistakes in public. As a result, we remove ourselves from many learning experiences except for those occurring in the most private of circumstances.

A Different Logic

7   From a practical point of view, "to err is wrong" makes sense. Our survival in the everyday world requires us to perform thousands of small tasks without failure. Think about it: you wouldn't last very long if you were to step out in front of traffic or stick your hand into a pot of boiling water. In addition, engineers whose bridges collapse, stock brokers who lose money for their clients, and copywriters whose ad campaigns decrease sales won't keep their jobs very long.

8   Nevertheless, too great an adherence to the belief "to err is wrong" can greatly undermine your attempts to generate new ideas. If you're more concerned with producing right answers than generating original ideas, you'll probably make uncritical use of the rules, formulae, and procedures used to obtain these right answers. By doing this, you'll by-pass the germinal phase of the creative process, and thus

spend little time testing assumptions, challenging the rules, asking what-if questions, or just playing around with the problem. All of these techniques will produce some incorrect answers, but in the germinal phase errors are viewed as a necessary by-product of creative thinking. As Yaz would put it, "If you want the hits, be prepared for the misses." That's the way the game of life goes.

Errors as Stepping Stones

9   Whenever an error pops up, the usual response is "Jeez, another screwup, what went wrong this time?" The creative thinker, on the other hand, will realize the potential value of errors, and perhaps say something like, "Would you look at that! Where can it lead our thinking?" And then he or she will go on to use the error as a stepping stone to a new idea. As a matter of fact, the whole history of discovery is filled with people who used erroneous assumptions and failed ideas as stepping stones to new ideas. Columbus thought he was finding a shorter route to India. Johannes Kepler stumbled on to the idea of interplanetary gravity because of assumptions which were right for the wrong reasons. And, Thomas Edison knew 1800 ways *not* to build a light bulb.

10   The following story about the automotive genius Charles Kettering exemplifies the spirit of working through erroneous assumptions to good ideas. In 1912, when the automobile industry was just beginning to grow, Kettering was interested in improving gasoline-engine efficiency. The problem he faced was "knock," the phenomenon in which gasoline takes too long to burn in the cylinder—thereby reducing efficiency.

11   Kettering began searching for ways to eliminate the "knock." He thought to himself, "How can I get the gasoline to combust in the cylinder at an earlier time?" The key concept here is "early." Searching for analogous situations, he looked around for models of "things that happen early." He thought of historical models, physical models, and biological models. Finally, he remembered a particular plant, the trailing arbutus, which "happens early," i.e., it blooms in the snow ("earlier" than other plants). One of this plant's chief characteristics is its red leaves, which help the plant retain light at certain wavelengths. Kettering figured that it must be the red color which made the trailing arbutus bloom earlier.

12   Now came the critical step in Kettering's chain of thought. He asked himself, "How can I make the gasoline red? Perhaps I'll put red dye in the gasoline—maybe that'll make it combust earlier." He looked around his workshop, and found that he didn't have any red dye. But he did happen to have some iodine—perhaps that would do. He added the iodine to the gasoline and, lo and behold, the engine didn't "knock."

13   Several days later, Kettering wanted to make sure that it was the redness of the iodine which had in fact solved his problem. He got

some red dye and added it to the gasoline. Nothing happened! Kettering then realized that it wasn't the "redness" which had solved the "knock" problem, but certain other properties of iodine. In this case, an error had proven to be a stepping stone to a better idea. Had he known that "redness" alone was not the solution, he may not have found his way to the additives in iodine.

Negative Feedback

14   Errors serve another useful purpose: they tell us when to change direction. When things are going smoothly, we generally don't think about them. To a great extent, this is because we function according to the principle of negative feedback. Often it is only when things or people fail to do their job that they get our attention. For example, you are probably not thinking about your kneecaps right now; that's because everything is fine with them. The same goes for your elbows: they are also performing their function—no problem at all. But if you were to break a leg, you would immediately notice all of the things you could no longer do, but which you used to take for granted.

15   Negative feedback means that the current approach is not working, and it is up to you to figure out a new one. We learn by trial and error, not by trial and rightness. If we did things correctly every time, we would never have to change direction—we'd just continue the current course and end up with more of the same.

16   For example, after the supertanker *Amoco Cadiz* broke up off the coast of Brittany in the spring of 1978, thereby polluting the coast with hundreds of thousands of tons of oil, the oil industry rethought many of its safety standards regarding petroleum transport. The same thing happened after the accident at the Three Mile Island nuclear reactor in 1979—many procedures and safety standards were changed.

17   Neil Goldschmidt, former secretary of transportation, had this to say about the Bay Area Rapid Transit (BART):

> It's gotten too fashionable around the country to beat up on BART and not give credit to the vision that put this system in place. We have learned from BART around the country. The lessons were put to use in Washington, in Atlanta, in Buffalo, and other cities where we are building mass transit systems. One of the lessons is not to build a system like BART.

We learn by our failures. A person's errors are the whacks that lead him to think something different.

Trying New Things

18   Your error rate in any activity is a function of your familiarity with that activity. If you are doing things that are routine and have a high likelihood of correctness, then you will probably make very few

errors. But if you are doing things that have no precedence in your experience or are trying different approaches, then you will be making your share of mistakes. Innovators may not bat a thousand—far from it—but they do get new ideas.

19   The creative director of an advertising agency told me that he isn't happy unless he is failing at least half of the time. As he puts it, "If you are going to be original, you are going to be wrong a lot."

20   One of my clients, the president of a fast-growing computer company, tells his people: "We're innovators. We're doing things nobody has ever done before. Therefore, we are going to be making mistakes. My advice to you: make your mistakes, but make them in a hurry."

21   Another client, a division manager of a high-technology company, asked his vice president of engineering what percentage of their new products should be successful in the marketplace. The answer he received was "about 50%." The division manager replied, "That's too high. 30% is a better target; otherwise we'll be too conservative in our planning."

22   Along similar lines, in the banking industry, it is said that if the credit manager never has to default on any of his loans, it's a sure sign he's not being aggressive enough in the marketplace.

23   Thomas J. Watson, the founder of IBM, has similar words: "The way to succeed is to double your failure rate."

24   Thus errors, at the very least, are a sign that we are diverging from the main road and trying different approaches.

Nature's Errors

25   Nature serves as a good example of how trial and error can be used to make changes. Every now and then genetic mutations occur—errors in gene reproduction. Most of the time, these mutations have a deleterious effect on the species, and they drop out of the gene pool. But occasionally, a mutation provides the species with something beneficial, and that change will be passed on to future generations. The rich variety of all species is due to this trial and error process. If there had never been any mutations from the first amoeba, where would we be now?

Summary

26   There are places where errors are inappropriate, but the germinal phase of the creative process isn't one of them. Errors are a sign that you are diverging from the well-traveled path. If you're not failing every now and then, it's a sign you're not being very innovative.

Tip #1:
If you make an error, use it as a stepping stone to a new idea you might not have otherwise discovered.

Tip #2:
Differentiate between errors of "commission" and those of "omission." The latter can be more costly than the former. If you're not making many errors, you might ask yourself, "How many opportunities am I missing by not being more aggressive?"

Tip #3:
Strengthen your "risk muscle." Everyone has one, but you have to exercise it or else it will atrophy. Make it a point to take at least one risk every twenty-four hours.

Tip #4:
Remember these two benefits of failure. First, if you do fail, you learn what doesn't work; and second, the failure gives you an opportunity to try a new approach.

Understanding the Content

Feel free to reread all or parts of the selection to answer the following questions.

1. Does von Oech believe "to err is wrong"? Why?

2. How does von Oech feel about the traditional grading system in schools? Why?

3. According to the author, what is wrong with "playing it safe"?

4. What are some of the "useful purposes" of making mistakes?

5. Explain what von Oech means when he says in his conclusion that we should differentiate between errors of "commission" and those of "omission" (26).

6. What two benefits of failure does the author propose?

7. To what audience do you think the author is writing? Why?

8. Is there an implied or stated thesis? What is it?

Looking at Structure and Style

1. How does von Oech use the first two paragraphs to lead us into his subject and thesis?

2. What is the cause–effect relationship discussed in paragraph 4?

3. What is the function of paragraphs 5 and 6?

4. What is being compared and contrasted in paragraphs 7 and 8?

5. Is this essay mostly formal or informal? List some words or phrases that support your answer.

6. For what purpose does the author use paragraphs 9–13? Are the paragraphs effective?

7. What writing pattern is used in paragraphs 14, 16, and 17?

8. How would you describe the author's attitude and tone?

Evaluating the Author's Viewpoints

1. Do you agree or disagree with von Oech's comments regarding the traditional educational grading system? Why?

2. In paragraph 6, the author says, "Most of us have learned not to make mistakes in public. As a result, we remove ourselves from many learning experiences except for those occurring in the most private of circumstances." Is this true? Is it true of you?

3. Respond to paragraph 25. What does von Oech mean? Do you agree?

4. Do you agree with von Oech that we should take at least one risk every twenty-four hours? Why? What kind of risks does he have in mind?

5. Where and when are errors inappropriate?

Pursuing Possible Essay Topics

1. Make a list of von Oech's arguments for the positive side of making errors. Write an essay that agrees with his thesis, but provide examples of your own. Or write an essay that disagrees with him.

2. Write about a time when you learned from an error you made.

3. Discuss your viewpoints on the traditional grading system. What are its pros and cons? How has it affected your learning?

4. Use this statement from the essay as the thesis for your own essay: "Most people consider success and failure as opposites, but they are actually both products of the same process" (2).

5. In his book *Escape from Childhood,* educator John Holt states:

> Young people should have the right to control and direct their own learning, that is, to decide what they want to learn, and when, where, how, how much, how fast, and with what help they want to learn it. To be still more specific, I want them to have the right to decide if, when, how much, and by whom they want to be *taught* and the right to decide whether they want to learn in a school and if so which one and for how much of the time.

Write an essay that supports or refutes Holt's radical statement about le ing. How would his ideas work? How would such an approach change present educational system?

6. With one or more of your classmates, discuss your individual learning styles. When you have finished your discussion, write a brief essay summarizing what you learned.

7. Brainstorm or freewrite on one or more of the following:

a. making mistakes   d. nature's errors

b. famous errors   e. negative feedback

c. grades   f. trying new things

8. Ignore these suggestions and find your own topic on some aspect of learning and write an essay about it.

Preparing to Read

Take a minute or two to look over the following reading selection. Note the title and author, read the opening paragraph, and check the essay's length. Make certain you have the time now to read it carefully and to do the exercises that follow it. Then, in the spaces provided, answer the following questions.

1. What do you think the title means? _____

_____

_____

2. What will be the subject of this essay? _____

_____

_____

3. What might you learn from reading it? _____

_____

_____

Vocabulary

Good comprehension of what you are about to read depends upon your understanding of the words below. The number following each word refers to the paragraph where it is used.

semiliterate (1) having only an elementary level of reading and writing ability

impediments (4) obstacles, barriers, hindrances

trump card (4) a card from the suit in a card game that outranks all other suits for the duration of the game

chemical dependency (9) addiction to drugs

In Praise of the F Word

Mary Sherry

Mary Sherry is a writer and adult literacy educator. This selection, "In Praise of the 'F' Word," originally appeared in Newsweek *magazine's* My Turn *column.*

1 Tens of thousands of 18-year-olds will graduate this year and be handed meaningless diplomas. These diplomas won't look any different from those awarded their luckier classmates. Their validity will be questioned only when their employers discover that these graduates are semiliterate.

2 Eventually a fortunate few will find their way into educational-repair shops—adult-literacy programs, such as the one where I teach basic grammar and writing. There, high-school graduates and high-school dropouts pursuing graduate-equivalency certificates will learn the skills they should have learned in school. They will also discover they have been cheated by our educational system.

3 As I teach, I learn a lot about our schools. Early in each session I ask my students to write about an unpleasant experience they had in school. No writers' block here! "I wish someone would have had made me stop doing drugs and made me study." "I liked to party and no one seemed to care." "I was a good kid and didn't cause any trouble, so they just passed me along even though I didn't read well and couldn't write." And so on.

4 I am your basic do-gooder, and prior to teaching this class I blamed the poor academic skills our kids have today on drugs, divorce and other impediments to concentration necessary for doing well in school. But, as I rediscover each time I walk into the classroom, before a teacher can expect students to concentrate, he has to get their attention, no matter what distractions may be at hand. There are many ways to do this, and they have much to do with teaching style. However, if style alone won't do it, there is another way to show who holds the winning hand in the classroom. That is to reveal the trump card of failure.

5 I will never forget a teacher who played that card to get the attention of one of my children. Our youngest, a world-class charmer, did little to develop his intellectual talents but always got by. Until Mrs. Stifter.

6 Our son was a high-school senior when he had her for English. "He sits in the back of the room talking to his friends," she told me. "Why don't you move him to the front row?" I urged, believing the embarrassment would get him to settle down. Mrs. Stifter looked at me steely-eyed over her glasses. "I don't move seniors," she said. "I flunk them." I was flustered. Our son's academic life flashed before my eyes. No teacher had ever threatened him with that before. I regained my

composure and managed to say that I thought she was right. By the time I got home I was feeling pretty good about this. It was a radical approach for these times, but, well, why not? "She's going to flunk you," I told my son. I did not discuss it any further. Suddenly English became a priority in his life. He finished out the semester with an A.

7   I know one example doesn't make a case, but at night I see a parade of students who are angry and resentful for having been passed along until they could no longer even pretend to keep up. Of average intelligence or better, they eventually quit school, concluding they were too dumb to finish. "I should have been held back," is a comment I hear frequently. Even sadder are those students who are high-school graduates who say to me after a few weeks of class, "I don't know how I ever got a high-school diploma."

8   Passing students who have not mastered the work cheats them and the employers who expect graduates to have basic skills. We excuse this dishonest behavior by saying kids can't learn if they come from terrible environments. No one seems to stop to think that—no matter what environments they come from—most kids don't put school first on their list unless they perceive something is at stake. They'd rather be sailing.

9   Many students I see at night could give expert testimony on unemployment, chemical dependency, abusive relationships. In spite of these difficulties, they have decided to make education a priority. They are motivated by the desire for a better job or the need to hang on to the one they've got. They have a healthy fear of failure.

10   People of all ages can rise above their problems, but they need to have a reason to do so. Young people generally don't have the maturity to value education in the same way my adult students value it. But fear of failure, whether economic or academic, can motivate both.

11   Flunking as a regular policy has just as much merit today as it did two generations ago. We must review the threat of flunking and see it as it really is—a positive teaching tool. It is an expression of confidence by both teachers and parents that the students have the ability to learn the material presented to them. However, making it work again would take a dedicated, caring conspiracy between teachers and parents. It would mean facing the tough reality that passing kids who haven't learned the material—while it might save them grief for the short term—dooms them to long-term illiteracy. It would mean that teachers would have to follow through on their threats, and parents would have to stand behind them, knowing their children's best interests are indeed at stake. This means no more doing Scott's assignments for him because he might fail. No more passing Jodi because she's such a nice kid.

12   This is a policy that worked in the past and can work today. A wise teacher, with the support of his parents, gave our son the opportunity to succeed—or fail. It's time we return this choice to all students.

Understanding the Content

Feel free to reread all or parts of the selection to answer the following questions.

1. What is the "F word" discussed in the essay?

2. What is Sherry's attitude toward the F word?

3. What reasons does the author give for believing that the threat of flunking students is a positive teaching tool?

4. What choice does the author want to give to students? Why is she particularly interested in the subject?

5. What is the point of this selection? What does it have to do with the subject of learning?

Looking at Structure and Style

1. How does paragraph 2 help to support paragraph 1?

2. What is the point of paragraph 3?

3. How does Sherry use paragraphs 5 and 6 to support her viewpoint?

4. What is the point of paragraphs 9 and 10?

5. What audience do you think the author had in mind when she wrote this essay?

Evaluating the Author's Viewpoints

1. Do you agree with the author that "flunking as a regular policy has just as much merit today as it did two generations ago" (11)? Why?

2. What are some good arguments for *not* flunking students?

3. The author contends that fear of failure can motivate students. Explain why you agree or disagree.

4. Would you like to have Mary Sherry as a teacher? Explain why or why not.

Pursuing Possible Essay Topics

1. Recall a time when fear of failure motivated you to accomplish something.

2. Summarize the reasons why the author is praising the F word.

3. Write an essay that takes the opposite viewpoint regarding the F word.

4. Explore the pros and cons of withholding high school diplomas from students who lack the ability to learn, despite fear of failure.

5. Brainstorm or freewrite on one or both of the following:
   a. fear of failure
   b. flunking

6. Ignore these topics and find your own topic related to giving or receiving a failing grade.

Preparing to Read

Take a minute or two to look over the following reading selection. Note the title and author, read the opening paragraph, and check the essay's length. Make certain you have the time now to read it carefully and to do the exercises that follow it. Then, in the spaces provided, answer the following questions.

1. What do you think the subject of this essay is? _____

_____

_____

2. What do you think the title means? _____

_____

_____

Vocabulary

Good comprehension of what you are about to read depends upon your under-standing of the words below. The number following each word refers to the paragraph where it is used.

mediocre (4) moderate to inferior in quality

hassled (5) bothered

offset (11) to make up for; counterbalance

asphalt (12) blacktop

menial (22) boring or tedious

Zero

PAUL LOGAN

When nineteen, Paul Logan flunked out of college and was forced to take a minimum wage job. Embarrassed by his failure, Paul decided to get serious and return to college. In the following essay from Making the Most of Your Life: Eight Motivational Stories & Essays, *Logan details what it took for him to go from a zero to a 4.0 grade point average.*

1   *Three F's and two I's.*

2   My first semester grades hit me like a kick in the stomach. The *F's* were for classes where my work was poor. The *I's* were "incompletes"— for courses in which I never finished my assignments. They eventually became F's too.

3   I crumpled the report card and shoved it deep in a trash can. I can't say I was surprised. A zero grade point average was what I deserved, no question about it. But seeing my name in print on the worst possible report card still hurt. It also lit a spark in me, one that changed my life.

4   I was nineteen when I bombed out my first year of college. I hadn't always been a poor student. During elementary and middle school, I was consistently at the top of my class. But when I transferred into a huge regional high school, everything changed. I started "underachieving." Guidance counselors, teachers, and members of my family noticed. "You have potential," they'd say when they heard of my mediocre performance. "You just don't apply yourself."

5   They didn't understand. The truth was I *did* apply myself—just not to academics. As a shy, acne-prone teenager thrown into an enormous and unfamiliar high school, grades were not my priority; survival was. During my freshman year, I was constantly hassled and teased by a group of older guys at my school. They shoved and threatened me on the bus, teased me in the halls, and mocked me during lunchtime. *Nerd. Geek. Loser.* These insults were fired at me like bullets. Sometimes they came with fists. I got scared.

6   This fear transformed me. Constantly stressed and distracted, I stopped worrying about classes. Too embarrassed to admit to teachers or my family what was happening, I quietly dropped from an A student in 8th grade to C student just a year later. My definition of success changed just as dramatically. To me, a good day at school was no longer about doing well in class. It was simply about getting home without being hassled. To achieve this goal, I learned to blend in to the crowd—to look, talk, and act like the popular kids. First, I changed my clothes and hairstyle. Then I started behaving differently, hanging out with new "friends" and teasing the few kids who fit in worse than me. By the end of my freshman year, I escaped being at the bottom of the social ladder, but I also gave up on being a good student.

7   Instead, my focus was on following the crowd and being a social success. In 10th grade, I got a job at a nearby mall, so I could buy what seemed important: name-brand clothes, expensive sneakers, the latest CD's, and movie tickets—things I thought I needed to be popular. So what if my grades tumbled because I neglected my studies? At least no one was laughing at me anymore. By 11th grade, a new girlfriend and my used car were what I cared most about. Classes were a meaningless activity I endured weekdays. Senior year was more of the same, though I took the SAT and applied to a few colleges—because classmates were doing it. Despite my mediocre grades, I managed to get accepted. The following September, thanks to my family's savings, I followed the crowd and floated straight to college.

8   That's when I started to sink. Years of putting social time and my job ahead of school left me without study habits to deal with college work. Years of coasting in class left me unready for assignments that

required effort and time management skills. Years of following others left me unequipped to make smart choices about my education. In addition to lacking skills, I also lacked motivation. College felt as meaningless to me as high school. Though I'd gotten accepted at a four-year university, nothing pushed me to succeed there. I arrived on campus in September without skills, goals, and a plan. I figured I could continue doing what I had done for years: coasting. It was a recipe for disaster.

9   My first week on campus, I coasted through freshman orientation, skipping activities because I didn't take them seriously. My second week, I attended a few parties, got home late, and overslept, missing a bunch of classes. No big deal, I thought. I'd just float by and hand in my homework late. But I quickly discovered, unlike high school, catching up was difficult in college. Readings in my English and History classes wore longer and more complicated than I was used to—too difficult for me to skim. Writing assignments were more numerous and required more time than I'd expected. Unaccustomed to the workload, I started cutting "easy" classes to complete overdue assignments from other courses. This strategy made me fall further behind, which, in turn, made it even more difficult to motivate myself to attend class.

10   *Why bother if you're already behind?* I thought.

11   Deadlines passed and work kept piling up, and I began to realize I was over my head. Halfway through the semester, I stopped going to classes regularly, hoping instead that I could score well on final exams to offset my missing assignments. But without attending class and taking notes, there was no way I could adequately prepare for tests. While coasting worked in high school, it didn't work in college. By the end of ten weeks, I knew I was done. No longer able to float, I'd sunk. My family was stunned and disappointed at my failure. I was, too, though the lesson hadn't yet fully sunk in.

12   That happened a few months later when I was working at a large warehouse store called Sam's Club—the one place near home that would hire an unskilled college dropout in the middle of winter. My job was to retrieve shopping carts from the store's massive parking lot and stack them in rows for customers. Days and nights, I trudged across the dismal asphalt, collecting carts and cleaning up piles of garbage and soiled diapers shoppers left behind. On this March afternoon, it was raw and stormy, and I was wearing a used yellow Sam's Club raincoat that made me stink of sweat and vinyl. My hair was dripping, and my shoes squished like soaked sponges with each step.

13   The store was crowded with shoppers, and I'd just shoved a heavy train of carts next to the front door when a cluster of young people walked out. I recognized them immediately: four popular classmates who'd gone to my high school. They were giggling about something—a sound that brought me back to the time, years earlier, when I feared being laughed at by my peers. My face began to burn.

14   "Oh my God, it's *Paul*," said one of them. They all looked at me. I felt trapped.

15   "What are *you* doing here?" said Ken, a guy who'd been in my English class in 10th grade. He glanced at my rain-soaked jacket.

16   "Working," I said. There was an awkward silence. I had spent years trying to fit in with people like them, and now I only wanted to get away. "What about you?" I asked, hoping to change the subject.

17   "We're home for spring break," Ken replied.

18   The burning on my face suddenly grew hotter. They were already finishing their first year of college, and I was pushing carts in the rain—pushing carts for them.

19   *"Paul, we need more carts in here! Hurry up!!!"* my supervisor yelled from inside the store.

20   My former classmates looked uncomfortable and embarrassed. I could see the questions in their eyes. *What happened to you? Weren't you in college too?* I felt as if my first semester grade point average was written across my face and they were reading it.

21   *Zero point zero.*

22   I nodded a quick goodbye and turned away. My eyes stung as the truth of my mistakes poured down on me like the rain. I had allowed myself to become what my grade point average said: a failure—a dropout without a plan, a goal, or a real future. A zero. Coasting wasn't going to carry me any further. Neither would the CD's, the parties, or the brand name sneakers I'd so valued in high school. By pursuing them and nothing else, I'd closed doors in my life. If I kept following the same path, I could spend years struggling in that dreary parking lot or some other menial job while my peers moved forward. I wanted to do more with my life than push shopping carts.

23   The spark which ignited at the sight of my report card erupted into a burning flame in my chest. Watching my friends drive off that afternoon, one thing was suddenly clear to me: it was time to get serious and take control of my life. College could help me do that, I realized. It could be a lifeline; I just had to grab it—no more coasting.

24   The following fall, with money saved from working nine months in the parking lot, I paid for classes at a local community college. This time, I attended every orientation activity—and I took notes. Learning from past mistakes, I also bought a calendar and jotted down each assignment, so I could see deadlines well in advance and plan accordingly. Instead of skipping classes for social time, I arranged social events after class with peers who seemed serious about their work. No longer a follower, I became a study group leader! This actually helped me become a popular student—the thing I had chased for so long in high school.

25   I am not going to say it was easy. After long days on the job, I spent longer nights at home doing my coursework. It took months of practice for me to learn the skills I'd missed in high school: how to take

good notes, how to take tests, how to write an effective essay, and how to get help when I needed it. But gradually I learned.

26   Throughout my second attempt at college, I sat beside many students who reminded me of myself during my first semester. I recognized them right away—students who seemed distracted or apathetic in class or who were frequently absent. They usually disappeared after a few weeks. Some were dealing with full lives that made it difficult to focus on their courses. Others, especially the ones straight out of high school, were coasting, unsure of why they were there or what they were doing. For these students, college is especially tough.

27   To thrive in college, you have to want to be there, and you have to be ready to focus on work. Some people aren't ready. They're likely to fail, just as I did. But even failure, as painful as it is, doesn't have to be an ending. It can be a learning experience—one that builds strength and gives direction. It can also serve as a wake-up call that turns a floating student into a serious one. It can even light a spark that sets the stage for future success. Take it from me, a former zero, who graduated from community college with a perfect 4.0 grade point average!

Understanding the Content

Feel free to reread all or parts of the selection to answer the following questions.

1. What was the event in Paul Logan's academic life that changed him as a student?

2. What was Logan's first semester of college like?

3. What did Logan end up doing after he left college?

4. What was the event that caused Logan to go back to college?

5. What was community college like for Paul Logan?

Looking at Structure and Style

1. Why do you think Paul Logan starts the essay with the story of his failing first-semester grades and then backtracks to his high school years?

2. What is the purpose of paragraphs 14–22?

3. Is this language in this essay mostly formal or informal? List some words or phrases that support your answer.

4. What writing pattern is used in paragraph 24?

5. In your own words, write a thesis statement for this essay.

6. What is the writing pattern used in paragraph 9? Paragraph 11?

Evaluating the Author's Viewpoints

1. What do you have to do to thrive in college, according to Paul Logan?

2. In freshman year of high school, what was Logan's "definition of success"? Did that definition change over time? If so, how?

3. Did Logan's plan—to follow the crowd in high school in the hopes of becoming a social success—work for him? What were the consequences of this decision?

4. Although Logan says that going to college the second time wasn't easy, what can we infer about how he feels now about the hard work and long hours?

5. What did Logan do the second time he went to college that was different from the first time? What were the results?

6. What are Logan's thoughts on the subject of failing?

Pursuing Possible Essay Topics

1. What is one failure that you've had in your life that has transformed you? Write an essay describing what you did and how you learned from the experience.

2. What have you done in college to help you succeed? Write an essay describing what you've done.

3. Do you think the author's decision to leave school, work, and then return to school was a good one? Or do you think he should have given four-year college another semester before dropping out? Write an essay discussing your viewpoint.

4. Do you think it is more difficult to be at a four-year college right out of high school or to be a returning student with family and work obligations? Why? Write an essay discussing your viewpoint.

5. Write an essay comparing and contrasting your high school experience with your college experience. Discuss how you've changed as a student and why.

6. Brainstorm or freewrite on one or more of the following:

   a. success
   b. failure
   c. learning from one's mistakes
   d. high school
   e. dropping out
   f. education

7. Don't like these suggestions? Find your own topic and write an essay about it.

Preparing to Read

Take a minute or two to look over the following reading selection. Note the title and author, read the opening paragraph, and check the essay's length. Make certain you have the time now to read it carefully and to do the exercises that follow it. Then, in the spaces provided, answer the following questions.

1. What do you think the title means? _____

_____

_____

2. What do you think the selection will say about cheating? _____

_____

_____

3. Why do you think the author uses the second person, "Your kid's going to pay

for cheating," in the title? _____

_____

_____

Vocabulary

Good comprehension of what you are about to read depends upon your understanding of the words below. The number following each word refers to the paragraph where it is used.

plagiarism (1) passing off as one's own the ideas or writings of another

syllabus (2) an outline or a summary of the main points of a text, lecture, or course of study

conspicuously (3) easily noticed

besieged (4) surrounded with hostile forces, harassed

crowing (5) boasting

condemnation (5) strong disapproval

amorality (8) lack of virtue

complicit (8) being involved as an accomplice to a wrongdoing or a crime

cribbing (10) copying, stealing, or cheating

Your Kid's Going to Pay for Cheating—Eventually

Leonard Pitts, Jr.

Leonard Pitts, Jr., a Pulitzer winning commentator, writes for the Miami Herald, *where his column runs every Monday and Friday. He is the author of* Becoming Dad: Black Men and the Journey to Fatherhood.

1   Last week, school officials in Piper, Kan., adopted an official policy on plagiarism—with punishments ranging from redoing an assignment to expulsion. Unfortunately, all that comes too late to help Christine Pelton.

2   She used to be a teacher. Taught biology at Piper High, to be exact. Then, last fall, she assigned her students to collect 20 leaves and write a report on them. The kids knew from the classroom syllabus—a document they and their parents both signed—that cheating would not be tolerated. Anyone who plagiarized would receive no credit for the assignment, which counted toward half their semester grade.

3   Maybe you've heard what happened next. Twenty-eight of Pelton's 118 sophomores turned in work that seemed conspicuously similar. It took only a little Web research for her to confirm that they had indeed cut-and-pasted their papers together.

4   True to her word, Pelton issued 28 zeroes. What followed was to moral integrity as the Keystone Kops are to law enforcement. Parents rose in outrage, some even making harassing, post-midnight phone calls to her home. Pelton offered the cheaters make-up assignments that would have allowed them to pass the class with D's. They refused. Besieged by angry mothers and fathers, the school board ordered the teacher to soften the punishment.

5   She went to school the next day and found the kids in a celebratory mood, cheering their victory and crowing that they no longer had to listen to teachers. By lunchtime, Pelton had quit. The school's principal and 13 of 32 teachers have also reportedly resigned. In the months since then, the cheaters have become the target of ridicule and condemnation in media around the world.

6   In spite of that, the parents of the 28 ethically challenged students continue to rally to their defense. One says it's not plagiarism if you only copy a sentence or two. Another expresses doubt the kids even know what plagiarism means.

7   To that, I can only say this: Please shut up. Haven't you already done enough damage?

8   Students have always cheated, yes. Always schemed to see the questions ahead of time, write notes on sweaty palms, peer over the shoulder of the teacher's pet. But what's most troubling here is not

the amorality of adolescents, but the fact that parents are so eagerly complicit, so ready to look the other way, so willing to rationalize the fact that their children are, in essence, liars and thieves. Lying about authorship of the work, thieving the grade that results.

9   Those students, their parents and the school board that caved in like cardboard in the rain are all emblematic of a society in which cheating has become not just epidemic but somehow, tolerated, even at the highest levels. As one senior told *CBS News*, "It probably sounds twisted, but I would say that in this day and age, cheating is almost not wrong."

10   Who can blame the kid for thinking that way when the news is full of noted historians cribbing from one another, Enron cooking the books well done, Merrill Lynch recommending garbage stock, a Notre Dame football coach falsifying his resumé. Whatever works, right? Ours is not to judge, right?

11   Wrong.

12   At the risk of being preachy, I'd like to point out the common thread between the historians, the coach, Enron and Merrill Lynch: They all got caught.

13   Cheaters almost always do. No, not necessarily in big, splashy stories that make *CBS News*. Sometimes, it's just in the small, quiet corners of inauthentic lives when they are brought up short by their own inadequacies and forced to acknowledge the hollowness of their achievements. To admit they aren't what others believe them to be.

14   Reputation, it has been said, is about who you are when people are watching. Character is about who you are when there's nobody in the room but you. Both matter, but of the two, character is far and away the most important. The former can induce others to think well of you. But only the latter allows you to think well of yourself.

15   This is the lesson of Piper High, for those who have ears to hear.

16   Turns out Christine Pelton is still teaching after all.

Understanding the Content

Feel free to reread all or parts of the selection to answer the following questions.

1. Who is Christine Pelton?

2. What did parents do after Christine Pelton issued the grades on her students' work, with 28 zeros handed out?

3. What did Christine Pelton do as a result of her students' and their parents' actions?

4. According to the author, what is the definition of reputation? Of character?

5. According to the author, what do almost all cheaters have in common?

6. What was the end result of the plagiarism scandal at Piper High?

Looking at Structure and Style

1. What is the thesis of this essay? Is it implied or stated? If stated, where is it stated?

2. What is the purpose of paragraph 10?

3. What is the author's attitude about the parents of Christine Pelton's students? How can you tell? What words or phrases does he use to convey his feelings?

4. Are paragraphs 15 and 16 effective as concluding paragraphs? Why or why not?

Evaluating the Author's Viewpoints

1. Does the author agree or disagree with the parents of Christine Pelton's students, who rallied to the students' defense? How can you tell?

2. How does the author feel about Christine Pelton and the stance she took regarding cheating and plagiarism?

3. How does the author feel about the students who plagiarized? Does he think that they plagiarized knowingly, or that they didn't really understand what plagiarism was? How can you tell? What words or phrases does he use to convey his feelings?

4. What does the author mean by "Turns out Christine Pelton is still teaching after all" (16)?

5. Based on your reading of this selection, who does the author think is most at fault here? The students? Their parents? The school officials? How can you tell?

Pursuing Possible Essay Topics

1. Write an essay about cheating in general. Is it ever morally right to cheat? Why or why not?

2. Do you agree or disagree with the statement, "Reputation . . . is about who you are when people are watching" (14)? Why? Give examples from either current events or from your own life to support your opinion.

 3. With a classmate, brainstorm on the topic of "plagiarism," "cheating," or "academic responsibility."

4. Would you have handled the situation in this selection differently? If so, how? Write an essay summarizing what you think school officials in Piper, Kansas, should have done when confronted with the issue of plagiarism, the outraged parents, and Christine Pelton's resignation.

5. Write an essay in opposition to Leonard Pitts's stance in this selection. Defend the students' actions and their right to cut and paste information from the Internet for their homework.

6. Ignore these topics and write about a topic of your choosing related to cheating.

 ## Opposing Viewpoints on Whether or Not Government Funding Should Be Given to Abstinence-Only Sex Education

The next two essays have different opinions about the value of government-funded sex education approaches. One author argues for the value in providing abstinence-only courses while the other believes abstinence-only sex education courses are not comprehensive enough.

Preparing to Read

Take a minute or two to look over the following reading selection. Note the title and author, read the opening paragraph, and check the essay's length. Make certain you have the time now to read it carefully and to do the exercises that follow it. Then, in the spaces provided, answer the following questions.

1. From the title and the opening paragraph, what do you think the essay will be about? _____

   _____

   _____

2. What do you learn about the author's viewpoint from the first two paragraphs?

   _____

   _____

3. Do you think you'll agree or disagree with the author's thesis? Why?

   _____

   _____

Vocabulary

Good comprehension of what you are about to read depends upon your understanding of the words below. The number following each word refers to the paragraph where it is used.

abstinence (1) the practice of refraining from an act or behavior

genocidal (1) the systematic killing of an entire group of people from a national, ethnic, or religious group

litigation (4) legal action or court case

imbue (6) to permeate or fill

sanitizing (6) making clean

glibly (12) without thought, preparation, or concern

Yes! Abstinence Is Working

KATHLEEN TSUBATA

Kathleen Tsubata is a regular contributor to the Washington Times *and co-director of the Washington AIDS International Foundation. She teaches HIV/AIDS prevention in public schools and community venues; she also trains teens as peer educators.*

1   The current tug-of-war between "abstinence-only" and "comprehensive" sexual-education advocates is distracting us from the real issue. We are in a war against forces far more unforgiving than we ever have encountered. We must look at what works to save lives. My work brings me to deal with teens every day, in public schools, churches and community organizations, teaching HIV/AIDS prevention. I train teens to teach others about this genocidal plague that is sweeping nations around the world and depleting continents of their most-productive population. I can tell you that most teens have a very superficial understanding of HIV and that many are putting themselves at risk in a wide variety of ways.

2   While teen pregnancy is serious, it is still, in one sense, the lesser evil. It's a difficult thing to bear a child out of wedlock, with the accompanying loss of education, financial stability and freedom. However, compared to HIV, it's a walk in the park. Make no mistake about it: The choice of sexual activity is a life-and-death matter, as Third World nations are finding out in stark terms.

3   Having multiple sexual partners is the No. 1 risk factor for contracting HIV and 19 percent of teens have had four or more sexual partners.

4   "So teach them to use condoms!" we are told. Studies indicate that condoms, if used correctly and consistently, may lower the transmission rate to 15 to 25 percent. That's not a fail-safe guarantee, as any condom manufacturer under litigation quickly would point out.

5   But there are two additional problems with condoms being the central pillar of HIV prevention. First, correct usage of condoms is hard to achieve in the dimly lit, cramped back seat of a car. Second, and more importantly, kids simply make decisions differently than adults. Janet St. Lawrence, of the Centers for Disease Control and Prevention (CDC), related the results of one behavioral study to me in a phone conversation last year. In that study, teens reported using a condom for their first sexual contact with someone, and subsequent contacts, "until they felt the relationship was permanent," St. Lawrence said. Then they stopped using condoms. These teens were asked what defines a "permanent" relationship. "Lasting 21 days or longer," was their response. In other words, such a teen could start a relationship, initiate sex using a condom, decide after three weeks

that it is "safe" to stop using a condom, break up and replay the whole cycle, convinced that this was responsible sexual behavior.

6   Teens are not realistic because they are young and not fully developed in key mental and emotional areas. They tend to imbue love with magical properties, as if the emotion is a sanitizing force, and that their trust can be shown by the willingness to take risks. Kids process information differently than adults. Parents know this. Saying "It's best not to have sex, but if you do, use a condom" is translated in their minds to "It's okay to have sex if you use a condom." Then, if they feel "this is true love," they convince themselves that even that is unnecessary. That's why during four decades of sex education we witnessed steep increases in sexual activity and the consequential increases in teen pregnancy, sexually transmitted diseases and poverty.

7   Only when abstinence education began in recent years did the numbers of sexually active teens go down a full 8 percentage points from 54 percent of teens to 46 percent, according to the 2001 *Youth Risk Behavior Surveillance*, published by the CDC. Simultaneously, teen pregnancies went down, abortions went down and condom use went up among those who were sexually active. Raising the bar to establish abstinence as the best method indirectly resulted in more responsible behavior in general.

8   You would think such good news would have people dancing in the aisles. Instead, the safe-sex gurus grimly predict that increased abstinence education will result in teens giving in to natural urges without the benefit of latex. Or, the critics of abstinence-until-marriage education insisted that their programs (which pay lip service to abstinence) somehow reached teens more effectively than the programs that focused on abstinence. A third interpretation is that contraception, not abstinence, has lowered the numbers.

9   However, a study of lowered teen-pregnancy rates between 1991 and 1995 (published in *Adolescent and Family Health* by Mohn, Tingle et al., April 2003) showed that abstinence, not contraceptives, was the major cause of the lowered pregnancy rate. Another 1996 study, by John Vessey, of Northwestern University Medical School, followed up on 2,541 teens, ages 13 to 16, who completed an abstinence-education program. He reported that one year after completing the program, 54 percent of formerly sexually active teens no longer were sexually active. This puts to rest the idea that "once a teen has sex, they will continue to be sexually active."

10   It often is claimed that most parents want pro-contraceptive education for their kids. In fact, a nationwide Zogby International poll of 1,245 parents in February (see poll results at www.whatparentsthink. com) commissioned by the pro-abstinence Coalition for Adolescent Sexual Health found that when shown the actual content of both comprehensive and abstinence-only sex-education programs,

73 percent of parents supported abstinence education and 75 percent opposed the condom-based education, with 61 percent opposing the comprehensive sex-ed programs.

11   But what do teens themselves think? In a 2000 study by the National Campaign to Prevent Teen Pregnancy, 93 percent of the teens surveyed said there should be a strong message from society not to engage in sex at least until graduation from high school. Will abstinence education cause sexually active teens to be unable to find out about contraception? The small amount in abstinence-education funding requested by Congress ($135 million among three programs) is miniscule compared with the $379 million funding of only six of the 25 federal programs teaching contraceptive-based education. This is Goliath complaining that David is using up all the rocks.

12   But, in all good conscience, can we teach something that would put kids in danger of contracting HIV, even if at a somewhat-reduced risk? Can we glibly decide, "Oh, only 15 percent of users will die?" That's acceptable? The stakes simply are too high. Even one life is too important to lose. When we're talking about life and death, we can't settle for the soggy argument of "Kids are going to do it anyway." That's what used to be said about racial discrimination, drunk driving and cigarette smoking, but when people became serious about countering these behaviors, they receded. If we realize the necessity of saving every teen's life, we can't help but teach them that because sex is wonderful, powerful and life-changing, it must be treated with great care.

13   Sex is most pleasurable and joyful when there is no fear of disease, when both partners feel absolute trust in the other, when the possibility of a pregnancy is not a destructive one and when each person truly wants the best for the other. This takes self-development, investment, emotional growth, responsibility and a whole host of other elements a typical teen doesn't possess, unless they are guided. In reality, every person already is aware of the need to limit sexuality to certain times and places, like many activities. Sexuality is far more complex than the physical mechanics of orgasm. That stuff is pretty much automatic. It's far more important to know that orgasm is the perfectly engineered system for creating life, and for experiencing the fulfillment of love.

14   Abstinence isn't a vague ideal but a practical, feasible life skill. Studies show that kids who are able to say no to sex also can say no to drugs, alcohol and tobacco. The skills in one area automatically transfer to other areas of health, Learning to delay gratification can have positive impacts on academic goals and athletic accomplishments.

15   Without the soap-opera distractions of sex, kids feel more confident and free to enjoy the process of making friends, developing their own individuality and working on their dreams. That's why virtually no one looks back on the decision to be sexually abstinent and says "I wish I had never done that." But 63 percent of teen

respondents who have had sex regretted it and said they wish they had waited, according to an International Communications Research of Media survey in June 2000 commissioned by the National Campaign to Prevent Teen Pregnancy. Further, 78 percent of the 12- to 17-year-old respondents said teens should not be sexually active, and only 21 percent thought sex for teens was okay if they used birth control.

16   Teens are telling us that they need support to resist the pressure to have sex. Even just making an abstinence pledge was found to delay sexual debut by 18 months on average, according to the National Longitudinal Study on Adolescent Health in 1997. And teens who know their parents have a strong belief and expectation of abstinence are far more likely to abstain, as shown in two 2002 studies released by the University of Minnesota Center for Adolescent Health and Development in which more than 80 percent of teens stayed abstinent when they knew their mothers strongly disapproved of premarital sex.

17   Even if it were only to end the spread of HIV/AIDS, that would be a valid reason to support abstinence education.

18   But teaching abstinence goes beyond preventing disease and unwanted pregnancy. It helps kids improve in the areas of self-esteem, academic attainments and future careers. It increases refusal skills toward drugs, alcohol and smoking. It equips teens with tools that they will use successfully throughout life, especially in their eventual marriage and family life. In other words, it has a positive ripple effect both in terms of their current and future life courses.

19   In my estimation, that definitely is worth funding.

Understanding the Content

Feel free to reread all or parts of the selection to answer the following questions.

1. Why does Tsubata call teen pregnancy "the lesser evil"? What does she consider more important?

2. What are the problems with condoms being the "central pillar of HIV prevention," according to the author?

3. According to the 2001 Youth Risk Behavior Surveillance, what was the result of abstinence education?

4. What type of sex education do parents want for their kids?

5. What do teens think is realistic and effective when it comes to sex education?

6. What are all of the benefits of teaching abstinence, according to Kathleen Tsubata?

Looking at Structure and Style

1. What is the thesis of this selection? Pick one sentence from the selection that effectively conveys the overall thesis.

2. Does Tsubata provide enough evidence to support her thesis?

3. Which paragraph best supports Tsubata's assertion that an abstinence-only education is best for teens?

4. List the outside sources that Tsubata uses to support her thesis. Are these inclusions effective?

5. Write a brief summary of Tsubata's argument.

6. What combination of writing patterns is used in paragraph 5?

Evaluating the Author's Viewpoints

1. What is the author's tone in this selection? What is her attitude toward those who take a different approach to sex education?

2. What does the author think of encouraging teens to use condoms as a way to prevent against pregnancy and disease?

3. What does Tsubata think about teens' ability to handle—both emotionally and physically—sexual activity?

4. Do you agree or disagree with Tsubata's thesis? Why?

5. What can you infer about Tsubata's feelings about those who disagree with her position? Use examples from the selection to support your opinion.

6. Does Tsubata feel that abstinence has further-reaching consequences than just preventing STDs (sexually-transmitted diseases) and teen pregnancy? If so, what does she say and how does she support her argument?

Pursuing Possible Essay Topics

Wait until you have read the following essay, "They'll Abstain If They're Given Good Reasons," by Deborah M. Roffman, before you write your next essay.

Preparing to Read

Take a minute or two to look over the following reading selection. Note the title and author, read the opening paragraph, and check the essay's length. Make certain you have the time now to read it carefully and to do the exercises that follow it. Then, in the spaces provided, answer the following questions.

1. From the title and the opening paragraph, what do you think the essay will be about? _____

    _____

    _____

2. What do you think the author's viewpoint toward abstinence will be?

    _____

    _____

3. Do you think you'll agree or disagree with the author's thesis? Why?

    _____

    _____

Vocabulary

Good comprehension of what you are about to read depends upon your understanding of the words below. The number following each word refers to the paragraph where it is used.

perplexed (1) filled with confusion; puzzled

advocated (7) pleaded or argued in favor of something

vociferous (8) a noisy or vehement outcry

conspiratorial (8) relating to, or characteristic of, an agreement to act together in an illegal, wrongful, or subversive act

demoralize (8) to undermine someone's confidence

curricula (9) a set of courses or coursework in a school setting

prudent (10) careful or discreet

chastity (11) the condition of being pure or chaste

indoctrination (19) to fill with a biased, partisan, or ideological point of view

disingenuous (20) not straightforward; crafty

 # They'll Abstain If They're Given Good Reasons

DEBORAH ROFFMAN

Deborah Roffman has worked as a health and human sexuality educator in the Baltimore/Washington, D.C. area since 1971. She is the author of Sex and Sensibility: The Thinking Parent's Guide to Talking Sense about Sex.

1 After learning about a congressional report offering evidence that many widely used abstinence-only courses grossly overestimate the failure rates for condoms, the seventh-grade students at one of the schools where I teach were perplexed.

2 "Well, if these courses are supposed to be health education," asked one, "why would anyone want to give wrong information about something as important as preventing AIDS?" Another added, "Are they trying to tell kids not to bother using condoms when they need them because they're useless anyway?" "None of this makes sense!" said a third. "Condoms can save lives." To which another retorted, "Well, maybe it's sex they're against, not AIDS!"

3 Many educators and parents I work with scratch their heads, too, when they learn that hundreds of millions of federal and state dollars are being spent on abstinence-only programs, in which contraception may be mentioned only in the context of its failure rates. Teachers and parents raise some important questions: Can abstinence-only be the best way to protect the nation's children against pregnancy and disease when we know, as Friday's National Center for Health Statistics report shows, that just under half of all teenagers have already had sexual intercourse? What's more, there is no evidence to prove that abstinence-only teaching actually keeps anyone abstinent, while numerous studies have demonstrated that more comprehensive programs do result in postponement and more responsible behavior. Parents are also confused about why abstinence-only came to be our government's official policy, since 85 percent of adults in the United States favor a comprehensive approach.

4 If 30 years of experience in this field has taught me one thing, it is that when talking with our children about sex, we need to make sure that we educate rather than dictate and that our approach is based on scientific evidence. Only then can we hope to arm young people against the escalating social and cultural pressures they face.

5   Many parents tell me that counseling children is not that easy. Adults I work with who readily understand the logic of what is referred to as the abstinence-plus approach (one that encourages postponement and also provides information about other methods of preventing unwanted pregnancy and disease) still worry about sending a mixed message: "Don't do that—but if you do, be sure to use a condom."

6   But there is another way to counsel teenagers that I know they don't find confusing at all: "First and foremost, we love you, and we want you to be safe. The best way to be safe is to abstain. And, for people who choose not to abstain there are steps they can take to lower the risks." Teenagers don't hear that as a Do/Don't message, but as straightforward evidence of how much adults care about their well-being and about how we expect them to take these decisions very seriously.

7   The abstinence-only legislation signed into law in 1996 is by no means the federal government's first foray into the field of sex education. During the first half of the 20th century, the government actually advocated strongly for sex education through, for example, Public Health Service conferences. Support for this position was also on the rise among private organizations, including the American Medical Association, the National Education Association and the American School Health Association.

8   There have always been people strenuously opposed to school-based programs for a variety of personal and religious reasons. By the mid-20th century, with new and growing visibility and acceptance of sex instruction in schools, some opponents began to organize themselves politically. They began to attack local schools and school districts in a systematic and sometimes vociferous fashion, openly characterizing sex education as a conspiratorial scheme designed to "demoralize youth, divide parents from children, and increase sexual activity among adolescents."

9   With the emerging AIDS crisis in the 1980s, these local groups—working with several highly sophisticated and recognized groups such as the Eagle Forum, Concerned Women for America, Focus on the Family and the Family Research Council—were uniquely positioned to take an active role in the shaping of school-based curricula. Capitalizing on the escalating fear of the disease, they shifted their strategy from keeping sex education out of the schools entirely to instituting abstinence-only teaching throughout the entire country. In other words, abstinence-only teaching was not suddenly born out of the desire to prevent AIDS or teenage pregnancy. AIDS provided the context and pretext for launching abstinence-only education as a national priority.

10 Don't get me wrong: I think the emphasis on abstinence in recent years has gone a long way toward making it a more acceptable option

for young people. There is no question in my mind that abstinence—as in the delay or postponement of sexual intercourse—is the prudent choice for anyone not yet ready to take on the physical, social, emotional and moral responsibilities inherent in the act of intercourse, or for anyone whose personal or religious values dictate that the proper place for this behavior is only within the context of marriage. I have yet to meet a responsible health educator who does not make these points clearly in his or her teaching.

11   However, the mandatory guidelines in the federal abstinence-only program reveal a very different agenda. Teachers in schools where these federal dollars are accepted are not permitted to frame abstinence or postponement as a recommended choice in the service of one's health, but as an obligatory state of being until marriage. In other words, abstinence is not to be portrayed as a means to an end (good health) but as an end in itself. The ultimate goal of the program is to promote premarital chastity rather than premarital health.

12   I meet parents all the time who confuse these concepts and as a result can't frame a clear message. They feel stuck. I suggest that first they have to decide: Do I want to give a message that emphasizes chastity before marriage over other considerations, or do I want to frame abstinence in the sense of postponement until a young person is able to handle the responsibilities involved? There is often much soul-searching involved in facing this question, but it is the key to communicating effectively.

13   Parents for whom the chastity message is the right one need to articulate persuasively the personal or religious reasons behind their beliefs. They'll also need to prepare themselves for equally persuasive counter-arguments that their children, especially the older ones, may offer. Parents who want to impart a postponement message can develop their case around the developmental, health, social, ethical and relationship issues they view as paramount. In either case, children are served well by parents who present well-supported views. Schools can best help by not taking sides and by ensuring that a wide range of parental views are treated with respect.

14   One of the challenges that all educators face is distinguishing religious teaching from health education. Individuals who believe in the doctrines associated with a particular religion do so as part of their faith in God, and they often consider that all morality stems from these deeply held beliefs. Were sexually transmitted infections suddenly out of the picture and preventing unwanted pregnancy a matter of putting a substance in the tap water, my hunch is that backers of abstinence-only would continue to insist on that approach.

15   Health education is a different matter. As an applied science, it is based on the most current evidence-based data available. It must also be objective: A health educator must not choose to eliminate or slant information—and certainly not potentially life-saving information—as a way of proving or promoting his or her beliefs.

16   Similarly, health educators can't "work backwards." That is, they can't begin with a preconceived notion of what is the right course of action for every person under every circumstance and then create curricula designed to meet that end. An approach such as abstinence-only education—which dictates the correct answer even before the first question is asked—is antithetical to the educational process.

17   Let's be clear, too, that quality health education is never "values free"—as if education of any kind could ever be values free. It endeavors to help individuals understand themselves and their personal or religious values, because informed decision-making is never purely about external facts. Good health education strives to highlight and reinforce core moral values, such as honesty, respect, caring and responsibility, as they relate to healthy choices.

18   There is much concern in the public health community that abstinence-only programs leave those young people who ultimately choose not to abstain in a dangerous information vacuum. I see an equally dangerous moral and ethical vacuum, because they are also left without guidance on how to apply the values they have absorbed to the sexual situations in which they will find themselves. How ironic that in the name of "morality" we may diminish young people's ability to think and behave ethically.

19   I have no problem whatsoever with the concepts of chastity, religion or religious instruction. Each has its place, and I often bring religious views into classroom discussions because they are essential to understanding ourselves and the cultural and political landscape of American society. My problem is with religion and indoctrination masquerading as public education, and with chastity masquerading as abstinence.

20   And make no mistake, teenagers have a kind of built-in radar for sensing when adults are trying to manipulate them—including those savvy 12- and 13-year-olds in my seventh-grade classroom the other day. Once they realize that what adults are telling them is in any way disingenuous, they stop listening, no matter how good that advice may be.

21   So let's stop calling the federal government's approach to sex instruction "abstinence-only education" and start calling it what it really is: chastity-only advocacy. And let's not expect that it will provide the kind of balanced, accurate information that our children need and deserve.

Understanding the Content

Feel free to reread all or parts of the selection to answer the following questions.

1. What was the reaction of Roffman's seventh grade students after learning about the congressional report on abstinence-only programs and their overestimation about the failure rates for condoms?

2. How does Roffman think that adults should talk to children and teens about sex?

3. According to Roffman, how did the abstinence-only programs come into being in the United States?

4. What is the goal of abstinence-only programs, according to Deborah Roffman?

5. What does Roffman think should be the real name of the government's "abstinence-only education" programs? Why?

Looking at Structure and Style

1. What is the thesis of this selection? Pick one sentence from the selection that effectively conveys the overall thesis.

2. Does Roffman provide enough evidence to support her thesis? If not, what could she have done to support her thesis more fully?

3. How does Roffman's thesis differ from Tsubata's in *Yes: Abstinence Is Working?* Are they alike in any way?

4. Which paragraph best supports Roffman's assertion regarding abstinence-only policies?

5. Does Roffman use any outside sources to support her argument? If so, list them.

6. Write a brief summary of Roffman's argument.

7. In your opinion, whose argument—Tsubata's or Roffman's—is better, more compelling? Which has the strongest support? Why?

Evaluating the Author's Viewpoints

1. What is the author's tone in this selection?

2. What is Roffman's position on chastity? What is her position on religion or religious instruction?

3. Does Roffman think that abstinence-only programs should be abolished?

4. Do you agree or disagree with Roffman's thesis? Why?

5. Now that you've read both articles, which author do you most agree with and why?

Pursuing Possible Essay Topics

1. Argue against either Tsubata's thesis in *Yes: Abstinence Is Working* or Roffman's thesis in *They'll Abstain If They're Given Good Reason.* For whichever thesis you choose, make sure you consider each of the main arguments and provide argumentative support for your views.

2. Write an essay expressing your own viewpoints on sex education, discussing your views about when sex education should start for children, if abstinence-only is the best approach, and how involved the school should be in the process.

3. Whose argument—Tsubata's or Roffman's—is closest to your own regarding sex education? Write an essay comparing and contrasting your views with the views of the author whose beliefs are closest to your own.

4. Do you think, as some opponents of sex instruction in schools do, that sex education is designed to "demoralize youth, divide parents from children, and increase sexual activity among adolescents"? Why or why not? Write an essay discussing your viewpoint.

5. Brainstorm or freewrite on one or more of the following:
   a. sex education
   b. abstinence-only programs
   c. more comprehensive sex education programs
   d. STD/AIDS prevention

Student Essay

Read the following narrative essay written when the author was a student at the University of North Carolina. She graduated in 2005 on the Chancellor's Honor List. As you read, look for answers to these questions:

1. Would this essay satisfy a writing assignment on some aspect of learning?

2. Why do you think she wrote it?

3. Does she follow the basic writing suggestions provided in Chapter 2, "Viewpoints on Writing Essay"?

4. What grade would you give her essay and why?

One Hundred Percent Half-Breed

Bridget W. Dimery

1   As it has always been within every culture, people are put into categories of society. Usually it is race that society categorizes a person in. But what do you do when you're two races, neither one more than the other? It is hard to fit in to one race when you are another at the same time. I fall into the category of bi-racial. Bi-racial is when you are two races, and both are exactly equal to each other. You see, my father is full-blooded Native American, and my mother is full-blooded white. So I've always had to defend myself to both races when one person out of their ignorance questions my claim to Native American. I think that being bi-racial has been the cause for my search of acceptance in the world, but mostly acceptance in the Native American world.

2   When I was in elementary school in Michigan, the majority of the students were white. I started there in the first grade, and some of the boys in my class asked me if I was an Indian. When I told them that I was, they laughed. They asked me where were my tomahawk and my tepee. They said I wasn't a real Indian because I didn't have a bow and arrow. Even at six years old, I knew what was going on. But I told those boys that those were just traditional ways of some tribes. I told them that we were modern day. We were just like every other average American. After those first

few days of school, nobody really paid attention to it anymore, and I was just a kid like them. The only time that it ever came up was around Thanksgiving when we talked about pilgrims and Indians or in social studies when we discussed the 1800's. I never felt like I didn't fit in because nobody had ever really made a point to pick on me about being different from him or her because kids are usually teased by their peers for being different.

3   When I was ten years old, we moved to my dad's hometown of Pembroke where the population is predominantly Native American. When I started the fifth grade, I knew that something was different. I was now labeled as the "white girl." I guess it was because I talked proper with a northern accent and my skin was a little bit lighter than most of my classmates. They would laugh at me when I would put down Native American as my race on my EOG tests and tell me I was just a white girl. I did the best that I could to fit in. As time went on, I made friends, but a few people still liked to call me the white girl, even in high school. I guess it was because my skin wasn't a dark copper color. They never paid attention to my dark hair and eyes, or to my Indian nose. So when my Dad would come pick me up from school they would be like "That's your dad? I thought you were white." I would get the last laugh when they accepted me after seeing my Dad. I think that they were taught at home that all Indians had nothing but dark skin. Since I was a lot lighter than the other kids, they thought of me as being as nonnative. And all I wanted from them was the acknowledgement of being an Indian.

4   Back in my primary school days and even in today's society, people have a view of Native Americans as dressed in buckskins, long black hair, copper skin and tepees. But that is just a typical stereotype. And since I don't fit the stereotype, I wasn't a "real Indian" to them. In Vine Deloria, Jr.'s *Custer Died for Your Sins: An Indian Manifesto*, he throws away the stereotypes and reveals who Native Americans really are; and that is nothing like the stereotypes. Also, by not being a full blood, I am looked down upon even more by some. In Deloria's chapter titled "Indians Today, The Real and the Unreal," he states, "The more we try to be ourselves the more we are forced to defend what we

have never been." It is difficult for me to be taken seriously as a Native American because my light skin doesn't fit the typical stereotype. And when I was in primary school, that was my only fault to the other students. I didn't have that bronze skin. I even used to wear self-tanner because I thought that I would be taken more seriously as a Native American and be accepted by my peers. But I can look back now and say I am a real Indian not just by blood but also by how I identify myself. And looking back now, I didn't need them to tell me who I am.

5   Looking back at those times now, I can laugh at how naïve we are as children. My Mom and I still joke about it now. I'll go places with my Mom and Dad, and she'll say stuff like "what's that white woman doing with two Indians?" One time I told her that, since I wasn't either white or Indian, I was a hundred percent half-breed. She told my Dad's friend, and he about laughed his head off. He said "gal, you're all right aren't you?" A lot of times though, people who are breeds (as they are usually labeled) can't find a place where they are wanted. In Louis Owens's *Mixed Blood Messages,* he takes narratives from other novels and movies and relates them to the mixed blooded Indian. In his chapter called "Mapping the Mixed Blood," he talks about half-breeds (people who are half Native American and half-white) and the struggles they face in acceptance from either world. He quotes Okanogan author Mourning Dove from her novel *Cogewea, The Halfblood: A Depiction of the Great Montana Cattle Range* of the issue she faces on being a breed. He quotes, "Our Caucasian brothers criticize us as a shiftless class, while the Indians disown us as abandoning our own race. We are maligned and traduced as no one but we of the despised 'breeds' can know". I can relate to this because even though a lot of people don't pay any attention to what you are, there are some who won't ever accept you because you have the other race in you. They can't look past your outside. I've had white people look down on me in places because I'm an Indian. But I've also had some Indians to look down on me because I am also white. But that doesn't mean that I couldn't be accepted into either world. I could fit myself into society as either one or the

other but never both. But I just choose to be Native American because those are my feelings that I have felt all of my life.

6   Many people would ask me why I feel so strong about being Native American. Since I am also white, then why are my feelings so strong? The truth is that I really don't know why. I can't explain how my heart feels when I hear about Native Americans in the media and society. Or why I hurt so much when I read about the genocide inflicted on the Native Americans. My favorite thing to read about is the history of Native Americans, good and bad. I just want to read all of the truth that I can and carry on the traditions for the generations to come. In Paula Gunn Allen's *The Sacred Hoop,* she writes about the struggles mainly Native American women face in society. Even though she is a half-breed herself, she is a strong believer in carrying on the traditions of Native America. Allen states, "The American idea that the best and the brightest should willingly reject and repudiate their origins leads to an allied idea—that history, like everything in the past, is of little value and should be forgotten as quickly as possible." Many times when people ask me what I am going to college for and I tell them American Indian Studies, the reaction is usually "why do you want to study that, why not go into something to make money?" It's hard to explain to someone that I don't care about money and don't want a job that I am miserable with. Today's society is so caught up in the future that they want to forget the past. I'm a believer in holding on to the traditions and values of the past to make the future better. I can't go to school and learn everything there is to know about Native Americans, but I can live my life through my feelings and experiences. I can help to keep the Native past alive through keeping it strong through the future. I'm not a full blood technically, but every other aspect of me is a Native American.

7   I think that being a non full-blooded Native American has been the cause for my search of acceptance in the Native American world. I just want my life to be fulfilled in a way that I can accept myself for who I am. I used to only care about what everybody else thought about me, but I think that as I grow older

I realize the shallowness of my worries. I can't go on living my
life worried about what everyone else thinks. But I can live my
life fully if I finally accept who I am myself. And then I will
be content with being a one hundred percent half-breed. Not full
Indian in blood, but a full Indian in heart.

Reaction

In your journal or on a separate sheet of paper, write your reaction to the student essay. What would you tell this student about her essay? Compare your comments with those of your classmates.

Viewpoints on Images

If your instructor assigned an essay that required research, why must you be cautious about using information found on the Internet, such as Wikipedia, the free encyclopedia? Why might library resources be a better source, at least to begin your research?

United States Declaration of Independence

From Wikipedia, the free encyclopedia

The **United States Declaration of Independence** is a statement adopted by the Continental Congress on July 4, 1776, announcing that the thirteen American colonies then at war with Great Britain were no longer a part of the British Empire. Written primarily by Thomas Jefferson, the Declaration is a formal explanation of why Congress had voted on July 2 to declare independence from Great Britain, more than a year after the outbreak of the American Revolutionary War. The birthday of the United States of America—Independence Day—is celebrated on July 4, the day the wording of the Declaration was approved by Congress.

Congress issued the Declaration of Independence in several forms. It was initially published as a printed broadside that was widely distributed and read to the public. The most famous version of the Declaration, a signed copy that is usually regarded as *the* Declaration of Independence, is on display at the National Archives in Washington, D.C. Contrary to popular mythology, Congress did not sign this document on July 4, 1776; it was created after July 19 and was signed by most Congressional delegates on August 2.

Philosophically, the Declaration stressed two Lockean themes: individual rights and the right of revolution. These ideas of the Declaration continued to be widely held by Americans, and had an influence internationally, in particular the French Revolution. Abraham Lincoln, beginning in 1854 as he spoke out against slavery and the Kansas-Nebraska Act[2], provided a reinterpretation[3] of the Declaration that stressed that the unalienable rights of "Life, Liberty and the pursuit of Happiness" were not limited to the white race.[4] "Lincoln and those who shared his conviction" created a document with "continuing usefulness" with a "capacity to convince and inspire living Americans."[5] The invocation by Lincoln in his Gettysburg Address of the Declaration of Independence defines for many Americans how they interpret[6] Jefferson's famous preamble:

We hold these truths to be self-evident, that all men are created equal, that they are endowed by their Creator with certain unalienable Rights, that among these are Life, Liberty and the pursuit of Happiness.

United States Declaration of Independence

1823 facsimile of the engrossed copy

Created June–July 1776

Ratified July 4, 1776

Location Engrossed copy: National Archives Original: lost Rough draft: Library of Congress

Authors Thomas Jefferson *et al.*

Signers 56 delegates to the Continental Congress

Purpose Announce and explain separation from Britain [1]

National Archives/Wikipedia text entry; all text is available under the terms of the GNU Free Documentation License, www.gnu.org/license/fdl-1.2.txt

On the Net

Learning and education are such broad topics that there are thousands of Internet sites devoted to various aspects of each. If you want to do your own research, do a search on one or more of the popular search engines such as Excite, Google, or Yahoo! by typing in the keyword "learning" or "education." You will then be presented with thousands of sites related to the word you chose; you can choose the sites you would like to explore or the subjects about which you would like to learn more.

However, as you probably know from "surfing the Web," you need to be as specific as possible to get the kind of information you need. One thing you can do is choose any topic of interest related to these two areas or one related to the readings in this chapter, such as "failure," "plagiarism," or "abstinence education," and you will get specific sites devoted to this subject.

If you want to learn more about any of the authors of the writings in this chapter, you can search the Internet by typing in the author's name or the title of one of the selections into the search field of the search engine of your choice. Try typing in and searching the sites that provide more information about Pitts and his viewpoints.

If you would like to try your hand at researching on the Web, do one or more of the following exercises.

1. Go to www.plagiarism.org and read through the site. Find out what the purpose of the site is and summarize your findings.

2. Go to your school's Web site and see if there is a stated plagiarism and/or cheating policy. Write a brief summary of what you found.

3. Do a web search on abstinence education. Evaluate the sites for their credibility and look for anything that might indicate a certain bias on the subject. For instance, who is the author of the site? What is the name of the site? What is the tone of the information presented? Write a brief summary of what you found.

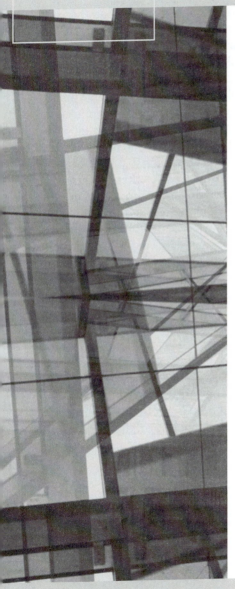

4 Viewpoints on Human Behavior

Focus on People's Behavior

To help you focus on the subject of this chapter, take a few minutes to prepare for the topic by pre-writing on one or more of the following prompts:

1. your private and public self
2. everybody is doing it
3. it's not my fault
4. fear of the unknown
5. conventional wisdom
6. my country right or wrong

What makes us behave the way we do? Sociologists and psychologists, among others, are still trying to find an answer to this question. Some answers have been found. It's clear that we humans have the ability to reason and make choices. But many aspects of our physical and social environment limit the choices available to us. Still, sociologists claim that given our options and our preferences, we choose to do what we expect will be most rewarding. Whether the rewards are candy, fame, money, a better life in the future, or affection, we act or choose primarily for self-interest.

The idea of self-interest as a motive for human behavior is one that many social scientists use to try to explain our actions. Economists, observing that we seek a variety of goods for ourselves, have developed their theories of supply and demand. And the success of advertising certainly depends on the self-interest of the consumer. Psychologists believe that behavior is shaped by reinforcement. That is, we repeat actions or behaviors that produce the results we desire. If our parents praise us for certain actions, we continue to act in those ways. Our reward is the praise we get. Sociologists believe that we seek what we expect will reward us and avoid what we perceive will cost us. Making our parents angry "costs" us; touching a hot fire "costs" us. If we are "normal," then we learn to behave according to these norms.

According to social scientists, we learn to see ourselves as others see us. In a sense, we look at ourselves from the outside. As infants and young children, we are not able to understand the meaning of the behavior of those around us. As we grow, we learn to know what we are like by seeing ourselves in others. We form an idea of what others want and expect and how they react to us. We settle into a pattern of behavior through interactions with others; we learn the "rules" of behavior for our particular environment. And even though we have choices, our behavior is frequently influenced by what those around us want or expect us to do.

Of course, we don't always follow the norm. Those who regularly don't follow the rules are considered abnormal. Some abnormal behavior is funny, some sad, some self-destructive, and some dangerous to others. The essays in this chapter deal with a variety of behavior: the good and the bad, the misunderstood, the so-called abnormal, the funny, and the unexplainable. You will recognize some of the actions described and wonder at others, but they are all part of the complex creatures called humans. It is hoped that you will both learn from the variety of readings and be stimulated by them to write your viewpoints on the subject.

Preparing to Read

Take a minute or two to look over the following reading selection. Note the title and the author, read the opening paragraph, and check the essay's length. Make certain you have the time now to read it carefully and to do the exercises that follow it. Then, in the spaces provided, answer the following questions.

1. What do you think is the subject of the essay? _____

   _____

2. How do you think the author feels about the mentally ill? Why? _____

   _____

   _____

3. What is the author's tone toward her subject in the first paragraph? _____

   _____

Vocabulary

Good comprehension of what you are about to read depends upon your understanding of the words below. The number following each word refers to the paragraph where it is used.

psychotic (3) relating to mental illness; sometimes relating to loss of contact with reality

calibration (4) adjustment or correction

keel (4) balance

vigilance (4) watchfulness

stint (5) a period of time

schisms (8) divisions

stigmatized (9) characterized as disgraceful, discredited

Call Me Crazy, But I Have to Be Myself

Mary Seymour

Mary Seymour works at Northfield Mount Herman School in Massachusetts. The following essay appeared in Newsweek's *"My Turn" section.*

1   Nearly every day, without thinking, I say things like "So-and-so is driving me crazy" or "That's nuts!" Sometimes I catch myself and realize that I'm not being sensitive toward people with mental illness. Then I remember I'm one of the mentally ill. If I can't throw those words around, who can?

2   Being a functional member of society and having a mental disorder is an intricate balancing act. Every morning I send my son to junior high school, put on professional garb and drive off to my job as alumni-magazine editor at a prep school, where I've worked for six years. Only a few people at work know I'm manic-depressive, or bipolar, as it's sometimes called.

3   Sometimes I'm not sure myself what I am. I blend in easily with "normal" people. You'd never know that seven years ago, fueled by the stress of a failing marriage and fanned by the genetic inheritance of a manic-depressive grandfather, I had a psychotic break. To look at me, you'd never guess I once ran naked through my yard or shuffled down the hallways of a psychiatric ward. To hear me, you'd never guess God channeled messages to me through my computer. After my breakdown at 36, I was diagnosed as bipolar, a condition marked by moods that swing between elation and despair.

4   It took a second, less-severe psychotic episode in 1997, followed by a period of deep depression, to convince me I truly was bipolar. Admitting I had a disorder that I'd have to manage for life was the hardest thing I've ever done. Since then, a combination of therapy, visits to a psychiatrist, medication, and inner calibration have helped me find an even keel. Now I manage my moods with the vigilance of a mother hen, nudging them back to center whenever they wander too far. Eating wisely, sleeping well, and exercising regularly keep me balanced from day to day. Ironically, my disorder has taught me to be healthier and happier than I was before.

5   Most of the time, I feel lucky to blend in with the crowd. Things that most people grumble about—paying bills, maintaining a car, working 9 to 5—strike me as incredible privileges. I'll never forget gazing through the barred windows of the psychiatric ward into the parking lot, watching people come and go effortlessly, wondering if I'd ever be like them again. There's nothing like a stint in a locked ward to make one grateful for the freedoms and burdens of full citizenship.

6   Yet sometimes I feel like an impostor. Sometimes I wish I could sit at the lunch table and talk about lithium and Celexa instead of *Will & Grace*. While everyone talks about her fitness routine, I want to brag how it took five orderlies to hold me down and shoot me full of sedatives when I was admitted to the hospital, and how for a brief moment I knew the answers to every infinite mystery of the blazingly bright universe. I yearn for people to know me—the real me—in all my complexity, but I'm afraid it would scare the bejesus out of them.

7   Every now and then, I feel like I'm truly being myself. Like the time the school chaplain, in whom I'd confided my past, asked me to help counsel a severely bipolar student. This young woman had tried to commit suicide, had been hospitalized many times and sometimes locked herself in her dorm room to keep the "voices" from overwhelming her. I walked and talked with her, sharing stories about medication and psychosis. I hoped to show by example that manic-depression did not necessarily mean a diminished life. At commencement, I watched her proudly accept her diploma; despite ongoing struggles with her illness, she's continuing her education.

8   I'm able to be fully myself with my closest friends, all of whom have similar schisms between private and public selves. We didn't set out to befriend each other—we just all speak the same language, of hardship and spiritual discovery and psychological awareness.

9   What I yearn for most is to integrate both sides of myself. I want to be part of the normal world but I also want to own my identity as bipolar. I want people to know what I've been through so I can help those traveling a similar path. Fear has kept me from telling my story: fear of being stigmatized, of making people uncomfortable, of being reduced to a label. But hiding the truth has become more uncomfortable than letting it out. It's time for me to own up to who I am, complicated psychiatric history and all. Call me crazy, but I think it's the right thing to do.

Understanding the Content

Feel free to reread all or parts of the selection to answer the following questions.

1. From what disorder or illness does the author suffer? What does it mean to have this condition?

2. What does the author do for a living? Has she shared her past with her co-workers? Why or why not?

3. What does the author do to control her mental illness?

4. Why is the author reluctant for "people to know me—the real me" (6)?

5. With whom is the author the most open about her mental illness, and why?

Looking at Structure and Style

1. What is the author's thesis? Is it stated or implied? If stated, where?

2. What is the purpose of paragraph 3?

3. What is the author's tone and attitude toward the subject of mental illness?

4. What message is the author trying to convey about mental illness? In what paragraph is this best expressed, and why?

5. What examples does the author give to illustrate why she feels like an "impostor"?

6. How effective is paragraph 9 as a concluding paragraph? Does this paragraph adequately convey the author's conflicted feelings about her life? Why or why not?

Evaluating the Author's Viewpoints

1. Seymour doesn't think that she should share with most people the fact that she is bipolar. Although she yearns "for people to know me—the real me" (6), she fears they will be afraid of her once they learn the truth. Do you agree or disagree with her, and why?

2. Based on your reading of the selection, do you think that the author thinks her mental illness is just a case of bad luck, heredity, or a combination of both? How can you tell?

3. Discuss the author's statement "Ironically, my disorder has taught me to be healthier and happier than I was before" (4). Does the author think she is lucky to have a mental illness? What does she mean by this statement?

4. Why do you think the author wants people to know of her "identity as bipolar" (9)? What would she gain by revealing that to the people in her life?

Pursuing Possible Essay Topics

1. Write an essay describing how you might feel to learn that someone in your life was mentally ill or suffering from bipolar disorder. Would you feel the same way toward that person?

2. Write an essay about how you think society treats people with mental illness. Do you think that people with mental illness are stigmatized? Why or why not?

3. Do you think the author should tell the people she works with about her mental illness? Why or why not? Write an essay urging the author to either tell the people she works with or keep her secret.

4. Write an essay from the point of view of the author's son. What do you think his life is like, imagining that he is fully aware of his mother's bipolar disorder?

5. Do you think mental illness is hereditary or just a random occurrence? Why?

6. Brainstorm or freewrite on one or more of the following:
   a. mental illness
   b. manic-depression
   c. Mary Seymour
   d. prejudice

7. Find your own topic related to mental illness and write an essay.

Preparing to Read

Take a minute or two to look over the following reading selection. Note the title and author, read the opening paragraph, and check the essay's length. Make certain you have the time now to read it carefully and to do the exercises that follow it. Then, in the spaces provided, answer the following questions.

1. What is suggested by the title? _____

   _____

2. What do you think the essay will be about? _____

   _____

3. Does the opening paragraph make you want to read on? Why? _____

   _____

Vocabulary

Good comprehension of what you are about to read depends upon your under-standing of the words below. The number following each word refers to the para-graph where it is used.

affluent (1) wealthy, well-to-do

impoverished (1) drained of wealth, poor

discreet (1) cautious, careful

uninflammatory (1) not arousing anger or emotion

unwieldy (2) difficult to handle

quarry (2) a hunted animal, prey

accomplice (2) one who aids a criminal

tyranny (2) absolute power, usually unjust and cruel; here, the power muggers have to terrorize women

elicit (3) bring out or cause

avid (4) enthusiastic, eager

taut (4) strained, tense

warrenlike (5) like a *warren*, a place where small animals live, but also refer-ring to places overcrowded with people

bandolier-style (5) the way a soldier wears an ammunition belt

solace (5) comfort

in retrospect (6) looking back on the past

bravado (6) false bravery

perilous (7) dangerous

ad hoc posse (7) a group formed for a special purpose (in this case, to chase him); *ad hoc* is Latin for "for this"

skittish (9) nervous

congenial (9) friendly, cooperative

constitutionals (10) healthy walks

Night Walker

BRENT STAPLES

Brent Staples writes for the New York Times. *His memoir,* Parallel Time: Growing Up in Black and White, *was the winner of the Anisfield Wolff Book Award, an award previously won by such writers as James Baldwin, Ralph Ellison, and Zora Neale Hurston.*

1 My first victim was a woman—white, well dressed, probably in her early 20s. I came upon her late one evening on a deserted street in Hyde Park, a relatively affluent neighborhood in an otherwise mean, impoverished section of Chicago. As I swung onto the avenue behind her, there seemed to be a discreet, uninflammatory distance between us. Not so. She cast back a worried glance. To her, the youngish black man—a broad six feet two inches with a beard and billowing hair, both hands shoved into the pockets of a bulky military jacket—seemed menacingly close. She picked up her pace and was soon running in earnest. Within seconds she disappeared into a cross street.

2 That was more than a decade ago. I was 22 years old, a graduate student newly arrived at the University of Chicago. It was in the echo of that terrified woman's footfalls that I first began to know the unwieldy inheritance I'd come into—the ability to alter public space in ugly ways. It was clear that she thought herself the quarry of a mugger, a rapist, or worse. Suffering a bout of insomnia, however, I was stalking sleep, not defenseless wayfarers. As a softy who is scarcely able to take a knife to a raw chicken—let alone hold one to a person's throat—I was surprised, embarrassed, and dismayed all at once. Her flight made me feel like an accomplice in tyranny. It also made it clear that I was indistinguishable from the muggers who occasionally seeped into the area from the surrounding ghetto. I soon gathered that being perceived as dangerous is a hazard in itself: Where fear and weapons meet—and they often do in urban America—there is always the possibility of death.

3   In that first year, my first away from my hometown, I was to become thoroughly familiar with the language of fear. At dark, shadowy intersections, I could cross in front of a car stopped at a traffic light and elicit the *thunk, thunk, thunk, thunk* of the driver—black, white, male, female—hammering down the door locks. On less traveled streets after dark, I grew accustomed to but never comfortable with people crossing to the other side of the street rather than pass me. Then there were the standard unpleasantries with policemen, doormen, bouncers, cabdrivers, and others whose business it is to screen out troublesome individuals *before* there is any nastiness.

4   I moved to New York nearly two years ago and I have remained an avid night walker. In central Manhattan, the near-constant crowd covers the tense one-on-one street encounters. Elsewhere, things can get very taut indeed.

5   After dark, on the warrenlike streets of Brooklyn where I live, I often see women who fear the worst from me. They seem to have set their faces on neutral, and with their purse straps strung across their chests bandolier-style, they forge ahead as though bracing themselves against being tackled. I understand, of course, that the danger they perceive is not a hallucination. Women are particularly vulnerable to street violence, and young black males are drastically overrepresented among the perpetrators of that violence. Yet these truths are no solace against the alienation that comes of being ever the suspect, an entity with whom pedestrians avoid making eye contact.

6   It is not altogether clear to me how I reached the ripe old age of 22 without being conscious of the lethality nighttime pedestrians attributed to me. Perhaps it was because in Chester, Pa., the small, angry industrial town where I came of age in the 1960s, I was scarcely noticeable against a backdrop of gang warfare, street knifings, and murders. I grew up one of the good boys, had perhaps a half-dozen fistfights. In retrospect, my shyness of combat has clear sources. As a boy, I saw countless tough guys locked away; I have since buried several, too. They were babies, really—a teenage cousin, a brother of 22, a childhood friend in his mid-20s—all gone down in episodes of bravado played out in the streets. I chose, perhaps unconsciously, to remain a shadow—timid, but a survivor.

7   The fearsomeness mistakenly attributed to me in public places often has a perilous flavor. The most frightening of these confusions occurred in the late 1970s and early 1980s, when I worked as a journalist in Chicago. One day, rushing into the office of a magazine I was writing for with a deadline story in hand, I was mistaken for a burglar. The office manager called security and, with an ad hoc posse, pursued me through the labyrinthine halls, nearly to my editor's door. I had no way of proving who I was. I could only move briskly toward the company of someone who knew me.

8   Relatively speaking, however, I never fared as badly as another black male journalist. He went to nearby Waukegan, Ill., a couple of summers ago to work on a story about a murderer who was born there. Mistaking the reporter for the killer, police officers hauled him from his car at gunpoint and but for his press credentials would probably have tried to book him. Such episodes are not uncommon. Black men trade tales like this all the time.

9   Over the years, I learned to smother the rage I felt at so often being mistaken for a criminal. Not to do so would surely have led to madness. I now take precautions to make myself less threatening. I move about with care, particularly late in the evening. I give a wide berth to nervous people on subway platforms during the wee hours. If I happen to be entering a building behind some people who appear skittish, I may walk by, letting them clear the lobby before I return, so as not to seem to be following them. I have been calm and extremely congenial on those rare occasions when I've been pulled over by the police.

10   And on late-evening constitutionals I employ what has proved to be an excellent tension-reducing measure: I whistle melodies from Beethoven and Vivaldi and the more popular classical composers. Even steely New Yorkers hunching toward nighttime destinations seem to relax, and occasionally they even join in the tune. Virtually everybody seems to sense that a mugger wouldn't be warbling bright, sunny selections from Vivaldi's "Four Seasons." It is my equivalent of the cowbell that hikers wear when they are in bear country.

Understanding the Content

Feel free to reread all or parts of the selection to answer the following questions.

1. What point is Staples making in his essay? Is his thesis implied or stated?

2. What event caused Staples to learn that "being perceived as dangerous is a hazard in itself" (2)? What does he mean?

3. How old was the author at the time? What was his reaction?

4. What other events have made him "thoroughly familiar with the language of fear" (3)?

5. Why does Staples feel that he is "often being mistaken for a criminal" (9)?

6. What tactics or precautions does he take to avoid being mistaken for a potential criminal?

Looking at Structure and Style

1. How effective is the author's first paragraph? Does it create an interest in the essay? Why?

2. Why does Staples wait until the middle of paragraph 2 to explain what was actually happening—that he was merely taking a walk?

3. What is the function of paragraph 3? What paragraph pattern is used there?

4. What attitude do you think is expressed in paragraph 9? What inferences can you draw from the author's statements?

5. Rewrite or explain the following passages from the essay:
   a. "It was in the echo of that terrified woman's footfalls that I first began to know the unwieldy inheritance I'd come into." (2)
   b. "Where fear and weapons meet—and they often do in urban America—there is always the possibility of death." (2)
   c. "I could cross in front of a car stopped at a traffic light and elicit the *thunk, thunk, thunk, thunk* of the driver—black, white, male, female—hammering down the door locks." (3)
   d. "They seem to have set their faces on neutral, and with their purse straps strung across their chests bandolier-style, they forge ahead as though bracing themselves against being tackled." (5)
   e. "It is my equivalent of the cowbell that hikers wear when they are in bear country." (10)

6. How effective is the title? Explain.

7. What suggestions for revision, if any, would you offer the author?

Evaluating the Author's Viewpoints

1. In paragraph 2, Staples says that he learned at age 22 that he had "the ability to alter public space in ugly ways." Explain what he means. Might the woman he describes in the opening paragraph be just as afraid of a white man in the same situation?

2. Reread the last sentence in paragraph 3. What attitude does the author reflect when he alludes to "standard unpleasantries" with people in authority? Is he exaggerating?

3. In paragraph 5, Staples says that "young black males are drastically over-represented among the perpetrators of . . . violence." Where do you think he believes this overrepresentation takes place? Do you agree?

4. Staples reveals to his audience negative attitudes toward black males that he has experienced firsthand and does not deserve. What is your reaction to the way he has responded?

Pursuing Possible Essay Topics

1. Write about a time when your identity was questioned or you were mistakenly accused of something. How were you made to feel? How did you react?

2. Write about a time when you were frightened or felt threatened by someone. Was the fear or threat real or imagined? What led up to the situation or incident? How was it resolved?

3. Skim through a newspaper for two or three days to see how many episodes of street violence are reported. What effect do these reports have on people's behavior? Is street violence exaggerated?

4. Staples is a victim of stereotyping. Write an essay about the way you may knowingly or unknowingly stereotype a certain ethnic or racial group. Examine the cause or basis for your doing so.

5. Examine a behavioral characteristic—of yourself or of someone you know—that you don't like. How did the trait or attitude develop? What harm has it caused? What can you do about it?

6. Brainstorm or freewrite on one or more of the following:

   a. fear   d. gangs
   b. anger   e. danger
   c. prejudice   f. tension

7. Find your own topic related to stereotyping and write an essay.

Preparing to Read

Take a minute or two to look over the following reading selection. Note the title and author, read the first three paragraphs, and check the essay's length. Make certain you have the time now to read it carefully and to do the exercises that follow it. Then, in the spaces provided, answer the following questions.

1. From the title and the opening paragraph, what do you think the essay will be about? _____

   _____

   _____

2. What do you learn about the author's viewpoint from the first two paragraphs?

   _____

   _____

3. Do you think you'll agree or disagree with the author's thesis? Why? _____

   _____

   _____

Vocabulary

Good comprehension of what you are about to read depends upon your understanding of the words below. The number following each word refers to the paragraph where it is used.

ironies (1) uses of words to express something different or opposite to the literal meaning

inference (2) the process of deriving logical conclusions from premises known to be true

mimicry (3) the act of imitation

diligence (4) persistent application to an undertaking

misbegotten (4) having an improper basis or origin

succumbed (5) gave in to or surrendered

hearsay (6) information heard from another source

corroborate (7) agree with or back up

fallacious (7) false or untrue

debacle (8) a sudden downfall or defeat

weaning (9) detaching from that to which one is devoted

ideologues (10) supporters of a particular ideology or group of ideas

dichotomous (10) divided into two parts

ciphers (10) nonentities

cynosures (10) objects that serve as focal points

venality (10) susceptibility to corruption or bribery

calcified (11) became inflexible or unchanging

The Species Called Homo-Simpsons

RANDY ALCORN

As a freelance journalist, Randy Alcorn has spent 23 years writing weekly columns for the Santa Barbara News Press. *This article appeared in* Noozhawk.com.

1   One of nature's curious ironies is how the defining gift that she bestowed on the human species is so sparingly used by so many of its members. The "sapiens" in homo-sapiens is Latin for "wise," but judging by the brainless behavior that humans increasingly exhibit, the biological classification for human beings might more aptly be homo-simpsons.

2   Too many people seem to find rational, analytical thought unpleasant, difficult and too time-consuming. Logic requires a mental discipline that applies a process of inference, inquiry and examination—a process that lazy or easily distracted minds quickly abandon.

3   Homo-simpsons want quick, short, simple answers to life's imposing questions. Therefore, they prefer to substitute critical thinking with standard philosophies to which they can adhere without the discomfort of doubt. They are contented with the conventional wisdom. As Oscar Wilde once noted, such people are not really individuals, "their thoughts are someone else's opinions, their lives a mimicry, their passions a quotation."

4   There are few instances where the lack of intellectual diligence and the unquestioning acceptance of conventional wisdom are more apparent than in American political behavior. It certainly explains how George W. Bush could be elected president not just once, but twice. It explains how a nation could be led into a misbegotten and unnecessary war in Iraq, and, most disturbingly, how a nation could

so easily be persuaded to surrender its founding principles of civil rights and individual liberty.

5   Boneheaded public polices and corrupt, incompetent politicians continue to be inflicted upon this nation in great part because so many people have succumbed to the delusion that they are thinking correctly if they accept commonly accepted reasoning and beliefs, especially those endorsed by celebrities and by political and religious leaders.

6   A recent study conducted by Germany's Max Planck Institute revealed that people will continue to believe gossip and rumors—especially if those are malicious—even when they are presented with clear evidence refuting the gossip and rumors. The German researchers speculated that people may be genetically programmed to base decisions on hearsay rather than on a rational evaluation of the evidence.

7   The disastrously lethal and costly war in Iraq may corroborate the German study. Ignoring all the evidence to the contrary, millions of Americans abandoned common sense, did not question authority, and accepted the politically motivated malicious gossip that Iraq was directly involved in the 9/11 terrorist attacks. Additionally, ordinary citizens, much of the mainstream media and most of Congress succumbed to groupthink and accepted the Bush administration's fallacious assertions that Iraq had weapons of mass destruction that would be made available to al-Qaeda terrorists.

8   Eventually, the rationale offered for continuing the Iraq debacle was the removal of a murderous tyrant and the establishment of democracy in Iraq. If that were the justification for war, Cuba would have been a more convenient place to start spreading democracy. But then, we don't need Cuba's sugar, we need oil.

9   Islamic terrorism against the United States was incited in great measure by the U.S. military presence in the Middle East—there to protect the oil supplies. Ironically, the money that is being spent on the war in Iraq and on the U.S. military presence in the Middle East could be better spent on weaning America from its dependence on foreign oil and on oil in general. For the cost of this war, nearly $500 billion already, how many homes in America could be made energy-independent with solar electric technology? How much research and development of alternate energy could be funded?

10   American politics and, therefore, its government are dominated by ideologues whose capability for rational thought and analysis is crippled by adherence to dichotomous doctrine—left or right, Democrat or Republican. It is no mystery why nothing that makes much sense gets done in Washington, D.C.—there is little clear, impartial thinking that happens there. We have ciphers in Congress and incompetents in the White House (doh!), but no real leaders, no cynosures guiding the nation to real solutions to its real problems.

Just partisan bickering, ideological platitudes, and reckless, salivating, venality.

11   There are certainly more rational approaches to the issues this nation confronts, but finding them would require many more citizens to have vigorous, independent minds engaged in logical thinking. More people would have to question conventional thinking, especially when it derives from authority figures and calcified ideologies.

12   When surveying the political landscape our vision has been conditioned to see only left or right, liberal or conservative. What we should be looking for is rational or irrational, intelligence or stupidity. Today, rational discretion is seldom found in the same old places—left or right, Democrat or Republican. We need to look with clear vision in new places. We must stop behaving like homo-simpsons and start living up to our namesake, homo-sapiens.

Understanding the Content

Feel free to reread all or parts of the selection to answer the following questions.

1. How does Alcorn define the term "homo-simpsons"?

2. According to Alcorn, what is the homo-simpson's thought process?

3. According to Alcorn, why do "boneheaded policies and corrupt, incompetent politicians continue to be inflicted upon this nation" (see paragraph 5)?

4. Why was the war in Iraq initially supported by many Americans, according to the author? What information did people use to make their decision about the war?

5. According to Randy Alcorn, how should Americans think about the political landscape?

Looking at Structure and Style

1. What is the thesis of this selection? Rewrite it in your own words.

2. Does Alcorn provide enough evidence to support his thesis?

3. Does Alcorn use outside sources to support his thesis? How effectively does he use these sources?

4. What is the organizing pattern used in paragraphs 4 and 5?

5. What is the author's tone in this selection? Identify some words and/or phrases that illustrate your answer.

6. What is the author's attitude towards his subject? How can you tell?

Evaluating the Author's Viewpoints

1. What is the difference between a homo-simpson and a homo-sapien? What examples does the author use to draw the distinction between the two?

2. Do you agree or disagree with the author that "too many people seem to find rational, analytical thought unpleasant, difficult, or too time-consuming (2)? Why?

3. What can you infer about Alcorn's opinion of George W. Bush as president?

4. Do you think Alcorn considers himself a homo-simpson or homo-sapien? How can you tell?

5. Reread the conclusion of this selection. Do you think that Alcorn thinks that we can develop the vision that he lays out in this paragraph? Why or why not?

Pursuing Possible Essay Topics

1. Do you consider yourself a homo-simpson or a homo-sapien? Why? Write an essay describing yourself using one of these two terms.

2. Why do you think—according to the study conducted by the Max Planck Institute (6)—that people will continue to believe gossip and rumors even if they are presented with clear evidence refuting them? Write an essay discussing your viewpoint.

3. Write an essay either agreeing with or disagreeing with Randy Alcorn's thesis.

4. If you hear a celebrity espouse a particular way of thinking, or state an opinion, are you less likely or more likely to believe what they are saying because they are a celebrity? Write an essay discussing your viewpoint.

5. Brainstorm or freewrite on one or more of the following:
   a. the war in Iraq
   b. homo-simpsons versus homo-sapiens
   c. politics in America
   d. liberals versus conservatives
   e. critical thinking

6. Write about your own topic on the subject of critical thinking to make decisions.

Preparing to Read

Take a minute or two to look over the following reading selection. Note the title and author, read the first paragraph, and check the essay's length. Make certain you have the time now to read it carefully and to do the exercises that follow it. Then, in the spaces provided, answer the following questions.

1. From the title and the opening paragraph, what do you think the essay will be about? _____

   _____

2. What do you learn about the author's viewpoint about his subject from the first paragraph? _____

   _____

Vocabulary

Good comprehension of what you are about to read depends upon your understanding of the words below. The number following each word refers to the paragraph where it is used.

meander (1) to move aimlessly without a set course

Abu Ghraib (2) a U.S. military prison in Iraq

plausible (3) credible; apparently valid or acceptable

mundane (10) commonplace or ordinary

rivulets (12) small brooks or streams

venerated (13) regarded with respect

fervently (14) showing or acting with great emotion or zeal

The Ballad of Lynndie England

JOSEPH L. BAGEANT

Joseph L. Bageant writes an online column, which can be found at www.jpebageant. com. The following selection is from his 2007 book Deer Hunting with Jesus: Dispatches from America's Class War.

1   Lynndie Rana England was born in 1982. I have a son her age. Like my son, she graduated high school in 2001. Folks in Fort Ashby say she did well in school, which is no great achievement in these places where the academic bar is set so damned low it is buried in the ground in hopes that any student who bothers to attend school will meander across it. After graduating, true to local form, she got married at age nineteen to James Fike, a nice local kid, a grocery stock boy. I'm sure she married mostly out of small-town boredom. I got married that way once, though I've got sense enough now to be positively embarrassed to tell you how young I actually was.

2   Anyway, Lynndie was married to James Fike when she enlisted in 2003. However, enlistment led to a "relationship" with a fellow reserve unit member at Abu Ghraib named Charles Graner, and pregnancy at age twenty-one. By the end of 2003 came the standard low-rent divorce papers exchange between Fike and England. This was four months before the Abu Ghraib scandal broke, but already there were clues. While home on leave, Lynndie told her divorce lawyer that "bad things" were going on at Abu Ghraib. She said prisoners were being forced to exercise until they dropped from exhaustion and to wear women's underwear on their heads. She said lots of OGAs (other government agencies) were involved. Anyone who was ever in the military knows that "other government agencies" means the CIA. You don't fuck with or question the CIA. Lynndie said, "They said, 'Good job. Keep it up.'" She thought it was weird, but she kept it up.

3   Lynndie has given only one interview, and a revealing one at that, to Tara McKelvey of *Marie Claire* magazine. Though under the close supervision of her lawyer, she alluded to hangings conducted in doorways at Abu Ghraib and to the sodomizing of young Iraqi boys by one of the contractors. But her overarching story is a common and plausible one to be found in any trailer court or blue-collar burg in America—falling for the wrong guy for the wrong reasons in the wrong place.

4   Lynndie was at Abu Ghraib during a particularly bad time. Prisoners tried to riot. Enemy mortars pounded the place at night, and the air was choked with concrete dust. Snipers picked away at guards during the day. There was terror inside, terror outside. Her former commander, Brigadier General Janis Karpinski, told McKelvey that "in situations like Iraq, the first thing some young female soldiers look for is a protector—a senior male" (all of which is oddly reminiscent of the domestic prison environment). "Enter Charles Graner," said Karpinski. "He's much older, and he's full of himself. He's just got that kind of personality... She was blown away."

5   Spc. Charles A. Graner Jr. is now pulling ten years. So we must presume that the former prison guard who loved taking close-ups of blow jobs in storage rooms, who loved anal sex with Lynndie, often

with her giving the thumbs-up gesture that would become infamous, has hung up his camera for most of the next decade. Still, there's that question: Why did she do those things?

6   "I just wanted to make him happy," she told her lawyer, Roy Hardy. "I didn't want him to take the pictures," she told McKelvey, "but he took pictures of everything. . . . He kept a camera in his cargo pocket. He was always taking his camera out."

7   Graner had his camera ready on the night he led a mentally ill prisoner nicknamed Gus—who, according to trial records, smeared feces on his body and threatened to kill the guards—out of his cell with a tie-down strap around his neck. He handed it to Lynndie so he could take a picture. One more time Lynndie helped Graner feel good. Graner snapped the picture and e-mailed it to his family in Pennsylvania. "Look what I made Lynndie do," he wrote.

8   Lynndie England is now serving out a thirty-six-month sentence in the Naval Consolidated Brig Miramar in San Diego. She no longer thinks much about chasing tornadoes like Helen Hunt. She was up for parole in the fall of 2006. No one believed she would get it, and they were right. So England is taking computer and electronic equipment repair classes. It's not storm chasing, but at least she will be employable when she gets out. . . .

9   We rural and small-town mutt people seem by an early age to have a special capacity for cruelty. For instance, as a child did you ever put a firecracker up a toad's ass and light it? George W. Bush and I have that in common. As nonwhites the world round understand, white people can be mean, especially if they feel threatened—and they feel threatened about everything these days. But when you provide certain species of white mutt people with the right incentives, such as approval from God and government, you get things like lynchings, Fallujah, the Birmingham bombers. You get Abu Ghraib.

10   Even as this is being written, we may safely assume that some of my tribe are stifling the screams of captives in America's secret "black site" prisons across the planet. On a more mundane scale, they might be (as seen in CBS footage) kicking and stomping hundreds of chickens to death every day at the Pilgrim's Pride plant in Moorefield, West Virginia, not too far from where I am writing, and where Lynndie once worked. Or consider the image of Matthew Shepard's body twisted on that Wyoming fence. That too is our handiwork. We, the mutt-faced working-class sons and daughters of the Scots-Irish republic, born to kick your chicken breast meat to death for you in the darkest, most dismal corners of our great land, born to kill and be killed in stock-car races, in drunken domestic rows, and of course in the desert dusty back streets at the edges of the empire.

11   Middle-class urban liberals may never claim us as brothers, much less as willing servants, but as they say in prison, we are your meat.

We do your bidding. Liberals' refusal to admit that we do your dirty work for you, not to mention international smackdowns and muggings for the Republic—from which you benefit more materially than we ever will—makes it no less true.

12   Literally from birth, we get plenty of conditioning to kill those "gooks" and "sand monkeys" and whoever else needs a lesson at any particular moment in history according to our leadership. Like most cracker kids in my generation, from the time I could walk I played games in which I pretended to kill Japanese, Indians, Germans, Koreans, Zulus (as seen in the movies *Zulu* and *Uhuru!*), variously playing the role of U.S. cavalry, Vikings a la Kirk Douglas, World War II GIs, colonial soldiers, and of course Confederate soldiers. As little white cracklets we played with plastic army men that we tortured with flame, firecracker, burning rivulets of gasoline, kerosene, lighter fluid, and, if atomic bombing was called for, M80s and ash cans. We went to sleep dreaming of the screams of the evil brutes we had smitten that day, all those slant-eyed and swasticated enemies of democracy and our way of life.

13   Later, as post-cracklets in high school, we rode around in cars looking to fight anyone who was different, be they black, brown, or simply from another school or county. As young men we brawled at dances and parties or simply while staring at one another bored and drunk. We bashed each other over women, less-than-weight bags of dope, money owed, and alleged insults to honor, wife, mother, or model of car—Ford versus Chevy—in other words, all of white trash culture's noblest causes. With the fighting tradition of Scots Irish behind us, we smash each other up ceaselessly in trailer court and tavern, night and day, in rain and summer heat, until finally we reach our midfifties and lose our enthusiasm (not to mention stamina) for that most venerated of Borderer sports.

14   Said meanness is polished to a high gloss of murderous piety most useful to the military establishment. Thus, by the time we are of military age (which is about twelve), we are capable of doing a Lynndie England on any type of human being unfamiliar to us. Sent to Iraq or Afghanistan, most of us, given the nod and enough stress, seem capable of torturing "the other" as mindlessly as a cat plays with a mouse. That we can do it so readily and without remorse is one of the darkest secrets underlying the "heroes" mythology the culture machine is so fervently ginning up about the series of wars now unfolding. When one of us is killed by a rooftop sniper in Baghdad, we weep and sweat, banding closer together as Borderer brothers in the ancient oath of ultimate fealty and courage.

15   It's been that way all my life, and I doubt it will end until the American empire declines and the reigning Caesar, Republican or Democrat, no longer needs the mutt people. Pure meanness is highly valued in Caesar's legions. Lots of Americans don't seem to mind

having a pack of young Scots-Irish American pit bulls savage some fly-blown desert nation, or run loose in the White House for that matter, so long as they are *our* pit bulls protecting Wall Street and the 401(k)s of the middle class.

16   The problem is this: Pit bulls always escalate the fight and keep at it until the last dog is dead, leaving the gentler breeds to clean up the blood spilled.

17   Sitting on her cot in her military prison cell, Lynndie England is no longer the waif in the Abu Ghraib photos. She smells like soap, writes Tara McKelvey. "She rubs her hands constantly, and her cuticles are raw and bleeding. Her hair is pulled back in four tortoiseshell clips, and it's streaked with premature gray," McKelvey reports. She has had visitors only once, and then only because McKelvey provided the opportunity to her mother, her sister Jesse, and her baby, Carter, son of Charles Graner Jr., the soldier who shot the pictures that outraged the world.

18   Even before Graner's pictures were made public, they seem to have been more public at the prison than the brass has ever admitted. The photograph of the human pyramid was used as a screen saver, according to military investigators. That it would seem safe to do such a thing in the usually ultrastrict military environment says a great deal about the attitudes of the higher-ups at Abu. You don't take chances in a terror-filled military prison just for laughs.

19   But maybe you do for love. Or to feel a sense of belonging. The girl from the trailer park next to the roadside beer joint of Fort Ashby, West Virginia, did. Monster of Abu or not, she once hung out with other kids at Evan's Dairy Dip and once was a member of the Future Farmers of America. No one in her family ever earned a college degree. She joined the army because she wanted the money for college. She quit her job at the infamous Pilgrims Pride chicken plant because "people were doing bad things. Management didn't care." Just like the people at Abu Ghraib were doing bad things. Management didn't care there either.

20   So she waits out her sentence as a high-profile prisoner. Unlike other inmates, she isn't allowed to take the flag down at day's end. After all, someone might snap another picture of her. And our empire definitely doesn't need any more shots of little Scots-Irish girls too damned eager to please.

Understanding the Content

Feel free to reread all or parts of the selection to answer the following questions.

1. Who is Lynndie England? Why is she in prison?

2. Who is Charles Graner and what relationship does he have to Lynndie England?

3. According to England, why did she do the things that Charles Graner asked her to do? What explanation does she provide?

4. What is the definition of "mutt people" according to Joseph Bageant? When defining, use your own words based on your reading of this selection.

5. Why do many mutt people end up in the military, according to Bageant?

Looking at Structure and Style

1. What is the thesis of this selection? Is it stated or implied? If stated, where? Rewrite it in your own words.

2. What was the author's purpose in writing this essay?

3. Does Bageant provide adequate support for his thesis?

4. What parallels does Bageant draw between himself and England? What effect does this have on your reading of this essay?

5. What organizing patterns are used in paragraph 9?

6. What purpose does it serve, in your opinion, for Bageant to change the subject of the essay from England to the mutt people? Is it effective?

Evaluating the Author's Viewpoints

1. Why do you think that the author wrote about Lynndie England? What was his purpose?

2. What is the author's attitude toward England? How can you tell?

3. What can you infer about the author's feelings toward "middle-class urban liberals"?

4. How does Bageant feel about the military, in general? Can you tell from the details given in this selection?

5. Why do you think that the title of this selection is "The Ballad of Lynndie England"? What is the author trying to convey by using that title?

Pursuing Possible Essay Topics

1. Joseph Bageant describes a culture that is familiar to him and outlines the similarities of his own life to Lynndie England's. Describe how and where you grew up. What comparisons can you draw to what Bageant describes? Contrasts?

2. With a classmate or in a group, discuss why you think people who grow up in the environment that Bageant describes might gravitate to the military. Use

examples to support your point. Have one member of the group take notes on the differing viewpoints discussed; together, write a summary.

3. Do you think that Lynndie England's punishment fit her crime? Write an essay discussing your viewpoint.

4. Do you think that the media coverage of the Abu Ghraib prison scandal was overblown? Not highlighted enough? Write an essay discussing your viewpoint.

5. Brainstorm or freewrite on one or more of the following:

   a. the military
   b. war crimes
   c. "groupthink"
   d. violence in America
   e. class distinctions in America

6. Don't like these topics? Pick your own topic and write about it.

Preparing to Read

Take a minute or two to look over the following reading selection. Note the title and author, read the first paragraph, and check the essay's length. Make certain you have the time now to read it carefully and to do the exercises that follow it. Then, in the spaces provided, answer the following questions.

1. From the title and the opening paragraph, what do you think the essay will be

   about? _____

   _____

2. What do you learn about the author's viewpoint about his subject from the

   first paragraph? _____

   _____

Vocabulary

Good comprehension of what you are about to read depends upon your understanding of the words below. The number following each word refers to the paragraph where it is used.

coup (1) a perfectly executed takeover; success

coercive (1) using force or threats to make someone to do something against their will

sanctioned (1) supported or encouraged, usually by public opinion

hypocrisy (3) falseness or two-facedness

dinars (3) a type of currency unit in some African, Asian, or southeastern European countries

propensity (5) a tendency or predisposition

imperative (7) obligation or necessity

insurgent (8) a member of a political party that revolts against the ruling party

tacitly (8) unspoken or inferred

equivocations (9) evasions; equivocal statements or expressions

Lessons of Abu Ghraib

Mark Bowden

Mark Bowden is a national correspondent for Atlantic Monthly, *as well as an author, journalist, screenwriter, and teacher of creative writing and journalism. His book* Black Hawk Down: A Story of Modern War *was a bestseller and finalist for the National Book Award.*

1   A committee of devils scheming to thwart American intentions in Iraq could have done no worse than turning a group of loutish, leering U.S. soldiers loose with a camera on bound, hooded, naked Iraqi prisoners.

2   The U.S. intervention in Iraq is troubled, to say the least, and now our own forces have handed our enemies a propaganda coup that trumps their best efforts. The photos from Abu Ghraib prison portray Americans as exactly the sexually obsessed, crude, arrogant, godless occupiers that our enemies say we are. They have even succeeded in uniting those on both sides of the war issue at home. Everyone is outraged and disgraced. The two sides are competing for adjectives to properly express the depths of their revulsion. And rightly so. There is no excuse for the abuses at Abu Ghraib. The individual soldiers involved ought to feel ashamed, as should our military and our nation. The photos we have seen so far come in two categories: one suggests a complete lack of order, the other, even more disturbing, a systematic, inappropriate use of coercive interrogation methods. In certain rare cases keeping a prisoner cold, uncomfortable, frightened, and disoriented is morally justified and necessary; but the danger in acknowledging as much has always been that such abusive treatment will become the norm. This is what happened in Israel, where a newly introduced regime of officially sanctioned "aggressive interrogation" quickly deteriorated into a system of routine physical abuse. (The Israeli Supreme Court reissued a ban on all such practices in 1999.) Routine physical abuse appears to have resulted already at Abu Ghraib, where such torments were apparently employed wholesale, and where a climate of dehumanization and sadism took root. The responsibility for that extends way up the chain of command, in ways that will become clear only with time and investigation. There are predictions (including one by Karl Rove, no less) that it will take a generation to repair the damage to America's image in the Middle East.

3   In the face of this horror even the most measured attempts to add context or perspective seem almost beside the point. Have there been exaggerations? The photos are said to prove that American forces are no better than Saddam Hussein's jailers. Well, no: whatever the Americans did, it is not the equivalent of cutting out tongues, gouging out eyes, lopping off limbs, stringing people up with piano

wire, and executing people by the tens of thousands. One former Iraqi prisoner was quoted by the Associated Press as saying that he would rather have been tortured by Saddam—an opinion that, like a boast of bravery, is easier to hold to when there is no danger of its being put to the test.

4   And, needless to say, there's plenty of hypocrisy. Maybe it's just me, but did I miss a similar storm of moral outrage from the Arab world over the pious Islamists who got out their video cameras to record the gruesome beheadings of Daniel Pearl and Nicholas Berg? Okay, those were renegade co-religionists, and maybe it's not a fair comparison. So let's look at official government policy. Any reader of the yearly reports on torture published by Amnesty International and Human Rights Watch would pay his weight in antique dinars to stay in an American military prison if the alternative was jail anywhere in the Arab world. Hayder Sabbar Abd, one of the men being abused in the Abu Ghraib photos, said he fully expected to be killed. Of course he did. That's what happens to men thrown in jail in his part of the world.

5   In the end, though, context and perspective cannot mask what is universal about the events at Abu Ghraib. I respect soldiers as much as anyone, but every group of young men (and, apparently, women) contains a few who get a thrill out of kicking somebody when he is helpless and down. Americans are not a superior race, and American soldiers are not morally superior to the soldiers of other nations. The best we can hope is that they are better trained and disciplined, and guided by policy that is morally sound. Sadly, this is not always the case.

6   The scenes depicted in the photographs are a graphic example of what often takes place in a prison environment where controls and supervision are inadequate. Prison guards have been abusing inmates for as long as there have been prisons. In a now infamous 1971 psychological experiment at Stanford University, in which one randomly selected group of students was permitted to play the role of "guards" over another group of "inmates," abuses began almost immediately, and at one point involved forcing inmates into sexually humiliating role-playing. People don't like to admit it, but the propensity for cruelty is in all of us, and it rises to the surface for many when they are given complete authority over other human beings. Add the unique environment of war, in which culture, religion, race, ethnicity, and ideology often separate guards from prisoners, and abuses are sadly and extremely likely.

7   The fact that the pictures were taken at all, and the cheerful expressions on the faces of the American bullies, suggest an atmosphere in which these soldiers had no reason to fear being punished for their behavior. It seems doubtful that the photos were meant to be used later to intimidate other prisoners, as has been suggested. If that had been so, the guards would probably have tried to look threatening.

These photos have the appearance of grotesque souvenirs. The smiling faces of the tormentors suggest that apart from lacking moral judgment, these soldiers felt licensed to abuse.

8   Why? By all accounts, military and CIA interrogators at the prison were using coercive tactics—sleep deprivation, deception, fear, or drugs—on large numbers of prisoners, and even recruiting prison guards to assist them. I have written in this magazine about the moral imperative for using these methods on uncooperative individuals withholding critical, life-saving information. No doubt there are some imprisoned in Iraq who fall into that category. But such instances are rare.

9   The only way to prevent interrogators from feeling licensed to abuse is to make them individually responsible for their actions. If I lean on an insurgent leader who knows where surface-to-air missiles are stockpiled, then I can offer the defense of necessity if charges are brought against me. I might be able to persuade the court or tribunal that my ugly choice was justified. But when a prison, an army, or a government tacitly approves coercive measures as a matter of course, widespread and indefensible human-rights abuses become inevitable. Such approval unleashes the sadists. It leads to severe physical torture (because there can never be a clear line between coercion and torture), to rape, and to murder.

10   These things may already have happened. The Bush Administration has tried to walk a dangerous line in these matters. The President has spoken out against torture, but his equivocations on the terms of the Geneva Convention suggest that he perceives wiggle room between ideal and practice. There are reports that Administration lawyers quietly drafted a series of secret legal opinions last year that codified the "aggressive" methods of interrogation permitted at U.S. detention facilities—which, if true, effectively authorized in advance the use of coercion.

11   Perhaps the most disturbing evidence of this mindset was Donald Rumsfeld's long initial silence on the Abu Ghraib photos. His failure to alert the President or congressional leaders before the photos became public—and he knew they were going to become public—leads one to conclude that he didn't think they were a very big deal. If so, this reveals him to be astonishingly tone-deaf, or worse. Maybe he simply wasn't shocked.

Understanding the Content

Feel free to reread all or parts of the selection to answer the following questions.

1. How do the photographs from Abu Ghraib portray Americans, according to Mark Bowden?

2. To whom does the responsibility of what happened at Abu Ghraib fall, according to Bowden?

3. Why does Bowden think the abuses at Abu Ghraib happened?

4. What types of coercive tactics are being used on prisoners by military and CIA interrogators at prisons like Abu Ghraib?

5. How is Bowden's thesis on Abu Ghraib different from Bageant's? Where do they place the major blame for what happened at Abu Ghraib?

Looking at Structure and Style

1. What is the thesis of this selection? Is it stated or implied? If stated, where? Rewrite it in your own words.

2. What was the author's purpose in writing this essay?

3. What is the author's tone? His attitude toward his subject? List some examples to support your answer.

4. What combination of patterns is used to organize paragraph 1?

5. Does the author use suitable and credible evidence to support his thesis?

6. What purpose do paragraphs 7 and 8 serve in this selection?

Evaluating the Author's Viewpoints

1. What can you infer about how Bowden feels about the American forces in Iraq? Those serving at the Abu Ghraib prison?

2. How does Bowden think that the United States can avoid in the future a situation like the one at Abu Ghraib?

3. Why does Bowden think that the abuses happened in the first place? What kind of culture existed that allowed people to act as they did?

4. What is Bowden's viewpoint on torture and aggressive interrogation in times of war?

5. What can you infer about how Bowden feels about the Bush administration, in office when the abuses took place? Former Secretary of Defense Donald Rumsfeld?

Pursuing Possible Essay Topics

1. Write an essay either agreeing or disagreeing with Bowden's thesis.

2. Do you think torture is something that is acceptable to use in certain situations, like wartime? If so, why? Write an essay discussing your viewpoint.

3. With a classmate or in a group, discuss this selection. In particular, read through paragraphs 7 and 8. Do you agree with what Bowden says in these paragraphs? Why or why not? Collectively, keep notes and write a summary that best expresses the discussion of the group.

4. Do you think Americans in particular have become desensitized to violence and images of violence? Why or why not? Write an essay discussing your viewpoint.

5. Freewrite or brainstorm on one or more of the following topics:

   a. the military

   b. abuses in the prison system

   c. violence

   d. desensitization to violence

   e. the use of torture in interrogation

6. Think about this essay and what was most compelling to you. Write an essay on a topic of your choosing related to this selection.

Opposing Viewpoints on the Causes of Violence and Who Is Ultimately Responsible for Violent Behavior

In one of the following essays, the author suggests that society is responsible for much of the violence committed, especially among the poor. The second essay suggests that genetic factors, not society alone, may be the cause of violence and needs to be studied.

Preparing to Read

Take a minute or two to look over the following reading selection. Note the title and author, read the first three paragraphs, and check the essay's length. Make certain you have the time now to read it carefully and to do the exercises that follow it. Then, in the spaces provided, answer the following questions.

1. What do you think is the subject of this essay? _____

_____

_____

2. What kind of behavior do you think will be discussed? _____

_____

_____

3. How do you define *ghetto*? _____

_____

_____

Vocabulary

Good comprehension of what you are about to read depends upon your understanding of the words below. The number following each word refers to the paragraph where it is used.

starkly (3) unmistakably, clearly

rendered (6) made, caused

fruitless (7) ineffectual, useless

eliciting (8) drawing out, causing

abhors (10) detests, offends

malady (10) ailment, disorder

exculpation (11) pardon, acquittal

sustained (14) endured, carried

debilitatingly (15) in a harmfully crippling manner

disparate (18) different, dissimilar

tacit (20) silent, unspoken

eradicate (20) abolish, destroy

propriety (30) appropriateness

"The Ghetto Made Me Do It"

Francis Flaherty

Freelance author Francis Flaherty first published the following essay in In These Times, *a biweekly magazine in Chicago dedicated to informing and analyzing popular movements for social, environmental, and economic justice; to providing a forum for discussing the politics that shape our lives; and to producing a magazine that is read by the broadest and most diverse audience possible.*

1   When Felicia "Lisa" Morgan was growing up, her parents would sit down to meals with guns next to their plates. They were defending themselves—against each other.

2   "This was Lisa's dinner," explains attorney Robin Shellow. "She was seven at the time."

3   If nothing else, Lisa Morgan's childhood in a poor, inner-city Milwaukee neighborhood starkly illustrates the tragic effects of urban violence. "Mom shot dad," Shellow says. "And Mom shot boyfriend. . . [Lisa's] uncle, who was actually her age, was murdered. Two days later, her other uncle was murdered. Her sister's boyfriend was paralyzed from the neck down by gunfire. Her brother was shot at and injured. Her mother once had set her father on fire."

4   If this weren't enough tragedy in one young life, Lisa Morgan's mother was a drug addict and Lisa was raped at age 12.

The "Ghetto Defense"

5   So perhaps it's not too surprising that Morgan, as a teenager, committed six armed robberies and one intentional homicide in the space of 17 minutes in October 1991. The victims were girls; the stolen objects were jewelry, shoes and a coat. The dead girl was shot at point-blank range.

6   What *is* surprising—to the legal establishment, at least—is the approach Robin Shellow used in defending Morgan. In the girl's neighborhood and in her family, Shellow argued, violence is a *norm*, an occurrence so routine that Morgan's 17 years of exposure to it have rendered her not responsible for her actions.

7   This "ghetto defense" proved fruitless in Morgan's case. In court, the young woman was found both sane and guilty. Unless Shellow wins on appeal, Morgan will be behind bars well into the next century.

8   But despite its failure for Morgan, Shellow's "cultural psychosis" or "psychosocial history" strategy has taken hold. "I've gotten hundreds of calls from interested attorneys," Shellow says. Already, the defense is being floated in courtrooms around the nation. It's eliciting both enthusiasm and outrage.

The Defense Is a Medical One

9   Technically, Shellow's defense is a medical one. She believes that Morgan suffers from post traumatic stress disorder (PTSD) and other psychological ailments stemming from her lifelong exposure to violence.

10   Like other good lawyers, Shellow knows that the law abhors broadly applicable excuses, so she emphasizes the narrowness of her claim. Morgan belongs to a very small group of inner-city residents with "tremendous intra-familial violence," only some of whom might experience PTSD. She also stresses the unrevolutionary nature of the defense, medically and legally. PTSD has been recognized as a malady in standard diagnostic texts since 1980, she says, and it has been employed as a criminal defense for Vietnam veterans, battered wives and many other trauma victims.

11   Despite Shellow's attempts to show that her defense is neither new nor broad, the case is ringing loud alarms. For, however viewed, her strategy sets up an inflammatory equation between inner-city conditions and criminal exculpation. The implication is that if you grew up in a poor, violent neighborhood and you commit a crime, you may go scot-free.

12   Yet why not a ghetto defense? After all, if a Vietnam veteran can claim PTSD from the shock of war, why shouldn't a similar defense be available for a young black reared in the embattled precincts of Bed-Stuy [Bedford-Stuyvesant neighborhood of New York City]? Sounds sensible, no? Isn't a ghetto like a battlefield?

Compare These Neighborhoods to War Zones

13   Alex Kotlowitz, who chronicled the lives of two Chicago black boys in *There Are No Children Here*, goes even further. He says the inner city can be worse than war. "You hear constant comparisons of these neighborhoods to war zones, but I think there are some pretty significant differences," he says. "In war, there's at least a sense that someday there will be a resolution, some vision that things could be different. That is not the case in the inner cities. There is no vision. And there's no sense of who's friend and who's foe."

14   There are other analogies that make the ghetto defense seem very legitimate. For instance, despite traditional self-defense principles, a battered wife in some jurisdictions can kill her sleeping husband and be legally excused for the homicide. The reason is the psychological harm she has sustained from her life of fear and violence.

15   Why not Lisa Morgan? Hasn't her life been debilitatingly violent and fearful?

16   These arguments make some lawyers hopeful about the future of Shellow's pioneering strategy. But most observers are pessimistic. "We'll get nowhere with it," says famous defense lawyer William Kunstler.

The Poor Instead of the Powerful

17   Why? One reason is that the American justice system often favors the powerful over the poor. For generations, for instance, the bloodiest crime in the nation—drunk driving—was punished with a relative wrist slap. By contrast, a recent federal law mandates that those convicted of the new crime of carjacking get socked with a minimum and mandatory 15-year sentence.

18   What explains these disparate approaches? Simple: protection of the affluent classes. Light penalties for drunk driving protect the affluent because they often drive drunk. Harsh carjacking penalties protect the affluent because they are the usual carjacking victims. "The middle class sees carjacking [laws] as protecting them from people coming out of some poor neighborhood and just showing up in *their* neighborhood and committing a crime in which they are at risk of dying," says Professor James Liebman of Columbia University School of Law.

19   Because the ghetto defense protects the poor instead of the powerful, Kunstler and others doubt it has a bright future. Other factors further dim the strategy's chances. Fear is a main one, says Professor Liebman. The ghetto defense brings a gulp from jurors because "their first thought is, 'If he's not responsible, then none of those people are,'" he reasons. And we all know what that means: riots, mayhem, Los Angeles.

20   Social guilt raises even higher the hurdles for the ghetto defense. To allow such a defense is a tacit admission that we—society—tolerate a situation so hobbling that its victims have become unaccountable for their actions. "If it ain't them who's guilty, it's us," says Michael Dowd, director of the Pace University Battered Women's Justice Center in New York. And "it's just too horrific for us to accept responsibility, too horrific to say, 'I'm responsible for what happened in L.A.' We will be able to accept the [ghetto] defense at the same moment that we are seriously moved to eradicate the realities behind that defense."

21   What are the biggest criticisms of the ghetto defense? One focuses on the victim's identity. Battered spouses and battered children are accused of killing precisely those who hurt them. This endows the crime with a certain rough justice. But in a ghetto defense case, the victim is usually an innocent stranger.

22   Others, like Kotlowitz, worry that the ghetto defense might dislodge the cornerstone of our justice system: personal responsibility. "We have to be careful not to view people growing up in neighborhoods completely as victims; they are both victims and actors," he warns. "We can't absolve them from responsibility."

23   Lisa Morgan "went up to someone she didn't know, stole a jacket from her, and then just blew her away," he says. "There's no way as a society that we can excuse that. We can understand it, but we can't excuse it."

24   He raises a fundamental question. Everyone can point to scars from the past—alcoholic parents, tragic love, etc.—and claim exculpation. And if all are excused, who is responsible?

25   Another worry is diminished standards. "[The ghetto defense] lowers expectations," Kotlowitz continues. "It says, 'OK, I understand what you've been through, so it's OK to go out and hurt somebody.' And once you lower your expectations, particularly with kids, they will meet only those lower expectations."

A Disease Is a Disease

26   It's only fair to note that other criminal defenses also have these weaknesses. For instance, the victim of a PTSD-afflicted veteran is often an innocent passerby, and the battered-spouse doctrine certainly raises questions about personal responsibility and lowered expectations.

27   And if, as seems likely, some ghetto residents do have PTSD largely as a result of their living conditions, it's hard to see why this ailment should be exculpatory for veterans, say, but not for ghetto residents. After all, a disease is a disease, and how you got it is irrelevant.

28   How deep go the wounds from the ghetto? Here are two incidents in Morgan's life: "When Felicia was about 11, her mother put a knife to her throat and threatened to kill her," according to a psychologist's report in the case. "Felicia escaped by running into the basement, where she 'busted the lights out with my hand' so that her mother could not see her." Then, when she was 12, the landlord attacked her. "Felicia fought him off by throwing hot grease onto him, but he finally subdued her, tied her hands to the bed, stuffed her mouth with a sock and raped her."

29   How does one live like this? Morgan gives a hint. "My ears be open," she told the psychologist, "even when I'm asleep."

30   This was a *child*. Society did nothing to stop these daily depredations upon her. While the legal propriety of the ghetto defense is an important question, the biggest question of all in this story has nothing to do with personal responsibility. It has to do with society's responsibility to poor children like Morgan. What does it say about our society that such a defense was conceived? How can things have come to this pass?

Understanding the Content

Feel free to reread all or parts of the selection to answer the following questions.

1. What is meant by the "ghetto defense"? Define it in your own words.

2. Reread paragraph 8. Define what Shellow means by the "'cultural psychosis'or 'psychosocial history' strategy." What does it have to do with the ghetto defense?

3. What is post-traumatic stress disorder (PTSD)? What causes it?

4. Why do legal experts worry about the ghetto defense being used and accepted in court cases? What would be the implications? How would it protect the poor instead of the powerful?

5. What are the biggest criticisms of the ghetto defense?

6. Does Flaherty's thesis favor the ghetto defense? Why or why not?

Looking at Structure and Style

1. The first four paragraphs of the essay deal with Felicia "Lisa" Morgan. Why? How effective is this as an introduction to the author's subject?

2. Flaherty frequently uses transitional words or phrases to move from one paragraph or idea to another. Find some examples of them. How effective are they?

3. In paragraphs 13 and 14, what pattern is primarily used?

4. In paragraphs such as 12, 15, 17, 18, and 21, Flaherty uses questions. For what purpose? Is this a good technique in this case? Explain.

5. Is Flaherty's thesis stated or implied? If stated, where?

Evaluating the Author's Viewpoints

1. Robin Shellow, Felicia Morgan's attorney, believes in the ghetto defense. Do you? Explain your reasoning.

2. Flaherty raises the question that if a Vietnam veteran can claim PTSD from the shock of the war, why shouldn't a similar defense be made for a young black reared in an embattled ghetto? How do you respond to the idea?

3. Flaherty believes the American justice system often favors the powerful over the poor (17). Is his support sufficient for the reader to accept his viewpoint? Do you agree? Support your views.

4. The ghetto defense suggests that society "tolerate[s] a situation so hobbling that its victims have become unaccountable for their actions" (20), implying that each of us is responsible for such things as the Los Angeles riots and the living conditions in the ghettos. Do you accept such responsibility? Explain.

5. Reread the last paragraph. Does society have a responsibility to poor children like Morgan? How do you answer Flaherty's questions?

Pursuing Possible Essay Topics

Wait until after you have read the following essay, "Seeking the Roots of Violence" by Anastasia Toufexis, before attempting to write an essay on violence and its causes.

Preparing to Read

Take a minute or two to look over the following reading selection. Note the title and author, read the first two paragraphs, and check the essay's length. Make certain you have the time now to read it carefully and to do the exercises that follow it. Then, in the spaces provided, answer the following questions.

1. What do you think is the subject of this essay? _____

_____

2. What kind of behavior do you think will be discussed? _____

_____

3. What do you think may be the roots of violence? _____

_____

Vocabulary

Good comprehension of what you are about to read depends upon your understanding of the words below. The number following each word refers to the paragraph where it is used.

predisposed (1) inclined, prone, liable

inflammatory (2) inciting anger, concern, or disagreement

genetics (2) the study of heredity, especially inherited characteristics

muster (3) assemble, gather, collect

incensed (3) furious, angry

tawdry (5) gaudy and cheap

disparity (7) difference, contrast

impulsive (10) acting without much thought

premeditated (10) deliberate, thought out

anomalies (14) oddities, peculiarities

Seeking the Roots of Violence

ANASTASIA TOUFEXIS

Anastasia Toufexis writes for Time *magazine on a variety of social concerns.*

1   It's tempting to make excuses for violence. The mugger came from a broken home and was trying to lift himself out of poverty. The wife beater was himself abused as a child. The juvenile murderer was exposed to Motley Crue records and *Terminator* movies. But do environmental factors wholly account for the seven-year-old child who tortures frogs? The teenager who knifes a teacher? The employee who slaughters workmates with an AK-47? Can society's ills really be responsible for all the savagery that is sweeping America? Or could some people be predisposed to violence by their genes?

2   Until recently, scientists had no good way to explore such questions—and little incentive: the issue was seen as so politically inflammatory that it was best left alone. But advances in genetics and biochemistry have given researchers new tools to search for biological clues to criminality. Though answers remain a long way off, advocates of the work believe science could help shed light on the roots of violence and offer new solutions for society.

3   But not if the research is suppressed. Investigators of the link between biology and crime find themselves caught in one of the most bitter controversies to hit the scientific community in years. The subject has become so politically incorrect that even raising it requires more bravery than many scientists can muster. Critics from the social sciences have denounced biological research efforts as intellectually unjustified and politically motivated. African-American scholars and politicians are particularly incensed; they fear that because of the high crime rates in inner cities, blacks will be wrongly branded as a group programmed for violence.

4   The backlash has taken a toll. In the past year, a proposed federal research initiative that would have included biological studies has been assailed, and a scheduled conference on genetics and crime has been canceled. A session on heredity and violence at February's meeting of the American Association for the Advancement of Science turned into a politically correct critique of the research; no defenders of such studies showed up on the panel. "One is basically under attack in this field," observes one federal researcher, who like many is increasingly hesitant to talk about his work publicly.

5   Some of the distrust is understandable, given the tawdry history of earlier efforts to link biology and crime. A century ago, Italian physician Cesare Lombroso claimed that sloping foreheads, jutting chins and long arms were signs of born criminals. In the 1960s, scientists advanced the now discounted notion that men who carry an

XYY chromosome pattern, rather than the normal XY pattern, were predisposed to becoming violent criminals.

6   Fresh interest in the field reflects a recognition that violence has become one of the country's worst public-health threats. The U.S. is the most violent nation in the industrialized world. Homicide is the second most frequent cause of death among Americans between the ages of 15 and 24 (after accidents) and the most common among young black men and women. More than 2 million people are beaten, knifed, shot or otherwise assaulted each year, 23,000 of them fatally. No other industrialized nation comes close: Scotland, which ranked second in homicides, has less than one-fourth the U.S. rate.

7   This cultural disparity indicates that there are factors in American society—such as the availability of guns, economic inequity and a violence-saturated culture—that are not rooted in human biology. Nevertheless, a susceptibility to violence might partly be genetic. Errant genes play a role in many behavioral disorders, including schizophrenia and manic depression. "In virtually every behavior we look at, genes have an influence—one person will behave one way, another person will behave another way," observes Gregory Carey, assistant professor at the University of Colorado's Institute for Behavioral Genetics. It stands to reason that genes might contribute to violent activity as well.

8   Some studies of identical twins who have been reared apart suggest that when one twin has a criminal conviction, the other twin is more likely to have committed a crime than is the case with fraternal twins. Other research with adopted children indicates that those whose biological parents broke the law are more likely to become criminals than are adoptees whose natural parents were law-abiding.

9   No one believes there is a single "criminal gene" that programs people to maim or murder. Rather, a person's genetic makeup may give a subtle nudge toward violent actions. For one thing, genes help control production of behavior-regulating chemicals. One suspect substance is the neurotransmitter serotonin. Experiments at the Bowman Gray School of Medicine in North Carolina suggest that extremely aggressive monkeys have lower levels of serotonin than do more passive peers. Animals with low serotonin are more likely to bite, slap or chase other monkeys. Such animals also seem less social: they spend more time alone and less in close body contact with peers.

10   A similar chemical variation appears to exist in humans. Studies at the National Institute on Alcohol Abuse and Alcoholism conclude that men who commit impulsive crimes, such as murdering strangers, have low amounts of serotonin. Men convicted of premeditated violence, however, show normal levels. As for aggressive behavior in women, some researchers speculate that it might be tied to a drop in serotonin level that normally occurs just before the menstrual period.

Drugs that increase serotonin, researchers suggest, may make people less violent.

11   Scientists are also trying to find inborn personality traits that might make people more physically aggressive. The tendency to be a thrill seeker may be one such characteristic. So might "a restless impulsiveness, an inability to defer gratification," says psychologist Richard Herrnstein of Harvard, whose theories about the hereditary nature of intelligence stirred up a political storm in the 1970s. A high threshold for anxiety or fear may be another key trait. According to psychologist Jerome Kagan, also of Harvard, such people tend to have a "special biology," with lower-than-average heart rates and blood pressures.

12   Findings like these may be essential to understanding—and perhaps eventually controlling—chronic wrongdoers, argue proponents of this research. "Most youth or adults who commit a violent crime will not commit a second," observes Kagan. "The group we are concerned with are the recidivists—those who have been arrested many times. This is the group for whom there might be some biological contribution." Kagan predicts that within 25 years, biological and genetic tests will be able to pick out about 15 children of every thousand who may have violent tendencies. But only one of those 15 children will actually *become* violent, he notes. "Do we tell the mothers of all 15 kids that their kids might be violent? How are the mothers going to react to their children if we do that?"

13   It is just such dilemmas that have so alarmed critics. How will the information be used? Some opponents believe the research runs the danger of making women seem to be "prisoners of their hormones." Many black scholars are especially concerned. "Seeking the biological and genetic aspects of violence is dangerous to African-American youth," maintains Ronald Walters, a political science professor at Howard University. "When you consider the perception that black people have always been the violent people in this society, it is a short step from this stereotype to using this kind of research for social control."

14   The controversy began simmering more than a year ago, when Louis Sullivan, then Secretary of Health and Human Services, proposed a $400 million federal research program on violence; 5 percent of the budget would have been devoted to the study of biochemical anomalies linked to aggressive behavior. The program was shelved before being submitted to Congress, and one reason may have been the reaction to an unfortunate statement by Dr. Frederick Goodwin, then director of the Alcohol, Drug Abuse and Mental Health Administration. Commenting about research on violence in monkeys, Goodwin said, "Maybe it isn't just the careless use of the word when people call certain areas of certain cities 'jungles.'" African-Americans were outraged. The ensuing furor forced Goodwin to resign, though

Secretary Sullivan then appointed him to head the National Institute of Mental Health, a job he still holds.

15   Soon after that episode, the federally endowed Human Genome Project agreed to provide the University of Maryland with $78,000 for a conference on violence. When the program's organizers announced that the session would look at genetic factors in crime, opponents torpedoed the meeting. "A scandalous episode," charges Harvard's Herrnstein. "It is beneath contempt for the National Institutes of Health to be running for cover when scholars are trying to share their views."

16   Dr. Peter Breggin, director of the Center for the Study of Psychiatry in Bethesda, Maryland, who led the opposition that scuttled the conference, has no apologies. "The primary problems that afflict human beings are not due to their bodies or brains, they are due to the environment," he declares. "Redefining social problems as public health problems is exactly what was done in Nazi Germany."

17   Some critics see the current interest in heredity as part of an ugly political trend. "In socially conservative times," argues political scientist Diane Paul of the University of Massachusetts at Boston, "we tend to say crime and poverty are not our fault and put the blame not on society but on genes."

18   Even staunch believers in heredity's influence do not discount environment. In fact, the two are intimately entwined, and separating cause and effect is not easy. Biology may affect behavior, but behavior and experience also influence biology. Serotonin levels, for example, are not only controlled by genes but, according to research in monkeys, they can be lowered by regular exposure to alcohol. By the same token, says Kagan, a child with a fearless personality may turn into a criminal if reared in a chaotic home, but given a stable upbringing, "he could well become a CEO, test pilot, entrepreneur or the next Bill Clinton."

19   No one thinks that discovering the roots of violence will be simple. There may be as many causes as there are crimes. The issue is whether to explore all possibilities—to search for clues in both society and biology.

Understanding the Content

Feel free to reread all or parts of the selection to answer the following questions.

1. What are the arguments for conducting genetic research for clues to violent behavior? What are the arguments against such research?

2. Compared with other industrialized countries, the United States ranks highest in violent crime rates. In Toufexis's essay, what factors are often given as causes?

3. According to some scientists, what effect does the neurotransmitter serotonin have on behavior? What is serotonin?

4. What role does environment play in the cause and effect of violent behavior?

5. What is the author's thesis? Is she for or against genetic research dealing with violent behavior?

Looking at Structure and Style

1. What is/are the basic paragraph pattern(s) used in the opening paragraph? Is/Are the pattern(s) effective here? Explain.

2. What is the function of paragraph 6? How does paragraph 7 build on the content of paragraph 6?

3. How well balanced are the pro and con arguments for genetic research into criminal behavior? Does the author present information fairly? Explain.

4. Describe the author's tone and attitude toward her subject. What words or phrases develop that tone and attitude?

5. Does the concluding paragraph draw a conclusion or summarize the content? Is it effective as a closing paragraph? Explain.

Evaluating the Author's Viewpoints

1. In paragraph 15, Richard Herrnstein is quoted as saying, "It is beneath contempt for the National Institutes of Health to be running for cover when scholars are trying to share their views." Do you think the author agrees? Do you? Why or why not?

2. Dr. Peter Breggin helped "scuttle" a proposed conference on genetic factors and violence, believing that "redefining social problems as public health problems is exactly what was done in Nazi Germany" (16). Do you agree? Why or why not?

3. The author believes that there may be as many causes as there are crimes. Do you agree? Explain.

Pursuing Possible Essay Topics

1. Write an essay explaining your views on genetic research into violence. Should the government fund such research? Is it important research?

2. Write an essay that compares and contrasts the causes for violence as discussed in Francis Flaherty's "The Ghetto Made Me Do It" and Toufexis's essay. Explain why you think environment and heredity are the major causes of violence.

3. Write an argument that supports or refutes Dr. Peter Breggin's statement in paragraph 16.

4. Write an essay on what effect you feel your environment has had on your behavior patterns.

5. Brainstorm or freewrite on one or more of the following:
   a. chronic wrongdoers
   b. violent behavior
   c. heredity
   d. aggression
   e. drugs
   f. impulsiveness

6. If you don't like these ideas, find your own topic on some aspect of behavior and write an essay.

Student Essay

Read the following narrative essay written by a student. As you read, look for answers to these questions:

1. Does the essay fulfill an assignment to write about some aspect of behavior?

2. How well does the narrative hold your interest?

3. Is the thesis clear and well supported?

My Private Prison

Jody Nelson

1   It was 3:00 A.M., my mother was tired and my eyes were bloodshot from lack of sleep and crying. She had just finished writing another essay for me. We could breathe now. The panic, the anguish, and the procrastination were over, but my secret fear of writing would continue to haunt me for a lifetime. I cannot recall exactly when my fear of writing began or why. Maybe it was a critical English teacher, or an unfavorable comparison to others, or worse my own inner critic reminding me of my inabilities. Whatever the cause, my fear of writing has severely limited me in my education and careers.

2   As a child, I enjoyed writing creative stories about travel and exploration and other people's lives, so as to escape my own. I was able to write freely without rules, restrictions, guidelines and criticism. However, my memory of writing shifted during adolescence. Writing papers became a frustrating painful event, one that I would avoid at all costs. This evasion shaped my view of education and what direction I would take to limit my exposure to this terrible task only taking classes with little or no writing. Much of my time was spent agonizing over papers, crying and begging my mother to write them. This put a strain on my family and myself. I never learned how to write for myself and concealing this truth took much of my energy and confidence.

3   Knowing my weakness, I forged ahead to college pursuing my strengths. I was a visual and kinesthetic learner, so art

and physical education were appropriate subjects to study, and I knew I wouldn't have to write very much. By doing this I limited myself in the studies of literature, poetry, writing, and reading and to this day I do not know very much about these topics and feel inadequately versed in literature-based conversations. Choosing art and physical education satisfied my inner critic for a while, as I received straight "A's" and graduated from college with honors. However, I *knew* that I had failed writing class four times and spent many hours stressing over each writing and eliciting help from others. These requests put undue strain on my friends and teachers. Having this degree did not set me free me from my fear, for I knew that I would have to find a job with little or no writing. Avoiding this took a lot of my valuable time and energy.

4   My strong verbal skills that I relied on so heavily landed me a job at a private school for gifted children, where I taught physical education. The first day of teacher training the director asked me to write a curriculum for the year. The word "write" sent me into a state of shock, which led to inertia as I told myself, "I can't do this!" and "I don't know how!" I panicked and once again turned to whomever I could for help. I went to the library and reviewed other curricula and asked for help from teachers and the administration. I asked others to write the curriculum and educational articles or avoided these tasks altogether. One time I even paid a parent to help write a piece of the curriculum for me.

5   This nagging fear continued as I explored new career avenues of being a teacher educator and working in the sports management industries. The concept of me doing these jobs was exciting, but I knew each direction would involve writing, so I moved forward with great hesitation. One by one, I tried each new career path, applying to four different graduate school programs over a period of three years. I got accepted to each program, but as soon I contemplated how much writing would be involved and realized that the schools might find out about my deficiency in writing, I quit.

6   However, I did study broadcasting at a local junior college and hosted a television show. I enjoyed both experiences tremendously and knew this was my next direction. Starting an internship at a local news station, I thought that most of the job would involve shooting and editing video. But once again, when the reporter asked me to write scripts for the video, I felt paralyzed by my fear, unable to write, and I quit. While I had this dream of becoming an interviewer I didn't want to fail or be exposed and most of all I didn't want to write.

7   My terrifying experience with writing has plagued me throughout most of my life, a nagging secret, an exasperating flaw, and a real detour to my dreams and aspirations. I no longer want to be weighed down and limited by this fear. As a first step to freedom and a chance to see what strengths I do have, I am taking a beginning writing course at Santa Barbara City College. Although this may seem like a small step, it is actually very significant, as I symbolically begin to confront my private prison. And someday I hope to write with ease and confidence.

Reaction

In your journal or on a separate sheet of paper, write your reaction to the student essay. How well does the essay fit the assignment to write on some aspect of behavior? Does the narrative hold your interest? Why or why not? Is the thesis well supported? What grade would you give the essay? Why?

Viewpoints on Images

Look at the photo. What do you think is happening? What kinds of activities bring out this type of behavior in people? Have you ever reacted this way in a crowd? Why or why not? Discuss the causes and effects of such crowd behavior.

© Lynne Fernandes/The Image Works

On the Net

Like education, human behavior is a broad topic that encompasses many different subject areas. You can search the Internet to find out more about any topics that interest you from the chapter or look up additional information about an author. Here are a couple of interesting sites that you might like to look at—after you have finished writing all of your essays for the chapter.

1. By going to *www.queendom.com*, you will have access to a number of interesting and fun personality tests that may give you some insight into your own behavior. Test topics range from general knowledge to personality tests, from nutrition and eating habits to career choice and preparation tests. This site, called Test Junkie, is mostly for fun. The site developers run a disclaimer that the tests may give you insight into your personality, but they also may not. The developers advise you to "go on this journey with your mind . . . and your eyes . . . wide open."

2. The Kaplan Minds games site, at *www1.kaplan.com,* has a more academic focus. Visit this site if you are interested in learning more about the standardized tests that will be given to you during your academic career (visit the "college" link on the site) and how to excel at them. This site also includes interesting information for those entering college and for those already enrolled. If you want to continue with your academic career, you can visit the "graduate" section or visit sites geared toward specific careers, like "education" or "nursing." You can take practice tests and assess where you need to spend time to pass and do well on specific tests.

If you'd like to explore some of the topics in the chapter, do a keyword search. Or, think about doing one or more of the following activities.

1. Choose a sports team that you enjoy following. If you don't have a favorite team, choose the local team. Visit the official team Web site, and then visit fan sites. Compare and contrast the information found on the official site and your favorite fan site.

2. Look at Web sites devoted to Brent Staples and learn more about this author. See if there are any links to additional readings by Staples, and read another one of his essays.

3. Visit two or three sites devoted to Mary Seymour and learn more about her life and other writings.

5 Viewpoints on Cultural Differences

To help you focus on the subject of this chapter, take a few minutes to prepare for the topic by prewriting on one or more of the following prompts:

1. your cultural heritage and its effect on you
2. attitudes toward women in different cultures
3. racial profiling
4. stereotypes of other cultures
5. judging people by their dress
6. the effect religion has on cultures

The history of the United States is filled with accounts of people who came from all over the world to settle here. Many came willingly to find a better life, some were forced to come as slaves or to be used as cheap labor, some were driven from their homelands for political reasons, some fled from war, and still others came hoping to get rich quickly and then go back home. Immigration, especially of people from western and southern Europe, was high between 1870 and 1920. Between the years 1880 and 1900 alone, a half million people came to this country *each year.* During the next fourteen years, over a million people immigrated to America *each year.* Whether born here or an immigrant, everyone living in America felt widespread cultural and institutional changes. The rise of an urban-industrial way of life that attracted thousands of people to cities, the growing interest in scientific knowledge and research, and the variety of new cultures that the immigrants brought with them all had an effect on education, science, fashion, food, music, art, literature, publishing, and politics. People referred to America as a "melting pot," a place where people of all types could blend together.

Times are changing. Some sociologists are concerned that the United States is no longer a "melting pot" but a "salad bowl." According to the March 2007 Census Bureau report, the nation's immigrant population (legal and illegal) reached a record of 37.9 million in 2007. Since 2000, 10.3 million immigrants have arrived—the highest seven-year period of immigration in U.S. history. More than half of post-2000 arrivals (5.6 million) are estimated to be illegal aliens. Immigrants account for one in eight U.S. residents, the highest level in 80 years. In 1970 it was one in 21; in 1980 it was one in 16; and in 1990 it was one in 13. Overall, nearly one in three immigrants is an illegal alien.

Unlike most earlier immigrants, who were willing to learn English and wanted to "melt" into American life, many of today's immigrants don't see the need to assimilate or blend in. While it is difficult for those coming here to adjust to a new language and way of life, it is often difficult for natives to accept the culture of the new arrivals. Can the mingling of the different cultures avoid prejudices and stereotyping? How will this rise in both legal and illegal immigration affect America's culture?

Preparing to Read

Take a minute or two to look over the following reading selection. Note the title and the author, read the first three paragraphs, and check the essay's length. Make certain you have the time now to read it carefully and to do the exercises that follow it. Then, in the spaces provided, answer the following questions.

1. What does the title tell you about this essay? _____

_____

2. What do you think this essay will be about? _____

_____

_____

3. Based on your reading of the first three paragraphs, how does the author feel

about covering her head? How can you tell? _____

_____

_____

Vocabulary

Good comprehension of what you are about to read depends upon your understanding of the words below. The number following each word refers to the paragraph where it is used.

antithetical (5) diametrically opposed

turbulent (6) causing unrest or disturbance

chagrin (7) a feeling of unease cause by failure or disappointment

degradation (8) to cause a reduction in rank, dignity, or esteem

posturing (10) a frame of mind that affects one's thoughts or behavior

fawned (13) to seek favor by flattery

subjugate (14) to conquer or bring under one's conrol

swathed (15) wrapped or swaddled as in clothing

extol (16) to praise highly

utopic (19) idyllic

egalitarian (23) democratic; equal

Veiled Intentions: Don't Judge a Muslim Girl by Her Covering

Maysan Haydar

Maysan Haydar is a social worker in New York City. She has written for The Nation, Spin, CMJ, *and* Venus. *The following essay appeared in* Body Outlaws: Rewriting the Rules of Beauty and Body Image, *edited by Ophira Edut.*

> O Prophet! Tell thy wives and daughters and the believing women that they should cast their outer garments over their persons. That is most convenient that they should be known and not be molested.
>
> —THE QURAN, Chapter 33, Verse 59

> And say to the believing women that they should lower their gaze and guard their modesty: that they should not display their beauty and ornaments except what ordinarily appears thereof; that they should draw their veils over their bosoms and not display their beauty . . .
>
> —THE QURAN, Chapter 24, Verse 30–31

1   I have a confession to make.

2   I've been covering my hair, as is prescribed for Muslim women, since I was twelve years old. And while there are many good reasons for doing so, I wasn't motivated by a desire to be different, to honor tradition, or to make a political statement.

3   I wanted the board game Girl Talk

4   When girls from our small, Midwestern Muslim community donned their first *hijab* (headscarf), their families rewarded them with parties and monetary gifts. At twelve, I wasn't nearly as physically developed as a Muslim girl is supposed to be when she starts covering, but I desperately wanted Girl Talk. I knew that if I announced my intention to begin veiling in the board game aisle at Kmart, I could ask for anything and receive it.

5   My choice of Girl Talk as reward for taking on a religious responsibility is amusing to me now, because it's so antithetical to what veiling is supposed to represent. Girl Talk was the ultimate slumber party game, where players performed gags or revealed embarrassing secrets, then got to choose from four kinds of fortune cards as a prize. My favorite cards hooked me up with the class president, the football captain, or a hunky lifeguard who saved me from drowning. And I still have a sheet of "zit stickers," which were meant to punish gamers who failed to share their dirt.

6   Now that I'm twenty-five and have worn a veil for more than half my life, I can admit to this shallow beginning, which is so far from my reason for veiling today. As an adult, I embrace the veil's modesty, which allows me to be seen as a whole person instead of a twenty-piece

chicken dinner. In spite of the seeming contradictions of my life—I'm married to a white man who was raised Catholic, I love heavy metal, I consider myself a feminist, and I sport a few well-disguised piercings—I follow my religion's standard of modesty and appearance. It's only now, after comparing my turbulent teen experiences with those of other women, that I can fully appreciate how much of a saving grace this small piece of cloth was.

7   Much to my chagrin, many Americans see veiling as an oppressive tool forced on Muslim women by the men in our culture. Yet, the practice of covering hair and body is a choice for many women—and it is not specific to Islam. All the monotheistic religious (Christianity, Judaism, and Islam) advocate modesty in dress, though the interpretation of "modesty" varies greatly. Ironically, the population that spends millions on beauty products, plastic surgery, and self-help guides is the same one that takes pity on me for being so "helpless" and "oppressed." On a New York City bus a couple weeks ago, I sat with another woman, also veiled, but wearing a traditional *jilbab* (a cloak that women wear over their clothing). A girl two seats over remarked to her friend, while flipping her hair for effect, that she couldn't understand how we could dress this way. "Me, I got to be *free*."

8   To my eyes, her idea of freedom involved a complicated hairstyle, loads of makeup and jeans she probably had to sew herself into. If anything, I would find that ensemble more caging, more oppressive and more painful than clothes that allow me to walk in front of construction sites confidently, with minimal risk of harassment. (Construction workers may feel obligated to say something to every passing woman, but I often get things like "I like your skirt!" or "Girl, I would marry you!"—harmless compared to the degradation I've heard many women complain about.)

9   As for freedom, my parents have a healthy understanding of Islam, especially the Quranic verse "Let there be no compulsion in religion" (2:256). Having been raised in religiously different homes themselves (Mom: very liberal, European-minded, not so religious: Dad: religious, culturally structured gender roles and expectations), they only practiced traditions that they understood, accepted, and believed. Thus, my mother knew the best way to introduce veiling to me was to emphasize its feminist, forward-thinking reasons: Covering removes that first level of being judged, of being assessed based on my measurements, and it absolves me of the need or desire to be wanted solely for my looks. My choice of Girl Talk didn't showcase a deep understanding of that idea. But reflecting back, I see that wearing a scarf greatly influenced how people viewed me and my goals, before I could ever appreciate that it was having that effect.

10   In high school, my interactions with the opposite sex were different than the norm. If I hadn't yet been inclined to deal with boys in

an unpressured, ungiggly, un-made-up way, the scarf shoved me in that direction. So, without being given handbooks or informative flyers about how they should curb their posturing and come-ons, guys sensed that they should treat me with respect.

11   I didn't watch boys and girls learn about each other from the sidelines. I have many rich friendships with men, and over the years a good number of them have made a go at becoming "more than friends." I didn't participate in dating games, but I was flattered by the attention, especially since I knew I was being liked for who I was beyond my body. What made me attractive was my ability to relate to everyone in a very natural way, without all the confusing sexual pressure. The weirdness that normally clouds boy-girl interactions was lifted, because most guys automatically assumed I wasn't available for dating. Of course, girls deserve to be treated with respect no matter what they wear. But since we live in a world of mixed messages, I got to bypass a lot of damaging experiences.

12   The veil bestowed other experiences upon me that I wouldn't quite classify as negative, but definitely educational. Like anyone else who's visibly different from the norm, I encountered ridiculous ideas about what a covered person should be, do, and enjoy. If someone overheard me talking about my interests, which included karate and skateboarding, I grew to enjoy their disbelief and shock. I didn't pick my hobbies to prove that stereotypes are often false, but it was nice to make people reconsider their notions of a Muslim girl.

13   Moving to New York City right after college and living alone was the most affirming thing I've done to solidify my resolve and truly understand what veiling means. Here, for the first time, people believed that I was wearing a scarf because I wanted to, not because my family coerced me into it. On the other hand, New York exemplifies what's wrong with our image-obsessed society. I worked for a couple of magazines and saw the way women acted out to draw attention to themselves. It was especially apparent at my anything-goes dot-com job, where women showed up to work in backless halter tops and were fawned over by male coworkers.

14   And now, as I write this, I can watch women subjugate themselves on reality dating shows. On a show about aspiring models I heard a woman say that her greatest goal would be to appear in *Stuff* magazine. I can't imagine centering my life on something as fleeting and meaningless as being admired simply for my body.

15   You might assume that because Muslim women traditionally don't display our bodies, we don't hold them as important or feel connected to them—or that we don't value ourselves as sexual beings. Guess again. While our degree of modesty is high, the value Muslim women place on the bodies underneath our veils is higher. In Sunday school, girls are taught that our bodies are beautiful ("God is beautiful

and loves beauty" is a *hadith,* or saying, of the prophet Muhammad) and that they're so valuable that they're only meant to be shared in an intimate relationship: husband and wife, mother and baby, among women, and in clinical or safe spaces (for example, with your doctor, among family members). Historically, the most severe-looking coverings used to be limited to the richest women in Arab society; being swathed in so much cloth was regarded as a sign of status.

16   People who have written about being in the secluded quarters of Arab homes or at their parties often express surprise at the degree to which these cloaked women maintain themselves via fitness, style, and decadent rituals. (Let's not even get started on the body hair-removal process in the Middle East.) I'm not one for creams and blushes, but I understand that there are women who enjoy the beauty process, and I see no harm in indulging it for the right reasons. Feminist author Geraldine Brooks, in her book *Nine Parts of Desire,* quotes women across the Middle East who extol the virtues of pretting up for their loved ones. To me, this demonstrates that Western priorities are out of line: American women spend hours getting ready for strangers to see them but don't give the same effort to those who see them in intimate settings.

17   As for the variation in Muslim women's dress, it demonstrates the wide-ranging interpretations of modesty. I often get asked what the most "right" version is: the Afighani *burqah,* the Iranian *chador,* the Pakistani *salwar kameez,*[1] the Arab *jilbab,* or a sweatshirt and jeans. The short answer is that the recommendations for modesty are to be interpreted and applied at the discretion of the woman picking her clothes.

18   All through high school, I wore a *jilbab* exclusively because I didn't have to spend any effort worrying about what was in season or what I would be expected to wear to fit in. I now cover my hair, but generally wear jeans and a long-sleeved shirt. My once-strict interpretation of modesty has been adapted to my urban lifestyle. Is wearing an *abaya* (the head-to-toe gown that completely covers the wearer) and a face veil a good idea in New York City? Probably not, since the *abaya* would likely get stuck in a subway door or pick up the dust off any floor you glide across. But not wearing an *abaya* in Saudi Arabia would probably make getting around very difficult for a woman.

19   It's utopic and ridiculous to assert that looks don't matter and that by veiling I'm avoiding the messiness—particularly after September 11th. Now some people hold their breath a bit longer, assuming I'm a fundamentalist or wondering if I'm there to cause them harm. I sense

[1] *burqah … salwar kameez:* The *burqah* covers a women from head to toe, with a mesh strip in front of the eyes to allow some vision; the *chador* also drapes the head and body, but not the face; the *salwar kameez* is a tunie-and-trouser set.

people studying me on the trains, reading the cover of the book in my hand and trying to gauge if I'm one of "us" or one of "them." I grapple with the frustration that I can't reassure everyone individually that my goals have everything to do with social justice and nothing to do with holy war. But I have seen suspicions fade in the eyes of the pregnant woman to whom I've given my subway seat, or the Hasidic[2] man whose elbow I've taken to help him up the stairs.

20   Though many of the stereotypes and incorrect assumptions people had while I was growing up still prevail (that Muslim equals backwards/oppressed/fundamentalist/terrorist), current events have pedestrians describing their secondhand "expertise" of Islam—the history of Wahhabi Islam,[3] the export of Sayyid Qutb[4] and the Muslim Brotherhood's[5] ideas—or trying to argue that the Quranic requirements for modesty don't include veiling. It's much harder to explain why I cover to those who think they have a full understanding of the culture and the faith than those whose "knowledge" of the Middle East is limited to *Aladdin* and *hummus*.

21   I do appreciate the status Islam and the Middle East have in the news these days—the interest has generated new scholarship on Arabia's history and anthropology and on Islamic law, all of which I'm interested in and am relieved is being researched. This research includes a pool of female scholars reexamining Islamic texts with a feminist lens, and separating actual religious commands from their long-held, culturally laden interpretations, which often smack of patriarchy.

22   Forcing women to veil or unveil usually has the opposite effect. When I attended elementary school in Saudi Arabia and flew home to Michigan each summer, a parade of women swathed in black *abayas* would head to the airplane bathrooms once we were safely in the air and emerge wearing short, tight ensembles. Conversely, banning the veil in Syria and Turkey sparked a resurgence in its popularity.

23   The question of veiling comes up once someone finds out that I've married into a family that celebrates Christmas, with my full participation. "If you have a daughter, what will she wear?" they ask. I haven't yet cracked a pregnancy or parenting book, but I hope that my policy will be similar to the egalitarian way I was raised. If she wants to, she

[2] *Hasidie:* Hasidism is a form of Jewish mysticism; Hasidie men typically wear long black coats and wide-brimmed black hats, while women cover their hair and wear long skirts and long sleeves for modesty.

[3] *Wahhabi Islam:* A Sunni fundamentalist form of Islam founded by Muhammad ibn Abdel al Wahhab (1703–1792), Wahhabism is the majority faith of Saudi Arabia and Qatar.

[4] *Sayyid Qutb:* Egyptian writer and intellectual (1906–1966) who condemned western values and promoted the idea of a fundamentalist Islamic state; affiliated with the Muslim Brotherhood.

[5] *Muslim Brotherhood:* Worldwide movement, founded in Egypt in 1928, that advocates government imposition of strict Islamic law.

24   can; if she doesn't want to, then she won't. It's far more important for her to respect herself, her body, and her life.

At the heart of my veiling is personal freedom. I dress this way because it has made it easier to get through adolescent phases and New York City streets with no self-loathing, body hang-ups, or sexual harassment. I wish more women emerged unscathed; no one should suffer for what they look like or what they wear.

Understanding the Content

Feel free to reread all or parts of the selection to answer the following questions.

1. Why did Haydar originally consent to covering her hair at age twelve?

2. Why does Haydar continue to wear the head scarf as an adult?

3. What happened to Haydar recently when riding a New York City bus? What was her reaction to this moment?

4. What kind of family background does the author come from? In other words, how do her parents view religion and its place in their lives?

5. How was Maysan Haydar treated by members of the opposite sex in high school? How was this different from the way other young women were treated?

6. How did moving to New York City after college affect Haydar?

7. Have things changed for Haydar and the way she is viewed as a Muslim woman since 9-11? If so, how?

Looking at Structure and Style

1. What is the thesis of this essay? Is it stated or implied? If stated, where?

2. What is the organizing pattern used in paragraph 13? What is that paragraph's relation to the paragraph that precedes it (paragraph 12)?

3. What is the purpose of paragraphs 1–5? Is beginning the essay in this way effective? Why or why not, in your opinion?

4. What is the purpose of paragraph 7? What is its relation to paragraph 8?

5. What was the author's purpose in writing this essay? Do you think she achieved her goal? Why or why not?

6. List the examples the author uses to support her statement that "the veil bestowed [other] experiences upon me that I wouldn't quite classify as negative, but definitely educational." (12) Does she provide enough examples to support this statement?

Evaluating the Author's Viewpoint

1. Compare and contrast Haydar's views on modesty with modern-day views on modesty. Do you see any merits to the idea of covering one's head? One's whole body?

2. Do you agree or disagree with Haydar's reaction and thoughts on the woman sitting on the New York City bus: "If anything, I would find that ensemble [hairstyle, loads of makeup, and jeans that she probably had to sew herself into] more caging, more oppressive, and more painful than clothes that allow me to walk in front of construction sites confidently . . ." (8) Why?

3. Do you agree or disagree with Haydar that women "subjugate themselves on reality dating shows" (14)? Why?

4. After reading this selection, has your opinion changed regarding women who cover their heads in public? Why or why not?

5. What were some of the things you learned from reading this selection?

6. Do you think Haydar adequately explores both the advantages and disadvantages of wearing a head scarf? Give support from the selection for your answer.

Pursuing Possible Essay Topics

1. Do you think it is "oppressive" for women in the Muslim culture to cover their heads? Why or why not? Write an essay defending your viewpoint.

2. In your opinion, how much do looks matter in today's society? Why do you think that is? Write an essay discussing your feelings on this topic.

3. Think about your own high school experience. What effect would wearing a head scarf (if you're a woman; if you're a man, imagine what it would have been like) have had on your high school experience? Would you have been accepted? Why or why not? Describe what you think life would have been like.

4. Brainstorm or freewrite on one or more of the following topics:
   a. stereotypes
   b. religious oppression
   c. religious tradition
   d. cultural differences
   e. cultural diversity
   f. prejudice

5. Find your own topic on the subject of cultural heritage and write an essay.

Preparing to Read

Take a minute or two to look over the following reading selection. Note the title and author, read the opening paragraph, and check the essay's length. Make certain you have the time now to read it carefully and to do the exercises that follow it. Then, in the spaces provided, answer the following questions.

1. What does the title tell you about this essay? _____

    _____

2. Does the opening paragraph tell you anything about what this essay might be

    about? _____

    _____

Vocabulary

Good comprehension of what you are about to read depends upon your understanding of the words below. The number following each word refers to the paragraph where it is used.

protagonist (1) main character in a story, leading role

regimes (7) governments or administrations

qualms (7) misgivings, bad feelings

arbitrary (10) random

incarcerated (10) jailed

It Could Happen Here
Laila Al-Marayati

Dr. Laila Al-Marayati is a gynecologist and former Presidential appointee to the U.S. Commission on International Religious Freedom (USCIRF). She is a founding member and former president of the Muslim Women's League, an organization formed to challenge discrimination against Muslim women. She is also the Chairwomen of KinderUSA, an organization dedicated to the well-being of Palestinian children. The following article appeared in the Los Angeles Times.

1   Not long ago I rented the movie *The Count of Monte Cristo* to watch with my two sons, who I thought would enjoy the exciting, action-packed tale. My 11-year-old surprised me, though, by becoming very

agitated as the protagonist, Edmond Dantes, was banished to the Chateau d'If, a grisly prison on a desolate island where torture was the order of the day.

2   "Are people tortured in prison today?" he asked.

3   "Well, yes," I admitted.

4   "What about here, here in America?"

5   "No, of course not," I reassured him. "It's something that only happens in other countries."

6   "Can they take you out of prison here and send you somewhere else to get tortured?" he asked.

7   I am usually honest with my children. But not this time. I had recently read that U.S. officials had admitted to sending detainees abroad to countries with regimes that have no qualms about using torture to get people to cooperate. This was not information my son needed to hear.

8   "Absolutely not!" I assured him. "Why are you so worried about this?"

9   "Well, what if they make a mistake and you get taken to jail even though you didn't do anything wrong? I mean, what if they sent you to jail just for being Muslim? Everyone thinks Muslims are terrorists and bad people."

10   His fear of arbitrary arrest and torture disturbed me, especially since this is the reality for some Muslims here and many more abroad who have been incarcerated as suspects in the "war on terrorism."

11   Our family has roots in Palestine and Iraq, so naturally we are preoccupied with events overseas, but we limit the exposure of our children to media coverage of the Middle East. We don't discuss the threats to their civil liberties at the dinner table.

12   Though our children are proud of their ethnic heritage, they identify themselves as Americans. At their Islamic school, parents and teachers reinforce the notion of an integrated Muslim American identity. Muslim values, they learn, can contribute to the betterment of their country. Some of the kids have ties "back home," visiting frequently, perhaps creating a dual allegiance. Not so in our family. We don't spend our summer vacations in Baghdad or the Gaza Strip.

13   I don't have the heart to tell my boys that, if pending legislation passes, our security as Muslims living in America—even as citizens by birth—will be at risk, or that my son's question might foretell his own future.

14   Earlier this year, the Justice Department prepared a draft proposal to revise the USA Patriot Act, a post-Sept. 11 law that greatly expanded the ability of law enforcers to track suspected terrorists. If the Domestic Security Enhancement Act of 2003 outlined in the memo (known widely as Patriot II) is ultimately passed by Congress, the government would, in the name of fighting terrorism, be granted sweeping new surveillance powers, more leeway to detain citizens indefinitely without charge and the ability to present secret evidence

against those accused of supporting terrorism. The death penalty would be expanded to include certain terror-related crimes. The government would also have the authority to strip Americans of their citizenship for providing support to an organization deemed a "terrorist group," a term that is broadly and vaguely defined.

15   I want to tell my children that as law-abiding American citizens, they have nothing to worry about. But I know that simply obeying the law won't keep them from being profiled at the airport, monitored while attending the mosque or wiretapped if they participate in Muslim-oriented activities on campus when they go to college. The truth is, they will be suspects, simply because of their identity as young adult Americans who also happen to be male, Muslim and of Arab descent.

16   We can hope that our elected officials won't agree to the further erosion of civil liberties and will refuse to pass Patriot II. But if they lack the resolve to question something that wouldn't make us more secure but would render America unrecognizable to our founding fathers, then we're all in trouble.

17   *The Count of Monte Cristo* raised frightening issues for my sons. But it also made an important point. When Dantes was at the height of despair during his imprisonment, he rejected God for having abandoned him. Later, when the words etched on his cell wall, "God will give me justice," were proved true, he vowed never to lose faith again. His troubles may have caused my son to agonize about the injustices that could befall him one day, but perhaps he also learned from the film that God's justice prevails despite man's injustice to man.

Understanding the Content

Feel free to reread all or parts of the selection to answer the following questions.

1. What movie are the author and her sons watching at the beginning of this essay? What effect does the story line of this movie have on one of her sons?

2. Why does the author lie to her son when he asks her if detainees can be sent somewhere else to get tortured?

3. What is Al-Marayati's ethnic background? How does this background feed into her and her son's fear of arbitrary arrest and torture?

4. Why do the author's children identify themselves as Americans first? How do the author and her husband help foster that American identity?

5. What are the USA Patriot Act and the Domestic Security Enhancement Act of 2003?

6. What would the result of a revised Patriot Act be on the government's powers, according to the author?

Looking at Structure and Style

1. What is the thesis of this selection? Pick one sentence from this selection that effectively conveys the overall thesis.

2. Why do you think the author begins this selection with a story about her and her sons watching a movie? What is the impact of this anecdote on the essay overall?

3. Does the author use credible evidence and support to prove her thesis?

4. What is the relationship of paragraph 14 to paragraph 13? Is paragraph 14 effective?

5. How effective is the last paragraph of this selection?

Evaluating the Author's Viewpoints

1. Is Al-Marayati objective or subjective in expressing her viewpoints in this selection?

2. Do you agree or disagree with the author that "simply because of their identity as young adult Americans who also happen to be male, Muslim and of Arab descent," (15) her sons will be viewed as suspects?

3. What does the author think will be the effects of the USA Patriot Act and the Domestic Security Enhancement Act of 2003?

4. Despite being law-abiding citizens, what does the author think could happen to Muslims if the Patriot II Act is passed?

5. Do you think that the author has hope for her sons' situation in this country? How can you tell?

Pursuing Possible Essay Topics

1. Do you think, as the author does, that the Patriot II Act will result in a "further erosion of civil liberties" (16)? If you need more information, go online and find some information on the Patriot II Act to see if you agree or disagree with the author. Write an essay defending your viewpoint.

2. With a classmate or a group, discuss the following question: In today's world, do you think there are other groups besides Arabs and Muslims that bear the brunt of racial profiling and prejudice? If so, describe the group and what its members endure in American society. Use examples to support your point.

3. Brainstorm or freewrite on one or more of the following:
   a. your cultural heritage   c. racial profiling   e. American
   b. prejudice   d. civil liberties

4. Pick your own topic on the subject of cultural heritage and write an essay.

Preparing to Read

Take a minute or two to look over the following reading selection. Note the title and author, read the opening paragraph, and check the essay's length. Make certain you have the time now to read it carefully and to do the exercises that follow it. Then, in the spaces provided, answer the following questions.

1. What do you think the essay will say about Latinos and Mexican immigrants?

    _____

2. What do you think the author means by the title? _____

    _____

    _____

3. What might you learn from reading this essay? _____

    _____

    _____

Vocabulary

Good comprehension of what you are about to read depends upon your understanding of the words below. The number following each word refers to the paragraph where it is used.

   embodies (7) represents, gives form to

   plagues (7) disturbs, annoys, bothers

   coupled (8) combined, joined

   naive (15) innocent, gullible

   acculturated (17) changed as a result of contact with another culture

   disaffection (25) alienation, separation

The Great Divide

Michael Quintanilla

Michael Quintanilla is a senior features writer for the San Antonio Express-News *and has also been on staff at the* Los Angeles Times. *He is an award-winning journalist, having won the* Los Angeles Times' *breaking news award in 2001 for his coverage of the World Trade Center attacks. The following selection originally appeared in the* Los Angeles Times.

1   Virginia Gomez wanted to share a story.

2   The 13-year-old eighth-grader and her friends—all American-born Latinas—were walking past three Mexican immigrant sixth-graders after school recently. One of the younger children was sipping from a soda can. Suddenly, one of Virginia's friends bopped the bottom of the can.

3   "Wham! The soda spilled all over the little girl," Virginia recalled. As she and her friends walked away, the immigrant student muttered a Spanish obscenity.

4   "What? You want to start something?" Virginia's friend asked the now-frightened girl. "Tell me to my face . . . Wetback!"

5   "We're all proud of being Mexican," said Virginia—who was born in Los Angeles to immigrant parents—as she talked about the on-campus incident the day after it occurred at Nimitz Middle School in Huntington Park.

6   "But the thing is we see ourselves as different even though we have the same culture," she said. "We're American and they're not."

7   Virginia's story embodies all the elements of a conflict that plagues many Latino students today: the alienation and prejudice that divide American-born Latino kids and their immigrant classmates. The students often segregate themselves during lunchtime, on the basketball court, at school dances, and while hanging out on campus before and after school.

8   A language barrier coupled with an unfamiliar teen culture—the culture of the popular American Latino kids who wear baggy clothes with Doc Martens or Nikes and listen to deep-house and hip-hop—adds to the problem of assimilation for immigrant students.

9   In most cases, students agree, it's the American-born Latinos who ridicule the immigrants.

10   They make fun of the immigrant boys who dress in white buttoned shirts instead of T-shirts and high-water cotton trousers instead of oversized jeans. They ridicule the immigrant girls in their ruffled starched blouses and pleated skirts and braids tied with bows. They make fun of the immigrant children's shyness, respectfulness and dedication to academics.

11   The U.S.-born Latinos call the Mexican kids "*quebradita* people" because of their banda music and *quebradita* dances. They make fun of the immigrants' "nerdy" Mickey Mouse–adorned backpacks and have even coined a term for them: "Wetpacks."

12   They call the immigrant students other names—"beaner," "Wehac" (a derogatory term for a Mexican immigrant of Indian descent) and tell them to "go back where you come from." Immigrant students at Nimitz reported that when they run around the track in gym class, American-born teens shout "Corrale! Corrale! La Migra! La Migra!" ("Run! Immigration!").

13   Brad Pilon, a bilingual school psychologist with the Los Angeles Unified School District, works with about 70 schools—most with a majority Latino enrollment—in the mid-city area, including Belmont High School's Newcomer Center, which helps hundreds of recent non-English speaking immigrants adjust in school.

14   "These kids feel the segregation, they live it," Pilon said. "They get beat up, get lunches stolen, are laughed at in their faces" by U.S.-born Latinos he said. Often the immigrant student is too scared to report the harassment. Also, Pilon said, students soon learn that if they were to report such incidents, "nothing would be done" because overloaded teachers and administrators often aren't aware the problem exists.

15   "The immigrant kids, especially the newest arrivals, are naive, open and most of all vulnerable when they come to school," Pilon said. "When they first come here, like anybody who moves anywhere, they are faced with the problem of fitting in."

16   For most, fitting in is their dream even though they often view American kids as lazy, unmotivated and disrespectful to their parents and teachers.

17   Ramon A. Gutierrez, director of the Center for the Study of Race and Ethnicity at the University of California, San Diego, said this Latino rift is not something new. He cited a 10-year-old study conducted in the San Jose area, where a researcher found four Latino groups that segregated themselves from each other in one school—"the recent lower-income Mexican immigrant; the middle-class Mexican immigrant; the acculturated Chicano kids and the cholo kids: lower-income Mexican Americans."

18   "There have always been tensions and stresses between individuals of a remote immigrant past and recent immigrants," he said. "What it boils down to is discrimination based not only on immigrant status," Gutierrez said, but also on language and social class.

19   "If you went to Beverly Hills High, you'd find lower-class white kids segregated from the wealthier kids. It's segregation based on social standing," he said.

20   Rene Estrella, a leadership class adviser and biology teacher at Belmont High School, where 90% of the 4,500 enrollment is Latino,

said immigrant Latino students "take the brunt of discrimination" from American-born students because "the people who are privileged to be born here think that they are superior to the person who was not.

21   "I think most kids who come to Belmont don't have too much to feel good about, growing up in the area. They don't get out of this area very much and anything they can hold onto to get a better identity, even if it means making others feel lower, makes them feel important."

22   Estrella said storytelling sessions in his classes helped bring students together last semester, and he probably will continue them. For several minutes at the start of each class, students shared their lives with other classmates. Immigrant students spoke about their homelands, family members killed in their war-torn countries and their adjustment to life in the United States.

23   "Hearing each other's stories united the students. It made the American-born kids understand the struggle so many of the newcomers have experienced and the struggle they still face, especially when they are segregated," Estrella said.

24   "We are oppressing each other and that bothers me," said Lupe Simpson, principal of Nimitz, the second-largest middle school in the country. The school has an enrollment of 3,200 students—97% Latino, one-fifth of that number recent immigrants.

25   Simpson said she is deeply concerned about the "anti-Mexican" feelings of some of her students as well as the isolation and disaffection immigrant children deal with daily. "But I don't see this as a defeat," she said. "It's a challenge."

26   She hopes students will embrace her plan for a buddy program that would pair native and immigrant Latinos so they could help and learn from each other. Another idea she is exploring is to have award assemblies for the whole student body, instead of the English as a Second Language students having their assemblies separately, as they do now. And she wants to speak to teachers and administrators about integrating students in classrooms, during sporting events and at school dances.

27   "We have to do something so the kids can see that that kind of thinking prevails in their lives and where does it end? We have to start ending it with ourselves. We have to show our kids that we are more alike than we are different," she said after listening to some of the students express their feelings in recent interviews at the school.

28   Gabriela Rico, 13, a Nimitz eighth-grader from Mexico, said she is mocked in gym class because she doesn't always understand the games.

29   "The Chicanos don't speak to us at all. They don't try to teach us. That's what we want most of all—to learn the games, to learn English, to be like them," she said, as other immigrant children nodded.

30   "I know they make fun of me," Gabriela said, her eyes on a book on her lap. "I tell my mother and she tells me not to be like them and show off, not to place value on materialistic things like clothes or shoes or to care too much about appearances."

31   Julio Bejarano, an 11-year-old sixth-grader also from Mexico, said he gets along fine with kids in his neighborhood, many of them American-born. But at school, it's a different world. He said he is not accepted "as a friend by the Latino Americanos," never invited to join in a game of basketball or to sit with them at lunchtime "because they think we are inferior to them because we were not born here." His eyes water. The room is silent for a few seconds.

32   Language is the biggest obstacle, he said, even though it should be the key to bridging the communications gap because an over-whelming majority of the American Latinos are bilingual.

33   "We talk to them in Spanish because we don't know English and even though they know how to speak Spanish, they talk to us in English. Why don't they want to communicate with us?" Julio said.

34   Nancy Garcia, also 11, said she has an American Latina "good friend," but still there's no escaping the prejudice. "My friend tells me that she *is* superior to me," Nancy said, even though Nancy's grades are better.

35   "I don't know why she says that," Nancy paused. "I think she might be envious of us because we are so proud of our culture."

36   Still, she said she yearns to one day be accepted by her American-born Latino classmates because "I love the get-togethers they have at school, the way they dress, the way they dance, their music."

37   Image, said American-born classmate Lisa Moreno, 13, plays a big role in the self-imposed segregation at her school. "You have to know how to dress so you can be in the 'in-crowd.' Immigrant girls wear Payless shoes."

38   Peer pressure keeps them from befriending the immigrants, students said. "If I were to hang around with them, then I wouldn't be in the in-crowd anymore," explained Lisa.

39   Said Virginia Gomez: "Straight out, we haven't welcomed the Mexicans with open arms. We're like, 'You want to be with us? I don't think so.'"

40   "It shouldn't be this way—two groups," said Virginia, who is student body president at Nimitz. "But what can you do to stop it? Some people are not going to change no matter what you do."

41   Rudy Lopez, a Los Angeles-born 13-year-old Latino at Nimitz, agreed that both groups should be united, especially "when they haven't done anything to us to treat them bad."

42   That's a sentiment shared by several students at Belmont.

43   Sandra Flores, 16, a 10th-grader born in Los Angeles, said, "I have newcomer friends and it's very hard for them. I think they are afraid to

talk to U.S. Latinos because they are expecting us to put them aside, you know, ignore them. That's why they come to their own little groups."

44   "It's sad to see us segregated like that, especially when the immigrant students have such a big enthusiasm for learning, for having better futures. They are really smarter than us," she said.

45   Ernesto, a 16-year-old Guatemalan (who preferred not to use his surname), said he chooses to remain a loner because he doesn't want to be rejected as he was last year in junior high school.

46   "We get rejected because of the way we dress, talk, the way we are," he said. So he and his immigrant friends hang out together, encourage each other, lift each other's spirits. As a group, they are secure and safe. It's what gets them through the day.

47   Still, it's unfathomable sometimes to Ernesto and other immigrant young people that they have left one war to face another.

48   "We come from war-torn countries," he said. "Our families have struggled to come here for a better future and then we still have to struggle with people who are from our own race."

Understanding the Content

Feel free to reread all or parts of the selection to answer the following questions.

1. To what does the title refer? What is the main reason for the divide?

2. What are some of the problems that prevent the assimilation of Mexican immigrants with American-born Latinos?

3. What types of segregation and harassment do some Mexican immigrants face?

4. What are some of the actions schools are taking to close the divide between Mexican immigrants and American-born Latinos?

Looking at Structure and Style

1. Because this selection originally appeared in a newspaper, paragraphs are short. If you were to edit the article, where might you combine paragraphs?

2. The opening uses an anecdote to draw reader interest. How effective is it? Would another method work just as well? Explain.

3. Quintanilla quotes from several sources. How helpful are these in supporting his story? Are the sources credible?

4. How would you describe the author's tone and attitude? What words or phrases help develop tone and attitude?

5. How effective is the last paragraph?

Evaluating the Author's Viewpoints

1. Is Quintanilla mostly objective or subjective in his reporting? Explain.

2. Ramon Gutierrez explains the "great divide" in paragraph 19 by stating, "If you went to Beverly Hills High, you'd find lower-class white kids segregated from the wealthier kids. It's segregation based on social standing." Do you agree with his viewpoint? Explain.

3. Storytelling sessions and buddy programs are cited as two initiatives intended to stop the prejudice against Mexican immigrants. Do you think these methods can be helpful in eliminating prejudice? Explain.

Pursuing Possible Essay Topics

1. Write about a time when you felt segregated from a group or felt prejudice against you. What was the cause? How did you feel? How did it affect your own prejudices?

2. Interview your parents or grandparents. What is their heritage? Have they ever experienced segregation or prejudice based on their heritage? How did it affect them?

3. What cultural groups in your neighborhood bear the brunt of segregation or prejudice? What is the cause? How might things be changed? Are you part of the problem?

4. Brainstorm or freewrite on one or more of the following:
   a. your heritage   d. immigrants
   b. language barriers   e. American
   c. prejudice   f. foreign

5. Ignore these topics and write an essay on some other aspect of culture or heritage.

Preparing to Read

Take a minute or two to look over the following reading selection. Note the title and the author, read the first paragraph, and check the essay's length. Make certain you have the time now to read it carefully and to do the exercises that follow it. Then, in the spaces provided, answer the following questions.

1. Does the title tell you anything about this essay? _____

_____

_____

2. What do you think this essay will be about? _____

_____

_____

3. What do you think this essay will say about being a Native American woman?

_____

_____

_____

Vocabulary

Good comprehension of what you are about to read depends upon your understanding of the words below. The number following each word refers to the paragraph where it is used.

inextricably (1) unavoidably or inescapably

diffuse (1) to soften; to scatter or disseminate

aplomb (1) self-confident; assurance

vacillate (4) to waver or be indecisive

ineradicable (4) impossible to remove

curios (5) unusual art objects

coffers (5) financial resources

perforce (6) unavoidably; forced by circumstances

formidable (7) bringing about fear or alarm

Where I Come From Is Like This

PAULA GUNN ALLEN

Paula Gunn Allen grew up on Cubero Land Grant in New Mexico. She is a feminist writer whose scholarly works promote Native American literature as a rich source of study. Some of her works include As Long As the Rivers Flow: The Stories of Nine Native Americans, A Cannon Between My Knees, Grandmothers of the Light: A Medicine Woman's Resource Book, *and* Life Is a Fatal Disease: Collected Poems 1962–1995.

1   Among the tribes, the occult power of women, inextricably bound to our hormonal life, is thought to be very great; many hold that we possess innately the blood-given power to kill—with a glance, with a step, or with a judicious mixing of menstrual blood into somebody's soup. Medicine women among the Pomo of California cannot practice until they are sufficiently mature; when they are immature, their power is diffuse and is likely to interfere with their practice until time and experience have it under control. So women of the tribes are not especially inclined to see themselves as poor helpless victims of male domination. Even in those tribes where something akin to male domination was present, women are perceived as powerful, socially, physically, and metaphysically. In times past, as in times present, women carried enormous burdens with aplomb. We were far indeed from the "weaker sex," the designation that white aristocratic sisters unhappily earned for us all.

2   I remember my mother moving furniture all over the house when she wanted it changed. She didn't wait for my father to come home and help—she just went ahead and moved the piano, a huge upright from the old days, the couch, the refrigerator. Nobody had told her she was too weak to do such things. In imitation of her, I would delight in loading trucks at my father's store with cases of pop or fifty-pound sacks of flour. Even when I was quite small I could do it, and it gave me a belief in my own physical strength that advancing middle age can't quite erase. My mother used to tell me about the Acoma Pueblo women she had seen as a child carrying huge ollas (water pots) on their heads as they wound their way up the tortuous stairwell carved into the face of the "Sky City" mesa, a feat I tried to imitate with books and tin buckets. ("Sky City" is the term used by the Chamber of Commerce for the mother village of Acoma, which is situated atop a high sandstone table mountain.) I was never very successful, but even the attempt reminded me that I was supposed to be strong and balanced to be a proper girl.

3   Of course, my mother's Laguna people are Keres Indian, reputed to be the last extreme mother-right people on earth. So it is no

wonder that I got notably nonwhite notions about the natural strength and prowess of women. Indeed, it is only when I am trying to get non-Indian approval, recognition, or acknowledgement that my "weak sister" emotional and intellectual ploys get the better of my tribal woman's good sense. At such times I forget that I just moved the piano or just wrote a competent paper or just completed a financial transaction satisfactorily or have supported myself and my children for most of my adult life.

4   Nor is my contradictory behavior atypical. Most Indian women I know are in the same bicultural bind: we vacillate between being dependent and strong, self-reliant and powerless, strongly motivated and hopelessly insecure. We resolve the dilemma in various ways: some of us party all the time; some of us drink to excess; some of us travel and move around a lot; some of us land good jobs and then quit them; some of us engage in violent exchanges; some of us blow our brains out. We act in these destructive ways because we suffer from the societal conflicts caused by having to identify with two hopelessly opposed cultural definitions of women. Through this destructive dissonance we are unhappy prey to the self-disparagement common to, indeed demanded of, Indians living in the United States today. Our situation is caused by the exigencies of a history of invasion, conquest, and colonization whose searing marks are probably ineradicable. A popular bumper sticker on many Indian cars proclaims: "If You're Indian You're In," to which I always find myself adding under my breath, "Trouble."

5   No Indian can grow to any age without being informed that her people were "savages" who interfered with the march of progress pursued by respectable, loving, civilized white people. We are the villains of the scenario when we are mentioned at all. We are absent from much of white history except when we are calmly, rationally, succinctly, and systematically dehumanized. On the few occasions we are noticed in any way other than as howling, bloodthirsty beings, we are acclaimed for our noble quaintness. In this definition, we are exotic curios. Our ancient arts and customs are used to draw tourist money to state coffers, into the pocketbooks and bank accounts of scholars, and into support of the American-in-Disneyland promoters' dream.

6   As a Roman Catholic child I was treated to bloody tales of how the savage Indians martyred the hapless priests and missionaries who went among them in an attempt to lead them to the one true path. By the time I was through high school I had the idea that Indians were people who had benefitted mightily from the advanced knowledge and superior morality of the Anglo-Europeans. At least I had, perforce, that idea to lay beside the other one that derived

from my daily experience of Indian life, an idea less dehumanizing and more accurate because it came from my mother and the other Indian people who raised me. That idea was that Indians are a people who don't tell lies, who care for their children and their old people. You never see an Indian orphan, they said. You always know when you're old that someone will take care of you—one of your children will. Then they'd list the old folks who were being taken care of by this child or that. No child is ever considered illegitimate among the Indians, they said. If a girl gets pregnant, the baby is still part of the family, and the mother is too. That's what they said, and they showed me real people who lived according to those principles.

7   Of course the ravages of colonization have taken their toll; there are orphans in Indian country now, and abandoned, brutalized old folks; there are even illegitimate children, though the very concept still strikes me as absurd. There are battered children and neglected children, and there are battered wives and women who have been raped by Indian men. Proximity to the "civilizing" effects of white Christians has not improved the moral quality of life in Indian country, though each group, Indian and white, explains the situation differently. Nor is there much yet in the oral tradition that can enable us to adapt to these inhuman changes. But a force is growing in that direction, and it is helping Indian women reclaim their lives. Their power, their sense of direction and of self will soon be visible. It is the force of the women who speak and work and write, and it is formidable.

8   Through all the centuries of war and death and cultural and psychic destruction have endured the women who raise the children and tend the fires, who pass along the tales and the traditions, who weep and bury the dead, who are the dead, and who never forget. There are always the women, who make pots and weave baskets, who fashion clothes and cheer their children on at powwow, who make fry bread and piki bread, and corn soup and chili stew, who dance and sing and remember and hold within their hearts the dream of their ancient peoples—that one day the woman who thinks will speak to us again, and everywhere there will be peace. Meanwhile we tell the stories and write the books and trade tales of anger and woe and stories of fun and scandal and laugh over all manner of things that happen every day. We watch and we wait.

9   My great-grandmother told my mother: never forget you are Indian. And my mother told me the same thing. This, then, is how I have gone about remembering, so that my children will remember too.

Understanding the Content

Feel free to reread all or parts of the selection to answer the following questions.

1. From where do Native American women derive their occult power, according to tribal lore?

2. What is Paula Gunn Allen's mother's background? What is unique about her mother's "people"?

3. What was Gunn Allen taught about Native Americans? In other words, what was their role in "white history"?

4. In what religion was Gunn Allen raised? What was she told about Native Americans in relation to how they interacted with people of that religion?

5. What are the "ravages of colonization," according to Paula Gunn Allen?

Looking at Structure and Style

1. What is the thesis of this essay? Is it stated or implied? If stated, where?

2. How does paragraph 1 relate to paragraph 2? To the rest of the selection?

3. What organizing pattern is used in paragraph 4?

4. What is the relation of paragraph 8 to the thesis of this selection?

5. What is the author's attitude about her subject? How can you tell? What words or phrases give you an idea of her attitude?

6. Comment on paragraph 9 as a concluding paragraph. Is it effective? Why or why not?

Evaluating the Author's Viewpoint

1. What is the "bicultural bind" that the author describes? How has this bicultural bind affected Gunn Allen?

2. What are the author's "notable nonwhite notions" about women?

3. What can you infer about the author's opinion of and relationship with her mother? Her grandmother?

4. How was what the author knew to be true about Indian life at odds with what she learned through history lessons?

5. How are women viewed in Indian culture, according to Paula Gunn Allen?

Pursuing Possible Essay Topics

1. Have you learned anything in history books or in school about your culture that you feel is untrue or misleading? If so, what is it? Write an essay discussing what you know to be true in relation to what you've been taught.

2. How are women thought of in your culture? How are they treated? Write an essay discussing the role of women in your particular cultural heritage.

3. Do you ever, like the author, find yourself in a "bicultural bind"? If so, write about it. Describe the bind and how it affects your life overall.

4. Brainstorm or freewrite on one or more of the following topics:

   a. history

   b. oppression

   c. tradition

   d. culture

   e. women

   f. family life

   g. cultural diversity

5. Think of another topic related to the subject of cultural heritage and write an essay about it.

Preparing to Read

Take a minute or two to look over the following reading selection. Note the title and the author, read the first paragraph, and check the essay's length. Make certain you have the time now to read it carefully and to do the exercises that follow it. Then, in the spaces provided, answer the following questions.

1. What does the title tell you about this essay? _____

   _____

   _____

2. What do you think this essay will be about? _____

   _____

   _____

3. Based on your reading of the first paragraph, how do you think the author

   will define the term "salad bowl"? Why? _____

   _____

   _____

Vocabulary

Good comprehension of what you are about to read depends upon your understanding of the words below. The number following each word refers to the paragraph where it is used.

implicitly (1) completely, absolutely, without a doubt

assimilation (1) the process of assimilating or becoming similar

jibe (1) to agree with or be in accord with

crucible (1) a severe test of belief

indoctrinate (2) to convince of an ideological point of view

admixture (2) the act of mixing; something produced by mixing

homogeneous (3) sameness; uniform

evanescence (4) to disappear like vapor

differential (4) showing a difference

anomalous (5) deviating from the usual order

amalgamation (6) a consolidation; merger

pablum (9) also spelled "pabulum": material whose intellectual content is bland or unsatisfying

Forget the "Melting Pot": Make Mine a Salad Bowl

HANNIBAL B. JOHNSON

Hannibal B. Johnson is an author and independent consultant who has received numerous awards for his human relations works and his writing. His works in-clude Black Wall Street, Up from the Ashes, Acres of Aspiration, Mama Used to Say, *and* No Place Like Home.

1   My 1960s-era elementary school social studies teachers routinely referred to America as the world's great melting pot. The metaphor implicitly characterized the history of race and ethnicity in America as one of inclusion, adaptation, and, ultimately, assimilation. This simplistic, superficially appealing slant on American history did not jibe with my own experience. My reality consisted of largely segregated schools and housing, overt racism and discrimination, and economic inequity. I wondered why African-Americans had not quite melted in my teachers' multicultural crucible. I pondered why we had not fully embraced—and had not been fully embraced by—the elusive American dream. Indeed, history and life in general made me wonder whether the mysterious concoction stewing in that great melting pot derived from a recipe that all but omitted African-American ingredients.

2   How could those teachers dutifully indoctrinate us with the melting pot mantra, knowing full well that little Black children like me had not, and likely would not, melt. Even though I stood out as one of a handful of African-American kids in my Mineral Wells, Texas elementary schools, and even though I excelled academically and socially, the prospect of full assimilation seemed Pollyannaish. I never overcame my difference. I always stood out. Within and outside the schoolhouse gates, the world sent an unmistakable message: The melting pot admixture repels that which threatens to darken the blend.

3   Even now, in Twenty-First Century America, the melting pot employs color control. Segregated schools still exist. Housing and neighborhoods continue to be remarkably racially homogeneous. Racism and discrimination, while palpably less overt, nonetheless continue to corrupt. Economic disparity persists. Total assimilation seems but

a theoretical fantasy—mere figments of the imaginations of those with but a tenuous grasp on reality.

4   Diane Sawyer's 1990s "True Colors" segment on the ABC news-magazine *Primetime Live* dramatically illustrates the evanescence of African-American assimilation. Sawyer took two males—one White, the other Black—of roughly the same age, intellect, and physical attractiveness to St. Louis, Missouri. The men separately undertook some mundane but important day-to-day tasks. (To control for the time factor, the men undertook these tasks separately, but within minutes of one another.) They went to the same car dealership to inquire into purchasing a car. They went shopping. They answered employment ads. They sought out housing. Without fail, the White male received vastly more favorable treatment. The car dealer offered him the car both men wanted at a price significantly lower than the price quoted to the Black male. The same anxious sales clerk who cheerfully greeted the White male in the department store tailed the Black male from aisle to aisle. The White male received warm greetings and leads from an employment agency. He got job leads from a potential employer. The Black male heard warnings about "laziness" at the same employment agency. He heard, "Sorry, no jobs here," at the same employment agency. The White male toured a vacant apartment. The landlord offered him a lease almost immediately. The same landlord coldly told the Black man, "No vacancies." In the end, the two men, friends from the outset, compared notes. Each man expressed his astonishment—indeed, horror—at the extent of their differential treatment.

5   "True Colors," the Diane Sawyer piece, cannot be dismissed as dated or anomalous. For most African-Americans, racism and discrimination continue to contaminate the American compound. Forget the melting pot. A more apt analogy—more accurate, less dismissive, and more empowering—of the history of race and ethnicity in America resides in the salad bowl.

6   I greatly value my identity as an American. I also value my identity as an African-American. I recognize that African-Americans have not, by and large, assimilated. But assimilation is only partially a choice. That which one aspires to assimilate into must be to some degree willing to allow the amalgamation.

7   Our lack of assimilation, dictated by a tortuous history of racism and discrimination, may not be such a bad thing. Assimilation, after all, requires sacrificing our cultural identity in favor of some imagined "average American" ideal. Without doubt, all of us, racial and ethnic identities aside, need to jump into the American mix. But we need not melt down so far as to lose our distinctive, defining culture and history.

8   What unites us—our shared humanity and our total embrace of America's lofty ideals—trumps our important, real racial and ethnic differences. Our differences, though, do not magically disappear. We all benefit from understanding our rich diversity. We learn and grow by sharing all of whom and what we as individuals, and all of whom at what we as various "peoples" [are] that make America great.

9   The concoction in our mythical melting pot looks, feels, and tastes like Pablum. Compare that with the richness and zest of the colorful assortment in my salad bowl. Each ingredient retains its individual integrity. Each ingredient adds unmistakable character to the whole. Together, they flavor a vibrant, all-American piece de resistance. Forget the melting pot. Make mine a salad bowl!

Understanding the Content

Feel free to reread all or parts of the selection to answer the following questions.

1. What is a melting pot as a metaphor for America, traditionally speaking? What was Hannibal B. Johnson's reaction to that term and what it implied?

2. Where did Johnson grow up? Did this area have a majority of African-Americans?

3. What was Diane Sawyer's "True Colors" segment? What did it seek to prove? Did it succeed?

4. What is the advantage to the salad bowl metaphor, according to Hannibal B. Johnson?

Looking at Structure and Style

1. What is the thesis of this essay? Is it stated or implied? If stated, where?

2. Does the author's use of metaphor strengthen this essay? Why or why not?

3. In addition to being an argumentative essay, what other predominant mode(s) of organization is/are used?

4. What is the purpose of paragraphs 4 and 5? Their relation to the rest of the essay?

5. What is the relation of paragraph 1 to paragraph 3 in this essay?

6. Is the introductory paragraph effective in setting the tone for the selection? In conveying what the subject of the selection will be? Why or why not?

7. In your opinion, does the author include an effective concluding paragraph? Explain why or why not.

Evaluating the Author's Viewpoint

1. Is Johnson mostly objective or subjective when approaching his subject? Explain.

2. What is the author's tone throughout this essay?

3. Why do you think Johnson includes a detailed description of Diane Sawyer's 1990 segment "True Colors" in this essay? Is it necessary? Effective?

4. Do you agree or disagree with the author that "in Twenty-First Century America, the melting pot employs color control" (3)? Why?

5. Do you think that the metaphor of the salad bowl is more "empowering," as the author contends?

Pursuing Possible Essay Topics

1. With your class or in small groups, discuss the idea of the American "melting pot." Write a brief summary of your discussion.

2. Hannibal Johnson writes that he always "stood out" when he was a child in school. Did you? If so, write an essay discussing how you felt.

3. Is total assimilation a "theoretical fantasy" in your opinion? Write an essay discussing your viewpoint.

4. What would help lessen some of the disparity that exists in the United States? Write an essay discussing one thing that you think would help.

5. Brainstorm or freewrite on one or more of the following topics:

   a. racial inequality

   b. the Melting Pot versus the Salad Bowl

   c. ethnic differences

   d. prejudice

   e. America

6. Find your own topic related to the subject of cultural heritage and write an essay.

Preparing to Read

Take a minute or two to look over the following reading selection. Note the title and author, read the opening paragraph, and check the essay's length. Make certain you have the time now to read it carefully and to do the exercises that follow it. Then, in the spaces provided, answer the following questions.

1. What does the title tell you about the essay? What do you think when you see the term "cultural baggage"? _____

   _____

   _____

2. What does the term "cultural heritage" mean to you? _____

   _____

   _____

3. Is your cultural heritage important to you? If so, how? _____

   _____

   _____

Vocabulary

Good comprehension of what you are about to read depends upon your understanding of the words below. The number following each word refers to the paragraph where it is used.

chauvinism (2) partiality to a group or place to which one belongs or has belonged

venerable (3) impressive by reason of age

militant (4) aggressive

ecumenism (4) a movement promoting unity among religious groups

tartans (5) garments with a plaid design, patterned to designate different clans

Seder (7) Jewish ceremonial dinner held on the first evening or first and second evenings of Passover

secular (8) not specifically religious

progenitors (9) ancestors in a direct line

epiphany (10) an illuminating discovery

spewed (11) came forth in a flood or gush

maxim (11) general truth, fundamental principle, rule of conduct

Cultural Baggage

BARBARA EHRENREICH

Barbara Ehrenreich has written thirteen books, including Nickel and Dimed, *and* Bait and Switch: The (Futile) Pursuit of the American Dream, *which revealed her findings as an undercover white-collar job seeker. Those experiences led her to form United Professionals, an organization for white-collar workers who find their lives disrupted by forces beyond their control. This selection is from her book* Snarling Citizen.

1   An acquaintance was telling me about the joys of rediscovering her ethnic and religious heritage. "I know exactly what my ancestors were doing 2,000 years ago," she said, eyes gleaming with enthusiasm, "and *I can do the same things now.*" Then she leaned forward and inquired politely, "And what is your ethnic background, if I may ask?"

2   "None," I said, that being the first word in line to get out of my mouth. Well, not "none," I backtracked. Scottish, English, Irish—that was something, I supposed. Too much Irish to qualify as a WASP; too much of the hated English to warrant a "Kiss Me, I'm Irish" button; plus there are a number of dead ends in the family tree due to adoptions, missing records, failing memories and the like. I was blushing by this time. Did "none" mean I was rejecting my heritage out of Anglo-Celtic self-hate? Or was I revealing a hidden ethnic chauvinism in which the Britannically derived served as a kind of neutral standard compared with the ethnic "others"?

3   Throughout the 60's and 70's, I watched one group after another— African-Americans, Latinos, Native Americans—stand up and proudly reclaim their roots while I just sank back ever deeper into my seat. All this excitement over ethnicity stemmed, I uneasily sensed, from a past in which *their* ancestors had been trampled upon by *my* ancestors, or at least by people who looked very much like them. In addition, it had begun to seem almost un-American not to have some sort of hyphen at hand, linking one to more venerable times and locales.

4   But the truth is, I was raised with none. We'd eaten ethnic foods in my childhood home, but these were all borrowed, like the pasties, or Cornish meat pies, my father had picked up from his fellow miners in

Butte, Montana. If my mother had one rule, it was militant ecumenism in all matters of food and experience. "Try new things," she would say, meaning anything from sweetbreads to clams, with an emphasis on the "new."

5   As a child, I briefly nourished a craving for tradition and roots. I immersed myself in the works of Sir Walter Scott. I pretended to believe that the bagpipe was a musical instrument. I was fascinated to learn from a grandmother that we were descended from certain Highland clans and longed for a pleated skirt in one of their distinctive tartans.

6   But in *Ivanhoe*, it was the dark-eyed "Jewess" Rebecca I identified with, not the flaxen-haired bimbo Rowena. As for clans: Why not call them "tribes," those bands of half-clad peasants and warriors whose idea of cuisine was stuffed sheep gut washed down with whisky? And then there was the sting of Disraeli's remark—which I came across in my early teens—to the effect that his ancestors had been leading orderly, literate lives when my ancestors were still rampaging through the Highlands daubing themselves with blue paint.

7   Motherhood put the screws on me, ethnicity-wise. I had hoped that by marrying a man of Eastern European–Jewish ancestry I would acquire for my descendants the ethnic genes that my own forebears so sadly lacked. At one point, I even subjected the children to a Seder of my own design, including a little talk about the flight from Egypt and its relevance to modern social issues. But the kids insisted on buttering their matzohs and snickering through my talk. "Give me a break, Mom," the older one said. "You don't even believe in God."

8   After the tiny pagans had been put to bed, I sat down to brood over Elijah's wine. What had I been thinking? The kids knew that their Jewish grandparents were secular folks who didn't hold Seders themselves. And if ethnicity eluded me, how could I expect it to take root in my children, who are not only Scottish-English-Irish, but Hungarian-Polish-Russian to boot?

9   But, then, on the fumes of Manischewitz, a great insight took form in my mind. It was true, as the kids said, that I didn't "believe in God." But this could be taken as something very different from an accusation—a reminder of a genuine heritage. My parents had not believed in God either, nor had my grandparents or any other progenitors going back to the great-great level. They had become disillusioned with Christianity generations ago—just as, on the in-law side, my children's other ancestors had shaken off their Orthodox Judaism. This insight did not exactly furnish me with an "identity," but it was at least something to work with: we are the kind of people, I realized—whatever our distant ancestors' religions—who do *not* believe, who do not carry on traditions, who do not do things just because someone has done them before.

10   The epiphany went on: I recalled that my mother never introduced a procedure for cooking or cleaning by telling me, "Grandma
did it this way." What did Grandma know, living in the days before
vacuum cleaners and disposable toilet mops? In my parents' general
view, new things were better than old, and the very fact that some
ritual had been performed in the past was a good reason for abandoning it now. Because what was the past, as our forebears knew it?
Nothing but poverty, superstition and grief. "Think for yourself," Dad
used to say. "Always ask why."

11   In fact, this may have been the ideal cultural heritage for my particular ethnic strain—bounced as it was from the Highlands of Scotland across the sea, out to the Rockies, down into the mines and
finally spewed out into high-tech, suburban America. What better
philosophy, for a race of migrants, than "Think for yourself"? What
better maxim, for people whose whole world was rudely inverted
every 30 years or so, than "Try new things"?

12   The more tradition-minded, the newly enthusiastic celebrants of
Purim and Kwanzaa and Solstice, may see little point to survival if
the survivors carry no cultural freight—religion, for example, or
ethnic tradition. To which I would say that skepticism, curiosity and
wide-eyed ecumenical tolerance are also worthy elements of the
human tradition and are at least as old as such notions as "Serbian"
or "Croatian," "Scottish" or "Jewish." I make no claims for my personal line of progenitors except that they remained loyal to the
values that may have induced all of our ancestors, long, long ago, to
climb down from the trees and make their way into the open
plains.

13   A few weeks ago, I cleared my throat and asked the children, now
mostly grown and fearsomely smart, whether they felt any stirrings
of ethnic or religious identity, etc., which might have been, ahem,
insufficiently nourished at home. "None," they said, adding firmly,
"and the world would be a better place if nobody else did, either." My
chest swelled with pride, as would my mother's, to know that the race
of "none" marches on.

Understanding the Content

Feel free to reread all or parts of the selection to answer the following questions.

1. What is the author's cultural heritage?

2. Why did certain groups proclaiming their heritage in the 1960s and 1970s
make the author uncomfortable?

3. How did the author strive for a cultural heritage as a child? What did she do
to identify and acknowledge her roots?

4. What did the author hope to gain for her children by marrying a man with an Eastern European-Jewish background?

5. What did the author do to try to introduce tradition and religious identity into her children's lives? How did her children react to her attempts?

6. How did the author's parents feel about tradition? What did her father tell her as a child that the author classifies as a "better philosophy, for a race of migrants" (11)?

7. How do the author's children feel about the way they were raised in terms of their ethnic and religious identity?

Looking at Structure and Style

1. What is the main function of paragraphs 1 and 2? Are these two paragraphs effective as an opening to the essay?

2. The author quotes her parents in several paragraphs. What is the purpose of these quotations?

3. How does paragraph 4 explain the author's viewpoint on cultural heritage and support her thesis? How does paragraph 10 help support what the author states in paragraph 4?

4. What is the function of paragraph 6?

5. Is paragraph 13 an effective conclusion? Why or why not?

6. The essay details the author's coming to terms with her cultural heritage. What stages of her life does she use to illustrate her journey?

Evaluating the Author's Viewpoints

1. What does the author think of people who embrace a strong cultural heritage?

2. How has the author's attitude toward cultural heritage changed throughout her life?

3. What is the author's religious background? How has this helped shape her views on cultural heritage?

4. Does the author feel a need to pass on traditions and rituals to her children? Explain.

5. Is the author proud of her Scottish-English-Irish background? Why or why not? What examples from history does the author give to support your conclusion?

Pursuing Possible Essay Topics

1. How important do you think it is that children grow up with a strong sense of their cultural heritage? Write an essay discussing your viewpoint.

2. What is your cultural background? Write an essay discussing how your ethnicity has defined who you are and who you will become.

3. Discuss some aspect of your culture of which you are particularly proud. What contributions has your culture made to society that make your culture stand out from other cultures?

4. Do you think the advice—"Think for yourself." "Always ask why." (10)—would be helpful to a child growing up in today's society? Why or why not?

5. Brainstorm or freewrite on one or more of the following:

   a. cultural heritage

   b. ethnicity

   c. diversity

   d. religious tradition

   e. rituals

6. Ignore these topics and write an essay about a topic of your own related to culture or cultural heritage.

Opposing Viewpoints on Culture's Influence

The next two selections deal with the effects American culture can have on someone from a different background. One author wants to become part of the American culture, while the other author wants little or nothing to do with it.

Preparing to Read

Take a minute or two to look over the following reading selection. Note the title and the author, read the first two paragraphs, and check the essay's length. Make certain you have the time now to read it carefully and to do the exercises that follow it. Then, in the spaces provided, answer the following questions.

1. What do you think this essay will be about? _____

    _____

    _____

2. Based on your reading of the first two paragraphs, what can you infer about Amy Tan and how she feels about her Chinese heritage? _____

    _____

    _____

Vocabulary

Good comprehension of what you are about to read depends upon your understanding of the words below. The number following each word refers to the paragraph where it is used.

appalling (2) dreadful; awful

clamor (4) demand noisily; shout loudly

Fish Cheeks

AMY TAN

Amy Tan is an Asian-American, award-winning writer whose works have won numerous awards and have been translated into 35 languages. Her novels are The Joy Luck Club, The Kitchen God's Wife, The Hundred Secret Senses, The Bonesetter's Daughter, *and* Saving Fish from Drowning, *all New York Times bestsellers and the recipient of various awards. She is also the author of a memoir,* The Opposite of Fate, *two children's books,* The Moon Lady *and* Sagwa, *and numerous articles for magazines, including* The New Yorker, Harper's Bazaar, *and* National Geographic.

1   I fell in love with the minister's son the winter I turned 14. He was not Chinese, but as white as Mary in the manger. For Christmas I prayed for this blond-haired boy, Robert, and a slim new American nose.

2   When I found out that my parents had invited the minister's family over for Christmas Eve dinner, I cried. What would Robert think of our shabby Chinese Christmas? What would he think of our noisy Chinese relatives who lacked proper American manners? What terrible disappointment would he feel upon seeing not a roast turkey and sweet potatoes but Chinese food?

3   On Christmas Eve I saw that my mother had outdone herself in creating a strange menu. She was pulling black veins out of the backs of prawns. The kitchen was littered with appalling mounds of raw food: a slimy rock cod with bulging fish eyes that pleaded not to be thrown in a pan of hot oil. Tofu, which looked like stacked wedges of rubbery white sponges. A bowl soaking dried fungus back to life. A plate of squid, their backs crisscrossed with knife markings so they resembled bicycle tires.

4   And then they arrived—the minister's family and all my relatives in a clamor of doorbells and rumpled Christmas packages. Robert grunted hello, and I pretended he was not worthy of existence.

5   Dinner threw me deeper into despair. My relatives licked the ends of their chopsticks and reached across the table, dipping them into the dozen or so plates of food. Robert and his family waited patiently for platters to be passed to them. My relatives murmured with pleasure when my mother brought out the whole steamed fish. Robert grimaced. Then my father poked his chopsticks just below the fish eye and plucked out the soft meat. "Amy, your favorite," he said, offering me the tender fish cheek. I wanted to disappear.

6   At the end of the meal my father leaned back and belched loudly, thanking my mother for her fine cooking. "It's a polite Chinese custom to show you are satisfied," explained my father to our astonished guests. Robert was looking down at his plate with a reddened face. The minister managed to muster up a quiet burp. I was stunned into silence for the rest of the night.

7   After everyone had gone, my mother said to me, "You want to be the same as American girls on the outside." She handed me an early gift. It was a miniskirt in beige tweed. "But inside you must always be Chinese. You must be proud to be different. Your only shame is to have shame."

8   And even though I didn't agree with her then, I knew that she understood how much I had suffered during the evening's dinner. It wasn't until many years later—long after I had gotten over my crush on Robert—that I was able to appreciate fully her lesson and the true purpose behind our particular menu. For Christmas Eve that year, she had chosen all my favorite foods.

Understanding the Content

Feel free to reread all or parts of the selection to answer the following questions.

1. What did Amy Tan pray for the Christmas that she met Robert?

2. What different kinds of foods did Amy Tan's mother serve at Christmas Eve dinner? Why did she choose the foods that she served?

3. How did Amy Tan's family behave at the dinner table? Robert's family?

4. What did Tan's mother give her for Christmas? Why?

Looking at Structure and Style

1. Write the thesis of this essay in your own words.

2. What is the organizing pattern used in paragraph 5? What is its function in relation to the rest of the essay?

3. What is Tan's attitude toward her family and their customs? How can you tell? What words or phrases does she use to convey how she feels?

4. What is the significance of the title "Fish Cheeks"? Is it effective as a title for this essay? Why or why not?

5. Does Tan do a good job of comparing and contrasting her Chinese family with Robert's American one? Explain.

Evaluating the Author's Viewpoint

1. What can you infer about how Robert's family felt during the dinner at the Tan house?

2. What can you infer about how Tan felt about her family?

3. How do you think Tan feels now about her Chinese family? Her heritage?

Pursuing Possible Essay Topics

Before writing an essay in response to any ideas you may have after reading Amy Tan's essay, wait until you have read the following essay by Liu Zongren, "After Two Years in the Melting Pot."

Preparing to Read

Take a minute or two to look over the following reading selection. Note the title and the author, read the first paragraph, and check the essay's length. Make certain you have the time now to read it carefully and to do the exercises that follow it. Then, in the spaces provided, answer the following questions.

1. What does the title tell you about this essay? _____

   _____

   _____

2. What do you think this essay will be about? _____

   _____

   _____

Vocabulary

Good comprehension of what you are about to read depends upon your understanding of the words below. The number following each word refers to the paragraph where it is used.

impatient (1) annoyed with

hastily (1) quickly

glistene (3) reflected off of

After Two Years in the Melting Pot

LIU ZONGREN

Liu Zongren came to the United States from China on a scholarship to study English. He wrote about his experience in a book entitled After Two Years in the Melting Pot, *from which the following selection is taken. After his return to China, he wrote* 6 Tanyin Alley and Hard Time: Thirty Months in a Chinese Labor Camp.

1   There were many American customs which puzzled me. I was very impatient with table formality. Why do people have to remember to change plates, forks, knives, and spoons so many times in one meal? I was especially bothered by that piece of cloth called a napkin. English gentlemen tuck a white napkin under their chins during a

meal and Americans put one on their laps. I had trouble remembering to do this even a year and a half after I had arrived and had been to a number of fancy restaurants. Even if I did place it on my lap, it always slipped onto the floor. I often remembered to use my napkin only when I saw someone wipe his mouth with one; I then hastily picked mine up and spread it across my lap, stealing a look to see if others had noticed my lack of etiquette.

2   The concept of [the Mao] jacket conforms with the Chinese teaching of modesty, taught very early to children. They are told not to differ from others in appearance, not to be conspicuous, or they will provoke gossip. "She is frivolous," people might say if a woman did her hair in a fancy way; or, if she wore western clothing, they might comment, "Her blouse is too open at the neck!"

3   Of course, this is not the way Americans judge each other. Everyone tries to be different—and sometimes this goes to an extreme. One morning I glanced out of a classroom window to see a bright-colored figure walking across the lawn in front of University Hall. The sun glistened on her scarlet dress and bright red boots; her huge gold earrings sparkled, yet the part that caught the sunshine most was her hair. It was dyed half-red and half-yellow. In China, even a crazy woman would not dare walk out in the open looking like that.

4   In America, the overriding need to be recognized as an individual is so often expressed in the way one dresses. The exceptions are the teenagers who choose to dress alike and happily submit to the styles dictated by their peers. Parents and schools may not approve of certain fads in clothing yet they find it virtually impossible to control the dress codes. Other than the teenagers, I discovered no restrictions on how people should dress. I never saw two persons dressed identically, except by choice; the businessmen and bank workers on LaSalle Street dressed in three-piece suits and ties, all wearing their wing-tipped shoes. Still, they had enough variety in their outfits to appear different from one another. A young professor at Circle wore a different tie and shirt every day, even if he wore the same suit. With all the clothing changes they made every day, there was little chance that two professors would show up looking alike. . . .

5   I bought few clothes in the United States, not wanting to spend two hundred dollars for a suit I would never wear back in China. Most of my western Chicago clothes would go into a storage trunk, as my father's had—mere reminders of his ten-year period of service abroad. I wore the same jacket and two pairs of pants all through the seasons, just as I had in Beijing. I thought little of this until two Chinese colleagues from Illinois State University told me they felt embarrassed when they wore the same clothes two days in a row. "Everyone in

America changes every day," they said. "We don't have many clothes but we don't want to look shabby. We learned a trick—don't laugh at us. We take off the clothes we wear today and hang them in the closet. Tomorrow we put on another set. The day after tomorrow, we will wear the first set again; then next day, we mix the two sets up and we thus have a new set of clothes."

6   I laughed, not at my two colleagues, but at people who spend time worrying about what clothes they should wear. It is a waste of time for people to fuss over clothes, and it is also a waste for Chinese to try to find ways to restrict others' manner of dress. I hope that Chinese society will become more open, as America is, about the matter of clothing. A few western suits and blue jeans can hardly change centuries of Chinese teaching—history has already proved that. A billion people are like an immense ocean which can easily accommodate a few drops of foreign pigment without changing color. Western life is very appealing to many young Chinese today, who think that a better life can be achieved by adopting western life-styles. Let them try—they will soon learn.

7   Home now meant much more than just my wife and our son. It also meant the life I was born into, the surroundings and environment that looked Chinese, the people with whom I shared a culture, and the job at my office which I had, in the past, sometimes resented. I longed for them all. As one Chinese saying goes, all water returns to the sea; all leaves go back to their roots. My roots were in China, in Beijing, in my family. It was time I went home. . . .

8   I reflected on the fact that most of the successful Chinese I had met in Chicago—doctors and professors—never thought of themselves as Americans. "China is my country. Someday I will go back," one professor told me. These Chinese have a deeper sense of homeland than members of other ethnic groups I met in the United States. They have preserved more ancient Chinese customs and traditions than have the Chinese on either the mainland or Taiwan. It appears easier for a European immigrant to adjust to American society; a Chinese always thinks of his homeland. It is not merely a difference of skin color; it is cultural. I was glad to have become more aware of the importance of upholding my cultural values. . . .

9   After twenty months of observing American life, I had become more satisfied with the idea of my simple life in China, and I hoped that our country would never be one in which money is of first importance. I would never in my lifetime have the many possessions my middle-class American friends have. Yet, it seemed to me as if they were really only living the same cycle of life that I do in China, except on a higher economic rung of the ladder. We shared the same fundamental needs: family, friends, a familiar culture.

Understanding the Content

Feel free to reread all or parts of the selection to answer the following questions.

1. Which American customs puzzled Zongren and why?

2. What is the difference between how Americans dress and how the Chinese dress, according to Liu Zongren? What does this difference signify about each culture?

3. How did Zongren's colleagues at Illinois State University deal with the fact that they didn't have a lot of clothing?

4. Why didn't most of the Chinese people that Zongren met in American think of themselves as American?

5. What did Zongren's American home signify for him, his wife, and their son?

Looking at Structure and Style

1. Is Zongren's thesis stated or implied? If it is implied, rewrite it in your own words.

2. What is the purpose of paragraphs 2 and 3? What is their function in relation to paragraph 4?

3. In which paragraphs does Zongren use the organizing pattern of comparison and contrast? How do these paragraphs relate to the thesis of the essay?

4. What example does Zongren use to illustrate the Chinese "teaching of modesty"? Why does he include this, in your opinion?

Evaluating the Author's Viewpoint

1. What can you infer about how happy Liu Zongren was while living in the United States? How can you tell?

2. What can you infer about Zongren's colleagues at Illinois State University and how they felt about living in the United States?

3. What is Zongren's attitude toward the American way of dress?

4. Why, in your opinion, does the author include the quote "all water returns to the sea..." (7)? What is its purpose in this essay? How does it relate to Zongren himself?

5. What lessons did Zongren learn about himself while living in America, do you think?

Pursuing Possible Essay Topics

1. Compare and contrast Amy Tan's essay with Liu Zongren's. Do they share any similar themes? If so, what are they? Write an essay.

2. Now that you've read both selections, with whom do you identify more: Tan or Zongren? Why? Write an essay discussing your viewpoint.

3. Write an essay comparing and contrasting your culture with that of the Chinese people described in both Tan's and Zongren's essays.

 4. With a classmate, discuss which essay you enjoyed more and why. Write an essay summarizing your discussion.

5. Brainstorm or freewrite on one or more of the following topics:

   a. ethnicity

   b. cultural traditions

   c. assimilation

   d. cultural differences

   e. American dress/clothing

6. Pick your own topic related to cultural heritage and write an essay.

Student Essay

Read the following narrative essay written by a student. As you read, look for answers to these questions:

1. Does the essay's subject fit the assignment to write about some aspect of cultural heritage?
2. How well does the narrative hold your interest?
3. Is the thesis clear and well supported?

On Being White

Mara Joseph

1   I admit it freely. I am a privileged individual. I grew up in a wealthy area outside of Los Angeles, went to a very good public high school and have had all the things I could possibly need or want provided for me by two loving parents.

2   Until one day last month, I have never felt like I was being discriminated against. That day, while sitting in an anthropology lecture about race, class and gender, I started to feel as though the color of my skin (a rather blinding white at this time of year) was putting me in an unfair position.

3   And recently, I discovered that I am not the only person to feel this way either.

4   Just the other day, a friend told me about the cultural English class he had taken, in which he was the only white person. The main assignment in the class? Write about your experience as an immigrant to America who does not speak English.

5   Needless to say, my blue-eyed and blonde friend, who is probably a fifth-or sixth-generation American, didn't do very well in the class.

6   Another friend had a similar experience in her Asian American studies class, in which she was expected to write about her life as an Asian American (clearly a bit difficult for a person of European descent).

7   Once again, she did poorly in the class, and so did the few other white people in it.

8   On a similar note, David Horowitz's article decrying repara-
     tions was published recently in my college newspaper, although
     it was quickly revealed as an oversight by the editor who
     extended sincere apologies for the mistake.

9   I never saw the article, but I know the general idea behind
     reparations: Payment should be given to African Americans to
     compensate for the atrocities their ancestors endured as slaves.

10   Of course, I agree that slavery was a horrible tragedy and a
     scar on our country's history, as it is among many other
     countries involved in the slave trade during previous centu-
     ries. But I don't see how I am in any way responsible for it.

11   In fact, I don't see how my ancestors are either, because,
     like many other Americans, I am descended from recent immigrants.

12   Just years before the civil rights movements began in
     this country, my relatives were busy dealing with their own
     problems—namely Hitler and Nazi Germany (they were
     Austrian Jews).

13   Even if any relatives were among early British colonizers in
     this country and owners of slaves, I would hope to not be held
     responsible for their ignorance and injustice. To punish
     someone for actions they didn't commit is as unjust as
     punishing someone for the color of their skin.

14   But instead of learning from the past and moving on, it seems
     that many people would rather dwell and seek revenge. Instead
     of using college courses to teach students what the immigrant
     or racial experience is like, the classes catered to members of
     that particular culture.

15   Because so many of the other comments I have made in my
     aforementioned anthropology class have been shot down or
     ignored, I am writing this in hopes of reminding others that
     we are all immigrants in the United States with the notable
     exception of Native Americans, and we all have our own unique
     stories and valid opinions to share.

16   I agree with those who say that people should never be judged
     based on the color of their skin—so why are these same people
     often the first to judge me for the color of mine?

Reaction

In your journal or on a separate sheet of paper, write your reaction to the student essay. What would you tell this student about her essay?

Viewpoints on Images

The people in the accompanying photo are taking the oath of citizenship so that they can live permanently in the United States as U.S. citizens. In your opinion, what impact does the "melting pot" aspect of this country have on society? Its citizens? Compare and contrast the United States and its many cultures living together to a more homogeneous country, such as Japan. What issues arise from living in a melting pot?

©Jeff Topping/Getty Images

On the Net

If you just type in the keywords "cultural heritage" into your Internet browser, you will be given a comprehensive list of sites related to just about every culture in the world. The search we did generated a list of more than one million sites.

Explore your own cultural heritage or a heritage about which you would like to learn more. Do your research exclusively on the Internet by finding articles and looking at various sites that offer good information about the particular culture. Keep a list of the sites and take notes on new things that you learn.

Answer the following questions:

1. How many sites did you visit?

2. Do you think the information on the sites was reliable? Why or why not?

3. Of the sites you visited, which ones were the most helpful? Why?

4. Which sites would you not visit again? Why?

5. What are three new things that you discovered while surfing the Web?

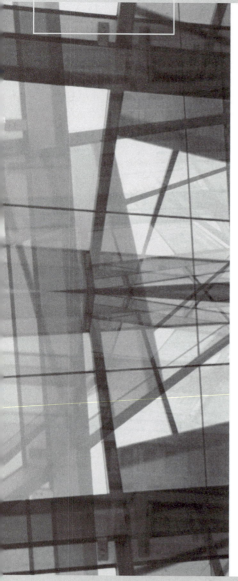

CHAPTER

6 Viewpoints on Social Concerns

Focus on Social Concerns

To help you focus on the subject of this chapter, take a few minutes to prepare for the topic by prewriting on one or more of the following topics:

1. punishment for smoking around children
2. advertising's effects on our body image
3. the American Dream defined
4. pollution from gasoline guzzlers
5. reasons to (or not to) reinstate the draft system
6. binge drinking

BEIJING, CHINA   A farmer who stole the head of a 3rd-century B.C. terra-cotta warrior and tried to sell it for $81,000 has been sentenced to death, an official Chinese newspaper reported Saturday.

SAN FRANCISCO   A man convicted and sentenced to prison for raping a young girl, then cutting off her arms and leaving her to die, was released today after serving three years of a twenty-year sentence.

In our society, most of us probably feel that a death sentence for stealing the head of a statue is too severe, while letting a man free after serving only a three-year term for raping and mutilating a child seems an outrage. But regardless of our reactions, the newspaper items reflect the social values of two different cultures.

As we live and grow, we learn the culture of the society in which we live. Sociologist Rodney Stark, in his book *Sociology,* tells us that the most significant elements of culture that we must learn are values, norms, and roles. Stark defines **values** this way: "The values of a culture identify its ideals—its ultimate aims and most general standards for assessing good and bad or desirable and undesirable. When we say people need self-respect, dignity, and freedom . . . we are invoking values." While values are rather general, **norms** are quite specific. "They are rules of governing behavior," Stark writes, "Norms define what behavior is required, acceptable, or prohibited in particular circumstances. Norms indicate that a person should, ought, or must act (or not act) in a certain way." A collection of these norms connected with a particular position in a society is called a **role.** For instance, in any given situation, each of us has "a relatively clearly defined role to fulfill: student, friend, woman, husband, shopper, pedestrian, cop, nun, bartender, wife, and so on." Thus, values, norms, and roles are connected.

How we think and act in the various roles we play is based on our society's values and norms. For instance, we generally expect a minister's behavior to follow certain norms: no smoking, no sexually deviant behavior, no using bad language, no wearing swim trunks while delivering a Sunday sermon. At the same time, your role while attending a church service also follows certain norms: no playing with your iPod or cellphone during the service, no shouting at friends across the aisle, no removing money from the collection plate.

History shows us that Americans have always been concerned with moral values. Chapters in textbooks are devoted to issues of right and wrong. Today we wonder how belief systems could ever have permitted the hanging of people as witches in Salem, the once widespread acceptance of slavery, the disregard for the rights of Native Americans, the long denial of voting rights and working privileges for women, the overt discrimination against Jews and other religious groups, the racial segregation from drinking fountains to schoolrooms, and the "blacklisting" and labeling as communists those who spoke out against government policies in the 1950s. Yet, at various times in our society, such norms were considered acceptable social behavior.

More recently, our society has had to deal with social clashes caused by the terrorist attacks of 9/11; the seemingly unending wars in Afghanistan and Iraq; the place of torture in dealing with terrorists; political scandals; attitudes toward gay rights, school prayer, and abortion; problems with homelessness; the shifting of jobs overseas for cheap labor; and illegal immigration, just to name a few. Disagreements over issues such as these create conflicts within our society that force us to reexamine our social values, norms, and roles. Doing so often brings about a change in attitudes and values from generation to generation. What was acceptable and valued in society yesterday may not be acceptable or valued today. What is acceptable or valued today may not be tomorrow.

The following reading selections reflect viewpoints and reactions to some current social concerns. Use them to practice your critical reading skills and to stimulate your own attitudes and thinking regarding social issues and values that are important to you.

Preparing to Read

Take a minute or two to look over the following reading selection. Note the title and author, read the opening paragraph, and check the essay's length. Make certain you have the time now to read it carefully and to do the exercises that follow it. Then, in the spaces provided, answer the following questions.

1. Based on your reading of the first paragraph, what do you think the subject of this essay will be? _____

_____

2. Why do you think the author uses an example in the opening paragraph?

_____

_____

Vocabulary

Good comprehension of what you are about to read depends upon your understanding of the words below. The number following each word refers to the paragraph where it is used.

fixated (2) obsessed, absorbed

grousing (5) complaining

recoiled (8) shrank back, backed away from

Your Mirror Image?

FRANCINE RUSSO

Francine Russo writes regularly for Time *magazine on a variety of subjects; she also writes a column called "Dear Francine," an advice column. The following selection was originally published in* Time.

1   Jenny Moran, 41, a sales executive in Ocean County, N.J., admits to being obsessed with her weight. But she was shocked when her 3½-year-old daughter suddenly began weighing herself several times a day. "I never thought she was paying attention," Moran says ruefully.

2   Moran has reason to be concerned. Study after study has found that mothers who are fixated on their body image are more likely to

have daughters with eating disorders than less self-conscious moms. Sure, you can blame the media for imposing a parade of surgically enhanced pop icons on your impressionable child, but the real danger to her self-image comes from closer to home: you!

3   Research shows that 80% of American women check out—and disapprove of—their reflections minutes after waking. On any given day, 45% say they are dieting. Scarier yet, a 1992 study found that 46% of girls 9 to 11 say they are "sometimes" or "very often" on a diet, and experts agree that the numbers have probably increased since then.

4   "We model our mothers," says psychology professor Lora Jacobi, who teaches a class on eating disorders at all-women Hollins University in Virginia. Of the students attracted to her class—typically those struggling with eating issues—virtually all report that their mothers were excessively worried about their size.

5   Your daughters are watching you, according to Jacobi. They observe you trying on jeans, overhear you grousing to your friends. They notice what you eat. If you declare yourself "good" for eating only salad and "bad" for eating cookies, they will judge their own goodness and badness the same way.

6   That was the case for Kristen Cole, a publicist in Northampton, Mass., who grew up watching her mother diet. Cake was pronounced "decadent." Cole, 33, believes such behavior helped pave the way for her struggles with anorexia and bulimia, which began at 12.

7   To avoid passing on an unhealthy obsession, it's wise to deal with weight and eating as health issues rather than moral ones, counsels Phyllis Cohen, a co-author of *You Have to Say I'm Pretty, You're My Mother.* And it's better to talk about bodies in terms of their strength and abilities rather than their appearance. If you're upset about gaining weight, Cohen urges, don't turn your anger inward. Self-loathing, most experts agree, is the root cause of eating disorders.

8   Do you hate your hips? Your butt? Be careful what you say. Self-contempt passes from generation to generation. Just recently, on a New York State college campus, Emily, 20, recoiled when her boyfriend squeezed her, exclaiming, "I love your arms!" Emily hated them. "My mother thought her arms were fat and flabby," she explains. "She'd never wear anything sleeveless. I thought that I was like her."

9   For your daughter to accept her body, you have to accept your own, insists Linda Perlman Gordon, a co-author of *Why Girls Talk—And What They're Really Saying.* "You must believe that you are more than just a pretty face."

10   What if you don't believe that? Start working on it. Try to like your body, and don't hide it from your daughter, suggests Boston family therapist Carleton Kendrick. "When she sees you in your bra and panties playing with the dog, she gets the message you're comfortable with your body and your sexuality," Kendrick says.

11   Also, let your kids know the things about yourself, apart from your body, that you're proud of—your resourcefulness, for example, or sense of humor. And, perhaps most difficult, don't communicate that you buy the distorted cultural messages that make thinness the essential ingredient for success, power and sexuality.

12   It's a tall order for most of us. If you can't overcome your hang-ups about your body, tell your daughters that it's a problem—your problem. With self-awareness and care, Kendrick says, you can avoid infecting them. Cole is now healthy, lean and active, a mother of two girls, 3 and 5. She tells them food is for energy and sweets are fine in moderation. "I keep the same Oreos in my cabinet as my mom did," she says, "but I took away the idea that some food is harmful." For her daughters, that may make all the difference.

Understanding the Content

Feel free to reread all or parts of the selection to answer the following questions.

1. According to the selection, what is the percentage of women who disapprove of their reflections within minutes after waking?

2. The selection states that on any given day, what percentage of women are dieting?

3. According to Francine Russo, how do daughters react to their mothers' issues with eating and body image?

4. How should women deal with weight and eating, according to this selection?

Looking at Structure and Style

1. What is the thesis of this selection? Is it stated or implied? If stated, where?

2. What is the purpose of paragraphs 9–11 in this selection? Do they support the author's thesis effectively?

3. How does the author use research and statistics to support her thesis? Is this effective? Are her sources credible?

4. What is Russo's attitude toward her subject? To whom is she writing, in your opinion? How does that affect her attitude and tone?

5. Do you think the author's use of Jenny Moran in the opening paragraph of this selection is effective? Why?

6. Does the concluding paragraph draw a conclusion or summarize the content? Is it effective as a closing paragraph? Explain.

Evaluating the Author's Viewpoints

1. What do you think of the statement, "it's wise to deal with weight and eating as health issues rather than moral ones" (7)?

2. Do you agree that "self-loathing . . . is the root cause of eating disorders" (7), or do you think that other factors influence poor body image and eating disorders?

3. Why do you think that almost half of girls surveyed said that they are sometimes or very often on a diet? What factors lead to this high number, in your opinion?

Pursuing Possible Essay Topics

1. If you are a woman, think about how much influence your mother may have had on your body image. Write an essay discussing your experience.

2. Do you think that men have body image issues? Write an essay discussing what you think some men experience with regard to weight, eating, and body image.

3. Write an essay discussing your views on the media's influence on body image. What role, if any, does the media play in shaping young girls' image of themselves?

4. Brainstorm or freewrite on one or more of the following topics:
   a. body image
   b. appearance
   c. being thin
   d. being fit
   e. exercise
   f. media influence on body image

5. If you don't like these topics, be creative and find your own topic related to a social concern and write an essay about it.

Preparing to Read

Take a minute or two to look over the following reading selection. Note the title and author, read the first two paragraphs, and check the essay's length. Make certain you have the time now to read it carefully and to do the exercises that follow it. Then, in the spaces provided, answer the following questions.

1. Based on your reading of the first two paragraphs, what do you think the subject of this essay will be? _____

_____

2. What is the author's tone in the opening paragraphs? _____

_____

Vocabulary

Good comprehension of what you are about to read depends upon your understanding of the words below. The number following each word refers to the paragraph where it is used.

jinked (6) tapped the end of the ash of a cigarette into an ashtray

demise (17) death, end

plié, pirouette, sissonne (19) terms used in ballet

Memories of a Sweet, Lethal, Smoke-Filled Home

DEAN P. JOHNSON

Dean Johnson teaches English at Camden Academy Charter School and is an adjunct professor at Rowan University in Glassboro, New Jersey. This essay appeared in the Los Angeles Times.

1   I half smiled when I heard the report about a Virginia woman who was sentenced to 10 days in jail for smoking in the presence of her children.

2   That's because my parents smoked.

3   Every night after dinner, my mother and father would lounge on the couch and put a match to a cigarette.

4   I remember watching them and feeling a little envious. It was like they were having another dessert. They seemed to enjoy it so thoroughly, and they looked so good doing it too.

5   They are young in this memory, their hair still dark, their faces still smooth, their bodies slender and strong. I remember sitting on the floor, just watching them, anxious for the day when I would be allowed to smoke.

6   We had ashtrays all through the house. The good ones were made of thick green or golden-bronze glass. There was a plastic one in the bathroom that sat on the back of the toilet or sometimes on the rim of the sink next to where we kept our toothbrushes. We even had a large ashtray with a fancy J on it, like a royal stamp. Whenever my father jinked his ash, his Army ring banged against the glass ashtray, making a tinkling sound and creating the illusion that the cigarette itself could chime.

7   I mostly enjoyed Sunday afternoons when my father would sit on the floor in front of the television, lean against the footstool and watch whatever sport happened to be in season. He would fix himself a tray of peanuts in the shell; a bottle of beer; a fresh, stiff pack of cigarettes and an ashtray.

8   I would often sit next to him with a bottle of soda and pretzel sticks that I would pretend were cigarettes.

9   There was a sunbeam that would slant through the living room window in the afternoon, slicing through the smoke that was always there. I loved watching the minuscule particles in a hazy spotlight, dancing in wild splendor.

10   Once, when no one was looking, I took two cigarettes from my dad's pack. My best friend Curt and I ran down into the woods and lighted them up. The menthol taste was so offensive to us that we could not get beyond a few puffs. "Let's try my dad's," Curt suggested, and he pulled out two regular cigarettes.

11   "Mmmmm, now that's a cigarette," I said.

12   Curt and I continued sneaking cigarettes from his dad as often as possible.

13   We even, upon occasion, bought our own packs. Because both of our fathers used to send us to the store to pick up a pack of cigarettes for them, like our moms would send us for a loaf of bread, it was easy and there were never any questions asked.

14   When I was in sixth grade, my mother stopped smoking. She told my brothers and me that it was a nasty habit. "But Dad smokes," we said. "It's bad for him too," she said.

15   I never remember seeing my mother with a cigarette in her hand again.

16   My father continued smoking—one to two packs a day. I smoked off and on from about the fifth grade through college.

17   When my father died of bladder cancer at the age of 56, it was clear that his smoking was a direct cause of his demise. The nicotine concentrates in the bladder, the doctors said, bathing the organ in carcinogens.

18   When my mother died of lung cancer at 56, only 17 months after my father, it was clear that my father's smoking was a direct cause of her early demise as well. Secondhand smoke, the doctors explained, is often more toxic because it is unfiltered.

19   The most beautiful smoke that balleted through the air—plié, pirouette and sissonne—ribboning with elegance in certain slants of light on Sunday afternoons was that unfiltered smoke that danced into my mother, my brothers and me from the warm, glowing tip of my father's cigarettes.

20   Ten days in jail for smoking around one's own children may seem like a severe punishment, but it just may be what it will take to beat an early death sentence.

Understanding the Content

Feel free to reread all or parts of the selection to answer the following questions.

1. What happened when Johnson and his friend smoked some of Johnson's father's cigarettes?

2. When did Johnson's mother stop smoking? What was her reason?

3. What was the cause of Dean Johnson's father's death? His mother's?

4. What was the punishment, according to Johnson, for the Virginia woman who smoked in the presence of her children?

Looking at Structure and Style

1. What pattern organizes the details of paragraphs 6–10?

2. What is the thesis statement of this selection? Write it in your own words.

3. What is the author's purpose in including the memory of his parents smoking in paragraphs 4 and 5?

4. The author uses some very descriptive words and phrases to describe his parents' smoking habit. Why do you think that is?

Evaluating the Author's Viewpoints

1. What does Johnson think of the punishment given to the Virginia woman for smoking in front of her children? Did he think the punishment was just or unjust? Do you agree?

2. Can you infer anything about how Johnson feels about people who smoke? Or, more specifically, about people who smoke in front of their children?

3. Do you think that Johnson's feelings toward smoking and smokers have changed over the years? How can you tell?

Pursuing Possible Essay Topics

1. What do you think of the punishment for the Virginia woman who smoked in front of her children? Do you feel that her punishment was just or unjust? Write an essay defending your position.

2. With a classmate, take both sides of the smoking argument—one of you in favor of smoking, one against. Discuss the various issues associated with smoking—the problem of secondhand smoke and its effects on nonsmokers, for example—and then write an essay in which you explore both sides of the debate.

3. Go online and do some research to find out the effects of smoking on one's health. Write an essay in which you detail what you learned.

4. Brainstorm or freewrite on one or more of the following:
   a. smoking
   b. secondhand smoke
   c. social concerns
   d. long-term health effects of smoking

5. Ignore the topics above and find a topic related to a social concern. Write an essay about it.

Preparing to Read

Take a minute or two to look over the following reading selection. Note the title and the author, read the first paragraph, and check the essay's length. Make certain you have the time now to read it carefully and to do the exercises that follow it. Then, in the spaces provided, answer the following questions.

1. What does the title tell you about this essay? _____

   _____

2. What do you think the author's viewpoint will be on trucks? _____

   _____

Vocabulary

Good comprehension of what you are about to read depends upon your understanding of the words below. The number following each word refers to the paragraph where it is used.

sneer (3) a scornful facial expression

correlated (8) brought into reciprocal relation

emissions (13) things discharged into the air; pollutants

Shut Up About My Truck

ACE ATKINS

Ace Atkins is a former staff reporter for the Tampa Tribune *and a Pulitzer Prize nominee. He currently writes novels and is a visiting professor in journalism at the University of Mississippi. The following article appeared in* Outside Magazine.

1   Picture this: You're at a stoplight, feeling smug in your new Prius, when a big Ford F-150 rumbles up. A large, scruffy guy in a baseball hat is behind the wheel, clearly enjoying his gas-guzzling V-8 engine, four-wheel drive, and oversize mud tires. You notice the tag: He's from Mississippi. Oh, great, you think—a red-stater. The son of a bitch probably never even saw *An Inconvenient Truth* and tunes in to Fox News between reruns of *Walker, Texas Ranger.*

2   Of course, the guy in the Prius may not be you. But the guy in the F-150 is definitely me—although, for the record, I don't watch Fox and I prefer the dearly departed *Deadwood* to Chuck Norris. And, yes,

on this page of this environmentally aware magazine, I'm here to declare that I don't feel bad about driving my truck. Not a bit. In fact, I love my truck. I love the power of the engine, the durable construction, and the way my 1-ELVIS license plate (proudly purchased at Graceland) looks above the front bumper.

3   But I also care a lot about the health of the planet. So let's talk about that sneer you're wearing when you see me on the road. When you do this, I'm reminded of the immortal words of Mississippi native Bo Diddley: "Before you accuse me, take a look at yourself."

4   Does your life match your ride?

5   I'm a writer by profession, but I own a farm and often haul hay and feed from the local co-op. I drive mainly on rural roads—some unpaved—where a quick thunderstorm can strand most cars. My wife and I grow much of our food, shunning chemicals for manure from a nearby pasture. What we don't grow, we try to buy at a farmers' market less than a mile up the road or at our local butcher and baker. We also run a dog-rescue group, transporting animals in large crates that would mean multiple trips in a smaller truck.

6   Now, to you. You drive an eco-friendly gas sipper. That's great. But after you park it, then what? Maybe you're a frequent business traveler, reading this on a plane. Did you know that the average commercial flight in the U.S. burns more than 22 gallons per passenger?

7   Lucky me; I work at home.

8   Speaking of homes, how big is yours? In the 1970s, the average new American house was 1,700 square feet. Today it's almost 2,500, and many homes are bigger than 3,000, which sounds great until you consider that household energy use is directly correlated with size.

9   I live in an 1,800 square-foot house built more than a century ago to withstand long summers of 100-degree heat and 80 percent humidity. Thanks to high ceilings, shade trees, and good ventilation, we use a window air-conditioning unit only at the hottest time in the afternoon. In the winter, we use sweaters, hats, and extra blankets to get through the coldest days.

10   Maybe your house has a nice TV room, where you watch the Sundance Channel's *The Green* on a sweet flat-screen—which, by the way, probably uses three times more juice than my old television. And that doesn't include TiVos, DVD players, Xboxes, computers, and chargers for cell phones and miscellaneous iThings. These "vampire" energy suckers use up to 600 million watts every day across the United States.

11   I read a lot of books.

12   Finally, since you're reading *Outside,* I bet you're careful to eat healthy. But many of you can't grow anything yourself, since tilling up your yard for a garden might bring on the wrath of the homeowners association. Too bad, since a recent study done at the University of

Alberta says that most of the environmental benefit of organic food disappears by the time it reaches your local supermarket.

13   I realize that not everyone can live the way I do—abandoning McMansions and high-tech toys to go rustic in the hills of north Mississippi. But as we roll together into an uncertain future, try to keep things in perspective. Contrary to the current fad, you don't become a better planetary citizen simply by investing in a more fuel-efficient car. That macrobiotic sushi wrap you just ate *may* have generated more emissions than my tailpipe did this week. And we're all entitled to a guilty pleasure or two—my truck, your flat-screen—as long as we do something to pay it back.

14   I work hard at doing just that. Do you?

Understanding the Content

Feel free to reread all or parts of the selection to answer the following questions.

1. What kind of car does Ace Atkins drive? Why?

2. How does Ace Atkins feel about his vehicle's impact on the planet? What, if anything, does he do to offset its impact?

3. Does Atkins's "life match his ride," in your opinion, based on the information he provides?

4. How big is the average American home today, according to Atkins? How has that changed since the 1970s?

Looking at Structure and Style

1. Rewrite the author's thesis in your own words.

2. What is the purpose of paragraph 5? Its relation to paragraph 6?

3. Does the author's use of outside sources, including relevant studies and statistics, support his thesis effectively? List all of the information that Atkins includes to support his thesis and then answer the question.

4. Is paragraph 14 an effective concluding paragraph, in your opinion? If you don't think so, rewrite the conclusion in your own words.

5. List all of the examples that Atkins gives which he thinks allow him to have a "guilty pleasure or two." Does he give enough examples, in your opinion?

Evaluating the Author's Viewpoint

1. Is Atkins mostly objective or subjective when approaching his subject? Explain.

2. What is the author's tone throughout this essay? His attitude toward his subject? How can you tell?

3. Did your opinion of Atkins change while you were reading the essay? If so, describe.

4. Has Atkins put forth an effective and credible argument for his use of a big truck to get around? Why or why not?

5. What can you infer about how Atkins feels about people who drive "gas-sippers"?

Pursuing Possible Essay Topics

1. Do you think it is acceptable to drive a gas-guzzling truck if you grow your own food and reduce your "carbon footprint" in other ways? In other words, do you agree or disagree with Atkins? Why or why not? Write an essay discussing your viewpoint.

2. Does "your life match your ride"? Write an essay either agreeing or disagreeing with this statement.

3. With a classmate, discuss how you could live a more energy-efficient life. When you're done, write an essay summarizing the points of your discussion.

4. Brainstorm or freewrite on one or more of the following topics:

   a. American dependence on foreign oil

   b. energy efficiency

   c. your carbon footprint

   d. McMansions

   e. organic food

5. Have another social concern that you want to write about? Think of a topic on your own on the subject of a social concern and write an essay.

Preparing to Read

Take a minute or two to look over the following reading selection. Note the title and the author, read the opening paragraph, and check the essay's length. Make certain you have the time now to read it carefully and to do the exercises that follow it. Then, in the spaces provided, answer the following questions.

1. From the title, what do you think this essay will be about? _____

_____

2. After reading the first paragraph, is the essay about what you thought? _____

_____

3. How does the author feel about her subject matter? _____

_____

Vocabulary

Good comprehension of what you are about to read depends upon your understanding of the words below. The number following each word refers to the paragraph where it is used.

flourished (2) prospered, thrived, benefited

argot (3) slang, jargon

supplicants (4) beggars

dovetailed (5) combined or connected into a unified whole

contingent (6) an assembled, representative group

bureaucratic (6) managerial, central

Our Tired, Our Poor, Our Kids

Anna Quindlen

Anna Quindlen is a Pulitzer Prize-winning journalist and bestselling author, having written five novels—including Blessings, Object Lessons, *and* One True Thing, *to name a few—and six nonfiction books. She currently writes the "The Last Word" column every other week in* Newsweek, *where the following essay was originally published.*

1   Six people live here, in a room the size of the master bedroom in a modest suburban house. Trundles, bunk beds, dressers side by side stacked with toys, clothes, boxes, in tidy claustrophobic clutter. One woman, five children. The baby was born in a shelter. The older kids can't wait to get out of this one. Everyone gets up at 6 A.M., the little ones to go to day care, the others to school. Their mother goes out to look for an apartment when she's not going to drug-treatment meetings. "For what they pay for me to stay in a shelter I could have lived in the Hamptons," Sharanda says.

2   Here is the parallel universe that has flourished while the more fortunate were rewarding themselves for the stock split with SUVs and home additions. There is a boom market in homelessness. But these are not the men on the streets of San Francisco holding out cardboard signs to the tourists. They are children, hundreds of thousands of them, twice as likely to repeat a grade or be hospitalized and four times as likely to go hungry as the kids with a roof over their heads. Twenty years ago New York City provided emergency shelter for just under a thousand families a day; last month it had to find spaces for 10,000 children on a given night. Not since the Great Depression have this many babies, toddlers and kids had no place like home.

3   Three mothers sit in the living room of a temporary residence called Casa Rita in the Bronx and speak of this in the argot of poverty. "The landlord don't call back when they hear you got EARP," says Rosie, EARP being the Emergency Assistance Rehousing Program. "You get priority for Section 8 if you're in a shelter," says Edna, which means federal housing programs will put you higher on the list. Edna has four kids, three in foster care; she arrived at Casa Rita, she says, "with two bags and a baby." Rosie has three, they share a bathroom down the hall with two other families. Sharanda's five range in age from 13 to just over a year. Her eldest was put in the wrong grade when he changed schools. "He's humiliated, living here," his mother says.

4   All three women are anxious to move on, although they appreciate this place, where they can get shelter, get sober and keep their kids at the same time. They remember the Emergency Assistance Unit, the city office that is the gateway to the system, where hundreds of families sit every day surrounded by their bags, where children sleep on benches until they are shuffled off dull-eyed for one night in a shelter or a motel, only to return as supplicants again the next day.

5   In another world middle-class Americans have embraced new-home starts, the stock market and the Gap. But in the world of these displaced families, problems ignored or fumbled or unforeseen during this great period of prosperity have dovetailed into an enormous subculture of children who think that only rich people have their own

bedrooms. Twenty years ago, when the story of the homeless in America became a staple of news reporting, the solution was presented as a simple one: affordable housing. That's still true, now more than ever. Two years ago the National Low Income Housing Coalition calculated that the hourly income necessary to afford the average two-bedroom apartment was around $12. That's more than twice the minimum wage.

6   The result is that in many cities police officers and teachers cannot afford to live where they work, that in Las Vegas old motels provide housing for casino employees, that in shelters now there is a contingent of working poor who get up off their cots and go off to their jobs. The result is that if you are evicted for falling behind on your rent, if there is a bureaucratic foul-up in your welfare check or the factory in which you work shuts down, the chances of finding another place to live are very small indeed. You're one understanding relative, one paycheck, one second chance from the street. And so are your kids.

7   So-called welfare reform, which emphasizes cutbacks and make-work, has played a part in all this. A study done in San Diego in 1998 found that a third of homeless families had recently had benefits terminated or reduced, and that most said that was how they had wound up on the street. Drugs, alcohol and domestic abuse also land mothers with kids in the shelter system or lead them to hand their children over to relatives or foster homes. Today the average homeless woman is younger than ever before, may have been in foster care or in shelters herself and so considers a chaotic childhood the norm. Many never finished high school, and have never held a job.

8   Ralth Nunez, who runs the organization Homes for the Homeless, says that all this calls for new attitudes. "People don't like to hear it, but shelters are going to be the low-income housing of the future," he says. "So how do we enrich the experience and use the system to provide job training and education?" Bonnie Stone of Women in Need, which has eight other residences along with Casa Rita, says, "We're pouring everything we've got into the nine months most of them are here—nutrition, treatment, budgeting. By the time they leave, they have a subsidized apartment, day care and, hopefully, some life skills they didn't have before."

9   But these organizations are rafts in a rising river of need that has roared through this country without most of us ever even knowing. So now you know. There are hundreds of thousands of little nomads in America, sleeping in the back of cars, on floors in welfare offices or in shelters five to a room. What would it mean, to spend your childhood drifting from one strange bed to another, waking in the morning to try to figure out where you'd landed today, without those things that confer security and happiness: a familiar picture on the wall, a

certain slant of light through a curtained window? "Give me your tired, your poor," it says on the base of the Statue of Liberty, to welcome foreigners. Oh, but they are already here, the small refugees from the ruin of the American dream, even if you cannot see them.

Understanding the Content

Feel free to reread all or parts of the selection to answer the following questions.

1. What is the "parallel universe" that Quindlen refers to in paragraph 2?

2. According to Quindlen, when was the last time in American history that so many "babies, toddlers and kids had no place like home" (2)?

3. According to the author, what is the result of the high cost of housing in this country?

4. Why does Anna Quindlen refer to shelters with programs for the homeless, such as Women in Need as "rafts in a rising river of need" (9)?

5. How long do women generally stay at Casa Rita, according to Bonnie Stone? What does the shelter hope to provide during that time?

Looking at Structure and Style

1. What is Quindlen's thesis? Is it stated or implied? If stated, where?

2. What sources does Anna Quindlen use to support her thesis? Are they sound sources? Why or why not?

3. How does the author compare and contrast middle-class Americans with the homeless? What examples of how both sides live in society does she use to show the disparity between the two groups?

4. What is the purpose of paragraph 1?

5. What is the purpose of paragraphs 5 and 6?

6. What reasons does the author give to explain how mothers with kids end up in the shelter system?

7. What effect does homelessness have on children, according to Anna Quindlen? List the effects she mentions in her essay.

Evaluating the Author's Viewpoints

1. How does the author view welfare reform? How can you tell?

2. What is Anna Quindlen's attitude toward homelessness?

3. What does the author want you to know about homeless people, and especially homeless children, in America? Which paragraph best summarizes the information that Quindlen wants you to take away from this essay?

4. How does the author describe the typical homeless woman?

Pursuing Possible Essay Topics

1. Write an essay discussing how you feel about the problem of homelessness in America.

2. What, if anything, do you think the government should do to help homeless people in America? Write an essay discussing your viewpoint.

3. Write an essay outlining what you think the women living in the shelter, as described by Anna Quindlen, need to do to avoid becoming homeless again.

4. What effects do you think homelessness has on children? What do you think is the worst lasting effect that homelessness has on an individual child?

5. Did this essay make you feel more sympathetic, less sympathetic, or about the same about the problem of homelessness? Write an essay discussing your reaction to this selection by Anna Quindlen.

6. Brainstorm or freewrite on the topic of homelessness.

7. Find your own topic about homelessness or homeless children and write an essay about it.

Preparing to Read

Take a minute or two to look over the following reading selection. Note the title and the author, read the first paragraph, and check the essay's length. Make certain you have the time now to read it carefully and to do the exercises that follow it. Then, in the spaces provided, answer the following questions.

1. What does the title tell you about this essay? _____

   _____

2. What do you think this essay will be about? _____

   _____

3. Based on your reading of the first paragraph, how do you think the author

   will define the term "salad bowl"? Why? _____

   _____

Vocabulary

Good comprehension of what you are about to read depends upon your understanding of the words below. The number following each word refers to the paragraph where it is used.

platoon (2) a subdivision of a company or troops consisting of two or more units, overseen by a lieutenant

trumped (3) a highly-valued resource or advantage

tenet (3) a doctrine or principle held as truth

fodder (4) a resource that is in demand and in abundant supply

deferments (7) official postponement of military service

protracted (8) long and drawn out

Why We Need a Draft

CPL. MARK FINELLI

Mark Finelli is an inactive noncommissioned officer in the Marine Corps who fought in Iraq. The following article appeared in Newsweek.

1   "MAYBE WE WOULD HAVE ONLY LOST THOSE three instead of 13," I thought to myself on a dusty Friday in Fallujah in early November 2005. I was picking up the pieces of a truck that hours before had been blown apart by an IED, wondering why our equipment wasn't better and why three more Marines were dead. My unit, Second Battalion Second Marines, had lost 13 men in the previous two weeks—not from fire fights but from increasingly powerful roadside bombs. Just then I noticed a big vehicle—what I would later learn was called an MRAP (for Mine Resistant Ambush Protected)—driving by, one owned by a private contracting company. This thing made our truck look like a Pinto in a Ferrari showroom. It was huge, heavy, ominous, indestructible. I wanted to commandeer it. I wanted to live in it.

2   I turned to my platoon sergeant. "Why are the private companies driving around in these things and not the Marine Corps?" I asked. He looked at me and rubbed together his thumb and forefinger. An MRAP costs five times more than even the most up-armored Humvee. That's when it became clear to me that America's greatest strength—its economic might—was not fully engaged in Iraq.

3   Why not? People need a personal, vested, blood-or-money interest to maximize potential. That is why capitalism has trumped communism time and again, but it is also why private contractors in Iraq have MRAPs when Marines don't. America isn't practicing the basic tenet of capitalism on the battle field, and won't be until we reinstitute the draft. Until the wealthy have that vested interest, until the sons of senators and the upper classes are sitting in those trucks, the best gear won't be paid for on an infantryman's timetable. Eighteen months after the Marines first asked for MRAPs, the vehicles are finally being delivered though still less than half the number the Pentagon had promised for this year.

4   It's not hard to figure out who suffers. Like previous generations of soldiers, the 160,000 servicemen and -women in Iraq are abundantly unrepresented in the halls of power. As a result, they've adopted what I find to be a disturbing point of view: many don't want the draft because they believe it will ruin the military which they consider their own blue-collar fraternity. They have heard the horror stories from their dads and granddads about "spoiled" rich officers. When a politician would come on TV in the Camp Fallujah chow hall talking about Iraq, the rank-and-file reaction was always something like, "Well, I am cannon fodder to this wealthy bureaucrat who never got shot at and whose kids aren't here. But I know I am making America safer, so I'll do my job anyway."

5   The real failure of this war, the mistake that has led to all the malaise of Operation Iraqi Freedom, was the failure to reinstitute the draft on Sept. 12, 2001—something I certainly believed would happen after I ran down 61 flights of the South Tower, dodging the carnage as I made my way to the Hudson River. (At the time I worked

at the World Trade Center as an investment adviser for Morgan Stanley.) But President Bush was determined to keep the lives of nonuniformed America—the wealthiest Americans—uninterrupted by the war.

6   I assure you, no matter who wins the 2008 election, we are staying in Iraq. But with the Marine Corps and the Army severely stressed after four and a half years of combat in Iraq—equipment needs replacing, recruitment efforts are a struggle—you tell me how we're going to sustain the current force structure without a draft. The president's new war czar, Lt. Gen. Douglas Lute, essentially said as much last month, when he announced that considering the draft "makes sense."

7   I don't favor a Vietnam-style draft, where men like the current vice president could get five deferments. Such a system is ultimately counterproductive because of the acrimony it breeds. Since it allows the fortunate and, often, most talented to stay home, those who cannot get out of the draft feel marginalized, less important than the cause they are asked to die for. At the end of the day, it was this bitterness that helped fuel the massive antiwar movement that pushed Nixon to end the draft in 1973.

8   No, I am talking about a fair, universal, World War II-style draft, with the brothers and sons of future and former presidents answering the call (and, unfortunately, dying, as a Roosevelt and a Kennedy once did) on the front line. Only then will the war effort be maximized. This war needs to be more discomforting to the average American than just bad news on the tube. Democracies waging a protracted ground operation cannot win when the only people who are sacrificing are those who choose to go.

Understanding the Content

Feel free to reread all or parts of the selection to answer the following questions.

1. Why does Finelli think that the draft should be reinstated?

2. Why don't some of Finelli's fellow servicemen and -women not want the draft reinstated?

3. What is the "real failure" of the war, according to Finelli?

4. Why is the Army and Marine Corps "severely stressed" according to Finelli?

5. According to Mark Finelli, what pushed Richard Nixon to end the draft in 1973?

Looking at Structure and Style

1. What is the thesis of this essay? Is it stated or implied? If stated, where?

2. Does Finelli make a credible argument for reinstating the draft? Why or why not? Does his status as a Corporal in the Marine Corps lend his argument more or less credence, in your opinion?

3. What is the overall organizing pattern of this selection? Are there any other patterns that are used more than once? If so, what are they, in what paragraphs are they used, and why do you think Finelli incorporates them?

4. What was Finelli's purpose, in your opinion, of including paragraphs 1 and 2 in this selection? Is this effective?

5. Overall, is Finelli's approach to his subject objective or subjective? Why?

Evaluating the Author's Viewpoint

1. Why doesn't Finelli favor a "Vietnam-style draft"?

2. Do you agree or disagree with Finelli that a draft should be reinstated? Why?

3. Do you think that a draft will ruin the military, like many of the enlisted men and women feel? Why or why not?

4. Do you think that having a draft would end the war in Iraq faster or would it have no effect? Why?

5. What can you infer about how Finelli feels about people who get deferments?

Pursuing Possible Essay Topics

1. Write an essay discussing your viewpoint on the invasion of Iraq by the United States in 2003. Do you feel it was warranted?

2. Has your opinion about the war in Iraq changed or has it always been the same? If it is has changed, write an essay discussing why that is the case.

3. Has the war in Iraq changed the United States or have most people, and the society at large, been unaffected by it? Why? Write an essay discussing your viewpoint.

4. How would you feel if you were drafted to serve in Iraq or Afghanistan? With a classmate or with the class, discuss what your reaction would be if you were drafted to fight overseas.

5. Brainstorm or freewrite on one or more of the following topics:

   a. war   c. the Iraq war   e. draft deferments

   b. the cost of war   d. the draft   f. the military

6. Think about a topic on your own on the subject of social concerns and write an essay.

Preparing to Read

Take a minute or two to look over the following reading selection. Note the title and the author, read the first two paragraphs, and check the essay's length. Make certain you have the time now to read it carefully and to do the exercises that follow it. Then, in the spaces provided, answer the following questions.

1. Does the title tell you what this essay will be about? _____

   _____

2. What do you think this essay will be about? _____

   _____

3. Based on your reading of the first two paragraphs, what do you think Mark Rothschild's opinion of the "Presidential Advance Manual" will be? _____

   _____

Vocabulary

Good comprehension of what you are about to read depends upon your understanding of the words below. The number following each word refers to the paragraph where it is used.

myriad (1) numerous; numberless

dissent (12) opposition; difference of opinion

Gagging Protesters by the Manual
MATTHEW ROTHSCHILD

Matthew Rothschild graduated from Harvard University where he was the editor for the Multinational Monitor, *a magazine founded by Ralph Nader. He has also worked at* The Progressive *as an associate editor, managing editor, publisher, and since 1994, as editor. Rothschild's latest book is* You Have No Rights. *The following selection was originally published in* The Progressive.

1   So the truth comes out. After a myriad of stories about people being excluded from events where the President is speaking, now we know that the White House has a policy manual on just how to do so.

2   Called the "Presidential Advance Manual," this 103-page document from the Office of Presidential Advance lays out the parameters for how to handle protesters at events.

3   "Always be prepared for demonstrators," says the document, which is dated October 2002 and which the ACLU [American Civil Liberties Union] discovered as part of a new lawsuit.

4   In a section entitled "Preventing Demonstrators," the document says: "All Presidential events must be ticketed or accessed by a name list. This is the best method for preventing demonstrators. People who are obviously going to try to disrupt the event can be denied entrance at least to the VIP area between the stage and the main camera platform. . . . It is important to have your volunteers at a checkpoint before the Magnetometers in order to stop a demonstrator from getting into the event. Look for signs they may be carrying, and if need be, have volunteers check for folded cloth signs that demonstrators may be bringing."

5   In another section, entitled "Preparing for Demonstrators," the document makes clear that the intention is to deprive protesters of the right to be seen or heard by the President: "As always, work with the Secret Service and have them ask the local police department to designate a protest area where demonstrators can be placed, preferably not in view of the event site or motorcade route."

6   The document also recommends forming "rally squads" to drown out protesters or block their signs. It states: "These squads should be instructed always to look for demonstrators. The rally squad's task is to use their signs and banners as shields between the demonstrators and the main press platform. If the demonstrators are yelling, rally squads can begin and lead supportive chants to drown out the protestors (USA!, USA!, USA!). As a last resort, security should remove the demonstrators from the event site."

7   The document offered advice on how to recruit members for such squads: "The rally squads can include, but are not limited to, college/young Republican organizations, local athletic teams, and fraternities/sororities."

8   The document does contain a warning in bold and underlined, however: "Remember—avoid physical contact with demonstrators!" It also advises the advance team to make sure that whatever action is taken to drown out the demonstrators does not "cause more negative publicity than if the demonstrators were simply left alone."

9   The ACLU obtained this document as part of a lawsuit against Gregory Jenkins, who was director of the White House Office of Presidential Advance. Bringing the suit are two couples that were booted from Presidential events.

10   Jeffrey Rank and Nicole Rank were arrested for protesting a Bush event at the West Virginia capitol on July 4, 2004. They were arrested

on the capitol grounds for wearing T-shirts that said, "Love America, Hate Bush," and "Regime Change Starts at Home." The front of their T-shirts had the word Bush with a line drawn through it.

11   Leslie Weise and Alex Young were hoping to attend a visit Bush made to Denver on March 21, 2005, where he was speaking on Social Security. Weise had a bumper sticker on her car that said, "No More Blood for Oil." That's why she and Young were kicked out of the Wings over the Rockies Air and Space Museum before Bush spoke.

12   "When the President attends a public event, the First Amendment does not allow him to speak or listen only to those who agree with him," says Arthur Spitzer, legal director of the ACLU of the National Capital Area. "Public places cannot be 'cleansed' of all dissent just to make the President look popular."

Understanding the Content

Feel free to reread all or parts of the selection to answer the following questions.

1. What is the purpose of the "Presidential Advance Manual"?

2. What has the ACLU done with the information they were given about the "Presidential Advance Manual"?

3. What are two things mentioned in the manual that people involved in planning Presidential appearances are instructed to do if confronted with demonstrators or think that demonstrators will be at an event?

4. What were Jeffrey Rank and Nicole Rank arrested for?

5. According to the selection, what does the manual define as "rally squads"? How are rally squads recruited?

Looking at Structure and Style

1. What is Rothschild's thesis? If it is not stated, rewrite it in your own words. If it is stated, identify where it is stated in the essay.

2. What is Rothschild's tone in this essay?

3. What is Rothschild's attitude toward his subject? How can you tell?

4. What is the relation of paragraphs 9–11 to the rest of this essay?

5. What was the author's purpose in writing this essay?

Evaluating the Author's Viewpoint

1. Is Matthew Rothschild mostly objective or subjective when approaching his subject? Does Rothschild exhibit any bias in this essay? Explain.

2. What can you infer about how Rothschild feels about the "Presidential Advance Manual"? About the ACLU and their lawsuit?

3. What can you infer about how Rothschild feels about demonstrators showing up at Presidential events? Rally squads?

Pursuing Possible Essay Topics

1. Do you think that demonstrators should be allowed at events where the President is speaking? Why or why not? Write an essay discussing your viewpoint.

2. Is there an issue about which you are passionate? Would you demonstrate or protest in order to be heard on this issue? If so, what is it? Write an essay about it.

3. What do you think about the "Presidential Advance Manual" and the things it recommends for handling demonstrators? Discuss your opinion with a classmate or with the entire class.

4. Brainstorm or freewrite on one or more of the following topics:

   a. freedom of speech

   b. the ACLU

   c. politics

   d. political repression

   e. government in the United States

5. Think about a social concern that troubles you or that is interesting to you and write an essay.

Opposing Viewpoints on the Effects of Binge Drinking

Reports of "binge drinking," particularly among college students, have been prevalent in the news. A Harvard Study of 119 colleges shows 44% of U.S. college students engaged in binge drinking during the two weeks before the survey. It is considered "binge drinking" when a male drinks 5 or more drinks in a row and when a woman downs 4 or more drinks in a row. According to the study, students more likely to binge drink are white, age 23 or younger, and are residents of a fraternity or sorority. If they were binge drinkers in high school, they were three times more likely to binge in college. Over half the binge drinkers, almost one in four students, were frequent binge drinkers, that is, they binged three or more times in a two-week period, while one in five students reported abstaining from drinking alcohol. The next two essays differ in their viewpoints on the dangers of binge drinking.

Preparing to Read

Take a minute or two to look over the following reading selection. Note the title and the author, read the first two paragraphs, and check the essay's length. Make certain you have the time now to read it carefully and to do the exercises that follow it. Then, in the spaces provided, answer the following questions.

1. What do you think is the subject of this essay? _____

_____

2. What opinion do you think Lis Wiehl holds on this issue? _____

_____

3. What is your reaction to the opening paragraph? _____

_____

Vocabulary

Good comprehension of what you are about to read depends upon your understanding of the words below. The number following each word refers to the paragraph where it is used.

detrimental (8) causing damage or harm

alleviate (10) reducing severity

Bottomless Drinking Ban on College Campuses

LIS WIEHL

Lis Wiehl is a FOX News Channel legal analyst. She also serves as a legal commentator on National Public Radio's "All Things Considered." She is the author of "The 51% Minority—How Women Still Are Not Equal and What You Can Do about It." The following essay is from the Web site "LIS ON LAW," www.foxnews.com.

1   College is a time of great pride and happiness for most kids and parents. Parents are excited that their children have gotten into a university and the teens are excited to embark on their first adventure away from the nest. College gives teens the freedom they have

been craving and gives parents that sense of self satisfaction that they raised a child on the path to success. The four glorious years of college are supposed to mold our children to become the future of our country. But not one cocktail at a time!

2   Nationally, college has come to symbolize frat parties and under-age drinking. After many recent deaths from alcohol poisoning at several universities, Minnesota is the first state to ban limitless drinking at college bars. The state may be the pioneer we need to prevent our children from drinking themselves into destruction.

3   Move over "land of 10,000 lakes," because Minnesota's new nick-name is going to be a lot dryer than that! A new law, which went into effect January 1 of this year, has effectively eliminated all "bottomless drinking" specials at bars, as well as all drinking specials after 11 P.M. That means that no longer can bars offer $20 all you can drink for the entire night, encouraging kids to drink. After the deaths of three col-lege students linked to alcohol in the past four months, Minnesota has put its collective foot down. Minnesota Congressman Lanning said, "All kinds of bad things happen to students as a result of binge drinking." Duh!

4   Bar owners disagree with this policy—not a shock-tail considering the business they have to lose. They responded by saying the ban is actually a bad thing. "You're just going to be pushing them to the house parties, the "keggers," to a totally unsupervised area," stated a Minnesota bar owner. While they do have a point, this mother of two still thinks their financial interests may outweigh their true concern for our childrens' [sic] safety.

5   But don't worry folks, bar owners have found ways around the bot-tomless drinking ban. Bars now simply offer $1 beers or $2 mixed drinks before 11 P.M.—effectively allowing students on a short budget to still drink like fish. Many are even worried that these restrictions may even encourage MORE drinking, in part because students are going to want to drink as much as they can before the deals end. So, is there a solution to our children's binge drinking problem? It doesn't look like frat parties will be serving Shirley Temples anytime soon.

6   You may be surprised to hear about a new study that showed Minnesota is home to more binge drinkers than almost anywhere in the nation, other states are not far behind. Nationally, a Harvard School of Public Health study found that 44 percent of collegians binge drink. The study also found that college may be the catalyst in these children's chain reaction into drinking so heavily. The col-lege graduation age, 21, has even been found to be the peak age for binge drinking across the country. To show how startling the college binge drinking epidemic is, would you be surprised to learn that 12,000,000 undergraduates drink four billion cans of beer every year? I sure was!

7   The long term risks of alcohol include everything from liver damage, to pancreatitis, to certain cancers, and even literal shrinkage of the brain. Not to mention the short term effects, alcohol poisoning and immediate death! Three Minnesota college students found out the hard way. In a $115 billion industry in the United States alone, it's not unusual for us parents to feel like its [sic] David vs. Goliath. Don't panic though, because we can help!

8   Although parents cannot physically be there every time our child is offered a drink, we can help to shape their decision making process. Parents are responsible for their children's upbringing up until they are 18, or go to college. The pressures to binge drinking can be avoided somewhat if we educate our children. Actively educating our children on the detrimental effects of alcohol could lead to a healthier, and hopefully dryer, solution.

9   And alcohol should not be some secret, mysterious thing that adults get to do! Something we don't talk about. Parents, your teens (even the honor students) have probably at least had an opportunity to try alcohol. Teaching kids about sex educates them about the consequences—alcohol-Ed if you will—should eliminate the mystery of drinking, and teach them the consequences of that choice.

10   Explaining to our children the dangers of alcohol in an accurate, caring, and unbiased way, could alleviate at least some of our worries. So, when talking to your kids be honest, be informative, and be straightforward. After all, binge drinking and college are not a good mix.

Understanding the Content

Feel free to reread all or parts of the selection to answer the following questions.

1. Which is the first state to ban limitless drinking at college bars and why, according to Lis Wiehl?

2. What is "bottomless drinking"?

3. How do bar owners feel about the ban on bottomless drinking? How do they plan to work around the ban?

4. What percentage of collegians binge drink?

5. What are the long-term risks associated with alcohol abuse? The short-term effects?

Looking at Structure and Style

1. Rewrite the thesis statement of this essay in your own words.

2. How does Wiehl's use of punctuation in this essay reveal her attitude toward her subject?

3. Does Wiehl use enough effective and credible evidence to support her thesis? List the pieces of evidence she uses and evaluate their effectiveness.

4. What is the organizing pattern used in paragraph 4? What is its relation to paragraph 3?

5. What is the purpose of including paragraph 7? What is its relation to the rest of the essay?

6. What was Wiehl's overall purpose in writing this essay?

Evaluating the Author's Viewpoint

1. What does Wiehl suggest that parents do to educate kids about alcohol?

2. What does Wiehl think about Minnesota's plan to ban "bottomless drinking"?

3. What can you infer about how Wiehl thinks about bar owners in Minnesota and their plans to deal with the ban?

4. What is Wiehl's tone in this essay? Her attitude toward the subject of binge drinking? Toward the Minnesota ban?

Pursuing Possible Essay Topics

Wait until after you have read the following essay, "Binge Drinking Is a Normal Impulse," by Jennie Bristow, before attempting to write an essay related to the issue of binge drinking.

Preparing to Read

Take a minute or two to look over the following reading selection. Note the title and the author, read the first two paragraphs, and check the essay's length. Make certain you have the time now to read it carefully and to do the exercises that follow it. Then, in the spaces provided, answer the following questions.

1. What do you think is the subject of this essay? _____

_____

2. What opinion do you think Jennie Bristow holds on this issue? _____

_____

3. What is your reaction to the first two paragraphs? _____

_____

Vocabulary

Good comprehension of what you are about to read depends upon your understanding of the words below. The number following each word refers to the paragraph where it is used.

liberalized (1) made more liberal or generous

dystopia (2) an imaginary place in which things are extremely bad

out on the lash (2) go out drinking or carousing

banal (3) commonplace and predictable

echelons (4) levels of hierarchy

feckless (5) feeble; careless or irresponsible

docilely (9) meekly

in thrall to (10) under the control of; under the influence of

Binge Drinking Is a Normal Impulse

JENNIE BRISTOW

Jennie Bristow is a member of the Libertarian LM Group, a loose collection of individuals and organizations characterized by an anti-environmentalist, apparently libertarian ideology and common heritage extending back to the British far-left

movement of the early 1980s. She is the commissioning editor of "Spiked Online," *and has also written for* Living Marxism *and* Novo, *its German sister publication.*

1   When Britain liberalized alcohol laws at the beginning of 2005, public officials worried that binge drinking would become more prevalent. The fear seemed unreasonable: despite governmental warnings about alcohol abuse, British citizens were living longer and healthier lives than ever. The warnings, then, are less representative of a real threat than of a contemporary obsession with micro-managing society. A carefree drunk, emotional, talkative, and happy-go-lucky, conflicts with these idealized values. An occasional binge, however, is a good way for people to lose their inhibitions and escape—for a short time—from their everyday lives.

2   What will British society look like under New Labour's proposed regime of licensing 24-hour drinking? Will it be the civilised café society of the political elite's dreams, where people sit around leisurely sipping from glasses of Chablis after a night at the theatre, or the anti-social dystopia of its nightmares, where teenagers spend all night out on the lash and schooldays snoozing at their desks?

3   Given the annual fad for debating the new licensing laws while doing nothing to change them, we may well never know. (Though a grasp of real life should tell us that the upshot will be neither dream nor nightmare, but really quite banal.) But the ongoing debate about the pros and cons of freeing pubs from their current 11 P.M. shutdown is a sobering reflection on the kind of society we live in today—one that is too passionless, uptight and risk-averse even to appreciate the importance of getting drunk.

4   Since the new year began, all 13 days ago [January 2005], we've been treated to headlined comments by medics, judges, politicians and policeman about the impact of the new licensing laws on individual health and public order. 'Binge drinking' (defined as more than two pints, and that's for the men) and 'anti-social behaviour' (defined as pretty much anything the authorities don't like) have become buzzwords in the phoney debate about whether it's better to have 11 P.M. curfews or bars with no happy hours that stay open all hours but encourage their clients to take a pledge of sobriety. While the upper echelons of state and society wrangle over the best way of regulating drinking, agreement is taken for granted on the key goal: Drunkenness Reduction. To which somebody, surely, has to ask—why?

5   What is it about getting drunk that today's society finds so hard to handle? It isn't as though we live in a nation of feckless alcoholics, too sodden to pour themselves out of bed and into work in the morning. For all the government's dire warnings about rising rates of liver cirrhosis and general alcohol-related health calamities, we should remember (again) that in reality, we are living longer and healthier lives than ever before.

6   And Britain 2005 is hardly a hotbed of inebriated violence. On 11 January [2005], a judge grabbed the headlines by attacking legalised 24-hour drinking on the grounds that easy access to alcohol is breeding 'urban savages' and turning town centres into no-go areas. The basis for his claim? That he was sentencing three men convicted of vicious assaults while out drinking and drug-taking after the European Championships, which left one of their victims in a coma. Maybe this judge knows more about town centres and urban savagery than the rest of us—even so, he surely must believe that behaviour like that above is the exception rather than the rule.

Losing Our Inhibitions

7   What we do have is a society in which sometimes, and for a variety of reasons, people like to get drink. Not because they think that wine goes better with dinner than Ribena [a British fruit drink]; not because they want to relax a little after a hard day's white-collar work; not because they believe the studies about a glass of red being good for their hearts (but two pints of lager being very bad indeed); but because they want to get off the plane of existence that is normal, humdrum, everyday life, and into that parallel universe of inebriation. What's wrong with doing that once in a while? Nothing. Indeed, there is a good deal that is very right about it.

8   We know that, every now and then, one very important reason to drink is to get drunk.

9   The key feature of alcohol, and the one that most worries today's uptight political class, is that it makes people lose their inhibitions. They become more aggressive, or more vulnerable to date-raping predators; they stop caring about what is good for their health or personal finances; they talk to strangers and pick arguments with their friends. In one night down the pub, these people, docilely on-message by day, manage to cock a snook at every principle of our carefully managed Therapeutic Society. Emotions rage, passions roar, and if it all ends in tears they are the messy, uncontrolled ones of the drunkard rather than the controlled closures of the counselling room. And for what? So they can wake up with a pounding hangover and a shiver of embarrassment, having achieved nothing more worthy than a good night out.

10   It is not the consequences of drunkenness that make it a modern bogeyman, but its simple out-of-controlness. For a political class hell-bent on micro-management of all aspects of everyday life, in thrall to etiquette, suspicious of spontaneity, and living by the code of 'everything in moderation', the image of the carefree drunk is one that it cannot comprehend, still less empathise with. For the rest of us, for whom the odd bender is not a political statement but a welcome fact of life, we should resist the temptation to buy into the cult

of 'responsible drinking' and remember what we are doing in the pub in the first place.

11   Already, there are too many twentysomething women on broken detox diets crying into their alcopops about how they know they drink too much. There are too many single men staying 'just for the one' before driving home to their X-box and pizza-and-Pepsi meal deal. There is too much consensus that we need to change the licensing laws because we have a cultural 'drinking problem' (rather than simply changing the law to allow us to have a drink when we want it). There is too much no smoking at the bar, no swearing at the bar, no standing at the bar and no going to the bar too many times.

12   We know that, every now and then, one very important reason to drink is to get drunk. We know that people with lost inhibitions generally don't get raped, beaten up or bankrupt, but generally do become sexier, funnier, more honest and more sociable (even if they appeal only to other drunk people). And we know that humdrum everyday life is often better escaped from in a pub with colleagues, friends and strangers than obsessed upon over a nice bottle of wine with a therapist or mentor.

13   So let's leave the official preoccupations with when we drink, how much we drink and why we drink to the medics, judges, politicians and policemen, and carry on drinking as we choose.

Understanding the Content

Feel free to reread all or parts of the selection to answer the following questions.

1. When did Britain liberalize alcohol laws? What effect did public officials fear would be the result of this liberalization?

2. What does Jennie Bristow think that Britain will "look like under New Labour's proposed regime of licensing 24-hour drinking"?

3. What "kind of society" does Bristow think the English live in today?

4. What is the British definition of "binge drinking," according to Bristow?

5. What is the "key feature" of alcohol, according to Bristow?

6. What kind of effects does alcohol have on people, in Jennie Bristow's opinion? How is this at odds with what the government in Great Britain thinks?

Looking at Structure and Style

1. Is Jennie Bristow's thesis statement implied or stated? If stated, where? If implied, rewrite it in your own words.

2. How many reasons does Jennie Bristow give for her opposition to Great Britain's law regarding alcohol? In your viewpoint, does she provide enough? Too many? Explain.

3. What is the implied main idea in paragraph 2? Why do you think Bristow has chosen to include a paragraph made up entirely of questions? Is it effective? Why or why not?

4. Does the author include credible evidence to support her thesis, in your opinion? Why or why not?

5. What is the function of paragraph 9? What is its relation to the rest of the essay? To paragraph 12?

6. Is paragraph 13 an effective concluding paragraph? If not, write a new one summarizing the information presented in the essay.

7. The spelling of some words in Britain differs from American spelling. Can you find some examples of those differences?

Evaluating the Author's Viewpoint

1. Do you think Jennie Bristow's political views—libertarian in nature—affect her opinion on this topic? Is it clear from the essay whether or not her political affiliation has any bearing on the argument?

2. Does Jennie Bristow present an objective or subjective view on this topic? Explain.

3. Who has written a better argument regarding this topic, in your opinion: Lis Wiehl or Jennie Bristow? Why?

4. Does Jennie Bristow think there are any advantages to drinking alcohol? If so, what are they?

5. What is Bristow's tone in this essay? Her attitude toward the subject of alcohol laws? Toward the British government and lawmakers?

Pursuing Possible Essay Topics

1. Compare and contrast the two selections and their thesis statements. Which author makes a more persuasive argument? Why? Write a short essay discussing how the author who did not make as good a case could strengthen her argument.

2. Write an essay exploring your viewpoint on the topic of legislating alcohol consumption.

3. Do you think that "binge drinking is a normal impulse"? Why or why not? Write an essay discussing your viewpoint.

4. Do you think that there should be a ban on bottomless drinking on college campuses? In bars outside of campuses? Why? Write an essay discussing your opinion.

 5. With a classmate or in class, discuss these two argumentative essays and determine who you think makes a better argument. Write a brief summary of your discussion.

6. Brainstorm or freewrite on one or more of the following topics:

   a. alcohol

   b. alcoholism

   c. bottomless drinking

   d. binge drinking

   e. personal freedom

7. If you don't like these, find your own topic on a concern or social issue and write an essay.

Student Essay

Read the following narrative essay written by a student. As you read, look for answers to these questions:

1. Does the essay deal with a social concern? If so, what?

2. Does the student have a clearly stated or implied thesis? What is the thesis?

3. Does the student sound genuinely concerned about the issue discussed? Explain.

Should I Believe in God?

Amy Kimoto

1   I do not believe in God.

2   From this point on, will I receive utter closed-mindedness from you? Are my views immoral and blasphemous? Will you listen to my beliefs, my ideas, me as a person?

3   I cannot believe in something that does not exist to me. I cannot believe in God just because everybody does.

4   I was not raised in an "abnormal" household. I even went to Bible studies and prayed to God when I was younger. I know many of the stories and I have read the Bible. As I grew older, my faith faded as my many questions about God and religion grew. Now, I believe not in God but the morals he represents—the Ten Commandments: You shall not murder, you shall not commit adultery, you shall not steal, honor your father and your mother, you shall not bear false witness, and so on. I must believe in these morals for they are the basis of our society. To cast down these morals is to cast down our way of governing and, therefore, our nation. But believing in the morals of God isn't the same as believing in God.

5   The Constitution also represents our rights, our beliefs, what is right, and what is wrong. I do not worship Thomas Jefferson and beg him to forgive me. I do not pray to Benjamin Franklin. I admire what they wrote, for they are certainly brilliant, but I in no way idolize them.

6   Religion may bring sanctuary and guidance to some people, but I object to some of the ideas preached by many religions, like the concept that one religion is right and the rest are wrong. This closed-mindedness has led to many wars and disputes. I think it is absurd that all of the religions are not united, since they are derived from the same or similar basic concepts. Even though it is human nature to believe that one religion is better than another, if all religions were united, they could serve a common cause—the betterment of humankind.

7   Another instance of closed-mindedness is the intolerance of homosexuals. Daily I hear and see degradation of homosexuality. Many religions teach that this lifestyle is morally wrong and that it goes against normal society.

8   This same closed-mindedness leads society to label me as a pagan or an atheist, as society needs to put a tag on everyone. I do not call myself antireligious but I am a realist. "How do you prove that God doesn't exist?" you ask. "How do you prove that Santa Claus doesn't exist?" I counter.

9   I will believe realistically and when the existence of God is proven, I will gladly convert.

Reaction

In your journal or on a separate sheet of paper, write your reaction to the student essay. What would you tell this student about her essay?

Viewpoints on Images

Since the United States soon needs to replace its dependency on oil, it must turn to alternate sources of energy. Do some research on wind, solar, or another alternate energy source and discuss its pros and cons as a possible major energy source.

© Kirk Hirota/Getty Images

On the Net

Spend some time thinking about the pro/con selections presented by Lis Wiehl and Jennie Bristow.

Do some more research on the topic of binge drinking, particularly as it relates to college students. Get several different viewpoints on the topic and answer the following questions:

a. What sites did you visit? What information did they present on binge drinking?

b. Remember to think about the credibility of the sites you visit. Who is the author of the individual sites? Can you detect any specific bias? Do the authors of the sites use credible sources and evidence to support the information that the sites contain?

c. Did you get any new information about the effects of binge drinking that were not discussed in the two opposing viewpoints that you read in this chapter? If so, what was it?

d. See if you can find information on other schools and what they have done to deal with this problem. Consider this information as you think about your own institution.

e. Is binge drinking a problem on your college campus? If so, what steps do you think your school could take to lessen the instances of binge drinking at your school? Based on the information you got on the various Web sites you visited, draft a proposal to your school's governing body, discuss the problems associated with binge drinking, and outline the steps you think your school could take to lessen the number of incidents related to it. If you think you have credible web sources, quote them in your proposal.

CHAPTER

7

Viewpoints on Family and Marital Relationships

Focus on Family and Marital Relationships

To help you focus on the subject of this chapter, take a few minutes to prepare for the topic by prewriting on one or more of the following topics:

1. a member of your family
2. mixed racial marriages
3. one of your family's traditions
4. your family values
5. traditions that should be broken
6. gay marriage and parenting

America is made up of family groups of many diverse cultures: the Asian–American family, the Hispanic family, the black family, the European family, the Middle Eastern family, and so on. Still, despite this wide range of backgrounds, some research* suggests that there are six major qualities shared by healthy families of all races and cultures:

1. a high degree of commitment to the family group and to promoting one another's happiness and welfare

2. an appreciation of one another; making the other person feel good about himself or herself

3. good communication patterns developed through spending time talking with and listening to one another

4. a desire to spend time together in active interaction

5. a strong value system, such as that found in a religious orientation

6. an ability to deal with crises and stress in a positive manner

Few families can live up to these ideals all the time. Just as an individual must work to keep mentally and physically fit, so must family members work to keep the family mentally and physically fit. Like individuals, even strong families have problems. Sometimes families break up. And just as there are no perfect parents, so there are no perfect children. But we have the option of changing our imperfect family relationships by working to develop those six characteristics of a strong family.

The subject of family relationships is one that concerns us all, no matter what our backgrounds. The following essays reveal some varied viewpoints on this broad subject, covering such aspects as gender differences, mother love, and the effects family breakups can have. Read them to understand how others feel about family and relationships, as well as to stimulate ideas for an essay of your own.

*N. Stinnet and J. DeFrain: *Secrets of Strong Families* (Boston: Little, Brown, 1985).

Preparing to Read

Take a minute or two to look over the following reading selection. Note the title and the author, read the first paragraph, and check the essay's length. Make certain you have the time now to read it carefully and to do the exercises that follow it. Then, in the spaces provided, answer the following questions.

1. What do you think is the subject of this essay? _____

   _____

2. What does the title mean? _____

   _____

3. What is your reaction to the first paragraph? What does it tell you about Kincaid? _____

   _____

Vocabulary

Good comprehension of what you are about to read depends upon your understanding of the words below. The number following each word refers to the paragraph where it is used.

entity (4) being; the fact of existence

incarnations (4) personifications of a given abstract quality or idea

disparaged (7) belittled

progenitor (12) a direct ancestor

The Estrangement

Jamaica Kincaid

Jamaica Kincaid was born Elaine Cynthia Potter Richardson in St. John's Antigua and Barbuda. In 1973, she changed her name to Jamaica Kincaid because of her family's disapproval of her writing. Her books include Annie John, A Small Place, My Brother, Mr. Potter, *and* Among Flowers. *In 2000 she was awarded the Prix Femina Étranger for* My Brother. *Her novel,* Lucy (1990), *is a fictional account of a woman coming into adulthood in a foreign country, a situation that echoed Kincaid's own life.*

1   Three years before my mother died, I decided not to speak to her again. And why? During a conversation over the telephone, she had once again let me know that my accomplishments—becoming a responsible and independent woman—did not amount to very much, that the life I lived was nothing more than a silly show, that she truly wished me dead. I didn't disagree. I didn't tell her that it would be just about the best thing in the world not to hear this from her.

2   And so, after that conversation, I never spoke to her, said a word to her of any kind, and then she died and her death was a shock to me, not because I would miss her presence and long for it, but because I could not believe that such a presence could ever be stilled.

3   For many years and many a time, her children, of which I was the only female, wondered what would happen to her, as we wondered what would happen to us; because she seemed to us not a mother at all but a God, not a Goddess but a God.

4   How to explain in this brief space what I mean? When we were children and in need of a mother's love and care, there was no better mother to provide such an ideal entity. When we were adolescents, and embracing with adolescent certainty our various incarnations, she could see through the thinness of our efforts, she could see through the emptiness of our aspirations; when we fell apart, there she was, bringing us dinner in jail or in a hospital ward, cold compresses for our temples, or just standing above us as we lay flat on our backs in bed. That sort of mother is God.

5   I am the oldest, by 9, 11, and 13 years, of four children. My three brothers and I share only our mother; they have the same father, I have a different one. I knew their father very well, better than they did, but I did not know my own. (When I was seven months in her womb, my mother quarreled with the man with whom she had conceived me and then ran away with the money he had been saving up to establish a little business for himself. He never forgave her.) I didn't mind not knowing my real father, because in the place I am from, Antigua, when people love you, your blood relationship to them is not necessarily the most important component. My mother's husband, the father of my brothers, loved me, and his love took on the shape of a father's love: he told me about himself when he was a boy and the things he loved to do and the ways in which his life changed for better and worse, giving me some idea about how he came to be himself, my father, the father of my brothers, the person married to my mother.

6   She was a very nice person, apparently; that is what everybody said about her at her funeral. There were descriptions of her good and selfless deeds, kindnesses, generosity, testaments of her love expressed in humor. We, her children, looked at one another in

wonder then, for such a person as described was not at all known to us. The person we knew, our Mother, said horrible things to us more often than not.

7   The youngest of my three brothers died of AIDS when he was 33 years of age. In the years he spent actively dying, our mother tended to him with the greatest tenderness, a tenderness that was absent all the time before he was dying. Before he got sick, before he became afflicted with that disease, his mother, my mother too, quarreled with him and disparaged him. This was enabled by the fact that he did not know how to go off somewhere and make a home of any kind for himself. Yes, he had been unable to move out into the world, away from this woman, his mother, and become the sole possessor of his own destiny, with all the loss and gain that this implies.

The two remaining brothers and I buried her right next to him, and we were not sure we should have done that: for we didn't know then, and still don't know even now, if he wanted to spend eternity lying beside her, since we were sure we would rather be dead than spend eternity lying next to her.

8   Is this clear? It is to me right now as I write it: I would rather be dead than spend eternity with our mother! And do I really mean that when I say it? Yes, I really mean just that: after being my mother's daughter, I would rather be dead than spend eternity with her.

9   By the time my mother died, I was not only one of her four children, I had become the mother of two children: a girl and then a boy. This was bliss, my two children in love with me, and I with them. Nothing has gone wrong, as far as I can see, but tears have been shed over my not being completely enthusiastic about going to a final basketball game in a snowstorm, or saying something I should have kept in my mind's mouth. A particularly unforgivable act in my children's eyes is a book's dedication I made to them; it read: "With blind, instinctive, and confused love to Annie and Harold, who from time to time are furiously certain that the only thing standing between them and a perfect union with their mother is the garden, and from time to time, they are correct."

10   I wrote this with a feeling of overbrimming love for them, my children. I was not thinking of my own mother directly, not thinking of her at all consciously at that exact time, but then again, I am always thinking of my mother; I believe every action of a certain kind that I make is completely influenced by her, completely infused with her realness, her existence in my life.

11   I am now middle-aged (59 years of age); I not only hope to live for a very long time after this, I will be angry in eternity if this turns out not to be the case. And so in eternity will my children want to be with me? And in eternity will I, their mother, want to be with them?

12   In regard to my children, eternity is right now, and I always want to be with them. In regard to my mother, my progenitor, eternity is beyond now, and is that not forever? I will not speak to her again in person, of that I am certain, but I am not sure that I will never speak to her again. For in eternity is she in me, and are even my children speaking to her? I do not know, I do not know.

Understanding the Content

Feel free to reread all or parts of the selection to answer the following questions.

1. What was Jamaica Kincaid's relationship with her mother like? Why?

2. What was the cause of the estrangement between Kincaid and her mother?

3. Was Jamaica Kincaid's mother always difficult to be around? If not, how did she change?

4. What was Kincaid's relationship with her brothers' father? Where was her biological father?

5. What is Jamaica Kincaid's relationship with her own children?

Looking at Structure and Style

1. Rewrite the thesis statement in your own words.

2. What is the purpose of paragraph 6? Its relation to paragraph 7? Its relation to the rest of the essay?

3. What examples does Kincaid provide to illustrate her negative impression of her mother? What examples does she give to prove that her mother could also be kind?

4. How effective is Kincaid's concluding paragraph as an ending to this essay? Is it powerful enough to end an essay that is so full of personal revelation? Why or why not, in your opinion?

5. What is the purpose of paragraph 9? Why do you think Kincaid chose to include this example in this selection?

Evaluating the Author's Viewpoint

1. What can you infer about how Kincaid feels about her decision to cut herself off from her mother three years prior to her mother's death?

2. What can you infer about how Kincaid feels about the people who thought her mother was kind? Does she think that her mother was kind? Or that people didn't really know her?

3. Why was her mother's death a shock to the author?

4. How did Kincaid's brothers feel about their mother?

5. With regard to her own death, what are Kincaid's wishes? Is she clear about what she desires?

Pursuing Possible Essay Topics

1. This is a very powerful essay because of the author's honesty in discussing a subject most people wouldn't have the courage to share. With a classmate or in class, discuss your reaction to it.

2. Have you ever had a relative with whom you have had a difficult relationship? If so, discuss in a brief essay how you deal with this person and the conflict you have.

3. Do you agree or disagree with Kincaid's decision to become estranged from her mother? Why? Write an essay discussing your viewpoint.

4. Brainstorm or freewrite on one or more of the following topics:
   a. motherhood
   b. parenting
   c. children
   d. estrangement
   e. family conflict

5. Or choose a topic that you like better on the subject of family and relationships and write an essay.

Preparing to Read

Take a minute or two to look over the following reading selection. Note the title and author, read the opening paragraph (including the footnote), and check the essay's length. Make certain you have the time now to read it carefully and to do the exercises that follow it. Then, in the spaces provided, answer the following questions.

1. What will the author probably say about family? _____

_____

2. Is your family "the perfect family"? Explain. _____

_____

_____

3. How would you define "family values"? _____

_____

_____

Vocabulary

Good comprehension of what you are about to read depends upon your understanding of the words below. The number following each word refers to the paragraph where it is used.

incriminating (4) accusing, indicating fault

ministered (4) attended, took care of

welts (5) bruises, discoloration or abrasions of the skin

encrusted (7) caked, covered over

factoring out (8) excluding

The Perfect Family

ALICE HOFFMAN

Alice Hoffman is a novelist (Here on Earth, Practical Magic, Property Of, At Risk, to name a few) and a screenwriter, having been author of the original screenplay

for "Independence Day." Her short fiction and non-fiction have been published in
The New York Times, The Boston Globe Magazine, Kenyon Review, Redbook, Architectural Digest *and other magazines.*

1. When I was growing up in the 50's, there was only one sort of family, the one we watched on television every day. Right in front of us, in black and white, was everything we needed to know about family values: the neat patch of lawn, the apple tree, the mother who never once raised her voice, the three lovely children: a Princess, a Kitten, a Bud[1] and, always, the father who knew best.

2. People stayed married forever back then, and roses grew by the front door. We had glass bottles filled with lightning bugs and brand-new swing sets in the backyard, and softball games at dusk. We had summer nights that lasted forever and well-balanced meals, three times a day, in our identical houses, on our identical streets. There was only one small bargain we had to make to exist in this world: we were never to ask questions, never to think about people who didn't have as much or who were different in any way. We ignored desperate marriages and piercing loneliness. And we were never, ever, to wonder what might be hidden from view, behind the unlocked doors, in the privacy of our neighbors' bedrooms and knotty-pine-paneled dens.

3. This was a bargain my own mother could not make. Having once believed that her life would sort itself out to be like the television shows we watched, only real and in color, she'd been left to care for her children on her own, at a time when divorce was so uncommon I did not meet another child of divorced parents until 10 years later, when I went off to college.

4. Back then, it almost made sense when one of my best friends was not allowed to come to my house; her parents did not approve of divorce or my mother's life style. My mother, after all, had a job and a boyfriend and, perhaps even more incriminating, she was the one who took the silver-colored trash cans out to the curb on Monday nights. She did so faithfully, on evenings when she had already balanced the checkbook and paid the bills and ministered to sore throats and made certain we'd had dinner; but all up and down the street everybody knew the truth: taking out the trash was clearly a job for fathers.

5. When I was 10, my mother began to work for the Department of Social Services, a world in which the simple rules of the suburbs did not apply. She counseled young unwed mothers, girls and women who were not allowed to make their own choices, most of whom had not been allowed to finish high school or stay in their own homes, none of whom had been allowed to decide not to continue their

---

[1]Nicknames of characters in a popular 1954–62 television show, *Father Knows Best.*

pregnancies. Later, my mother placed most of these babies in foster care, and still later, she moved to the protective-services department, investigating charges of abuse and neglect, often having to search a child's back and legs for bruises or welts.

6   She would have found some on my friend, left there by her righteous father, the one who wouldn't allow her to visit our home but blackened her eye when, a few years later, he discovered that she was dating a boy he didn't approve of. But none of his neighbors had dared to report him. They would never have imagined that someone like my friend's father, whose trash cans were always tidily placed at the curb, whose lawn was always well cared for, might need watching.

7   To my mother, abuse was a clear-cut issue, if reported and found, but neglect was more of a judgment call. It was, in effect, passing judgment on the nature of love. If my father had not sent the child-support checks on time, if my mother hadn't been white and college-educated, it could have easily been us in one of those apartments she visited, where the heat didn't work on the coldest days, and the dirt was so encrusted you could mop all day and still be called a poor housekeeper, and there was often nothing more for dinner than Frosted Flakes and milk, or, if it was toward the end of the month, the cereal might be served with tap water. Would that have meant my mother loved her children any less, that we were less of a family?

8   My mother never once judged who was a fit mother on the basis of a clean floor, or an unbalanced meal, or a boyfriend who sometimes spent the night. But back then, there were good citizens who were only too ready to set their standards for women and children, factoring out poverty or exhaustion or simply a different set of beliefs.

9   There are always those who are ready to deal out judgment with the ready fist of the righteous. I know this because before the age of 10 I was one of the righteous, too. I believed that mothers were meant to stay home and fathers should carry out the trash on Monday nights. I believed that parents could create a domestic life that was the next best thing to heaven, if they just tried. That is what I'd been told, that in the best of all worlds we would live identical lives in identical houses.

10   It's a simple view of the world, too simple even for childhood. Certainly, it's a vision that is much too limited for the lives we live now, when only one in 19 families are made up of a wage-earner father, a mother who doesn't work outside the home and two or more children. And even long ago, when I was growing up, we paid too high a price when we cut ourselves off from the rest of the world. We ourselves did not dare to be different. In the safety we created, we became trapped.

11   There are still places where softball games are played at dusk and roses grow by the front door. There are families with sons named Bud,

with kind and generous fathers, and mothers who put up strawberry preserves every June and always have time to sing lullabies. But do these families love their children any more than the single mother who works all day? Are their lullabies any sweeter? If I felt deprived as a child, it was only when our family was measured against some notion of what we were supposed to be. The truth of it was, we lacked for little.

12   And now that I have children of my own, and am exhausted at the end of the day in which I've probably failed in a hundred different ways, I am amazed that women alone can manage. That they do, in spite of everything, is a simple fact. They rise from sleep in the middle of the night when their children call out to them. They rush for the cough syrup and cold washcloths and keep watch till dawn. These are real family values, the same ones we knew when we were children. As far as we were concerned our mother could cure a fever with a kiss. This may be the only thing we ever need to know about love. The rest, no one can judge.

Understanding the Content

Feel free to reread all or parts of the selection to answer the following questions.

1. What type of family was typical when Hoffman was growing up? How similar or different were real-life families from those on television?

2. What was the "bargain" (3) Hoffman's mother could not make?

3. Hoffman says "it almost made sense when one of my best friends was not allowed to come to my house" (4). Why?

4. Hoffman contrasts suburban families with the families her mother worked with. What is the basic difference?

5. Reread the last sentence in paragraph 10. What does the author mean?

6. What is it that Hoffman feels is "the only thing we ever need to know about love" (12)?

Looking at Structure and Style

1. Is Hoffman's thesis stated or implied? If stated, where? Make a one-sentence statement of her thesis.

2. Hoffman uses comparison and contrast throughout her essay. What are some examples of this? Are they effective? Explain.

3. Hoffman uses several images throughout, such as silver-colored trash cans, neat lawns, and so forth. What is her purpose in doing this? Is her method effective? Explain.

4. To whom do you think Hoffman is writing? Why do you think so?

5. How would you describe Hoffman's tone? What words or phrases help develop that tone?

Evaluating the Author's Viewpoints

1. How does Hoffman define "family values"? Do you agree with her? Explain.

2. Is Hoffman's idea of "family" more the norm today than the so-called ideal norm of the 1950s?

3. What place do fathers seem to take in Hoffman's definition of "family values"?

4. How do you define "family"? "family values"?

Pursuing Possible Essay Topics

1. Write an essay that discusses erroneous concepts of family and family values. Who holds these concepts? From where do they come?

2. Interview some older people to discover what a "traditional" family lifestyle was like 40 years ago. Compare it to today's lifestyle.

3. Write an essay that supports or refutes the idea of the father taking care of the family while the mother works.

4. Talk to some immigrants about what their traditional family lifestyle was like before and after coming to this country. How much has it changed, if at all?

5. What other trends in our society are changing the traditional family unit as many people have known it? Write an essay on the forces in society that are changing the family unit.

6. Brainstorm or freewrite on one or more of the following:

   a. motherhood/fatherhood   d. the perfect parent

   b. perfect love   e. divorce

   c. maternal instincts   f. single parenting

7. If none of the above topics suit you, find your own topic on family or relationships and write an essay.

Preparing to Read

Take a minute or two to look over the following reading selection. Note the title and author, read the opening paragraph, and check the essay's length. Make certain you have the time now to read it carefully and to do the exercises that follow it. Then, in the spaces provided, answer the following questions.

1. What does the title tell you about this essay? _____

_____

2. Does the opening paragraph tell you anything about what this essay might be about? _____

_____

Vocabulary

Good comprehension of what you are about to read depends upon your understanding of the words below. The number following each word refers to the paragraph where it is used.

fortitude (1) strength, courage

Bedouin (5) a member of a nomadic tribe of Arabs

propriety (5) politeness, conformity to prevailing customs

A Worldwide Family

DIANA ABU-JABER

Diana Abu-Jaber is the author of the Pen Center USA Award-winning Crescent, *which was named one of the twenty best novels of 2003 by The Christian Science Monitor. She is also the author of* Arabian Jazz, *which won the 1994 Oregon Book Award and was nominated for the PEN/Faulkner. She teaches at Portland State University.*

1 Growing up, there was no escape from family. My strict Jordanian father believed that the behavior of his children reflected directly on the family. This meant that, although my sisters and I were born in the United States, we weren't supposed to act like American girls. We

wanted to wear short skirts, stay out late, go to parties. But these things were considered taboo in my household. We were supposed to be gleaming models of purity, fortitude and virtue.

2   My father admired Americans, especially their drive to work hard and succeed. But, like many other Arabs, he also felt that Americans were too loose and wild. My girlfriends had their own rooms with locks on the doors, private phones and TVs. They also had families disrupted by affairs and divorce; they barely knew their grandparents, and some of them had never met their cousins.

3   I did my share of sneaking out of my bedroom window to attend late-night parties and meet friends. But I was also immersed in family. We gathered for huge dinners. Relatives moved in and out of our house at my father's invitation. At the time, I envied my friends their freedom: When one of them complained that her father ignored her, I just thought she was lucky not to have her parents hovering over her. I took for granted the connection, identity and family unity that I grew up with.

4   Now that I've spent more time in Jordan, where my father was born, I've got a fuller perspective. One thing I've figured out is that the great thing about life in the Middle East is that you're never alone—and the great problem with life in the Middle East is that you're never alone.

5   My father's Bedouin sensibility was deeply traditional, frequently to the point of rigidity. He worked hard to instill in us his notions of propriety and modesty. At the dinner table, he lectured us on how we must protect the weak, share with others, never gloat and preserve our integrity. Without a sense of justice and honor, he said, people are little more than animals.

6   I rolled my eyes and dreamed of the day I could go off and be a "normal American".

7   But as I grew older, I began to appreciate the "normal Arab" world too. When we returned to the Middle East to visit my father's relatives, I saw how extended families lived together, parents adding rooms and apartments to their houses to accommodate spouses, children, widowed aunts. There were no homeless, no lonely elderly, no dispossessed. This reality was a powerful echo of my father's motto, repeated over and over when I was a child: "The family is absolutely sacred."

8   Now, I wonder what concepts like shame and honor, evil and sacred mean to us normal Americans, especially when we are faced with seemingly ceaseless images of prisoner torture and brutality at the hands of both Americans and Iraqis.

9   President Bush reminds me of my father in this sense: Neither really gets "the other." Bush doesn't recognize that Arabs may value their ancient, deeply cultivated sense of honor, tradition and family devotion above the American notion of individual freedom and liberty. The American focus on the pursuit of wealth and material goods leaves many Arabs in this country feeling lonely and short-changed.

10   It shouldn't be much of a stretch to imagine Iraqis' perspective: Their country has been bombed, invaded and occupied by a foreign army that claims to be a liberator even as it attempts to impose its cultural values and beliefs. Arbitrary detentions break apart Iraqi families. Iraqi men are abused and humiliated in jail. Is it any wonder that Iraqis, according to one recent poll sponsored by the U.S. government, overwhelming view the United States as an occupier and want U.S. troops to leave? Iraq's culture and traditions extend back centuries, yet Bush claims to know better what Iraqis need than the Iraqis themselves.

11   A friend returning from a year in the Middle East summed up the difference between the cultures this way: "Arabs have family," he said. "Americans have work."

12   My upbringing was full of shalts and shalt-nots. Too many to remember, and many of which I willfully broke. But it gave me a world with known boundaries, and this is something we must create by taking responsibility for our actions in Iraq; we must all be parents in transforming our nation. Each of us must be responsible for creating a nation of compassion and honor.

13   The human capacity for self-deception is profound, but we are now beyond a question of honor. We face the question of our humanity. The issue is no longer whether we can democratize Iraq or find weapons of mass destruction. These goals are discarded shells of political manipulation. The question now is whether we can save ourselves.

Understanding the Content

Feel free to reread all or parts of the selection to answer the following questions.

1. What is the author's ethnic background? How did this background affect how she was raised?

2. How does Abu-Jaber's father feel about Americans and their way of life?

3. How did the author feel about her strict upbringing?

4. According to Abu-Jaber, what is the Iraqi perspective regarding the United States' occupation of their country?

Looking at Structure and Style

1. Why does the author include information about her upbringing and her father's "Bedouin sensibility" (5) in the early paragraphs of this selection? How do these paragraphs relate to paragraphs 9–12?

2. What kind of mental image do you get of Abu-Jaber's father from her description of him?

3. What is the organizing pattern of paragraphs 1–3?

4. What is the author's tone in this essay? Does it change or stay the same?

Evaluating the Author's Viewpoints

1. What is the author's attitude toward her father and his beliefs?

2. Do you agree or disagree with the statement "Arabs have family. . . . Americans have work" (11)? Why?

3. Do you think the author agrees or disagrees with the statement in question 2? How can you tell?

4. How does the author feel about Middle Eastern life, in which "the great thing about life in the Middle East is that you're never alone—and the great problem with life in the Middle East is that you're never alone" (4)? Does she have an appreciation for the way of life in the Middle East?

5. What can you infer about how the author thinks her family life shaped her view of the world?

Pursuing Possible Essay Topics

1. Do you agree or disagree with the statement, "The family is. . . sacred" (7)? Write an essay discussing your viewpoint.

2. What do you think it means to be a "normal American" (6)? Write an essay discussing the term and what it means to you.

3. With a classmate, research the country of Jordan and find out what you can about its culture, everyday life, and politics. Then write a paper discussing what your research revealed.

4. What is your cultural background? Are there any members of your family who hold onto the "old" ways of your heritage? If so, write an essay describing this person and how living in two cultures affects his or her life, if at all.

5. What do you think of the statement, "Americans have work" (11)? Do you think this is true? Write an essay discussing your opinion of this statement.

6. Brainstorm or freewrite on one or more of the following:

   a. traditional family values   c. a "global community"

   b. Arab culture   d. the sacredness of family

7. Don't like these topics? Find a topic of interest to you regarding family and write about it.

Preparing to Read

Take a minute or two to look over the following reading selection. Note the title and author, read the opening paragraph, and check the essay's length. Make certain you have the time now to read it carefully and to do the exercises that follow it. Then, in the spaces provided, answer the following questions.

1. What do you think is meant by the title, "Black Unlike Me"? _____

   _____

   _____

2. What do you think the selection is going to be about? _____

   _____

3. Why do you think the author uses the incident in the first paragraph to open

   the essay? _____

   _____

   _____

Vocabulary

Good comprehension of what you are about to read depends upon your understanding of the words below. The number following each word refers to the paragraph where it is used.

diatribe (3) prolonged discourse

anonymous (3) not named or identified

indignation (4) anger aroused by something unjust, unworthy, or mean

earnest (4) exhibiting a serious or intent state of mind

tchotchkes (5) Yiddish word for trinkets or nicknacks

internalize (6) incorporate within the self as conscious or subconscious guiding principles

constructs (6) things constructed by the mind, working concepts

Black Unlike Me

JANA WOLFF

Jana Wolff, the author of Secret Thoughts of an Adoptive mother, *has written several articles for* Adoptive Families, *a magazine and leading source of adoption information for families before, during, and after adoption. This article appeared in the* New York Times Magazine.

1   "I hate collars," shouts my 7-year-old son into his mattress, where he has thrown himself, 20 minutes before we need to leave for school. I just woke him and we're in the middle of a fight I can't remember starting. It's no surprise that a second-grade boy would prefer to wear an oversize sleeveless jersey—Chicago Bulls red, No. 23—rather than a button-down shirt with a collar. But this is a school day, I explain to Ari, and you go to school not to play but to learn.

2   I didn't like the mini-sermon I felt coming on, but I couldn't stop myself. I chose that moment to make the connection between collared shirts and racism to my black son. I said that it was really important for him to look his best and do his best because there were idiots in the world who actually thought that people with dark skin were not as clean, or as smart, or as good as others. My son could prove them wrong on all counts.

3   Even before I finished, Ari crumbled before my eyes. From face down on his mattress, where he was trying to dig a cave under his blanket, came his muffled voice: "I hate this." And I knew just what he meant. He has heard me talk about prejudice since he learned his colors at 2½: "People with pink skin aren't always nice to people with brown skin." Truth is, the beginnings of this dawn-hour diatribe started many years ago, when my husband and I adopted our infant son. That's when I woke up from a deep, white sleep. Suddenly, racism, which had always existed outside my focus, became my focus. When children of color become your children, anonymous struggles become personal ones with names and faces that you know.

4   I wanted to walk out of Ari's bedroom and go back in as if none of this had happened. But it was too late. I had already done that thing again. That thing that white parents who have black children do: we move from racially clueless to racially conscious in the most clumsy of ways, never turning off our radar or putting down our dukes. Then we pass along our loaded agendas to our children and scare them with an edginess that is characteristic of late learners. I jumped in to fight the battle against racism with an indignation that was earnest but not earned.

5   It must be very hard for a child to have, as tour guides, parents who are tourists themselves. The risk is that the culture being visited will be reduced to its souvenirs. All I have to do is look around Ari's

room—past the clutter of Lego pieces, open books and plastic swords—to see my son's life as a pathetic collection of props: the Michael Jordan poster on the wall; the knitted Senegalese cap hanging from the doorknob; the framed autograph of Tiger Woods by his bed. The process of becoming black must lie somewhere beyond ethnic tchotchkes like these. I'm just not sure where. Ari's preference for peers over parents at this age gives me more satisfaction than most mothers experience as their young children mature. In looking toward his black friends for clues, he lands on the symbols that they value most, and he makes them his own. The day he got his hair cut exactly the way he wanted—a severe buzz on the sides with just enough hair left on top for the barber to carve a Nike swoosh—Ari walked out of that shop as if he had grown a foot taller. I had his buddies to thank for that boost.

6   I want to expand the ways for my son to be black, beyond cool haircuts and athletic heroes. The images of success in Ari's bedroom invite him to aspire to narrowly defined black standards; I'd rather my son experience the white privilege of believing that there are no limitations on who he can be and what he can do. I want Ari to internalize truths that aren't yet true: that to get straight A's is a black thing; that to set a positive example is a black thing; that to be a success in any arena is a black thing. But you can't decorate your room with these constructs. It dawned on me that morning that you can't rely on collared shirts to ward off bigotry or enhance self-esteem. "It's O.K. with me, Babe, if you wear a different shirt." Ari started heading for the dresser, when I added that it couldn't be sleeveless and it had to be clean. From the top drawer he pulled out an oversize black T-shirt with Grant Hill's picture on it. Then he sped downstairs for breakfast before I could change my mind or bring up the subject of racial pride again.

7   It is with a mixture of sadness and relief that I've begun to understand this much: becoming black is an inside job—my son's job. I can help by bringing black friends and customs and even props into our lives, but Ari's evolution into a proud black man will occur largely outside the walls of our home. And most of his growing, I'm convinced, will happen well beyond the reach of my loving white arms.

Understanding the Content

Feel free to reread all or parts of the selection to answer the following questions.

1. Why does the author object to her son's wearing an oversize sleeveless jersey to school?

2. How does her son react to her "mini-sermon" (2)?

3. What does the author say "white parents who have black children do" (4)?

4. What does the author's son, Ari, have in his room that the author classifies as "ethnic tchotchkes" (5)?

5. Why, toward the end of the essay, does the author compromise with Ari about the type of shirt he wants to wear? What has she learned by evaluating her reaction to Ari's choice of shirt?

6. What does the author mean in paragraph 5 when she writes, "It must be very hard for a child to have, as tour guides, parents who are tourists themselves"?

Looking at Structure and Style

1. How does the author use the first two paragraphs to illustrate some of the deeper struggles she has with her son's ethnicity and its impact on his life?

2. How does the author develop the incident that begins in paragraph 1 throughout the essay? Why does she choose to let her son pick out his own shirt at the end of the essay?

3. How does the author use the retelling of the disagreement with her son to discuss the larger issue of racism? What examples does she give of how she thinks her son will be affected by racism in his life?

4. The author quotes her son twice. How do the two quotes illustrate the conflict between mother and son?

5. What is the significance of a shirt with a collar? What does the author think it will say about her son if he wears that type of shirt?

Evaluating the Author's Viewpoints

1. The author has taught her son about prejudice by telling him that "people with pink skin aren't always nice to people with brown skin" (3). Do you agree with her statement? If you had to introduce your child to the subject of racism, how would you do it?

2. How does the author think white parents with black children can help the children develop their own identities?

3. What attempts has the author made to bring symbols of black culture and pride into her son's life? Do you agree with how she has gone about this? Why or why not?

4. Why does the author call herself and her husband "tour guides" (5) and "tourists" (5) with regard to their parenting of Ari?

5. In general, how does the author think black men are viewed in today's society? Do you agree with her assessment? Why or why not?

Pursuing Possible Essay Topics

1. Have you ever been a victim of racism? If so, describe what happened and how you reacted to the situation.

2. With what issues would you be confronted if you adopted a child of a different race? How would you help your child assimilate into your culture and society in general?

3. Write an opinion piece on one of the following:

   a. Why is it a good idea for people from one race to adopt a child of a different race?

   b. Why is it a bad idea for people from one race to adopt a child of a different race?

4. Pick one of the following topics for an essay:

   a. Do you think people should be judged by the way they dress or by their overall appearance?

   b. Do you think people are judged by the way they dress or by their overall appearance?

5. Brainstorm or freewrite on one or more of the following:

   a. racism in America

   b. multiculturalism

   c. adoption

   d. ethnicity

6. Choose a topic of your own on family or relationships and then write an essay about it.

Preparing to Read

Take a minute or two to look over the following reading selection. Note the title and author, read the first two paragraphs, and check the essay's length. Make certain you have the time now to read it carefully and to do the exercises that follow it. Then, in the spaces provided, answer the following questions.

1. What do you think this essay will say about the division of labor in the home?

   _____

   _____

2. What do you think the title means? _____

   _____

3. Do the first two paragraphs do an adequate job of letting you know what this

   essay will be about? Why or why not? _____

   _____

Vocabulary

Good comprehension of what you are about to read depends upon your understanding of the words below. The number following each word refers to the paragraph where it is used.

perpetuating (2) causing to continue indefinitely

divvying (3) dividing up

aggregate (5) the whole; total

weasel out of (9) to avoid; get out of doing

Boys Mow Lawns, Girls Wash Dishes

SUE SHELLENBARGER

Sue Shellenbarger is a columnist and news editor for The Wall Street Journal, *writing the "Work and Family" column that appears most Wednesdays in the publication. She is also the author of* Work and Family: Essays from the 'Work and Family' Column of The Wall Street Journal.

1   I've always considered myself tuned-in to the gender politics of the Chore Wars—the household battles between husbands and wives over who does what at home.

2   Imagine my surprise when I realized I'm guilty of perpetuating this conflict into the next generation. While reporting on the topic, I saw that I myself expect different things of my son, 16, and my daughter, 18: I want him to handle more fix-it jobs, while my daughter does more cleaning.

3   The latest research suggests I'm not alone. The way parents are divvying up and paying kids for chores suggests this is one family battle that will extend well into the next generation and beyond.

4   A nationwide study by the University of Michigan's Institute for Social Research shows boys ages 10 through 18 are more likely than girls to be getting paid for doing housework—even though boys spend an average 30% less time doing chores. Boys are as much as 10 to 15 percentage points more likely than girls at various ages to be receiving an allowance for doing housework, says the institute's newly completed analysis of data on 3,000 children ages 10 through 18.

5   Boys may be handling more of the kinds of chores that are re-garded as a job that should be paid, such as lawnmowing, speculates Frank Stafford, the University of Michigan economics professor heading the research. Chores such as dishwashing or cooking, often regarded as routine and done free, may fall more often to girls. (The analysis is based on aggregate samples, and doesn't compare treat-ment of siblings within individual families.)

6   Also, girls ages six through 17 perform two hours more of house-work each week than boys, the institute found. That echoes previous studies showing a similar gap, and mirrors an even bigger gulf be-tween adult women's and men's housework time. Women now do about 19.4 hours a week to men's 9.7 hours, according to research by Suzanne Bianchi, a sociology professor at the University of Mary-land, and others. "Girls hang around with their moms, boys with their dads, and they follow the patterns they grow up with," says Con-stance Gager, assistant professor, social and family dynamics, at Ari-zona State University.

7   Like me, many parents are unconscious of any gender gap among their own kids. Ann Barlow regards her family as gender-neutral, saying she and her husband treat their son, 13, and their daughter, 16, pretty much alike. "I don't think we discriminate," the San Ramon, Calif., mother. But she acknowledges that they do different tasks.

8   "We stick my son with taking out the garbage," she says. "I never even thought about it. It's just, 'Chris, take out the garbage.'" Her son also cleans the garage and handles household repairs more often

than her daughter. And her daughter spends about an hour more each week doing housework—three, compared with two by her son.

9   He uses humor to slip off the hook, Ms. Barlow says. "He'll be the first guy to weasel out of his chores. He'll say, 'Oh, I dropped a plate, you probably don't want me to handle those any more.'"

10   Some research shows that as adults, women are content doing more housework if they perceive the setup as fair. If a husband is working longer hours outside the home, for example, wives may willingly shoulder more chores.

11   But with kids, in addition to doing more housework, daughters are spending more time than sons performing paid jobs—1.9 hours a week for girls, vs. 1.3 hours for boys, Dr. Bianchi and others report in a 2006 book, "Changing Rhythms of American Family Life." Dr. Gager, who found a similar pattern in a 2004 study, likens these girls to "supermoms—they're superkids who do it all."

12   In many busy households, housework simply isn't a high priority any more; couples' combined housework time is down 25% from the 1960s, Dr. Bianchi says. In the resulting war against dustballs, many families value pragmatism over gender politics. Raoul and Jackie Pascual acknowledge that chores haven't been evenly distributed among their three children. A daughter, 22 and living at home, has always handled more cleaning than their son, now 19, or another daughter, 14. Their son takes out the trash and helps with such jobs as assembling furniture, says Ms. Pascual, of South Pasadena, Calif. But the Pascuals aren't concerned. "It doesn't make a difference" who does what, Mr. Pascual says, "as long as it's done."

13   Housework is a problem at Mike Grandin's house, but gender politics are the least of his worries. His daughter, 18, cooks meals and helps out more at home than his son, 15. But neither clean up messes to Mr. Grandin's satisfaction. The San Francisco stockbroker says he winds up doing a lot of the dishes and tidying up while his kids stay busy with extracurricular activities, studying and jobs. His response is gender-blind. "I come down just as hard on either one when they leave a mess."

Understanding the Content

Feel free to reread all or parts of the selection to answer the following questions.

1. How is the household labor divided in the Shellenbarger home?

2. What does research say about how chores are divvied up in the American home?

3. What does research say about women and household chores?

4. In today's households, where on the priority list does housework fall? Why?

Looking at Structure and Style

1. What is the thesis of this essay?

2. What effect does Shellenbarger's use of anecdotal information have on her essay? Is it useful and effective? Why or why not?

3. Are the outside sources that Shellenbarger uses credible and effective? Why or why not? How does she incorporate sources in this essay and for what purpose?

4. What is the organizing pattern used in paragraph 5? What is its relation to paragraph 6?

5. What is the author's tone in this selection? Her attitude toward her subject? How can you tell?

Evaluating the Author's Viewpoints

1. Why does Shellenbarger think that the "divvying up and paying kids for chores . . . is one family battle that will extend well into the next generation and beyond" (3)?

2. How does Shellenbarger feel about the division of labor in American households? How can you tell?

3. Was Shellenbarger aware of the "gender gap" before she wrote this article? Were you?

4. According to this selection, why isn't housework a priority anymore?

Pursuing Possible Essay Topics

1. In pairs or with your entire class, discuss "chore wars". Do you see any similarities to your experience in this selection? Any differences? Discuss.

2. Do you think that having clear designations on who does what—based on gender—is acceptable? Why or why not? Write an essay discussing your viewpoint.

3. Is getting the other members of your household to do chores a problem? Or do the other people in your house help out? Write an essay describing the division of labor in your house.

4. What non-gender specific tasks do you perform in your household, if any? Write an essay describing what you do and why.

5. What is your favorite household chore? Why? Write an essay describing it and why you enjoy it so much.

6. Brainstorm or freewrite on one or more of the following topics:

   a. the gender gap

   b. division of household labor

   c. male "jobs" versus "female" jobs

   d. housework

   e. chores

7. You know what else you can do . . . If you don't like these topics, find your own topic and write an essay

---

Opposing Viewpoints on Gay Marriage

One of the following essays strongly opposes gay marriage, believing that homosexual marriage would be bad for marriage, bad for children, and bad for society. The other believes that you we cannot deny an entire group of countrymen basic civil rights and call ourselves Americans.

Preparing to Read

Take a minute or two to look over the following reading selection. Note the title and author, read the first paragraph, and check the essay's length. Make certain you have the time now to read it carefully and to do the exercises that follow it. Then, in the spaces provided, answer the following questions.

1. From the title and the opening paragraph, what do you think the essay will be

   about? _____

   _____

2. The authors ask a question in the first paragraph. How do you think they will

   answer it? In other words, what will their opinion be? _____

   _____

Vocabulary

Good comprehension of what you are about to read depends upon your understanding of the words below. The number following each word refers to the paragraph where it is used.

sanctions (3) authoritative approvals that make an action valid

spawned (4) gave birth to

denomination (8) a large group of religious congregations under a common faith

monogamous (9) a relationship with one person

pathogens (13) things that cause disease

imposition (16) a burdensome or unfair demand

exacerbate (16) to make worse; intensify

entitlements (18) privileges

Speaking Out: Why Gay Marriage Would Be Harmful

ROBERT BENNE AND
GERALD McDERMOTT

Robert Benne and Gerald McDermott, who both teach religion at Roanoke College, wrote an earlier version of this article for the Public Theology Project. *Viewpoints published in "Speaking Out" do not necessarily represent those of* Christianity Today.

1   Now that the Massachusetts Supreme Court has ruled that marriage be open to gays and lesbians, it is time to consider the question that pops up more than mushrooms after a spring rain. How would the legalization of gay marriage harm current and future heterosexual marriages?

2   The answer at first glance is that it wouldn't, at least not in individual cases in the short run. But what about the longer run for everyone?

3   It is a superficial kind of individualism that does not recognize the power of emerging social trends that often start with only a few individuals bucking conventional patterns of behavior. Negative social trends start with only a few aberrations. Gradually, however, social sanctions weaken and individual aberrations became a torrent.

4   Think back to the 1960s, when illegitimacy and cohabitation were relatively rare. At that time many asked how one young woman having a baby out of wedlock or living with an unmarried man could hurt their neighbors. Now we know the negative social effects these two living arrangements have spawned: lower marriage rates, more instability in the marriages that are enacted, more fatherless children, increased rates of domestic violence and poverty, and a vast expansion of welfare state expenses.

5   But even so, why would a new social trend of gays marrying have negative effects? We believe there are compelling reasons why the institutionalization of gay marriage would be 1) bad for marriage, 2) bad for children, and 3) bad for society.

6   *1. The first casualty of the acceptance of gay marriage would be the very definition of marriage itself.* For thousands of years and in every Western society marriage has meant the life-long union of a man and a woman. Such a statement about marriage is what philosophers call an analytic proposition. The concept of marriage necessarily includes the idea of a man and woman committing themselves to each other. Any other arrangement contradicts the basic definition. Advocates of gay marriage recognize this contradiction by proposing "gay unions" instead, but this distinction is, we believe, a strategic one. The ultimate goal for them is the societal acceptance of gay marriage.

7   Scrambling the definition of marriage will be a shock to our fundamental understanding of human social relations and institutions. One effect will be that sexual fidelity will be detached from the commitment of marriage. The advocates of gay marriage themselves admit as much. "Among gay male relationships, the openness of the contract makes it more likely to survive than many heterosexual bonds," Andrew Sullivan, the most eloquent proponent of gay marriage, wrote in his 1996 book, *Virtually Normal.* "There is more likely to be a greater understanding of the need for extramarital outlets between two men than between a man and a woman. . . . Something of the gay relationship's necessary honesty, its flexibility, and its equality could undoubtedly help strengthen and inform many heterosexual bonds."

8   The former moderator of the Metropolitan Community Church, a largely homosexual denomination, made the same point. "Monogamy is not a word the gay community uses," Troy Perry told *The Dallas Morning News.* "We talk about fidelity. That means you live in a loving, caring, honest relationship with your partner. Because we can't marry, we have people with widely varying opinions as to what that means. Some would say that committed couples could have multiple sexual partners as long as there's no deception."

9   A recent study from the Netherlands, where gay marriage is legal, suggests that the moderator is correct. Researchers found that even among stable homosexual partnerships, men have an average of eight partners per year outside their "monogamous" relationship.

10   In short, gay marriage will change marriage more than it will change gays.

11   Further, if we scramble our definition of marriage, it will soon embrace relationships that will involve more than two persons. Prominent advocates hope to use gay marriage as a wedge to abolish governmental support for traditional marriage altogether. Law Professor Martha Ertman of the University of Utah, for example, wants to render the distinction between traditional marriage and "polyamory" (group marriage) "morally neutral." She argues that greater openness to gay partnerships will help us establish this moral neutrality (Her main article on this topic, in the Winter 2001 *Harvard Civil Rights and Civil Liberties Law Review,* is not available online, but she made a similar case in the Spring/Summer 2001 *Duke Journal Of Gender Law & Policy*). University of Michigan law professor David Chambers wrote in a widely cited 1996 *Michigan Law Review* piece that he expects gay marriage will lead government to be "more receptive to [marital] units of three or more" (1996 *Michigan Law Review*).

12   *2. Gay marriage would be bad for children.* According to a recent article in *Child Trends,* "Research clearly demonstrates that family

structure matters for children, and the family structure that helps the most is a family headed by two biological parents in a low-conflict marriage." While gay marriage would encourage adoption of children by homosexual couples, which may be preferable to foster care, some lesbian couples want to have children through anonymous sperm donations, which means some children will be created purposely without knowledge of one of their biological parents. Research has also shown that children raised by homosexuals were more dissatisfied with their own gender, suffer a greater rate of molestation within the family, and have homosexual experiences more often.

13   Gay marriage will also encourage teens who are unsure of their sexuality to embrace a lifestyle that suffers high rates of suicide, depression, HIV, drug abuse, STDs, and other pathogens. This is particularly alarming because, according to a 1991 scientific survey among 12-year-old boys, more than 25 percent feel uncertain about their sexual orientations. We have already seen that lesbianism is "chic" in certain elite social sectors.

14   Finally, acceptance of gay marriage will strengthen the notion that marriage is primarily about adult yearnings for intimacy and is not essentially connected to raising children. Children will be hurt by those who will too easily bail out of a marriage because it is not "fulfilling" to them.

15   *3. Gay marriage would be bad for society.* The effects we have described above will have strong repercussions on a society that is already having trouble maintaining wholesome stability in marriage and family life. If marriage and families are the foundation for a healthy society, introducing more uncertainty and instability in them will be bad for society.

16   In addition, we believe that gay marriage can only be imposed by activist judges, not by the democratic will of the people. The vast majority of people define marriage as the life-long union of a man and a woman. They will strongly resist redefinition. Like the 1973 judicial activism regarding abortion, the imposition of gay marriage would bring contempt for the law and our courts in the eyes of many Americans. It would exacerbate social conflict and division in our nation, a division that is already bitter and possibly dangerous.

17   In summary, we believe that the introduction of gay marriage will seriously harm Americans—including those in heterosexual marriages—over the long run. Strong political measures may be necessary to maintain the traditional definition of marriage, possibly even a constitutional amendment.

18   Some legal entitlements sought by gays and lesbians might be addressed by recognizing non-sexually defined domestic partnerships. But as for marriage, let us keep the definition as it is, and strengthen our capacity to live up to its ideals.

Understanding the Content

Feel free to reread all or parts of the selection to answer the following questions.

1. Which Supreme Court has ruled that marriage be open to gays and lesbians?

2. What are the "negative social effects" of illegitimacy and cohabitation, according to the authors?

3. What is the authors' definition of marriage?

4. What does Andrew Sullivan say about the homosexual "contract" concerning relationships?

5. What effect would the legalization of gay marriage have on teens "who are unsure of their sexuality," according to the authors?

6. What is the relationship between the traditional definition of marriage and procreation, according to Benne and McDermott? What effect would the legalization of gay marriage have on this relationship?

Looking at Structure and Style

1. What is the thesis of this selection? Is it stated or implied? If stated, where? Rewrite it in your own words.

2. What was the authors' purpose in writing this essay?

3. What is the authors' tone? What words and/or phrases help you to ascertain the tone?

4. What is the organizing principle of paragraph 5?

5. Do the authors use suitable and credible evidence to support their thesis?

6. In your opinion, have the authors created a reasonable and supported argument to prove their point that "the institutionalization of gay marriage would be 1) bad for marriage, 2) bad for children, and 3) bad for society"? If not, how could they have done a better job?

7. What was the authors' purpose in including a quote from Andrew Sullivan in paragraph 7? Does this inclusion strengthen or hurt their argument, in your opinion?

Evaluating the Author's Viewpoints

1. What do you think the authors' opinion of bearing children outside of marriage (illegitimacy) and living together (cohabitation) is? How can you tell?

2. Do you agree or disagree with the authors that "the institutionalization of gay marriage would be 1) bad for marriage, 2) bad for children, and 3) bad for society"? Why?

3. Do you agree or disagree with the authors' definition of marriage? Why?

4. Do you agree or disagree with the authors that "if we scramble the definition of marriage, it will soon embrace relationships that will involve more than two persons"? Why? Do you think the authors have presented a valid argument on this point?

5. How do the authors think that teens "unsure of their sexuality" will be affected by gay marriage? Do you agree?

6. What do you think the authors mean by "some legal entitlements sought by gays and lesbians might be addressed by recognizing non-sexually defined domestic partnerships"? What could some of those entitlements be? Do you agree with this statement, on the whole?

Pursuing Possible Essay Topics

Before beginning an essay on family or relationships, read the following essay, *Who Cares If Gays Marry?* by Gregory Blair.

Preparing to Read

Take a minute or two to look over the following reading selection. Note the title and author, read the first two paragraphs, and check the essay's length. Make certain you have the time now to read it carefully and to do the exercises that follow it. Then, in the spaces provided, answer the following questions.

1. What do you think this essay will say about gay marriage? _____

   _____

2. Do you think Gregory Blair will support or refute Benne and McDermott's

   thesis in *Speaking Out: Why Gay Marriage Would Be Harmful?* _____

   _____

3. What do you think the title means? _____

   _____

Vocabulary

Good comprehension of what you are about to read depends upon your understanding of the words below. The number following each word refers to the paragraph where it is used.

proponents (3) supporters or advocators

polygamous (3) having multiple spouses

permutations (3) complete changes or transformations

augment (4) to make something that is developing or already exists greater in size

myopic (5) narrow-minded or intolerant

tenet (6) a principle or ideology

Who Cares If Gays Marry?

GREGORY BLAIR

Gregory Blair is a Los Angeles-based writer who has produced plays, screenplays, and a novel, Spewing Pulp.

1   Apparently, most Americans. The interesting thing is, we don't agree on whether or not there should be a Constitutional amendment banning gays and lesbians from federally recognized marriage. While almost all of us agree that discrimination is ugly and un-American, most Americans seem to feel it's okay to ban gays from having the right to marry. Why is that?

2   Opponents claim that gay marriage is against definition, against God and against American values. So let's see whether that's true.

3   Let's look at the "definition" argument. This is two-fold. First, proponents of this stance would argue that marriage has always been defined as being between one man and one woman. This is certainly not true. Look at other cultures around the globe; many of them have different variations of what constitutes a marriage. The Muslim countries of the Middle East, Asia and North Africa often have polygamous marriages. Several central Asian cultures and others often have accepted polyandry—a custom in which a woman may have multiple husbands. Even in our own Mormon culture, here in America, polygamy was a viable option for quite some time. Similarly, in the past decades, many gays and lesbians have been married in various types of ceremonies around the nation and the globe. Whether we individually agree or approve of all of those types of marriage is irrelevant; what matters is that we must recognize that the definition of marriage has many permutations. Simply put, the word "marriage" itself is not discriminatory . . . and neither should we be.

4   Second, those who would argue "marriage" by definition is an exclusively heterosexual state of being do so by declaring that God intended marriage only for the procreation of children and that homosexuals cannot biologically fulfill this function. (We'll talk about the "God" part later.) The proposition that marriage is only for procreation immediately proves fallacious if you look honestly at history. Heterosexual marriage actually began and continued for centuries with several functions: in addition to procreation, marriage was also used to form and/or affirm alliances, augment familial wealth and status, and trace inheritance rights. To argue that homosexuals do not have the right to marry because they cannot procreate becomes even more invalid when you consider that if we define "marriage" as only being a right for people who can procreate, then infertile men and women, those beyond their child-bearing years, and people who simply choose not to have children should also not be allowed to

marry. Thus, the argument denies the rights to even more Americans, becoming at once even more ridiculous and unacceptable.

5   And now we come back to that "God" issue. The second argument those opposing gay marriage make is that homosexuality is against God. The credibility of this stance is shattered with two words: "Whose God?" We are being myopic, egocentric exclusionists if we are to only consider the Judeo-Christian God. What does that say to Americans with different religious backgrounds and cultures? Not to mention American Atheists, Agnostics and those who don't necessarily believe in a god at all. It is uncharitable and unforgivable to impose religious beliefs into the secular arena of the government. Or, more simply put: it is one thing to hold a religious belief; it is quite another to force it on a country.

6   This leads us directly into the argument that gay marriage is un-American. Nothing could be further from the truth. Our country was formed on the ideals that "all men are created equal" and that a separation of church and state would sanctify one's right to practice one's own belief system. This tenet protects those who believe in the Judeo-Christian God to live by certain rules of conduct. Similarly, it protects those who have other belief systems to live by *their* rules of conduct. It is meant to *equally* prevent people from being persecuted or discriminated against because of their beliefs. And embracing the idea that homosexuality is a sin—or that it is an acceptable lifestyle—are simply two different beliefs that are equally protected under that ideal. To even consider creating a law that discriminates against a whole class of people for what they believe (that homosexuality is not a sin, for example) goes against the separation of church and state and the basic freedom it protects. In truth, homosexuality is not un-American; denying homosexuals their rights *is*.

7   There are other arguments that people have presented against gay marriage. But, like the ones discussed above, they all are based on religious beliefs or simple fallacies. The fact remains that the only thing to do—even if you believe homosexuality to be a sin—is oppose a ban on gay marriage. You can preach to homosexuals, reach out to council them in your beliefs, and try to "save" them if you feel you must—but you cannot deny an entire group of countrymen basic civil rights and call yourself an American.

Understanding the Content

Feel free to reread all or parts of the selection to answer the following questions.

1. Who does Blair think cares that gays marry?

2. What does Blair say that opponents of gay marriage claim?

3. How do other cultures and religions look at marriage? How is the way they view marriage different from the way Americans view it?

4. Why does Blair think that the argument that gay marriage is un-American is faulty?

5. In Blair's opinion, what is the "only thing to do—even if you believe homosexuality to be a sin"?

Looking at Structure and Style

1. What is the thesis of this essay?

2. How does Blair use opposing viewpoints to structure his argument? Is this effective? Why or why not?

3. What organizing pattern is used in paragraphs 3 and 4?

4. Who uses evidence more effectively in their argument about gay marriage—Blair or Benne and McDermott? Why?

5. Describe Blair's tone and attitude in this essay. What words or phrases help develop this tone and attitude? How similar is Blair's tone and attitude to Benne and McDermott's?

6. How effective is paragraph 7—Blair's conclusion—in summarizing and bolstering his argument? Do you think it could be more effective? If so, rewrite it in your own words.

Evaluating the Author's Viewpoints

1. How does Blair refute the claim that God intended marriage only for the procreation of children?

2. How does Blair deal with the argument from those opposing gay marriage that homosexuality is against God? Does he do an adequate job? Why or why not?

3. Does Blair think that gay marriage is un-American? Why or why not?

4. What can you infer about how Blair defines marriage? In what ways do Blair and Benne and McDermott disagree about what the definition of marriage should be?

5. Benne and McDermott believe that "gay marriage can only be imposed by activist judges, not by the democratic will of the people". How do you think Blair would react to that statement, now that you have read both arguments?

6. What role, if any, should religion play in the decision as to whether or not gay marriage should be legal, according to Blair? According to Benne and McDermott?

Pursuing Possible Essay Topics

1. Write an essay that shows why either Benne and McDermott or Blair offers better support for his or her viewpoint. Use examples from the essays to support your thesis.

2. Write an essay outlining your opinion of the legalization of gay marriage.

3. What is the definition of marriage, in your opinion? Write an essay discussing your viewpoint.

4. What effect, do you think, would the legalization of gay marriage have on the children of gay couples? If possible, use statistics or outside sources to support your viewpoint.

 5. This is a controversial topic and people likely will have differing opinions on it. Get together with a classmate or a group of classmates to discuss it. Does either one or more of your classmates disagree with your opinion on the topic of the legalization of gay marriage? If so, why? Do they have a legitimate argument, in your opinion?

6. Brainstorm or freewrite on one or more of the following topics:
   a. the separation of church and state
   b. the definition of marriage
   c. family values
   d. gay marriage
   e. homosexuality
   f. the modern American family

7. Don't like these topics? Find your own topic on family and relationships and write about it.

Student Essay

Read the following narrative essay written by a student. As you read, look for answers to these questions:

1. Does the essay fit the assignment to write on some aspect of family or relationships?

2. Is there a thesis? If so, is it well supported and convincing? Has the student considered her audience? Is the title appropriate?

3. What would you suggest to the student to make the essay better?

My Younger Sibling

Anne Rishi

1   When we were growing up, I never paid too much attention to my little sister Jill. She had her friends and I had mine, but it was almost as if we took each other for granted, like a piece of furniture that was always there. This was especially so when I became a teenager and spent more time away from home. But back then, I had no idea what an influence I was having on her. If I had, I hope that I would have done things differently, because it may be too late now.

2   In high school I started hanging out with some students you could say were less than academically oriented. We were bored and found little value in school. So we ditched as often as we could and would hang out at the beach, smoking and acting like we were cool. Of course, being cool meant having sex with a guy I thought I was in love with. And just like in some sad teenage tale, I found myself pregnant.

3   When my parents found out, they took it better than I thought they would. Not that they liked it one bit. No, I got my share of "how-could-you-do-it-what-were-you-thinking" comments. But my parents finally accepted the situation. When the boy involved found out, he agreed to marry me and we moved in with his parents. So my senior year was spent being pregnant and married to a boy I really didn't know all that well. We never did get to know each other very well. He took off after the baby was born. My parents didn't think it was a good idea for me to move back home with a baby, not

while Jill was still in school. So they helped me with the paper work involved and soon I began collecting welfare checks and moved into a cheap apartment. Now I'm starting city college on a special program and hope I can complete my education.

4   At that time, I was so wound up in my problems that I don't remember what Jill thought about it all. I didn't care.

5   I should have.

6   Last week Jill came over to visit me and the baby. She told me she envied me living on my own and having a baby to love. I told her it wasn't as easy as it looked and that I was pretty lonely. She told me she is seeing a boy and hopes to get pregnant like I did so that she can leave home and live like me. She shocked me even more when she said that she feels our mother pays more attention to me and the baby now than she does to her. Jill admits she doesn't really want a baby, but she thinks the money she'd get from the government like I do would help her get out of the house and then Mom would pay more attention to her.

7   I tried to convince her she would ruin her life, but she looks at me and thinks I'm doing just fine. She can't see that I'm struggling with raising a baby alone, trying to pass my classes, and not having any fun. Now I see I've become an unwitting role model for my sister, a role I can only hope she doesn't follow. If only I'd realized the impact of my life on my little sister.

Reaction

In your journal or on a separate sheet of paper, write your reaction to the student essay. Use the questions posed before the essay as a guide for your comments.

Viewpoints on Images

In small groups, discuss everyone's first reaction to the photo. Share the types of jobs each member of the group has held and describe the type of jobs each member hopes to have in the future and the skills required.

© Rob Crandall/The Image Works

On the Net

This chapter explores many aspects of family and relationships. If you would like to learn more about your own family, check out *www.rootsweb.com/~rwguide*. This Web site will help you learn more about genealogy and will help you construct your family tree.

After you have had some time to look into your family's roots, do some research on a specific topic, such as adoption. Adoption is discussed in the article "Black Unlike Me" by Jana Wolff. Search the Web for resources on adoption and choose three sites that you think have the best, most unbiased information. Then answer the following questions:

1. How many sites did you explore?

2. What criteria did you use in choosing the three best sites?

3. Do you think the sites that you chose have the best information about adoption, or would you need to access more sites to compile the best information possible?

4. What is the best site you visited? Why?

If you do not want to do further research on the topic of adoption, choose another topic from the chapter and answer the questions above.

8

Viewpoints on Work

Focus on Work

To help you focus on the subject of work, take a few minutes and prewrite on one or more of the following topics:

1. the influence of parents on the work we choose
2. do our jobs define who we are
3. spending more than we earn
4. varied working conditions (office work, field hand, burger flipper, and so forth)
5. the ideal job
6. should career women marry
7. sweatshops

For many people, the real reason for working is not the work itself but the money or the status or the power that the work may bring. Sociologists claim that the average person more or less puts up with a job because of personal and family needs that are considered to be important, such as food, clothing, and shelter.

The style of our lives is often based on the type of work we do. Some jobs allow for flexible schedules, which means that we can take advantage of convenient times to meet personal or family needs; however, flexible schedules can be a disadvantage if we decide to take our work home with us. Other jobs are inflexible, even requiring us to punch time clocks. Such work means that we cannot easily take time off to tend to personal or family needs, leaving only evenings and weekends. Yet this type of work can be left behind at the job site. The time that we have for ourselves and our families, then, is determined by the type of job we have.

The work we do not only determines the quality of our lives by shaping our time, our leisure, our buying power, and our ability to travel; it even shapes our identities. When we meet someone for the first time, we generally ask, "What do you do?" The meaning behind the question is understood: "What do you do for a living?" And when the answer is waitress, police officer, doctor, writer, sales clerk, or whatever, we generally categorize that person to fit our stereotype of that particular jobholder.

As our economy changes, so do our jobs. Many of us find that we must move from community to community to keep up with jobs that require our skills or to find new ones when we have been laid off. Many of us attend college in preparation for a particular line of work, only to discover that there are no positions available, or to realize that what we've prepared for is not what we really want to do. Many of us who have been in the same job for years suddenly find that we must go back to school to retrain in order to meet the advances made in our field.

Changes in traditional family roles are also changing our work habits. In some families, both parents must work for economic reasons. Some men are discovering that they would rather stay home and raise their children while their wives go off to work. Many women are realizing that they prefer a career to the traditional mother or housewife role. Such changes are redefining the term *homemaker*.

The reading selections in this unit supply a wide range of viewpoints toward work. Use them to discover and to stimulate your own views on work.

▦ Preparing to Read

Take a minute or two to look over the following reading selection. Note the title and author, read the opening paragraph, and check the essay's length. Make certain you have the time now to read it carefully and to do the exercises that follow it. Then, in the spaces provided, answer the following questions.

1. Is the first paragraph an effective opening to the essay? Why or why not?

_____

_____

2. What do you think the essay will be about? _____

_____

_____

3. What is the "glass ceiling"? _____

_____

_____

Vocabulary

Good comprehension of what you are about to read depends upon your understanding of the words below. The number following each word refers to the paragraph where it is used.

mettle (3) courage, fortitude, spirit

flamboyant (4) showy

overwhelmingly (10) characterized by overpowering effect or strength

spate (12) a sudden outpouring

swath (13) path, strip

unconscionable (14) unscrupulous

Women Still Fighting for Job Equality
DeWayne Wickham

DeWayne Wickham is a columnist for USA Today *and the Gannett News Service. He has worked as an analyst for CBS News; as a reporter for both* The Evening Sun *and* The Sun of Baltimore; *as a Capitol Hill correspondent for* U.S. News and World Report; *and as a contributing editor for* Black Enterprise *magazine.*

1   The first time boxing promoter Diane Fischer showed up at a prefight weigh-in, all 14 boxers in the room stripped down to their birthday suits before stepping onto the scale.

2   "They were trying to embarrass me," Fischer said matter-of-factly of that 1997 incident, "but I didn't let them get to me."

3   In the 2½ years since she got a license to promote prizefights, Fischer has tried mightily not to let the resistance she has encountered from men bent on testing her mettle or running her out of the fight game get to her. But it hasn't been easy.

4   "No doubt about it, I'm still bumping up against that glass ceiling," she said of her long struggle to win acceptance in a profession dominated by flamboyant men with large egos.

5   Last week, on the eve of Women's Equality Day, the anniversary of the constitutional amendment that gave women the right to vote, Fischer put on eight fights at The Big Kahuna, a Wilmington [Delaware] theme restaurant whose sprawling outdoor deck was transformed into a noisy boxing arena.

6   Seated at ringside were former heavyweight champions Joe Frazier and Michael Spinks, and Butch Lewis, one of this country's leading fight promoters. That they showed up to watch the fights was a small victory for Fischer, who has been told more than a few times that she's a fish out of water.

7   "I've been bad-mouthed by a lot by men who say this is a man's job, not something a woman should be doing," Fischer said.

Cracking the Job Barriers

8   In fact, Fischer is a rare breed. More women in this country are employed as teachers, secretaries and cashiers than work in any other jobs. To break out of this box, an increasing number of the 64 million women in the labor force must find work in what the Department of Labor calls "nontraditional occupations"—areas of employment in which women now comprise 25% or less of the workforce.

9   This long list includes pilots, truck drivers, funeral directors, dentists, architects, bellhops, barbers, meter readers and construction workers. These are jobs women must get their fair share of as they assume a larger part of the burden of raising a family: Last year in this country, a woman headed nearly one of every four families that had children under the age of 18.

10   "The glass ceiling is thickest in areas where women are employed in jobs that are overwhelmingly dominated by men," said Elizabeth Toledo, a vice president of the National Organization for Women. "In general, jobs that are overwhelmingly male-dominated tend to have more issues."

11   Translation: They have more barriers for women to scale.

Good News—and Bad

12   It's easy to lose sight of this harsh reality, given the spate of good news about women on the employment front this year. There was a lot of happy talk about breaks in the glass ceiling when Carly Fiorina was named head of Hewlett-Packard, Eileen Collins became the first woman to command a space shuttle flight, and Karen Jurgensen got the editor's job here at *USA Today,* the nation's largest newspaper.

13   But despite these highly visible gains, there continues to be a wide swath of jobs with great earnings potential that are largely closed to women—and far too many work environments that are openly hostile to them.

14   NOW's two-year-old "Women-Friendly Workplace Campaign" has found no shortage of businesses to brand as "merchants of shame"—a tag the group bestows on firms it accuses of "unconscionable" abuse of female employees. The sex-discrimination lawsuits that have sprung from this campaign have ensnared some of the nation's biggest companies.

15   Still it's people such as Diane Fischer, not class action lawsuits, who put a human face on the sexism that robs millions of working women of the level playing field that Women's Equality Day symbolizes. Her efforts to win broad acceptance as a fight promoter will get a boost next month, when she and former lightweight boxing champion Roberto Duran team up to promote seven bouts in Panama.

16   But, sadly, her ultimate victory—like the jobs that millions of women seek in other occupations dominated by men—seems to be a long shot.

Understanding the Content

Feel free to reread all or parts of the selection to answer the following questions.

1. What did the boxers do to first-time boxing promoter Diane Fischer to embarrass her?

2. What event does Women's Equality Day commemorate?

3. What are the three occupations that the author says are the predominant occupations of women?

4. What are "nontraditional occupations"? Define the term and give a few examples.

5. What examples of breaks in the glass ceiling does the author give?

6. Where is the glass ceiling thickest?

7. What is the "Women-Friendly Workplace Campaign" (14)?

Looking at Structure and Style

1. How do paragraphs 1–3 help Wickham develop his thesis? How does he use these three paragraphs to set up the rest of the essay?

2. What purpose do the quotes serve in the essay? Are they effective?

3. How does the author use statistics to support his thesis? Give some examples of the statistics included in the essay.

4. Do you think paragraphs 15 and 16 are effective as concluding paragraphs? Why or why not?

5. Does the title tell you anything about the author's view on women's roles in the workplace? How can you tell?

Evaluating the Author's Viewpoints

1. Diane Fischer said, "I've been bad-mouthed by a lot by men who say this is a man's job, not something a woman should be doing" (7). Does the author support Fischer in her quest to become a successful boxing promoter? How can you tell?

2. Is there one paragraph in particular that tells you how the author feels about women in nontraditional occupations? If so, which one?

3. Do you agree with the author that jobs such as pilot, truck driver, funeral director, and dentist "are jobs women must get their fair share of as they assume a larger part of the burden of raising a family" (9)? Why or why not?

4. Why is the glass ceiling thickest in areas where women are employed in jobs that are dominated by men?

5. Do you think the author makes a good argument for having women employed in nontraditional occupations? If not, what would be a better argument?

6. What do you think of NOW's "Women-Friendly Workplace Campaign" (14)?

7. Does the author think that Diane Fischer will be successful in her quest to become a successful boxing promoter?

Pursuing Possible Essay Topics

1. Write an essay explaining why you think many women in this country are employed as teachers, secretaries, and cashiers.

2. What types of issues do you think women will face in "jobs that are overwhelmingly dominated by men" (10)? Write an essay describing the types of

issues women face when they hold jobs such as truck driver, funeral director, barber, and meter reader.

3. Write an essay that supports your viewpoint on women in nontraditional occupations.

4. With a classmate, discuss whether or not you think Diane Fischer should pursue her dream of becoming a boxing promoter. Write an essay summarizing your discussion.

5. Brainstorm or freewrite on one or more of the following:
   a. women in the workplace
   b. jobs for women in the 21st century
   c. equality for women in the workforce
   d. the glass ceiling
   e. sex discrimination in the workplace

6. Find a topic of your own related to women and work, and write an essay.

Preparing to Read

Take a minute or two to look over the following reading selection. Note the title and author, read the first two paragraphs, and check the essay's length. Make certain you have the time now to read it carefully and to do the exercises that follow it. Then, in the spaces provided, answer the following questions.

1. What will the author probably say about work? _____

_____

_____

2. What is a workaholic? _____

_____

_____

3. What is a company man? _____

_____

Vocabulary

Good comprehension of what you are about to read depends upon your understanding of the words below. The number following each word refers to the paragraph where it is used.

obituary (2) death notice

coronary thrombosis (2) a form of heart attack

discreetly (16) cautiously, modestly

The Company Man

Ellen Goodman

Ellen Goodman started her career as a researcher and reporter for Newsweek *magazine, and has worked as an associate editor the* Boston Globe *since 1967. The following article is taken from her book,* At Large.

1   He worked himself to death, finally and precisely, at 3:00 A.M. Sunday morning.

2   The obituary didn't say that, of course. It said that he died of a coronary thrombosis—I think that was it—but everyone among his friends and acquaintances knew it instantly. He was a perfect Type A, a workaholic, a classic, they said to each other and shook their heads—and thought for five or ten minutes about the way they lived.

3   This man who worked himself to death finally and precisely at 3:00 A.M. Sunday morning—on his day off—was fifty-one years old and a vice-president. He was, however, one of six vice-presidents, and one of three who might conceivably—if the president died or retired soon enough—have moved to the top spot. Phil knew that.

4   He worked six days a week, five of them until eight or nine at night, during a time when his own company had begun the four-day week for everyone but the executives. He worked like the Important People. He had no outside "extracurricular interests," unless, of course, you think about a monthly golf game that way. To Phil, it was work. He always ate egg salad sandwiches at his desk. He was, of course, overweight, by 20 or 25 pounds. He thought it was okay, though, because he didn't smoke.

5   On Saturdays, Phil wore a sports jacket to the office instead of a suit, because it was the weekend.

6   He had a lot of people working for him, maybe sixty, and most of them liked him most of the time. Three of them will be seriously considered for his job. The obituary didn't mention that.

7   But it did list his "survivors" quite accurately. He is survived by his wife, Helen, forty-eight years old, a good woman of no particular marketable skills, who worked in an office before marrying and mothering. She had, according to her daughter, given up trying to compete with his work years ago, when the children were small. A company friend said, "I know how much you will miss him." And she answered, "I already have."

8   "Missing him all these years," she must have given up part of herself which had cared too much for the man. She would be "well taken care of."

9   His "dearly beloved" eldest of the "dearly beloved" children is a hard-working executive in a manufacturing firm down South. In the day and a half before the funeral, he went around the neighborhood researching his father, asking the neighbors what he was like. They were embarrassed.

10   His second child is a girl, who is twenty-four and newly married. She lives near her mother and they are close, but whenever she was alone with her father, in a car driving somewhere, they had nothing to say to each other.

11   The youngest is twenty, a boy, a high-school graduate who has spent the last couple of years, like a lot of his friends, doing enough

odd jobs to stay in grass and food. He was the one who tried to grab at his father, and tried to mean enough to him to keep the man at home. He was his father's favorite. Over the last two years, Phil stayed up nights worrying about the boy.

12   The boy once said, "My father and I only board here."

13   At the funeral, the sixty-year-old company president told the forty-eight-year-old widow that the fifty-one-year-old deceased had meant much to the company and would be missed and would be hard to replace. The widow didn't look him in the eye. She was afraid he would read her bitterness and, after all, she would need him to straighten out the finances—the stock options and all that.

14   Phil was overweight and nervous and worked too hard. If he wasn't at the office, he was worried about it. Phil was a Type A, a heart-attack natural. You could have picked him out in a minute from a lineup.

15   So when he finally worked himself to death, at precisely 3:00 A.M. Sunday morning, no one was really surprised.

16   By 5:00 P.M. the afternoon of the funeral, the company president had begun, discreetly of course, with care and taste, to make inquiries about his replacement. One of three men. He asked around: "Who's been working the hardest?"

Understanding the Content

Feel free to reread all or parts of the selection to answer the following questions.

1. Goodman's essay is an extended definition of "a company man." Define a company man in your own words in one or two sentences.

2. What is Goodman's thesis? What is she saying through the definition of the company man?

3. What does Phil's wife, Helen, mean when a company friend says, "I know how much you will miss him," and she answers, "I already have" (7)?

4. Why were Phil's neighbors "embarrassed" (9) when his eldest son went around the neighborhood asking what his father was like? Why did his son need to ask?

5. What kind of relationship did Phil have with his daughter and younger son?

6. What kind of man is the company president looking for to replace Phil?

Looking at Structure and Style

1. Is Goodman's thesis stated or implied? If stated, where?

2. Reread paragraphs 1 and 15. Why does Goodman repeat this information?

3. Describe Goodman's tone and attitude. What words or phrases help develop her tone and attitude?

4. Look over the essay and find the places where Goodman uses dialogue. What effect does the use of dialogue have in those places?

5. Goodman frequently highlights certain words with quotation marks, as in paragraph 4. Why? What purpose does this serve?

Evaluating the Author's Viewpoints

1. What is Goodman's attitude toward Phil? Is she sympathetic? How do you know? Do you agree with her? Explain.

2. In paragraph 4, Goodman says, "He [Phil] worked like the Important People." To whom is her sarcasm being directed? Is it deserved? Explain.

3. Based on this essay, what values does Goodman seem to hold about work and its importance in the scheme of things? Do you agree with her? Explain.

Pursuing Possible Essay Topics

1. Write an essay that examines the importance of work in your parents' life. Did work take priority over family for them? Did they balance work and family time?

2. Write a plan for a better workweek (or workday, work year) than the traditional 40-hour week and hourly wage.

3. Argue the need for hard work and long hours.

4. What would you do with your life if you did not have to work?

5. Brainstorm or freewrite on one or more of the following:
   a. workaholism   d. free time
   b. work conditions   e. working overtime
   c. the ideal job   f. minimum wage

6. Lay off these ideas and fire away at one of your own concerning some aspect of work or jobs.

Preparing to Read

Take a minute or two to look over the following reading selection. Note the title and the author, read the first two paragraphs, and check the essay's length. Make certain you have the time now to read it carefully and to do the exercises that follow it. Then, in the spaces provided, answer the following questions.

1. What does the title tell you about this essay? _____

   _____

   _____

2. What does the title and the first two paragraphs tell you about the author and

   his philosophy? _____

   _____

   _____

Vocabulary

Good comprehension of what you are about to read depends upon your understanding of the words below. The number following each word refers to the paragraph where it is used.

austerity (4) strictness; adhering to economy

chutzpah (5) sassiness; nerve

epiphany (9) a sudden realization or ability to understand something previously not understood

Less Is More

JEFF YEAGER

Jeff Yeager spent 24 years working as a CEO and senior executive with national nonprofit organizations in Washington, D.C., before becoming a freelance writer, public speaker, and broadcast journalist. Specializing in offering advice for living a better life with less, Yeager was dubbed "The Ultimate Cheapskate" by the NBC Today show, where he appears as a guest correspondent.

1   "WHY WOULD YOU WANT to live like that?" friends ask me. "You can do so much better."

2   That's something I've heard ever since I left my career as a well-paid professional fundraiser to become, as I like to say, "selfishly employed" as a freelance writer. It finally hit me when one friend said, "If I were you, I'd go back to fundraising in a nanosecond. You could be earning five times what you're making as a writer."

3   The bolt that hit me wasn't that I'd settled for less. It was that for the first time in my life I was, finally, happily, settled. I was totally content with my work and the lifestyle that came with it. If the alternative to settling for less is to live a life of always wanting more, then I know I made the right choice.

4   Call it author's austerity—the frugal lifestyle most freelancers must embrace to pursue their passion full time. But the fact is, that's been one of the best fringe benefits of my new life. When I left my 25-year career to write, and my income retreated to what it was during the Reagan administration, I developed a new appreciation for the relationship between work, money, things and happiness.

5   Of course, the bankroll I squirreled away during my earlier career bolstered my chutzpah when it came time to forsake a regular paycheck, although I've never needed to tap it. That's not because I've become an overnight success (I haven't). It's primarily because of my success at a most un-American practice: living within my means.

6   For the first time since the Great Depression, Americans now have a negative savings rate, spending more than we earn after taxes. But at the same time, it's oddly comforting to those of us downsizing our lifestyles to accommodate a downsized income. You see, unlike during the Depression, income isn't the problem; in fact, even when adjusted for inflation, U.S. incomes have never been higher.

7   The problem is spending—we're simply consuming too much, and ironically, that's not making us happier, as we thought it would. The things we buy often disappoint us, and the debt we're racking up to buy them keeps us awake at night. That's the comforting thing: knowing that more isn't necessarily better and understanding that controlling spending is more important than maximizing income.

8   In the interest of full disclosure, I'm no newbie when it comes to pinching pennies. In fact, my freelance career is built around the topic of enjoying life more by spending less. But it was my transition to the writing life that made me fully realize that I could never write a book about the relationship between money and happiness. There'd be nothing to write.

9   We all know—or at least we've been told—that time is money. The implication is that when you waste your time, you're wasting an opportunity to be out there earning more money. The epiphany that accompanied my career change is that money is also time.

10   As a result, I now value time and the things I can do with it—write, for example—more than money and the things I can buy with it. How

much money I earn (or more commonly don't earn) from my writing isn't unimportant. But it's no longer the reason I do what I do.

11   Last year, I finished writing a short story that I thought was the best thing I'd written. After enthusiastically pitching it to every editor who might be remotely interested in buying it, I ended up giving first rights to a literary publication, free of charge.

12   My wife said, comfortingly, "It's too bad you couldn't sell it. It's really good. But once you're more established, things will be different."

13   Thinking back on how much I enjoyed writing the piece and how proud I was of the story, I said, "I don't know, honey. I think it's the best money I never made."

Understanding the Content

Feel free to reread all or parts of the selection to answer the following questions.

1. What did Yeager do previously as a career? What does he do now?

2. How do most Americans manage their finances, according to Jeff Yeager?

3. What is the relationship between money and happiness in the author's opinion?

4. What is "author's austerity"?

5. What happened after Yeager wrote a short story?

Looking at Structure and Style

1. The author uses dialogue to begin the essay. Is this an effective device? Why or why not?

2. What organizing pattern does Yeager use in paragraph 7?

3. What is Yeager's thesis? Is it stated or implied? If stated, where?

4. Does the use of an anecdote in paragraphs 11–13 serve as an effective conclusion to this essay? Write a non-anecdotal conclusion to this essay.

5. What is Yeager's tone in this essay? His attitude toward the subject?

Evaluating the Author's Viewpoint

1. In your opinion, is this essay about money, happiness, or a combination of both? Explain your answer.

2. How does Jeff Yeager feel about the concept of time?

3. How does Jeff Yeager feel about how Americans manage their money?

4. Does Yeager think that having money and being happy go hand in hand?

5. What can you infer about why Jeff Yeager left his well-paying job to become a freelance writer?

6. Do you think Jeff Yeager is happier in his current career as a freelance writer than he was as a well-paid professional fundraiser? What makes you think this?

Pursuing Possible Essay Topics

1. Write an essay discussing your future career plans. What do you plan on doing and why?

2. Would you rather make a lot of money in your career or be happy with what you're doing and make less money? Why? Write an essay discussing your viewpoint.

3. Are you good at saving money or do you spend all of the money that you earn? Write an essay discussing how you manage your money and if you think that you are good at it.

4. What does it mean to be happy, in your opinion? Write an essay discussing your viewpoint.

5. Is it really "work" if you love what you do for a living? Write an essay discussing this concept.

6. Brainstorm or freewrite on one or more of the following:
   a. work
   b. happiness
   c. debt
   d. saving money
   e. career

7. Don't like these topics? Find a topic that interests you related to some aspect of work and write an essay on it.

▦ Preparing to Read

Take a minute or two to look over the following reading selection. Note the title and the author, read the first two paragraphs, and check the essay's length. Make certain you have the time now to read it carefully and to do the exercises that follow it. Then, in the spaces provided, answer the following questions.

1. What does the title tell you about this essay? _____

_____

_____

2. What do you think this essay will be about? _____

_____

_____

Vocabulary

Good comprehension of what you are about to read depends upon your understanding of the words below. The number following each word refers to the paragraph where it is used.

sloth (1) aversion to work or exertion

battery (8) an impression sequence or array; succession

reverence (9) feeling of awe and respect; veneration

tycoon (13) a wealthy or successful businessperson

emulate (14) imitate or try to be like

A Father's Character, Not His Success, Shapes Kids' Careers

Hal Lancaster

Hal Lancaster recently retired after a thirty-one year career as a reporter, editor, bureau chief, and columnist for The Wall Street Journal.

1   As a semipro baseball player, my father had a wicked curveball and enough dash in the outfield to earn the nickname "Speed." My nickname was "Sloth" and I couldn't even make my high-school junior varsity team.

2   "Some people just aren't cut out for athletics," my father said without a trace of disappointment when I told him about the bungled tryout. "You know, a lot of guys who didn't make it in sports ended up writing about it."

3   Like most muscle-headed teens, I had no clue what to do with my life. But my father's commonsense wisdom somehow seemed right. I enrolled in a journalism class the next semester and found my calling.

4   "The father's role in our society in terms of an offspring's career choice is very powerful," says Martin Fine, a Chicago psychiatrist who works with young professionals. Until women started entering the work force in numbers, he says, fathers were the primary career role models.

5   A father's influence derives more from his character than his success, Dr. Fine says. Children often rebel against the career preferences of a successful but negligent father, while a proud but impoverished peddler's dedication and sacrifice can serve as his children's career inspiration.

6   And that doesn't just apply to sons. Women with encouraging fathers are more likely to venture into traditionally male fields such as law and medicine, psychoanalyst Jacki Marton concluded from a survey of young career women. "Fathers who shared their work with daughters expanded their horizons," Dr. Marton says.

7   Certainly, accomplished fathers can create impossible expectations. Jeffrey Sonnenfeld, an Emory University leadership expert, tells of the CEO who, after a distinguished career, still felt he hadn't measured up to his father, who built a major company from scratch. "How do you beat a guy like that?" the anguished CEO asked Prof. Sonnenfeld.

8   My father boosted my career by giving me the freedom to choose my own path and by proudly devouring every word I ever wrote. Still, it always amazed me that my career direction came not from a guidance counselor studying a battery of test results or a sage teacher, but from my father, a working-class guy who would have laughed if I had ever called him wise. These recent reflections made me wonder how much successful people were influenced by their fathers. So I asked a few:

9   Kim B. Clark's father was in publishing and advertising. Before that, though, Merlin Clark grew up a cowboy, put himself through college—the first in his family to attend—taught in a country school and imparted to his son a reverence for education. "To be a teacher, in my family, was a high calling," says Mr. Clark, dean of Harvard Business School.

10   Mr. Clark says he also learned a lot about leadership and how to see the big picture from his father, who led by example and by the force of his character. "My father had a favorite saying: Ride the high country," he recalls. "That is, get out of the scrub brush and get into the mountains. See forever and dream big dreams."

11   None of J. Michael Cook's three children became accountants. Perhaps it's the shadow cast by the chairman and CEO of Deloitte & Touche. "If I worked in the accounting industry, the expectations would be enormous and there would be undue pressure," says Angela Cook, a senior marketing manager for American Express. "Luckily for me, that wasn't where my interests were."

12   Still, her father provided gentle career guidance. Early on, he counseled her to think about her strengths and what she liked to do. Later, as she considered specific opportunities at American Express, he posed questions to help her decide: Is it a long-term or short-term move? Would it make her happy? Would it give her work satisfaction?

13   As the son of legendary oil tycoon H.L. Hunt, Ray Hunt knows about long shadows. "I decided a long time ago not to compete with anybody," says Mr. Hunt, who has nonetheless built his Hunt Oil Co. into a major exploration company.

14   Mr. Hunt tries to emulate his father's guiding principles, such as hire quality people and treat them well. He says his father once borrowed money to pay Christmas bonuses. Most of all, he remembers the wildcatter denying that he was a gambler in business. "Ray, I've never made a decision where, if everything went wrong, I couldn't keep going," Mr. Hunt recalls him saying. "That's among the top five sentences I remember from my father and I don't remember the other four."

15   Sons also learn from their father's mistakes. James Champy, chairman of CSC Index and co-author of the best-selling "Re-Engineering the Corporation," learned the importance of a balanced life from his workaholic father, a general contractor, who suffered his third heart attack while working on a Saturday and died at age 54. "He never enjoyed the fruits of what he built," he said.

16   The elder Champy's lessons on self-reliance and independence also left his son with an "almost genetic" reluctance to work for a large corporation, which led him to consulting.

17   So, for all these people, and especially for me, I want to say, "thanks, Dad."

18   In loving memory: William Merrit Lancaster (9/2/14–2/16/96).

Understanding the Content

Feel free to reread all or parts of the selection to answer the following questions.

1. What was the author's father's nickname in baseball? The author's nickname?

2. What was Lancaster's father's reaction when his son didn't make the junior varsity baseball team?

3. What effect does a father's influence have on children, according to Dr. Martin Fine?

4. What did James Champy learn from his father?

5. What was H.L. Hunt's "guiding principle," according to his son?

Looking at Structure and Style

1. What is the thesis of this essay? Is it stated or implied? If stated, where?

2. What organizing pattern is used in paragraph 1? How does it help Lancaster develop his thesis?

3. What is the purpose of paragraphs 9–14? What is their relationship to paragraph 15?

4. Is the author's use of outside sources effective? Why or why not? Do they help him develop his overall thesis?

5. Does the title of this essay adequately convey the message of this essay? If so, use examples to support your answer.

Evaluating the Author's Viewpoint

1. What can you infer about how the author feels about his father? What can you infer about their relationship?

2. What can you infer about the author as a teenager? How can you tell?

3. What do you think was the author's purpose in writing this essay?

4. Why do you think Lancaster includes the example of James Champy and his father in this essay? Is it effective?

Pursuing Possible Essay Topics

1. Write an essay discussing your relationship with your father. How has he influenced you?

2. Who has had more of an influence on you, your mother or your father? Or is it another family member entirely? Write an essay describing this person and their influence on you.

3. Do you think a father's character or his success is more important? Why? Write an essay discussing your viewpoint.

4. What is your main career goal? Has anyone in your family been especially supportive of that goal? Write an essay discussing this support.

5. With a classmate or a group of classmates, discuss this article. Do you think Lancaster has sufficiently supported his thesis? Why or why not? Collect the notes from the discussion and write a brief essay describing what you discussed.

6. Brainstorm or freewrite on one or more of the following:

   a. parenting

   b. fatherhood

   c. success

   d. character

7. Have your own ideas on another topic? Find a topic that interests you related to some aspect of work and write an essay on it.

Preparing to Read

Take a minute or two to look over the following reading selection. Note the title and the author, read the first two paragraphs, and check the essay's length. Make certain you have the time now to read it carefully and to do the exercises that follow it. Then, in the spaces provided, answer the following questions.

1. What does the title tell you about this essay? _____

_____

_____

2. What do you think this essay will be about? _____

_____

_____

3. How do you think the authors feel about their subject matter? How can you tell?

_____

_____

Vocabulary

Good comprehension of what you are about to read depends upon your understanding of the words below. The number following each word refers to the paragraph where it is used.

sinewy (2) lean and muscular

vantage (9) a position that affords a broad overview

aghast (11) struck by amazement; astounded

per capita (22) equally to each individual in a population

moribund (23) on the verge of becoming obsolete

engender (28) to bring into existence

precarious (28) lacking in security or stability

Two Cheers for Sweatshops

NICHOLAS D. KRISTOF AND SHERYL WUDUNN

Nicholas D. Kristof has been the New York Times *bureau chief in Hong Kong, Beijing, and Tokyo. Sheryl WuDunn has served as a foreign correspondent in Beijing and Tokyo. This essay was excerpted in the* New York Times Magazine *from their book* Thunder from the East: Portrait of a Rising Asia.

1   It was breakfast time, and the food stand in the village in northeastern Thailand was crowded. Maesubin Sisoipha, the middle-aged woman cooking the food, was friendly, her portions large and the price right. For the equivalent of about 5 cents, she offered a huge green mango leaf filled with rice, fish paste and fried beetles. It was a hearty breakfast. If one didn't mind the odd antenna left sticking in one's teeth.

2   One of the half-dozen men and women sitting on a bench eating was a sinewy, bare-chested laborer in his late 30's named Mongkol Latlakorn. It was a hot, lazy day, and so we started chatting idly about the food and, eventually, our families. Mongkol mentioned that his daughter, Darin, was 15, and his voice softened as he spoke of her. She was beautiful and smart, and her father's hopes rested on her.

3   "Is she in school?" we asked.

4   "Oh, no." Mongkol said, his eyes sparkling with amusement. "She's working in a factory in Bangkok. She's making clothing for export to America." He explained that she was paid $2 a day for a nine-hour shift, six days a week.

5   "It's dangerous work," Mongkol added. "Twice the needles went right through her hands. But the managers bandaged up her hands, and both times she got better again and went back to work."

6   "How terrible," we murmured sympathetically.

7   Mongkol looked up, puzzled. "It's good pay," he said. "I hope she can keep that job. There's all this talk about factories closing now, and she said there are rumors that her factory might close. I hope that doesn't happen. I don't know what she would do then."

8   He was not of course, indifferent to his daughter's suffering; he simply had a different perspective from ours—not only when it came to food but also when it came to what constituted desirable work.

9   Nothing captures the difference in mind-set between East and West more than attitudes toward sweatshops. Nike and other American companies have been hammered in the Western press over the last decade for producing shoes, toys and other products in grim little factories with dismal conditions. Protests against sweatshops and the dark forces of globalization that they seem to represent have become common at meetings of the World Bank and the World Trade Organization and this month, at a World Economic Forum in Australia,

livening up the scene for Olympic athletes arriving for the competition. Yet sweatshops that seem brutal from the vantage point of an American sitting in his living room can appear tantalizing to a Thai laborer getting by on beetles.

10   Fourteen years ago, we moved to Asia and began reporting there. Like most Westerners, we arrived in the region outraged at sweatshops. In time, though, we came to accept the view supported by most Asians: that the campaign against sweatshops risks harming the very people it is intended to help. For beneath their grime, sweatshops are a clear sign of the industrial revolution that is beginning to reshape Asia.

11   This is not to praise sweatshops. Some managers are brutal in the way they house workers in firetraps, expose children to dangerous chemicals, deny bathroom breaks, demand sexual favors, force people to work double shifts or dismiss anyone who tries to organize a union. Agitation for improved safety conditions can be helpful, just as it was in 19th-century Europe. But Asian workers would be aghast at the idea of American consumers boycotting certain toys or clothing in protest. The simplest way to help the poorest Asians would be to buy more from sweatshops, not less.

12   On our first extended trip to China, in 1987, we traveled to the Pearl River delta in the south of the country. There we visited several factories, including one in the boomtown of Dongguan, where about 100 female workers sat at workbenches stitching together bits of leather to make purses for a Hong Kong company. We chatted with several women as their fingers flew over their work and asked about their hours.

13   "I start at about 6:30, after breakfast, and go until about 7 P.M.," explained one shy teenage girl. "We break for lunch, and I take half an hour off then."

14   "You do this six days a week?"

15   "Oh, no. Every day."

16   "Seven days a week?"

17   "Yes." She laughed at our surprise. "But then I take a week or two off at Chinese New Year to go back to my village."

18   The others we talked to all seemed to regard it as a plus that the factory allowed them to work long hours. Indeed, some had sought out this factory precisely because it offered them the chance to earn more.

19   "It's actually pretty annoying how hard they want to work," said the factory manager, a Hong Kong man. "It means we have to worry about security and have a supervisor around almost constantly."

20   It sounded pretty dreadful, and it was. We and other journalists wrote about the problems of child labor and oppressive conditions in both China and South Korea. But, looking back, our worries were excessive. Those sweatshops tended to generate the wealth to solve

the problems they created. If Americans had reacted to the horror stories in the 1980's by curbing imports of those sweatshop products, then neither southern China nor South Korea would have registered as much progress as they have today.

21   The truth is, those grim factories in Dongguan and the rest of southern China contributed to a remarkable explosion of wealth. In the years since our first conversations there, we've returned many times to Dongguan and the surrounding towns and seen the transformation. Wages have risen from about $50 a month to $250 a month or more today. Factory conditions have improved as businesses have scrambled to attract and keep the best laborers. A private housing market has emerged, and video arcades and computer schools have opened to cater to workers with rising incomes. A hint of a middle class has appeared—as has China's closest thing to a Western-style independent newspaper, *Southern Weekend*.

22   Partly because of these tens of thousands of sweatshops, China's economy has become one of the hottest in the world. Indeed, if China's 30 provinces were counted as individual countries, then the 20 fastest-growing countries in the world between 1978 and 1995 would all have been Chinese. When Britain launched the Industrial Revolution in the late 18th century, it took 58 years for per capita output to double. In China, per capita output has been doubling every 10 years.

23   In fact, the most vibrant parts of Asia are nearly all in what might be called the Sweatshop Belt, from China and South Korea to Malaysia, Indonesia and even Bangladesh and India. Today these sweatshop countries control about one quarter of the global economy. As the industrial revolution spreads through China and India, there are good reasons to think that Asia will continue to pick up speed. Some World Bank forecasts show Asia's share of global gross domestic product rising to 55 to 60 percent by about 2025—roughly the West's share at its peak half a century ago. The sweatshops have helped lay the groundwork for a historic economic realignment that is putting Asia back on its feet. Countries are rebounding from the economic crisis of 1997–98 and the sweatshops—seen by Westerners as evidence of moribund economics—actually reflect an industrial revolution that is raising living standards in the East.

24   Of course, it may sound silly to say that sweatshops offer a route to prosperity, when wages in the poorest countries are sometimes less than $1 a day. Still, for an impoverished Indonesian or Bangladeshi woman with a handful of kids who would otherwise drop out of school and risk dying of mundane diseases like diarrhea, $1 or $2 a day can be a life-transforming wage.

25   This was made abundantly clear in Cambodia, when we met a 40-year-old woman named Nhem Yen, who told us why she moved

to an area with particularly lethal malaria. "We needed to eat," she said. "And here there is wood, so we thought we could cut it and sell it."

26   But then Nhem Yen's daughter and son-in-law both died of malaria, leaving her with two grandchildren and five children of her own. With just one mosquito net, she had to choose which children would sleep protected and which would sleep exposed.

27   In Cambodia, a large mosquito net costs $5. If there had been a sweatshop in the area, however harsh or dangerous, Nhem Yen would have leapt at the chance to work in it, to earn enough to buy a net big enough to cover all her children.

28   For all the misery they can engender, sweatshops at least offer a precarious escape from the poverty that is the developing world's greatest problem. Over the past 50 years, countries like India resisted foreign exploitation, while countries that started at a similar economic level—like Taiwan and South Korea—accepted sweatshops as the price of development. Today there can be no doubt about which approach worked better. Taiwan and South Korea are modern countries with low rates of infant mortality and high levels of education; in contrast, every year 3.1 million Indian children die before the age of 5, mostly from diseases of poverty like diarrhea.

29   The effect of American pressure on sweatshops is complicated. While it clearly improves conditions at factories that produce branded merchandise for companies like Nike, it also raises labor costs across the board. That encourages less well established companies to mechanize and to reduce the number of employees needed. The upshot is to help people who currently have jobs in Nike plants but to risk jobs for others. The only thing a country like Cambodia has to offer is terribly cheap wages; if companies are scolded for paying those wages, they will shift their manufacturing to marginally richer areas like Malaysia or Mexico.

30   Sweatshop monitors do have a useful role. They can compel factories to improve safety. They can also call attention to the impact of sweatshops on the environment. The greatest downside of industrialization is not exploitation of workers but toxic air and water. In Asia each year, three million people die from the effects of pollution. The factories springing up throughout the region are far more likely to kill people through the chemicals they expel than through terrible working conditions.

31   By focusing on these issues, by working closely with organizations and news media in foreign countries, sweatshops can be improved. But refusing to buy sweatshop products risks making Americans feel good while harming those we are trying to help. As a Chinese proverb goes, "First comes the bitterness, then there is sweetness and wealth and honor for 10,000 years."

Understanding the Content

Feel free to reread all or parts of the selection to answer the following questions.

1. What does Mongkol Latlakorn's daughter do for a living? How old is she? How does Latlakorn feel about his daughter's occupation?

2. When did the authors move to Asia and what was their purpose, do you think?

3. What effect has the sweatshop system had on China's economy?

4. What is the "Sweatshop Belt"?

5. What has been the effect of American pressure on sweatshops, according to Kristof and WuDunn?

Looking at Structure and Style

1. What is the thesis of this essay? Is it stated or implied? If stated, where?

2. What is the organizing pattern used in paragraph 21? What is that paragraph's relation to the rest of the essay?

3. What is the purpose of paragraphs 1–7? Is beginning the essay in this way effective? Why or why not, in your opinion?

4. What was the authors' purpose in writing this essay?

5. What does the title of this essay mean? Does it adequately convey the main point of this essay? Why or why not?

6. Is paragraph 31 an effective concluding paragraph for this essay? Is the use of the Chinese proverb in that paragraph effective? Why or why not?

7. What is the overall purpose of this essay? Were the authors successful in their execution? Why or why not?

Evaluating the Author's Viewpoint

1. Compare and contrast the difference in mind-set between the East and the West when it comes to sweatshops, as discussed by the authors.

2. What was the authors' viewpoint on sweatshops when they first moved to Asia fourteen years ago and now? What changed their minds?

3. After reading this essay, do you agree or disagree with Kristof and WuDunn's viewpoint? Why or why not?

4. What can you infer about how the authors feel about Mongkol Latlakorn's support of his daughter's working when they first meet him? How can you tell?

5. Are Kristof and WuDunn completely supportive of the sweatshop system? Use examples to support your answer.

Pursuing Possible Essay Topics

1. After reading this essay, do you think there are any benefits to the existence of sweatshops, either here or in Asia? If so, what are they? Write an essay discussing your viewpoint.

2. What are a few things you learned from reading this essay that you didn't know before? Write an essay discussing some things that were new to you.

3. Do you think that with the proper regulation and monitoring, sweatshops are an acceptable way to employ people? Why or why not? Write an essay discussing your viewpoint.

4. Do you think that it is acceptable to import low-priced consumer items from countries like Cambodia and Thailand or would you rather pay more and have the items produced here in the United States? Why? Write an essay discussing your viewpoint.

5. Brainstorm or freewrite on one or more of the following:
   a. sweatshops
   b. child labor
   c. globalization
   d. Asia
   e. cheap goods
   f. work

6. Don't like any of these topics? Find a topic that interests you related to some aspect of work and write an essay on it

Opposing Viewpoints on Work

The next two selections are concerned with the pros and cons of outsourcing jobs. Many companies have found that they can save money and still get the job done by hiring workers in countries overseas where the labor is cheaper. However, some say that shifting jobs overseas is unfair for American families who not only lose their jobs but can't find comparable jobs because they have been shifted overseas.

Preparing to Read

Take a minute or two to look over the following reading selection. Note the title and the author, read the first paragraph, and check the essay's length. Make certain you have the time now to read it carefully and to do the exercises that follow it. Then, in the spaces provided, answer the following questions.

1. What does the title tell you about this essay? The author's viewpoint? _____

_____

_____

2. What, if anything, do you know about outsourcing? What do you think you

will learn from this essay about this topic? _____

_____

_____

Vocabulary

Good comprehension of what you are about to read depends upon your understanding of the words below. The number following each word refers to the paragraph where it is used.

buzzword (1) catchphrase

reckon (8) determine; consider

forte (8) strong point; specialty

How Outsourcing Can Benefit Your Business

As found at www.productivitytools.com

The following selection appears on a recent posting of the Productivity Tools
Web site.

1   Outsourcing is the new buzzword in the business community. However, the question of why businesses outsource their business process is still being asked by a lot of people. Surely outsourcing would create a lot of profit for a business. Besides, why would businesses outsource their business process if they won't make any money out of it?

2   Aside from saving a lot of money from outsourcing, companies that want to unburden themselves from heavy workloads caused by the growing demand of their work by the public resort to outsourcing to do the job they should be doing. Businesses today hire outsourcing companies from different countries to do a part of the business process in order to save money on labor and also expand their capabilities.

3   Since there are a lot of skilled individuals in developing countries with little chance of employ, outsourcing became one of the best industries considered by a lot of talented and skilled individuals in developing countries. In terms of earnings, outsourcing provides brassy labor compared to getting your companies [sic] work done in-house. For instance, in the United States, you would pay a qualified professional about 100 dollars to get the job done. However, outsourcing the job to other countries will only ask you to pay twenty dollars to get the same job done with an equally qualified professional and at the same time, keep them happy.

4   The minimum earnings rate in developing countries is much lower compared in the United States. This is why outsourcing can save your company a lot of money in terms of earnings payments.

5   These are the benefits that your company can take advantage of in outsourcing. Cheap labor with equally qualified professionals in other countries can definitely save your company a lot of money on salaries.

6   However, before you try and outsource part of your companys [sic] work, you have to find if the outsourcing company is the right company for you. Find out if the company is hiring qualified professionals with skills related to your business. This will guarantee the best quality for your outsourced jobs.

7   By first checking out the quality of work from an outsourcing company, you will be able to find if the work done by them is up to par or not. If it is not, you can always go to other outsourcing companies and check out the quality of their work. Doing this will enable you to find the company that will meet your standards.

8   You also have to reckon if the professionals who will be handling your outsourced work is qualified to do the job. Besides, you don't want a talented programmer to do the job of a mechanic. You have to know the forte of the outsourcing company and find if they will be able to perform the job you will offer them with quality and efficiency.

9   Outsourcing will answer your business's financial and production problems. If you are looking for a way to save money and at the same time increase productiveness, outsourcing is the right choice for your company. Not only will you save a lot of money because of cheaper labor compared as to the rate in your state, but you will also have the same quality of work that the equally qualified professionals in your state can do at a much lower price.

10   With outsourcing, your business will be able to turn and also decrease the burden of heavy work load.

Understanding the Content

Feel free to reread all or parts of the selection to answer the following questions.

1. According to Waller, why do companies outsource?

2. What advantages does outsourcing hold for developing nations?

3. How can a company figure out if outsourcing is the right choice for their company?

4. What effect does outsourcing have on productiveness, according to the author?

5. Generally, what is the quality of outsourced work, according to the author?

Looking at Structure and Style

1. What is Waller's thesis? Is it stated or implied?

2. What is Corcoran's attitude toward the subject? Her tone?

3. How does the author support her thesis? Use examples in your response.

4. What is the purpose of this essay? Has Waller achieved her goal?

5. What is the organizing pattern used in paragraph 6?

6. Do you think the author does an adequate job of supporting her concluding paragraph: "With outsourcing, your business will be able to turn and also decrease the burden of heavy workload." (10) Why or why not?

Evaluating the Author's Viewpoint

1. After reading this selection, do you agree or disagree with the author that the outsourcing of work and jobs is beneficial to both the company doing the outsourcing and the company taking on the work? Why?

2. Based on the information that Waller includes in this selection, has she convinced you of her thesis? Why or why not?

3. Do you think that Waller exhibits any bias in her article? If so, give examples.

4. Do you think that someone considering outsourcing jobs would read this essay and be convinced that this would be an effective use of their company's time, money, and efforts? Why or why not?

Pursuing Possible Essay Topics

Before beginning an essay on family or relationships, read the following essay, *Outsourcing Jobs Leaves the American White-Collar Worker Behind* by Susan Galowicz.

Preparing to Read

Take a minute or two to look over the following reading selection. Note the title and the author, read the first paragraph, and check the essay's length. Make certain you have the time now to read it carefully and to do the exercises that follow it. Then, in the spaces provided, answer the following questions.

1. What does the title tell you about this essay? The author's viewpoint? _____

   _____

   _____

2. How might the thesis of this essay be different from the one put forth in the previous essay? Based on your reading of the first paragraph of this essay, do you have an opinion about who will make a better argument? Why? _____

   _____

   _____

Vocabulary

Good comprehension of what you are about to read depends upon your understanding of the words below. The number following each word refers to the paragraph where it is used.

voiceless (2) unspoken; unvoiced

pitting (7) to set in opposition

rhetoric (9) speech-making

Outsourcing Jobs Leaves the American White-Collar Worker Behind
A revised and updated 'Outsourcing America' calls for action

SUSAN GALOWICZ

The following selection appears on EurekaAlert, an online, global news service operated by AAAS, the science society, providing "a central place through which universities, medical centers, journals, government agencies, corporations and their organizations engaged in research can bring their news to the media." Susan Galowicz wrote the original news release, a shorter version, for the online "RIT news and events," published by the Rochester Institute of Technology.

1   Outsourcing might be good for American corporations, but it's not necessarily good for American workers, and it's likely to be bad for the American economy, even in the long run.

2   The revised edition of *Outsourcing America: The True Cost of Shipping Jobs Overseas and What Can Be Done about It* (AMACOM) written by Ron Hira, assistant professor of public policy at Rochester Institute of Technology, and Anil Hira, professor of political science at Simon Fraser University in Vancouver, brings attention to the voiceless white-collar American worker.

3   Moving jobs overseas is reshaping the American economy to suit corporate America. It also compromises American workers, the authors maintain. The trend has increased significantly since *Outsourcing America* was first published in 2005 and now includes different skill levels and types of jobs, says Ron Hira.

4   Released this spring, *Outsourcing America* updates the outsourcing debate and critically assesses the role corporations play in setting policy for high-skill immigration and outsourcing, the practice of moving American jobs across national borders. The authors also look at outsourcing trends in Europe, Canada and Australia, and other developed countries.

5   *Outsourcing America* closely examines the message businesses send when they threaten to outsource more jobs if not allowed to import cheaper guest workers.

6   "What they're saying is that increasing the guest worker program (H-1B and L-1 visa programs) will keep jobs here and save jobs from being offshored," says RIT's Hira. "When in reality those programs are being used to do knowledge transfer to transfer jobs overseas. The business community is on the one hand saying outsourcing is good, and on the other using the threat of outsourcing to change immigration policy. It's quite clever."

7   Instead of American companies competing against foreign rivals— which was the case in the 1980s when American semiconductor, auto and steel manufacturers lost market share to Japanese manufacturers— companies are now pitting their American workers against their overseas counterparts. According to Hira, this changes the political dynamics, but more importantly, changes which policies will be effective.

8   The white-collar worker has no representation in the outsourcing debate controlled by business interests, he notes. Likewise, the U.S. government has taken no policy response to outsourcing, an issue that has surfaced in the 2008 election season.

9   "The presidential candidates have tried to use the issue of outsourcing to their advantage, but once you cut through the rhetoric, there isn't much substance behind the policy proposals from either candidate," Hira says.

10   The authors recommend establishing a new organizational institution that represents American workers, something akin to the influential AARP, but on issues that directly affect the workplace.

11   "We don't have an organization for people who work," Hira says. "There's almost no awareness even that people aren't represented in Washington. And I don't see anybody talking about it."

Understanding the Content

Feel free to reread all or parts of the selection to answer the following questions.

1. What source does the author use to support her contention that "outsourcing might be good for American corporations, but it's not necessarily good for American workers"? Is this a credible and effective source? Why or why not?

2. What are the results put forth in *Outsourcing America*?

3. What are American companies doing when it comes to competing against foreign rivals, according to Ron Hira? What is the effect of these actions?

4. What effect does outsourcing have on the white-collar worker, according to Ron Hira?

5. What does Hira think of the presidential candidates' rhetoric on outsourcing?

6. What do Hira and his coauthors recommend for American workers, according to this essay?

Looking at Structure and Style

1. What is the thesis of this selection? Is it stated or implied?

2. What is the author's attitude toward the subject? Her tone? Compare and contrast it to the tone and attitude in the previous essay.

3. How does the author use outside sources in this essay? Are they effective? Should there have been more or fewer outside sources incorporated to support the thesis?

4. Who does a better job of supporting their thesis: this author or Waller? Why? Be specific in detailing who you think does a better job and why.

5. What is the purpose of including paragraphs 7 and 8 in this selection? Do they support the author's thesis? Why or why not?

Evaluating the Author's Viewpoint

1. How does the author feel about outsourcing?

2. Do you agree or disagree with the author that "companies are not pitting their American workers against their overseas counterparts" based on what you've read in this selection? Why?

3. Based on the information that the author includes in this selection, has she convinced you of her thesis? Why or why not?

4. Is there any evidence of bias in this article? If so, give examples.

Pursuing Possible Essay Topics

1. Write an essay comparing and contrasting how outsourcing is portrayed, vis a vis the American worker in each of these selections.

2. Write an essay discussing who you think does a better job of defending their viewpoint, Waller or Gawlowicz. In your essay, include support for (or examples that support) your viewpoint.

3. With whose essay do you agree more, Waller's or Gawlowicz's? Write an essay defending your position.

4. Write an essay discussing your viewpoint about outsourcing. Is outsourcing good for America? Why or why not?

5. Brainstorm or freewrite on one or more of the following:
   a. work
   b. outsourcing
   c. the global economy
   d. cheap goods
   e. white-collar workers

6. If none of these ideas works for you, select your own topic on some aspect of work and write an essay about it.

Student Essay

Read the following narrative essay written by a student. As you read, look for answers to these questions:

1. Does the essay fit the assignment to write on some aspect of work?

2. Does the essay have a thesis and adequate support?

3. Does the essay hold your interest?

"Oh, I'm Just a Housewife"

Roy Wilson

1   After watching my mother deal with our family of five, I can't understand why her answer to the question "What do you do?" is always "Oh, I'm just a housewife." JUST a housewife? Anyone who spends most of her time in meal preparation and cleanup, washing and drying clothes, keeping the house clean, attending PTA meetings, leading a cub scout troop, playing taxi driver to us kids when it's time for school, music lessons or the dentist, doing volunteer work for her favorite charity, and making sure that all our family needs are met is not JUST a housewife. She's the real Wonder Woman.

2   Why is it that so many mothers like mine think of themselves as second-class citizens or something similar because they don't have a job? Where has this notion come from? Have we males made them feel this way? Has our society made "going to work" outside the home seem more important than what a housewife must face each day?

3   I would be very curious to see what would happen if a housewife went on strike. Dishes would pile up. Food in the house would run out. No meals would appear on the table. There would be no clean clothes when needed. Hobbed-nailed boots would be required just to make it through the cluttered house. Walking and bus riding would increase. Those scout troops would have to disband. Charities would suffer.

4   I doubt if the man of the house would be able to take over. Oh, he might start out with the attitude that he can do just as good a job, but how long would that last? Not long, once he had to come home each night after work to more chores. There would be no more coming home to a prepared meal; he'd have to fix it himself. The kids would all be screaming for something to eat, clean clothes and more bus fare money. Once he quieted the kids, he'd have to clean the house (yes, housewives do windows), go shopping (either take the kids or get a baby sitter), make sure that the kids got a bath (after cleaning out all the dog hairs from the bathtub), and fix lunches for the next day. Once the kids were down for the night, he might be able to crawl into an unmade bed and try to read the morning newspaper.

5   No, I don't think many males are going to volunteer for the job. I know I don't want it. So, thanks, Mom! I'll do what I can to create a national holiday for housewives. It could be appropriately called Wonder Working Woman Day.

Reaction

In your journal or on a separate sheet of paper, write your reaction to the student essay. Use the questions posed before the essay as a guide for your comments.

Viewpoints on Images

While looking at the photo, think about how the idea of work has changed over the past few decades. What impact has technology had on the types of jobs that people do today?

© Ed Kashi/Corbis

On the Net

Chances are, at some point in your life, you'll need a résumé. If you would like to create one, revise the one you have, or get advice, visit one or more of the many Web sites that deal with résumés. About.com, which you can visit at *http://jobsearchtech.about.com/msub12-builders.htm,* has a complete site with help for creating a résumé from scratch or updating an existing résumé, and it also gives information on how to create your own Web page, which may help in a future job search. There are also links on this site that might prove helpful if you are undecided on your career path.

If you are more interested in getting career advice so that you don't end up like the "company man" described in the Goodman selection, visit one or more of the following sites to get the information you want: *www.ajb.dni.us* (America's Job Bank), *www.careercity.com* (Career City), or *www.cweb.com* (Career Web). Then answer the following questions:

1. What is the most important information you found on the site?

2. Which site would you visit again if you were actively looking for a job? Why?

3. Which sites, if any, were not helpful? Why? What kind of information would make them more helpful to people looking for jobs?

Now, do your own search on a topic of your choice related to "work" and answer the questions above.

9 Viewpoints on the Media and Technology

Focus on the Media and Technology

To help you focus on the subject of this chapter, take a few minutes to prepare for the topic by prewriting on one or more of the following prompts:

1. the importance of newspapers on your life
2. your use of the Internet
3. iPods and MP3 players
4. your favorite television programs
5. censorship of the media
6. the effects of playing video games
7. cell phones

Getting through a day without being touched by the media and technology would be unusual. We have daily newspapers (though readership seems to be slipping due to television and the Internet), weekly newsmagazines to recap what we might have missed in the daily papers, and digest magazines that gather articles and even books from a variety of sources and condense them for us so that we can keep up without straining ourselves intellectually. We have books and magazines on everything from how to have better sex to how to make a bomb. We stand in line for hours to be among the first to see the latest blockbuster movie. We wouldn't think of owning a car without an AM/FM radio with cassette and CD player and maybe a GPS system thrown in for good measure. We can't seem to get enough music: stores fill our ears with filtered music; parks and streets fill up with people wired to their headsets or cell phones. More than 90 million homes in the United States alone have television sets, each one turned on for an average of seven hours a day. According to one study done by the Roper Organization, 64 percent of the American public turns to television for most of its news, and 53 percent rank television as the most believable news source.

Collectively, the power that the media have over us is worth examining. Both directly and indirectly, the media have a profound effect on our lives. What we eat, what we buy, what we do, even what we think, is influenced by the media.

Concern for the direction in which the media are taking us has prompted such books as Marie Winn's *The Plug-In Drug* and *Unplugging the Plug-In Drug*, which deal with the negative effects of television; David Halberstam's *The Powers That Be*, an account of the people who create, control, and use the media to shape American policy and politics; Norman Corwin's *Trivializing America: The Triumph of Mediocrity*, a look at the way the media have contributed to a lowering of our cultural standards; Ben Bagdikian's *The Media Monopoly*, in which it is revealed that only 26 corporations control half or more of all media, including book publishers, television and radio stations, newspapers, and movie companies; Mark Hertsgaard's *On Bended Knee: The Press and the Reagan Presidency*, which reveals how the press gets conned by the candidates and ignores election issues; Patricia Greenfield's *Mind and the Media: The Effects of Television, Video Games, and Computers*, which shows the media's effects on us; James Fallow's *Breaking the News: How the Media Undermine American Democracy;* and Susan Jacoby's *The Age of American Unreason.*

Is all this attention uncalled-for? How believable, how revealing, how comprehensive, how good is what the media provide us? What effect will the Internet—and technology in general—have on our lives? What are the benefits—and the pitfalls—of technology and the Internet? How much influence do advertising sponsors have on the media? What effect is the violence portrayed in movies and on television having on our society? Is rap music causing harm? Should we be more concerned with media effects than we are? Just what effects *do* the media have on our lives? These are questions that the reading selections in this unit may prompt you to ask. It is hoped that reading them will stimulate both your thinking and your writing.

Preparing to Read

Take a minute or two to look over the following reading selection. Note the title and the author, read the opening paragraph, and check the essay's length. Make certain you have the time now to read it carefully and to do the exercises that follow it. Then, in the spaces provided, answer the following questions.

1. What do you think the subject of this essay will be? _____

_____

_____

2. What is the author's tone? _____

_____

3. What is Poniewozik's attitude toward Dennis Pluchinsky? How can you tell?

_____

_____

_____

Vocabulary

Good comprehension of what you are about to read depends upon your understanding of the words below. The number following each word refers to the paragraph where it is used.

squelch (1) suppress, crush

mealymouthed (1) insincere, unwilling to be direct

infrastructure (1) understructure, foundation

in retrospect (4) in reviewing the past

innocuous (8) inoffensive, harmless

expeditiously (11) quickly and efficiently

conscientious (14) dedicated, devoted, thorough

fiefdoms (15) empires

prerogatives (15) privileges, freedoms

mea culpas (17) acts of contrition, amends

Calling the C-Word the C-Word

James Poniewozik

James Poniewozik writes for TIME *magazine as a media and television critic. He is also a regular radio commentator for NPR's "All Things Considered" and "On the Media." The following essay appeared in* TIME *magazine.*

1   Three cheers for Dennis Pluchinsky. These days, too many people who would squelch reporting and expression couch their threats in mealymouthed terms—"watch what you say," and so on—so as to avoid being accused of favoring censorship. Not so Pluchinsky, a State Department analyst who has studied terrorism for the past 25 years. Writing in the *Washington Post* Sunday, Pluchinsky accuses the U.S. media of "treason" for reporting in detail on infrastructure and government weaknesses that make the country vulnerable to terrorists. These reports, he says, are easily available for terrorists to peruse and exploit. And he doesn't mince words about his solution: "This type of reporting—carrying specifics about U.S. vulnerabilities— must be stopped or censored."

2   You've got to admire a man who's willing to call the c-word the c-word, though his candor is not likely to win him many friends in the media. The knee-jerk journalistic reaction is to call Pluchinsky an alarmist, to say that reports in the press give no aid to terror- ists that they don't already have. Considering the man's quarter- century of experience, that would be arrogant. But for his own part, Pluchinsky doesn't seem to have thought much about the utility of a free press at all. Puzzling over post-9/11 terrorism coverage of our terror vulnerabilities, he writes, "I do not understand the media's agenda here."

3   Let me try to explain it. A large part of that agenda, idealism aside, is to stay alive. The bulk of the journalists with the highest profile in cov- ering the war on terrorism—and its occasional embarrassments—are not just in war zones overseas but in cities like Washington and New York. They rightfully see themselves as potentially the next victims of another large-scale terrorist attack. And Pluchinsky does nothing to counter the argument that aggressive reporting might actually do a thing or two to prevent one.

4   The basic failure to prevent the Sept. 11 attacks was not that so many of us imagined the possibility, but that so few of us did. In retro- spect, the idea that terrorists might use airplanes as flying bombs— and were planning to do so—seems obvious to any one looking at the pieces of information available before Sept. 11. It evidently didn't occur to the right people in the government, though, or for that mat- ter in the media: a terrorist searching pre-Sept. 11 reporting for that scheme would be out of luck.

5   The kind of scenario-spinning that the press has engaged in since Sept. 11 can seem like reckless brainstorming. When a journalist suggests that a terrorist might give himself Ebola and spread the disease in public, or blow up one of America's numerous chemical trucks to produce a crude gas attack, it may shock you or me. But that's because you and I are not soulless murdering bastards. The enemy that wants to kill us consists of people who look at any object they encounter—a truck, an airplane-dinner fork—and think, "How can I use this to kill as many people as possible?"

6   It flatters journalists to assume they can compete at that game. Look at one of the headlines Pluchinsky considers irresponsible: "Chemical Plants Are Feared As Targets." Can anyone plausibly argue that it never occurred to the folks who perpetrated Sept. 11 to hit a chemical plant?

7   Pluchinsky's stronger argument is that journalists endanger us when they report on specific vulnerabilities to terrorists or mistakes past terrorists have made. "Al Qaeda terrorists now know to pay a speeding ticket promptly," he writes. "They now know not to pay for things with large amounts of cash. They now know to buy some furniture for their apartments or rooms....They know now that they should have a phone installed in their apartments or rooms." But he doesn't note that sales clerks, local cops and landlords now know to look for that too. In a war on terrorism that requires tips from an informed public, how else does Pluchinsky suggest getting that information to law-abiding citizens? He doesn't.

8   More disturbingly, Pluchinsky leaves the method of determining what needs to be censored open-ended. After all, he himself acknowledges that "dangerous" information is sometimes composed of many pieces of information that are in themselves innocuous. In other words, you can't tell from reading an individual story whether it's dangerous or not. So how small does a tidbit of information have to be—a security snafu at the local airport, a photo taken near a nuclear power plant—to escape government scrutiny? (And I'm not exaggerating "government scrutiny" for effect; he writes, "It seems reasonable to me that a process should be established where such articles are filtered through a government agency such as the proposed Department of Homeland Security.")

9   But most unsettling of all, Pluchinsky's attack could let our guardians off the hook for their failures, in ways that are not just self-serving but dangerous. Consider one example he gives: "Abu-Ubayd al-Qurashi, believed to be a close aide to Osama bin Ladin [*sic*], commenting on the 9/11 operatives, stated that 'the suicide hijackers studied the lives of Palestinian Yehiya Ayash [a Hamas bomb maker who was himself assassinated] and Ramzi Yousef [operational planner of the 1993 World Trade Center bombing] and the security

mistakes that led to their downfall while they were preparing for the September 11 operation.' How did al Qaeda know about the security mistakes that led to the death of Ayash and the capture of Yousef? The media, at home and abroad."

10   It's a chilling passage, but not just for the reasons Pluchinsky argues. The "open sources" of vulnerability reporting he deplores are just that—open. They were available to law-enforcement officials, immigration officials and anyone else responsible for keeping those leaks plugged. It is at best a cop-out to claim that reporting weaknesses helps terrorists exploit them without acknowledging that that reporting also can spur changes in change-resistant bureaucracies.

11   Ah, but wouldn't it be better if we could make that information available only to the people on our side? Maybe, if we could assume that the folks on our side would act expeditiously and be held accountable, even though they know it won't get out to the public if they don't. (After all, if it's treasonous to report on a vulnerability, it's treasonous to report on someone's failure to correct it.)

12   This is more or less Pluchinsky's suggestion. He recommends that anyone who spots a potential vulnerability, rather than making it public, should instead report it to the government. "If the department determined that these vulnerabilities indeed existed," he says, "then it could award 'Homeland Security Protective Security' certificates to individuals or 'Homeland Security Gold Stars' to newspaper or Internet sites that put the country first during a time of war."

13   After issuing the gold star—or perhaps a decorative smiley-face sticker—presumably the government would fix the problem pronto. Problem is, that assumption flies in the face of what we've seen since Sept. 11, let alone before—be it intelligence sharing between the FBI and CIA, getting marshals onto airplanes or expediting the screening of bombs hidden in airplane luggage (an idea which, don't worry, occurred to terrorists long before I wrote it down).

14   The cynical interpretation is that the gold-star system would provide officials incentive to sweep their failures under the rug, knowing that a press not wishing to be treasonous would never call them on it, or that it would allow officials to label as "dangerous" reports that are merely embarrassing or politically dangerous. And I have no doubt some officials would use it that way, though I doubt that that is why Pluchinsky proposes it. Let's give him the benefit of the doubt and assume that he is not only sincere in his concern but good at and conscientious about his job: that, were a newspaper or other snoop to discover a flaw in our nation's security and bring it to his attention, he would set about to make it right, putting aside any questions of careerism, politics, pride or self-interest to act for the common good.

15   Pluchinsky seems to assume that every single one would. But a cursory glimpse at the intelligence failures before Sept. 11 and efforts

to bolster America's security afterward makes clear that not everyone responsible for safeguarding the nation and its infrastructure is a Dennis Pluchinsky. Too many responsible people in government and industry have shown that nothing short of public exposure and embarrassment will get them to take steps to improve security, if those steps endanger their business, bureaucratic fiefdoms or personal prerogatives.

16   "What also infuriates me," Pluchinsky writes, "is when the media publish follow-up reports noting that security measures or procedures around a specific target or system still have not been implemented. Not only do the media identify potential target vulnerabilities for the terrorists but they also provide our foes with progress reports!" It never seems to occur to him that, if not for "open sources" of information, those measures might never be implemented, leaving us more vulnerable to terrorists—who, Pluchinsky himself notes, have other ways of finding vulnerabilities besides watching the news.

17   That is the main lesson of the Coleen Rowley FBI memo, which produced mea culpas and commitments to reform that plainly should have seemed obvious to FBI insiders long before her memo—and that, just as plainly, were not in the offing until she wrote the memo and it broke to the public.

18   Is Coleen Rowley a traitor? Are the journalists who reported her story? Maybe Pluchinsky would say so. But then what does that make the superiors who ignored her until she wrote it? No doubt many of them would rather she, and the journalists who reported on her complaint, would have quietly handed them her complaint, to be filed away in some bottom drawer, in exchange for a shiny new gold star.

Understanding the Content

Feel free to reread all or parts of the selection to answer the following questions.

1. Who is Dennis Pluchinsky? What is his attitude toward the U.S. media?

2. What does Dennis Pluchinsky propose and why?

3. What was, according to Poniewozik, the "basic failure to prevent the Sept. 11 attacks" (4)?

4. How do the media, in general, feel about Pluchinsky and his suggestions regarding the dissemination of information?

Looking at Structure and Style

1. What is Poniewozik's thesis? Is it stated or implied? If stated, where?

2. What words or phrases does Poniewozik use throughout this selection to convey his feelings about Dennis Pluchinsky?

3. What is Poniewozik's tone throughout this essay?

4. What is the purpose of paragraphs 5–6? Do they help to support the author's thesis?

5. Rewrite paragraphs 17–18 so that they effectively conclude the essay, summarizing the information presented and restating Poniewozik's thesis statement.

Evaluating the Author's Viewpoints

1. What is Poniewozik's attitude toward Pluchinsky's suggestion that the media be censored?

2. What is Poniewozik's attitude toward the U.S. government and its intelligence gathering? How can you tell?

3. Based on your reading of the selection and what you know about the events surrounding September 11, do you agree or disagree that "too many responsible people in government and industry have shown that nothing short of public exposure and embarrassment will get them to take steps to improve security, if those steps endanger their business, bureaucratic fiefdoms or personal prerogatives" (15)? Why?

4. What do you think of Dennis Pluchinsky's suggestion that "anyone who spots a potential vulnerability, rather than making it public, should instead report it to the government" (12)?

5. Do you think that "journalists endanger us when they report on specific vulnerabilities to terrorists or mistakes past terrorists have made" (7)? Why?

Pursuing Possible Essay Topics

1. Poniewozik mentions Coleen Rowley in paragraphs 17–18 of his essay. Do some research on Coleen Rowley. Who is she, and why does the author mention her? Write an essay describing Coleen Rowley and summarizing the latest events in her life.

2. Write an essay either in support of Dennis Pluchinsky's viewpoint or in opposition to it. Use facts to support your opinion.

3. What measures do you think the United States should take to ensure the safety of its citizens? Write an essay discussing one aspect or measure that should be taken.

4. Do you think the United States government could have done more to stop the terrorist attacks of September 11? If so, what could it have done?

5. Is there any time when censorship of the media should be enforced? If so, when would that be and why?

6. Brainstorm or freewrite on one or more of the following topics:

   a. censorship

   b. the media

   c. freedom of speech

   d. terrorism

   e. U.S. intelligence

   f. airport security

7. Ignore these topics and find your own topic related to the media and censorship.

Preparing to Read

Take a minute or two to look over the following reading selection. Note the title and the author, read the opening paragraph, and check the essay's length. Make certain you have the time now to read it carefully and to do the exercises that follow it. Then, in the spaces provided, answer the following questions.

1. What do you think the title means? _____

    _____

    _____

2. What subject does the essay discuss? _____

    _____

    _____

3. What do you think is the author's viewpoint on the subject? _____

    _____

    _____

Vocabulary

Good comprehension of what you are about to read depends upon your understanding of the words below. The number following each word refers to the paragraph where it is used.

grisly (1) gruesome, horrible

allegedly (2) supposedly

Mrs. Grundy (3) an extremely conservative, prudish person

garroting (3) strangling

desecrating (4) abusing something sacred

denunciations (5) formal condemnations or accusations

advocates (7) recommends, supports

purveyors (7) distributors

lepers (7) outcasts

proffers (7) offers

Walter Cronkite (8) a popular TV news announcer, now retired

sanction (9) authorize, approve

cerebral (10) intellectual, theoretical

propagandists (11) advocates, those who spread their doctrines and beliefs

rampant (13) widespread

endemic (14) prevalent, common in our society

forum (15) a medium for open discussion

bluenoses (15) puritanical people

The Issue Isn't Sex, It's Violence

CARYL RIVERS

Caryl River is a Professor of Journalism at Boston University and the author of many books, including Slick Spins and Fractured Facts: How Cultural Myths Distort the News; Indecent Behavior; She Works, He Works *(co-authored with Rosalind Barrett); and a novel,* Camelot. *She is a regular contributor to the* Los Angeles Times, Philadelphia Inquirer, Newsday, *and the* Boston Globe, *from which the following essay was taken.*

1   After a grisly series of murders in California, possibly inspired by the lyrics of a rock song, we are hearing a familiar chorus: Don't blame rock and roll. Kids will be kids. They love to rebel, and the more shocking the stuff, the better they like it.

2   There's some truth in this, of course. I loved to watch Elvis shake his torso when I was a teen-ager, and it was even more fun when Ed Sullivan wouldn't let the cameras show him below the waist. I snickered at the forbidden "Rock with Me, Annie" lyrics by a black Rhythm and Blues group, which were deliciously naughty. But I am sorry, rock fans, that is not the same thing as hearing lyrics about how a man is going to force a woman to perform oral sex on him at gunpoint in a little number called "Eat Me Alive." It is not in the same league with a song about the delights of slipping into a woman's room while she is sleeping and murdering her, the theme of an AC/DC ballad that allegedly inspired the California slayer.

3   Make no mistake, it is not sex we are talking about here, but violence. Violence against women. Most rock songs are not violent—they are funky, sexy, rebellious, and sometimes witty. Please do not mistake me for a Mrs. Grundy. If Prince wants to leap about wearing only a purple jock strap, fine. Let Mick Jagger unzip his fly as he gyrates, if he wants to. But when either one of them starts garroting, beating, or sodomizing a woman in their number, that is another story.

4   I always find myself annoyed when "intellectual" men dismiss violence against women with a yawn, as if it were beneath their dignity to notice. I wonder if the reaction would be the same if the violence were directed against someone other than women. How many people would yawn and say, "Oh, kids will be kids," if a rock group did a nifty little number called "Lynchin," in which stringing up and stomping on black people were set to music? Who would chuckle and say, "Oh, just a little adolescent rebellion" if a group of rockers went on MTV dressed as Nazis, desecrating synagogues and beating up Jews to the beat of twanging guitars?

5   I'll tell you what would happen. Prestigious dailies would thunder on editorial pages; senators would fall over each other to get denunciations into the Congressional Record. The president would appoint a commission to clean up the music business.

6   But violence against women is greeted by silence. It shouldn't be.

7   This does not mean censorship, or book (or record) burning. In a society that protects free expression, we understand a lot of stuff will float up out of the sewer. Usually, we recognize the ugly stuff that advocates violence against any group as the garbage it is, and we consider its purveyors as moral lepers. We hold our nose and tolerate it, but we speak out against the values it proffers.

8   But images of violence against women are not staying on the fringes of society. No longer are they found only in tattered, paper-covered books or in movie houses where winos snooze and the scent of urine fills the air. They are entering the mainstream at a rapid rate. This is happening at a time when the media, more and more, set the agenda for the public debate. It is a powerful legitimizing force—especially television. Many people regard what they see on TV as the truth; Walter Cronkite once topped a poll as the most trusted man in America.

9   Now, with the advent of rock videos and all-music channels, rock music has grabbed a big chunk of legitimacy. American teen-agers have instant access, in their living rooms, to the messages of rock, on the same vehicle that brought them *Sesame Street.* Who can blame them if they believe that the images they see are accurate reflections of adult reality, approved by adults? After all, Big Bird used to give them lessons on the same little box. Adults, by their silence, sanction the images. Do we really want our kids to think that rape and violence are what sexuality is all about?

10   This is not a trivial issue. Violence against women is a major social problem, one that's more than a cerebral issue to me. I teach at Boston University, and one of my most promising young journalism students was raped and murdered. Two others told me of being raped. Recently, one female student was assaulted and beaten so badly she had $5,000 worth of medical bills and permanent damage to her back and eyes.

11   It's nearly impossible, of course, to make a cause-and-effect link between lyrics and images and acts of violence. But images have a tremendous power to create an atmosphere in which violence against certain people is sanctioned. Nazi propagandists knew that full well when they portrayed Jews as ugly, greedy, and powerful.

12   Violence against women, particularly in a sexual context, is being legitimized in two ways: by the increasing movement of these images into the mainstream of the media in TV, films, magazines, albums, videos, and by the silence about it.

13   Violence, of course, is rampant in the media. But it is usually set in some kind of moral context. It's usually only the bad guys who commit violent acts against the innocent. When the good guys get violent, it's against those who deserve it. Dirty Harry blows away the scum, he doesn't walk up to a toddler and say, "Make my day." The A Team does not shoot up suburban shopping malls.

14   But in some rock songs, it's the "heroes" who commit the acts. The people we are programmed to identify with are the ones being violent, with women on the receiving end. In a society where rape and assaults on women are endemic, this is no small problem, with millions of young boys watching on their TV screens and listening on their Walkmans.

15   I think something needs to be done. I'd like to see people in the industry respond to the problem. I'd love to see some women rock stars speak out against violence against women. I would like to see disc jockeys refuse air play to records and videos that contain such violence. At the very least, I want to see the end of the silence. I want journalists and parents and critics and performing artists to keep this issue alive in the public forum. I don't want people who are concerned about this issue labeled as bluenoses and book-burners and ignored.

16   And I wish it wasn't always just women who were speaking out. Men have as large a stake in the quality of our civilization as women do in the long run. Violence is a contagion that infects at random. Let's hear something, please, from the men.

Understanding the Content

Feel free to reread all or parts of the selection to answer the following questions.

1. What does Rivers mean by her title, "The Issue Isn't Sex, It's Violence"? Violence against whom?

2. Why is Rivers concerned that teenagers who were raised on *Sesame Street* might be misled by some rock videos and all-music channels?

3. Rivers says that violence is rampant in the media, mentioning the Dirty Harry movies and the now-canceled television show *The A Team*. Why does she consider this type of violence less harmful than some of the rock lyrics and rock videos? How do the heroes in these shows differ from the "heroes" in the rock videos?

4. What examples from her personal life does Rivers offer to support her view that violence against women "is not a trivial issue" (10)? Are they persuasive examples?

5. What suggestions does Rivers offer to people in the music industry as a way to combat violence against women? Who else does she wish would speak out? Why?

Looking at Structure and Style

1. In paragraph 2, Rivers mentions that she "loved to watch Elvis shake his torso" and "snickered" at certain rock lyrics that were "deliciously naughty" (2). What function does this serve?

2. What function does paragraph 3 serve?

3. How do paragraphs 4–6 work together to make Rivers's point? Why does she make paragraph 6 two short sentences?

4. How do paragraphs 7 and 8 work together? Why does she make it clear that she is not talking about censoring rock lyrics or videos?

5. What is the function of paragraphs 13 and 14? How do they work together to help support her thesis?

6. Concluding paragraphs 15 and 16 present Rivers's suggestions for curtailing the problem. Would it make much difference if she reversed the order of the two paragraphs? Explain.

7. Explain or rewrite the following passages from the essay:
   a. "I always find myself annoyed when 'intellectual' men dismiss violence against women with a yawn, as if it were beneath their dignity to notice" (4).
   b. "Usually, we recognize the ugly stuff that advocates violence against any group as the garbage it is, and we consider its purveyors as moral lepers" (7).
   c. "It [the media] is a powerful legitimizing force" (8).
   d. "I don't want people who are concerned about this issue labeled as bluenoses and book-burners and ignored" (15).

Evaluating the Author's Viewpoints

1. Rivers believes that some rock lyrics and music videos express a violence toward women, frequently a sexual violence. Do you agree? Have you listened to enough rock lyrics or seen enough MTV to speak from experience?

2. Look at the suggestions Rivers offers in paragraph 15. Do you think each suggestion is worth considering? Would implementing her suggestions be better than applying censorship laws? Explain.

3. In paragraphs 4 and 16, Rivers implies that men are not doing enough, that they are too silent about the problem. Do you agree? On what do you base your answer?

4. What is your response to paragraph 12? Is this a fairly good statement of her thesis?

Pursuing Possible Essay Topics

1. If you are not familiar with some recent rock lyrics or music videos, turn on the radio or MTV. Do you see or hear any violence toward women? Write an essay that agrees or disagrees with Rivers's thesis.

2. Analyze the lyrics of a popular rock song. What is being said? What is being implied? Do the words have any merit?

3. Write an essay that describes a rock video that appears on MTV (or some other all-music channel). What is happening? Do the images fit the lyrics? Are the images suggestive? What values are being portrayed that young viewers might accept simply because they admire the musician or singer?

4. Defend or refute the need for some type of censorship in the music industry as a way to protect young children and teenagers from exposure to sexual looseness or violence in songs and videos.

5. Brainstorm or freewrite on one or more of the following:

   a. MTV

   b. punk rock

   c. the Top 40

   d. rock-and-roll

   e. your favorite music group

   f. the influence of music

6. Come up with your own topic on some aspect of the media and write an essay on the topic.

Preparing to Read

Take a minute or two to look over the following reading selection. Note the title and author, read the first two paragraphs, and check the essay's length. Make certain you have the time now to read it carefully and to do the exercises that follow it. Then, in the spaces provided, answer the following questions.

1. What is the tone of the first two paragraphs of this selection? _____

   _____

   _____

2. What do you think this essay will be about? _____

   _____

Vocabulary

Good comprehension of what you are about to read depends upon your understanding of the words below. The number following each word refers to the paragraph where it is used.

sabotage (1) interference with, destruction

wares (13) goods, products

Making Them Squirm

JOHN TIERNEY

John Tierney is a twice-weekly contributor to the Op-Ed page of the New York Times, *from which the following essay was taken. He has written exclusively about science and technology, economics, and environmental controversies, and his article "Recycling Is Garbage" drew a record number of letters from readers of the* New York Times Magazine.

1   Last year a German teenager named Sven Jaschan released the Sasser worm, one of the costliest acts of sabotage in the history of the Internet. It crippled computers around the world, closing businesses, halting trains and grounding airplanes.

2   Which of these punishments does he deserve?
A) 21-month suspended sentence and 30 hours of community service.
B) Two years in prison.

C) A five-year ban on using computers.

D) Death.

E) Something worse.

3   If you answered A, you must be the German judge who gave him that sentence last week.

4   If you answered B or C, you're confusing him with other hackers who have been sent to prison and banned from using computers or the Internet. But those punishments don't seem to have deterred hackers like Mr. Jaschan from taking their place.

5   I'm tempted to say that the correct answer is D, and not just because of the man-years I've spent running virus scans and reformatting hard drives. I'm almost convinced by Steven Landsburg's cost-benefit analysis showing that the spreaders of computer viruses and worms are more logical candidates for capital punishment than murderers are.

6   Professor Landsburg, an economist at the University of Rochester, has calculated the relative value to society of executing murderers and hackers. By using studies estimating the deterrent value of capital punishment, he figures that executing one murderer yields at most $100 million in social benefits.

7   The benefits of executing a hacker would be greater, he argues, because the social costs of hacking are estimated to be so much higher: $50 billion per year. Deterring a mere one-fifth of 1 percent of those crimes—one in 500 hackers—would save society $100 million. And Professor Landsburg believes that a lot more than one in 500 hackers would be deterred by the sight of a colleague on death row.

8   I see his logic, but I also see practical difficulties. For one thing, many hackers live in places where capital punishment is illegal. For another, most of them are teenage boys, a group that has never been known for fearing death. They're probably more afraid of going five years without computer games.

9   So that leaves us with E: something worse than death. Something that would approximate the millions of hours of tedium that hackers have inflicted on society.

10   Hackers are the Internet equivalent of Richard Reid, the shoe-bomber who didn't manage to hurt anyone on his airplane but has been annoying travelers ever since. When I join the line of passengers taking off their shoes at the airport, I get little satisfaction in thinking that the man responsible for this ritual is sitting somewhere by himself in a prison cell, probably with his shoes on.

11   He ought to spend his days within smelling range of all those socks at the airport. In an exclusive poll I once conducted among fellow passengers, I found that 80 percent favored forcing Mr. Reid to sit next to the metal detector, helping small children put their sneakers back on.

12   The remaining 20 percent in the poll (meaning one guy) said that wasn't harsh enough. He advocated requiring Mr. Reid to change the Odor-Eaters insoles of runners at the end of the New York City Marathon.

13   What would be the equivalent public service for Internet socio-paths? Maybe convicted spammers could be sentenced to community service testing all their own wares. The number of organ-enlargement offers would decline if a spammer thought he'd have to appear in a public-service television commercial explaining that he'd tried them all and they just didn't work for him.

14   Convicted hackers like Mr. Jaschan could be sentenced to a life-time of removing worms and viruses, but the computer experts I consulted said there would be too big a risk that the hackers would enjoy the job. After all, Mr. Jaschan is now doing just that for a soft-ware security firm.

15   The experts weren't sure that any punishment could fit the crime, but they had several suggestions: Make the hacker spend 16 hours a day fielding help-desk inquiries in an AOL chat room for computer novices. Force him to do this with a user name at least as uncool as KoolDude and to work on a vintage IBM PC with a 2400 baud dial-up connection. Most painful of all for any geek, make him use Windows 95 for the rest of his life.

16   I realize that this may not be enough. If you have any better ideas, send them along.

Understanding the Content

Feel free to reread all or parts of the selection to answer the following questions.

1. Who is Sven Jaschan and what was he convicted of doing? What was his punishment?

2. Who is Professor Landsburg and what does he think should happen to people who spread computer viruses?

3. According to John Tierney, what would be the "public service for Internet sociopaths" (13)?

4. What is Sven Jaschan doing for a living now?

Looking at Structure and Style

1. What is the thesis of this selection? Rewrite it in your own words.

2. What is the author's tone in this essay?

3. What is the purpose of paragraphs 2–4? Do they help develop the author's thesis?

4. What is the purpose of paragraphs 13–15?

5. What pattern organizes paragraph 10?

Evaluating the Author's Viewpoints

1. What is the author's opinion of Sven Jaschan's punishment?

2. What does the author think should happen to people who perpetrate Internet crimes, like hacking and spreading viruses? Do you agree?

3. Why do you think the author uses the tone he does in this selection?

Pursuing Possible Essay Topics

1. What do you think of Professor Landsburg's proposition that spreaders of computer viruses are more logical candidates for capital punishment than murderers are? Write an essay either in defense of this idea or against it.

2. Have you ever had to deal with a computer virus? If so, write an essay describing what happened and how you felt.

3. Brainstorm or freewrite on one or more of the following:
   a. technology
   b. computers
   c. computer viruses
   d. hackers

4. Write an essay exploring how dependent you are on your computer.

5. Find a topic of your own related to technology and write an essay.

Preparing to Read

Take a minute or two to look over the following reading selection. Note the title and the author, read the first two paragraphs, and check the essay's length. Make certain you have the time now to read it carefully and to do the exercises that follow it. Then, in the spaces provided, answer the following questions.

1. What do the title and the subtitle tell you about this essay? _____

_____

_____

2. What do you think this essay will be about? _____

_____

_____

3. Why does Jacoby include a quote by Ralph Waldo Emerson? _____

_____

_____

Vocabulary

Good comprehension of what you are about to read depends upon your understanding of the words below. The number following each word refers to the paragraph where it is used.

prescience (1) knowledge of events before they occur

virulent (1) intensely harsh

pejoratives (2) disparagements; belittlements

convulsions (3) spasms or seizures

apocalyptic (3) involving or pertaining to doom and/or destruction

disjunction (4) the act of separating or disjoining

jeremiads (7) lengthy complaints

atrophy (7) a wasting away or deterioration

cumbersome (10) difficult to handle because of large size of heft

per se (15) intrinsically

rote (16) mechanical routine; know by memorizing

The Dumbing of America
Call Me a Snob, but Really, We're a Nation of Dunces
SUSAN JACOBY

Susan Jacoby has been a contributor to such publications as the New York Times Magazine, Washington Post Book World, Los Angeles Times Book Review, Harper's, Vogue, The Nation, *and* Mother Jones, *to name a few. Her latest book is* The Age of American Unreason. *The following article appeared in the* Washington Post.

1   "The mind of this country, taught to aim at low objects, eats upon itself." Ralph Waldo Emerson offered that observation in 1837, but his words echo with painful prescience in today's very different United States. Americans are in serious intellectual trouble—in danger of losing our hard-won cultural capital to a virulent mixture of anti-intellectualism, anti-rationalism and low expectations.

2   This is the last subject that any candidate would dare raise on the long and winding road to the White House. It is almost impossible to talk about the manner in which public ignorance contributes to grave national problems without being labeled an "elitist," one of the most powerful pejoratives that can be applied to anyone aspiring to high office. Instead, our politicians repeatedly assure Americans that they are just "folks," a patronizing term that you will search for in vain in important presidential speeches before 1980. (Just imagine: "We here highly resolve that these dead shall not have died in vain . . . and that government of the folks, by the folks, for the folks, shall not perish from the earth.") Such exaltations of ordinariness are among the distinguishing traits of anti-intellectualism in any era.

3   The classic work on this subject by Columbia University historian Richard Hofstadter, "Anti-Intellectualism in American Life," was published in early 1963, between the anti-communist crusades of the McCarthy era and the social convulsions of the late 1960s. Hofstadter saw American anti-intellectualism as a basically cyclical phenomenon that often manifested itself as the dark side of the country's democratic impulses in religion and education. But today's brand of anti-intellectualism is less a cycle than a flood. If Hofstadter (who died of leukemia in 1970 at age 54) had lived long enough to write a modern-day sequel, he would have found that our era of 24/7 info-tainment has outstripped his most apocalyptic predictions about the future of American culture.

4   Dumbness, to paraphrase the late senator Daniel Patrick Moynihan, has been steadily defined downward for several decades, by a combination of heretofore irresistible forces. These include the triumph of video culture over print culture (and by video, I mean every form of digital media, as well as older electronic ones); a disjunction between Americans' rising level of formal education and their shaky grasp

of basic geography, science and history; and the fusion of anti-rationalism with anti-intellectualism.

5   First and foremost among the vectors of the new anti-intellectualism is video. The decline of book, newspaper and magazine reading is by now an old story. The drop-off is most pronounced among the young, but it continues to accelerate and afflict Americans of all ages and education levels.

6   Reading has declined not only among the poorly educated, according to a report last year by the National Endowment for the Arts. In 1982, 82 percent of college graduates read novels or poems for pleasure; two decades later, only 67 percent did. And more than 40 percent of Americans under 44 did not read a single book—fiction or nonfiction—over the course of a year. The proportion of 17-year-olds who read nothing (unless required to do so for school) more than doubled between 1984 and 2004. This time period, of course, encompasses the rise of personal computers, Web surfing and video games.

7   Does all this matter? Technophiles pooh-pooh jeremiads about the end of print culture as the navel-gazing of (what else?) elitists. In his book "Everything Bad Is Good for You: How Today's Popular Culture Is Actually Making Us Smarter," the science writer Steven Johnson assures us that we have nothing to worry about. Sure, parents may see their "vibrant and active children gazing silently, mouths agape, at the screen." But these zombie-like characteristics "are not signs of mental atrophy. They're signs of focus." Balderdash. The real question is what toddlers are screening out, not what they are focusing on, while they sit mesmerized by videos they have seen dozens of times.

8   Despite an aggressive marketing campaign aimed at encouraging babies as young as 6 months to watch videos, there is no evidence that focusing on a screen is anything but bad for infants and toddlers. In a study released last August, University of Washington researchers found that babies between 8 and 16 months recognized an average of six to eight fewer words for every hour spent watching videos.

9   I cannot prove that reading for hours in a treehouse (which is what I was doing when I was 13) creates more informed citizens than hammering away at a Microsoft Xbox or obsessing about Facebook profiles. But the inability to concentrate for long periods of time—as distinct from brief reading hits for information on the Web—seems to me intimately related to the inability of the public to remember even recent news events. It is not surprising, for example, that less has been heard from the presidential candidates about the Iraq war in the later stages of the primary campaign than in the earlier ones, simply because there have been fewer video reports of violence in Iraq. Candidates, like voters, emphasize the latest news, not necessarily the most important news.

10   No wonder negative political ads work. "With text, it is even easy to keep track of differing levels of authority behind different pieces of information," the cultural critic Caleb Crain noted recently in the New Yorker. "A comparison of two video reports, on the other hand, is cumbersome. Forced to choose between conflicting stories on television, the viewer falls back on hunches, or on what he believed before he started watching."

11   As video consumers become progressively more impatient with the process of acquiring information through written language, all politicians find themselves under great pressure to deliver their messages as quickly as possible—and quickness today is much quicker than it used to be. Harvard University's Kiku Adatto found that between 1968 and 1988, the average sound bite on the news for a presidential candidate—featuring the candidate's own voice— dropped from 42.3 seconds to 9.8 seconds. By 2000, according to another Harvard study, the daily candidate bite was down to just 7.8 seconds.

12   The shrinking public attention span fostered by video is closely tied to the second important anti-intellectual force in American culture: the erosion of general knowledge.

13   People accustomed to hearing their president explain complicated policy choices by snapping "I'm the decider" may find it almost impossible to imagine the pains that Franklin D. Roosevelt took, in the grim months after Pearl Harbor, to explain why U.S. armed forces were suffering one defeat after another in the Pacific. In February 1942, Roosevelt urged Americans to spread out a map during his radio "fireside chat" so that they might better understand the geography of battle. In stores throughout the country, maps sold out; about 80 percent of American adults tuned in to hear the president. FDR had told his speechwriters that he was certain that if Americans understood the immensity of the distances over which supplies had to travel to the armed forces, "they can take any kind of bad news right on the chin."

14   This is a portrait not only of a different presidency and president but also of a different country and citizenry, one that lacked access to satellite-enhanced Google maps but was far more receptive to learning and complexity than today's public. According to a 2006 survey by National Geographic-Roper, nearly half of Americans between ages 18 and 24 do not think it necessary to know the location of other countries in which important news is being made. More than a third consider it "not at all important" to know a foreign language, and only 14 percent consider it "very important."

15   That leads us to the third and final factor behind the new American dumbness: not lack of knowledge per se but arrogance about that lack of knowledge. The problem is not just the things we do not

know (consider the one in five American adults who, according to the National Science Foundation, thinks the sun revolves around the Earth); it's the alarming number of Americans who have smugly concluded that they do not need to know such things in the first place. Call this anti-rationalism—a syndrome that is particularly dangerous to our public institutions and discourse. Not knowing a foreign language or the location of an important country is a manifestation of ignorance; denying that such knowledge matters is pure anti-rationalism. The toxic brew of anti-rationalism and ignorance hurts discussions of U.S. public policy on topics from health care to taxation.

16   There is no quick cure for this epidemic of arrogant anti-rationalism and anti-intellectualism; rote efforts to raise standardized test scores by stuffing students with specific answers to specific questions on specific tests will not do the job. Moreover, the people who exemplify the problem are usually oblivious to it. ("Hardly anyone believes himself to be against thought and culture," Hofstadter noted.) It is past time for a serious national discussion about whether, as a nation, we truly value intellect and rationality. If this indeed turns out to be a "change election," the low level of discourse in a country with a mind taught to aim at low objects ought to be the first item on the change agenda.

Understanding the Content

Feel free to reread all or parts of the selection to answer the following questions.

1. According to Susan Jacoby, to what are Americans "in danger of losing our hard-won cultural capital"?

2. What is the "classic work" on the subject of anti-intellectualism, according to Susan Jacoby? What was the main thrust of this book?

3. What are the "irresistible forces" that have contributed to the rise of "dumbness" in America, according to Susan Jacoby?

4. What is "first and foremost among the vectors of the new anti-intellectualism"? How has this affected how politicians deliver their messages?

5. How does Susan Jacoby define "anti-rationalism"?

Looking at Structure and Style

1. What is the thesis of this essay? If it is stated, paraphrase it. If it is implied, write it in your own words.

2. What role does politics play in Jacoby's argument?

3. Does Jacoby use credible sources to support her argument? If you think so, list all of the credible sources that she uses. If not, explain why you think she needs more or better ones.

4. What is the purpose of paragraph 13? What is its relation to the essay as a whole?

5. Overall, this is an argumentative essay. However, Jacoby uses another organizing pattern in the essay, particularly when she is talking about the factors that led to the "dumbing of America." What organizing pattern is used? Is it effective in laying out the basic theme of the essay? Why or why not?

Evaluating the Author's Viewpoints

1. What is Susan Jacoby's tone in this essay? Her attitude toward her subject? How can you tell? List the words or phrases that she uses that give you an idea of her tone and attitude.

2. Why do you think that Jacoby uses politics as a springboard for talking about the anti-intellectualism that she feels is "flooding" America?

3. What can you infer about how Susan Jacoby feels about Richard Hofstadter and his work? How can you tell?

4. Do you agree or disagree with the assertions made by Steven Johnson in his book "Everything Bad Is Good for You," particularly when it comes to watching television and playing video games? Why?

5. Do you agree or disagree with the author that "reading for hours in a tree-house" creates more informed citizens than playing video games or creating online profiles for Facebook? Why? Do you think there is a "happy medium"? If so, describe.

Pursuing Possible Essay Topics

1. What is your opinion regarding allowing children to watch television and play video games? Write an essay discussing your viewpoint.

2. Do you think that today's Americans are less intellectual than people, say, of your parents' and grandparents' generations? Why? Write an essay discussing your viewpoint.

3. Write an essay discussing whether or not you agree with Susan Jacoby's thesis regarding Americans and their intellectualism.

4. Do you think reading is important? Why? Write an essay discussing your viewpoint.

5. Brainstorm or freewrite on one or more of the following:

    a. American education

    b. reading

    c. video games

    d. media

    e. technology

6. Find a topic that interests you on some aspect of American education, media, intelligence, or intellectualism and write an essay about it.

Preparing to Read

Take a minute or two to look over the following reading selection. Note the title and the author, read the first paragraph, and check the essay's length. Make certain you have the time now to read it carefully and to do the exercises that follow it. Then, in the spaces provided, answer the following questions.

1. What do the title and the subtitle tell you about this essay? _____

   _____

   _____

2. What do you think this essay will be about? _____

   _____

   _____

3. Based on your reading of the title and the first paragraph of this selection,

   what do you think Andrew Sullivan's attitude toward his subject will be?

   _____

   _____

Vocabulary

Good comprehension of what you are about to read depends upon your understanding of the words below. The number following each word refers to the paragraph where it is used.

   chutzpah (1) a Yiddish word meaning "utter nerve"

   monastic (7) relating to a monastery; secluded and contemplative

   ether (11) a gas used to anesthetize or make a patient unconscious

   serendipity (14) good fortune; kismet

Society Is Dead: We Have Retreated into the iWorld

ANDREW SULLIVAN

Andrew Sullivan has been a columnist for TIME *magazine since 2002, and appears frequently on HBO's "Real Time with Bill Maher" and NBC's "Chris Matthews' Show." He writes daily for his online "Daily Dish" blog,* www.andrewsullivan. theatlantic.com. *The following article appeared in the* Sunday Times *of London.*

1   I was visiting New York last week and noticed something I'd never thought I'd say about the city. Yes, nightlife is pretty much dead (and I'm in no way the first to notice that). But daylife—that insane mish-mash of yells, chatter, clatter, hustle and chutzpah that makes New York the urban equivalent of methamphetamine—was also a little different. It was quieter.

2   Manhattan's downtown is now a Disney-like string of malls, riverside parks and pretty upper-middle-class villages. But there was something else. And as I looked across the throngs on the pavements, I began to see why.

3   There were little white wires hanging down from their ears, or tucked into pockets, purses or jackets. The eyes were a little vacant. Each was in his or her own musical world, walking to their soundtrack, stars in their own music video, almost oblivious to the world around them. These are the iPod people.

4   Even without the white wires you can tell who they are. They walk down the street in their own MP3 cocoon, bumping into others, deaf to small social cues, shutting out anyone not in their bubble.

5   Every now and again some start unconsciously emitting strange tuneless squawks, like a badly tuned radio, and their fingers snap or their arms twitch to some strange soundless rhythm. When others say "Excuse me" there's no response. "Hi", ditto. It's strange to be among so many people and hear so little. Except that each one is hearing so much.

6   Yes, I might as well own up. I'm one of them. I witnessed the glazed New York looks through my own glazed pupils, my white wires peeping out of my ears. I joined the cult a few years ago: the sect of the little white box worshippers.

7   Every now and again I go to church—those huge, luminous Apple stores, pews in the rear, the clerics in their monastic uniforms all bustling around or sitting behind the "Genius Bars", like priests waiting to hear confessions.

8   Others began, as I did, with a Walkman—and then a kind of clunkier MP3 player. But the sleekness of the iPod won me over. Unlike other models it gave me my entire music collection to rearrange as I saw fit—on the fly, in my pocket.

9   What was once an occasional musical diversion became a compulsive obsession. Now I have my iTunes in my iMac for my iPod in my iWorld. It's Narcissus heaven: we've finally put the "i" into Me.

10   And, like all addictive cults, it's spreading. There are now 22m iPod owners in the United States and Apple is becoming a mass-market company for the first time.

11   Walk through any airport in the United States these days and you will see person after person gliding through the social ether as if on autopilot. Get on a subway and you're surrounded by a bunch of Stepford commuters staring into mid-space as if anaesthetised by technology. Don't ask, don't tell, don't overhear, don't observe. Just tune in and tune out.

12   It wouldn't be so worrying if it weren't part of something even bigger. Americans are beginning to narrow their lives.

13   You get your news from your favourite blogs, the ones that won't challenge your view of the world. You tune into a satellite radio service that also aims directly at a small market—for new age fanatics, liberal talk or Christian rock. Television is all cable. Culture is all subculture. Your cell phones can receive e-mail feeds of your favourite blogger's latest thoughts—seconds after he has posted them—get sports scores for your team or stock quotes of your portfolio.

14   Technology has given us a universe entirely for ourselves—where the serendipity of meeting a new stranger, hearing a piece of music we would never choose for ourselves or an opinion that might force us to change our mind about something are all effectively banished. Atomisation by little white boxes and cell phones. Society without the social. Others who are chosen—not met at random. Human beings have never lived like this before. Yes, we have always had homes, retreats or places where we went to relax, unwind or shut out the world.

15   But we didn't walk around the world like hermit crabs with our isolation surgically attached.

16   Music was once the preserve of the living room or the concert hall. It was sometimes solitary but it was primarily a shared experience, something that brought people together, gave them the comfort of knowing that others too understood the pleasure of a Brahms symphony or that Beatles album.

17   But music is as atomised now as living is. And it's secret. That bloke next to you on the bus could be listening to heavy metal or a Gregorian chant. You'll never know. And so, bit by bit, you'll never really know him. And by his white wires, he is indicating he doesn't really want to know you.

18   What do we get from this? The awareness of more music, more often. The chance to slip away for a while from everydayness, to give our lives its own soundtrack, to still the monotony of the commute, to listen more closely and carefully to music that can lift you up and keep you going.

19   We become masters of our own interests, more connected to people like us over the internet, more instantly in touch with anything we want, need or think we want and think we need. Ever tried a Stairmaster in silence? But what are we missing? That hilarious shard of an overheard conversation that stays with you all day; the child whose chatter on the pavement takes you back to your early memories; birdsong; weather; accents; the laughter of others. And those thoughts that come not by filling your head with selected diversion, but by allowing your mind to wander aimlessly through the regular background noise of human and mechanical life.

20   External stimulation can crowd out the interior mind. Even the boredom that we flee has its uses. We are forced to find our own means to overcome it.

21   And so we enrich our life from within, rather than from white wires. It's hard to give up, though, isn't it.

22   Not so long ago I was on a trip and realised I had left my iPod behind. Panic. But then something else. I noticed the rhythms of others again, the sound of the airplane, the opinions of the taxi driver, the small social cues that had been obscured before. I noticed how others related to each other. And I felt just a little bit connected again and a little more aware.

23   Try it. There's a world out there. And it has a soundtrack all its own.

Understanding the Content

Feel free to reread all or parts of the selection to answer the following questions.

1. What comments does Andrew Sullivan have to say about life in New York both during the day and at night? On what does he blame this shift?

2. When Sullivan refers to "church," what is he really referring to?

3. How many people own iPods in the United States, according to Andrew Sullivan?

4. How are people "narrowing their lives," according to Sullivan?

5. How has technology affected people and how they interact with others, according to the author?

Looking at Structure and Style

1. What is the thesis of this essay? State it in your own words.

2. To what does Sullivan compare the Apple stores and why? Is this an effective comparison from the reader's point of view? Why or why not?

3. What is the organizing pattern used to organize paragraph 13? What is its relation to paragraph 12?

4. What is Sullivan's attitude toward the subject of technology? How can you tell?

5. Is paragraph 23 an effective concluding paragraph, in your opinion? Why or why not?

Evaluating the Author's Viewpoints

1. Why does Andrew Sullivan think that people wear iPods?

2. When Andrew Sullivan forgot to bring his iPod on a recent trip, how did he feel? What happened as a result?

3. What does Sullivan think of technology, as a whole? What effect, ultimately, has it had on society?

4. How would you describe Andrew Sullivan's relationship to his iPod? Compare and contrast the author's relationship with his iPod with your own.

Pursuing Possible Essay Topics

1. If you were traveling, even if it were just a short trip, and you forgot your iPod, what would your reaction be? Write an essay discussing whether or not forgetting your iPod would impact your mood or your day.

2. With a classmate or a group, discuss when you got your first iPod and why. Take notes and summarize your discussion for the entire class.

3. Do you think that technology—like iPods—alienate people from one another? Why or why not? Write an essay discussing your viewpoint.

4. What are the advantages of owning an iPod? Discuss in a brief essay.

5. Brainstorm or freewrite on one or more of the following:
   a. iPods
   b. isolation
   c. the iWorld
   d. media
   e. technology

6. Find a topic that interests you on some aspect of media and technology and write an essay.

Preparing to Read

Take a minute or two to look over the following reading selection. Note the title and the author, read the first two paragraphs, and check the essay's length. Make certain you have the time now to read it carefully and to do the exercises that follow it. Then, in the spaces provided, answer the following questions.

1. What does the title mean? _____

_____

_____

2. What do you think this essay will be about? _____

_____

_____

Vocabulary

Good comprehension of what you are about to read depends upon your understanding of the words below. The number following each word refers to the paragraph where it is used.

decrying (3) openly condemning

ubiquitous (4) seeming to be everywhere at the same time

depravity (4) moral corruption

ceding (8) surrendering possession of

plausibly (8) reasonably; credibly

voyeuristic (9) interest in obsessively observing something illicit or sordid

venerable (15) commanding respect by virtue of age or stature in society

Televising Humiliation

ADAM COHEN

Adam Cohen, the assistant editor at the New York Times *editorial board, is a lawyer and author with a particular interest in legal issues, politics, and technology. Before joining the* Times, *he was a senior writer at* TIME *magazine, where he wrote about a variety of topics, including Internet privacy and the Microsoft antitrust case. The following article appears in the* International Herald Tribune.

1   In November 2006, a camera crew from NBC's "Dateline" and a police SWAT team descended on the Texas home of Louis William Conradt Jr., a 56-year-old assistant district attorney. The series' "To Catch a Predator" team had allegedly caught Conradt making online advances to a decoy who pretended to be a 13-year-old boy. When the police and TV crew stormed Conradt's home, he took out a handgun and shot himself to death.

2   "That'll make good TV," one of the police officers on the scene reportedly told an NBC producer. Deeply cynical, perhaps, but prescient. "Dateline" aired a segment based on the grim encounter.

3   After telling the ghoulish tale, it ended with Conradt's sister Patricia decrying the "reckless actions of a self-appointed group acting as judge, jury and executioner, that was encouraged by an out-of-control reality show."

4   Patricia Conradt sued NBC for more than $100 million. Last month, Judge Denny Chin of U.S. District Court in New York ruled that her lawsuit could go forward. Chin's thoughtful ruling sends an important message at a time when humiliation television is ubiquitous, and plumbing ever lower depths of depravity in search of ratings.

5   NBC's "To Catch a Predator" franchise is based on an ugly premise. The show lures people into engaging in loathsome activities. It then teams up with the police to stage a humiliating, televised arrest, while the accused still has the presumption of innocence.

6   Each party to the bargain compromises its professional standards.

7   Rather than hold police accountable, "Dateline" becomes their partners—and may well prod them to more invasive and outrageous actions than they had planned. When Conradt did not show up at the "sting house"—the usual "To Catch a Predator" format—producers allegedly asked police as a "favor" to storm his home. Patricia Conradt contends that the show encourages police "to give a special intensity to any arrests, so as to enhance the camera effect."

8   The police make their own corrupt bargain, ceding law enforcement to TV producers. Could Conradt have been taken alive if he had been arrested in more conventional fashion, without SWAT agents, cameras and television producers swarming his home? Chin said a jury could plausibly find that it was the television circus, in which the police acted as the ringleader, that led to his suicide.

9   "To Catch a Predator" is part of an ever-growing lineup of shows that calculatingly appeal to their audience's worst instincts. The common theme is indulging the audience's voyeuristic pleasure at someone else's humiliation, and the nastiness of the put-down has become the whole point of the shows.

10   Humiliation TV has been around for some time. "The Weakest Link" updated the conventional quiz show by installing a viciously insulting host, and putting the focus on the contestants' decision

about which of their competitors is the most worthless. "The Apprentice" purported to be about young people getting a start in business, but the whole hour built up to a single moment: when Donald Trump barked "You're fired."

11   But to hold viewers' interest, the levels of shame have inevitably kept growing. A new Fox show, "Moment of Truth," in a coveted time slot after "American Idol," dispenses cash prizes for truthfully (based on a lie-detector test) answering intensely private questions.

12   Sample: "Since you've been married, have you ever had sexual relations with someone other than your husband?" If the show is as true as it says it is, questions in two recent episodes seemed carefully designed to break up contestants' marriages.

13   There are First Amendment concerns, of course, when courts consider suits over TV shows. But when the media act more as police than as journalists, and actually push the police into more extreme violations of rights than the police would come up with themselves, the free speech defense begins to weaken.

14   Patricia Conradt's lawsuit contains several legal claims, including "intentional infliction of emotional distress," for which the bar is very high: conduct "so outrageous in character, and so extreme in degree, as to go beyond all possible bounds of decency, and to be regarded as atrocious, and utterly intolerable in a civilized community."

15   Reprehensible as "Moment of Truth" is, it doubtless falls into the venerable category of verbal grotesquery protected by the First Amendment. The producers of "To Catch a Predator," however, appear to be on the verge—if not over it—of becoming brown shirts with television cameras. If you are going into the business of storming people's homes and humiliating them to the point of suicide, you should be sure to have some good lawyers on retainer.

Understanding the Content

Feel free to reread all or parts of the selection to answer the following questions.

1. What television shows does Cohen use to prove his point that humiliation is rampant on television?

2. Which show—and its "ugly premise"—produced the most drastic effect to this "televised humiliation"?

3. With respect to "To Catch a Predator," what role, according to Cohen, do the police play in the sting operation?

4. In order to "hold viewers' interest," what have television shows been doing, of late?

5. When referring to "brown shirts" and "storming people's homes," in paragraph 15, to whom is Cohen comparing the producers of "To Catch a Predator"? Why?

Looking at Structure and Style

1. What is the thesis of this essay? State it in your own words.

2. How many examples does Cohen use to prove his point? Does he use enough? Or does he need more? Explain your answer.

3. Does Cohen define the term "Humiliation TV" outright or does he rely only on examples to provide an illustration? Create a definition, using your own words.

4. What is the purpose of paragraphs 10–12? What is their relationship to the rest of the essay?

5. What is Cohen's tone in this selection? List some of the words and phrases that he uses that illustrate his tone.

Evaluating the Author's Viewpoints

1. What can you infer about how Cohen feels about Patricia Conradt's lawsuit against NBC?

2. How does Adam Cohen feel about the recent spate of "humiliation TV" shows? Do you agree or disagree with him? Why?

3. What can you infer about how Cohen views people who watch these shows? The people who appear on them voluntarily?

Pursuing Possible Essay Topics

1. Do you enjoy watching the types of shows that Andrew Cohen discusses in this essay? Why or why not? Write an essay discussing your viewpoint.

2. Do you think the First Amendment should cover the types of situations and speech that are found in these types of shows? In other words, do you think that Patricia Conradt has a case? Explain in an essay.

 3. With a classmate or in a group, compare and contrast the types of shows you grew up watching with the ones that are on television today. Summarize your notes in a report to your class.

4. Do you think reality television is entertaining or not? Write an essay discussing your viewpoint.

5. Do you think that reality television shows are actually "real"? Why or why not? Write an essay about it.

6. Brainstorm or freewrite on one or more of the following:

   a. television

   b. televised humiliation

   c. the First Amendment

   d. media

   e. technology

7. Using a topic of your own, write an essay on some aspect of media and technology.

 ## Opposing Viewpoints Dealing with the Internet's Future

The next two essays reveal a difference of opinion on what the future may hold for the Internet. As you read, look for their agreements and disagreements.

Preparing to Read

Take a minute or two to look over the following reading selection. Note the title and the author, read the first paragraph, and check the essay's length. Make certain you have the time now to read it carefully and to do the exercises that follow it. Then, in the spaces provided, answer the following questions.

1. What do you think the author will say about technology? _____

_____

_____

2. Do you think you will agree or disagree with what he has to say? Why?

_____

_____

Vocabulary

Good comprehension of what you are about to read depends upon your understanding of the words below. The number following each word refers to the paragraph where it is used.

piecemeal (1) by a small amount at a time

cinch (12) a certainty or sure thing

logistics (13) management of the details of an operation

wend (13) proceed or make one's way

protocol (17) a code of correct conduct or way of doing things

niche (17) a situation or activity particularly suited to one's interests

collegial (20) mutually respectful

conjecture (27) guess; speculation

The Future of the Web

JOSEPH COATES

Joseph Coates currently writes columns for Technological Forecasting and Social Change; Research and Technology; *and* Personnel Management. *He gives speeches*

on the future of technology all over the world. The following article appears in
The World & I.

1   Through a series of scientific, technological, and business coincidences, the evolution of information technology has led to a disjointed, competitive, and piecemeal communications system.

2   The telegraph, telephone, and radio resulted from separate inventions, each converted into businesses by people with different objectives. Television came about as a spin-off from radio to compete with film. About 30 years ago the latest technological marvel, the Internet, was dropped into the middle of this communications chaos.

3   Unlike anything that came before, the Internet was free, or nearly so, in the minds of the early user. It featured video screens, computer keyboards, and communication to anyone, anywhere in the world, who was part of the Internet network. It has become increasingly sophisticated in quality and reliability, more convenient to use, and immeasurably more popular and valuable with the creation of the World Wide Web. Its democratic feature—open to anyone, anonymously, if you choose—was most appealing.

Considering the Future

4   Looking ahead 15 to 20 years, the Internet will be unrecognizable. The rest of the telecommunications industry will also be unrecognizable as we approach the goal of universal, seamless communication from anyplace to anyplace, at any time.

5   Technological integration will be required through patchwork arrangements, either voluntarily or by government intervention. Businesses may evolve in an intelligent way to assume more and more of the total information package needed to serve all customers. AOL-Time Warner is taking a slow start in that direction.

6   On the technological side, the biggest thing affecting the future of the Internet, aside from the integration of media, is the emergence of wireless telecommunications. The new third-generation wireless service In the United States has enough broad-band-width capacity to service the Internet. Broadband means the capacity to speedily carry voice, text, photographs, graphics, movement, and interaction.

7   Wireless Internet will become as familiar as wireline Internet, with which it will be seamlessly integrated. Continually decreasing computer size, declining cost, and increasing numbers of users worldwide will define the total emerging system.

8   Existing applications are being substantially enhanced or expanded. Let's look at a number of these and see where they are going. Keep in mind that if costs drop as technology becomes more familiar and commonplace, it will expand the range of people,

organizations, and institutions that will be on the system. As Internet pioneer Robert Metcalfe proposed years ago, the value of a network increases geometrically as the square of the number of people on the network.

Business Uses

9   Shopping by Internet is now widespread, in competition with catalog buying or visiting the mall. It is especially attractive where there is no shop, supplier, or boutique nearby. Despite exaggerated expectations, Internet shopping is enormously successful. As the quality of images and the capability of interaction grow, the Net will be the big challenge to catalogs, which derive their strength from small size, convenience, and use of color.

10   The Internet will allow you to see yourself, having sent a picture and your measurements to a vendor. If you are buying clothes, you will be able to examine a wide range of outfits, and place an order without ever leaving your chair, desk, or plane seat. You will be able to see yourself walking, sitting, or rotated at various angles in your outfits. (Some people will always want to shop traditionally because that is recreation for them.)

11   As with most new uses, it will not be either-or but will offer a widening of choices based on people's preferences and short term pressures. Comparison shopping will be a cinch on the Internet and will drive down prices. Business-to-business network commerce is already flourishing and will expand tremendously. Auctions and various forms of bidding are already common and will become ubiquitous.

12   One consequence of Internetbased [sic] purchasing will be a radical change in logistics regarding the shipping of goods. As more things in smaller or larger packages are delivered to homes, offices, and business facilities, trucks themselves will change. The big ones will still be necessary, but there will be a lot more midsize and smaller ones to wend their way through the neighborhoods.

13   Some communities may resort to the Tokyo system, in which people place and pick up their Internet orders at a local chain, like 7-Eleven. The reason is that in Tokyo the street naming is so complex that it would be too expensive to deliver to individual addresses.

14   Wireline and wireless will help business operate not only around the clock but around the world, in the sense that any element of the business personnel or unit can contact any other element, anytime and anywhere. Out of that capability will come enhanced efficiency and effectiveness, tighter management, or looser reins where that is appropriate.

15   There will be more interpersonal action between people who are now normally distant. Groupware, the ability of multiple locations to

simultaneously communicate, exchange ideas, discuss matters, and work on projects, will be a cohesive factor in global business.

16   On the other hand, we will develop an etiquette that will be a constraint on who has the right to contact whom, when, for what purpose, and under what circumstances. After all, the system could easily drive everyone to a frazzle without proper protocol. Small businesses will benefit: the global Internet will allow any size enterprise to market worldwide and find (or be found by) members of niche markets.

Emergence of Cyberunions

17   Some markets will shrivel and even wither away when it is cheaper, faster, and more reliable to do a task yourself. Examples include travel agents, financial service advisers, and automobile dealers. Their individual survival will depend on innovations in customer service.

18   Arthur Shostak, a longtime student of organized labor, foresees the emergence of cyberunions. The Internet will not just improve the old tools of unionism but will open up new levels of excellence, making strategic planning more feasible, flexible, and practical. As unions gain international breadth, their actions will become more sophisticated.

19   In negotiations, if unions are able to call up the same in-depth information about the firm available to the employer, this will make solutions more mutually significant. The Internet will also allow unions to become more collegial, restoring the socialization and important to group cohesion and action.

20   Paralleling the new business-union relations will be public interest groups and nongovernmental organizations dealing with national or international governing bodies. The ability to gather, collect, process, and deliver information in depth and on demand during a negotiation or discussion will change relationships. The ability to confront solid information with solid information will reduce hostile confrontations. In almost all interorganizational negotiations, the best route is establishing cooperation on as much common ground as possible.

21   Surveys and panel voting will be common. Most promising will be real-time voting during TV programs on individual characters, acts, sequences, and outcomes. The questionable judgments of those who manage the media may be replaced by the more practical and down-to-earth judgments of viewers.

22   A surprisingly high percentage of people require supervision, whether as a condition of parole or for medical reasons. The availability of wireless-bandwidth capabilities will make it practical to have two-way audio, video, and data communication with them, ensuring that they remain law abiding, safe, and healthy. The Internet will be

able to identify where people are, remind them of what they must do—take a pill, exercise—and where they must go, and verify the safety of those who are at risk.

23   There will be a great deal more interaction through wireless Internet as the devices shrink in size and capacity grows. We might have wrist TVs, from the size of a wristwatch face up to anything that will be comfortable on your forearm.

24   The events of September 11 have reminded all of us that oral communication is invaluable in an emergency. We will add to that the capability of imagery, which will be a primary improvement in dealing with physical, medical, social, occupational, or traffic emergencies. In a disaster, a picture will be invaluable in allocating resources, mobilizing, setting priorities, and managing rescue workers.

Contacting the Best Coach

25   When you take part in sports and recreation using the Internet, you will be able to have outstanding coaches watch you swing the club, toss the caber, or race the horse. The ability to have expert knowledge brought to a sports activity without the tremendous burden of cost and time will open up new capabilities to enhance individual performance. A related benefit will be the correction of potentially dangerous patterns or maneuvers that occur in every sport.

26   The Internet will lead to public voting on sports in real time to conjecture on the next move, as the rugby or football team moves into action. Fox TV used this technology during the recent Super Bowl, when it asked fans to submit answers to upcoming plays by the Patriots and Rams. Instant display of results will add an exciting element to watching sports. Other kinds of recreation will be opened up by wireless devices: tiny cameras will allow us to see what a snorkeler sees, or to view the face of a person bungee jumping or driving a race car.

27   The Internet can be a factor in automobile safety. Some 42,000 people die each year in traffic accidents in the United States. The most dangerous drivers are the young and the elderly. Technology will provide real-time monitoring of their performance, reporting to the driver vocally while driving ("You took that turn too fast," "You are closing too quickly," or "You are delaying too long in applying the brakes").

28   Real-time reporting can become a combination of training and monitoring for young drivers and a refresher course and safety device for older drivers, who have slower responses. The feedback could be sent to your parents by Internet, or it could be replayed in the evening when you return home. For those with questionable driving records, monitoring could be mandated as a condition for maintaining one's license, with feedback continually sent to the traffic department.

Using a New Language—RUOK?

29   The Internet developed in the United States as if all the world spoke English and will do so forever. This is far from the truth, although English will be the dominant language for the English speaking nations, most professionals, and big business.

30   Communications among multinational corporations and their principal suppliers will be in English. But when one gets down to the nitty-gritty, consumers' side of life, it seems unlikely that people who speak Turkish or Polish will search for and buy a washing machine using English rather than their native tongue.

31   A large expansion in new languages on the Internet is already under way. Keyboards will become more complex. In his book *Alpha Beta*, John Man points out that there is a universal Unicode, which stores 143 characters to represent the alphabets in all languages. Complex graphic languages such as Arabic will have keyboards that can be flipped back and forth between the local language and English.

32   The Chinese will use a Roman keyboard for email using a script called Pinyin, which converts the sounds of Chinese into Roman letters. The system can even take into account the tonal differences that are so important in Chinese.

33   The lexicographer David Crystal claims that Netspeak is emerging as a third form of communication, the other two types presumably being speech and text. The Internet will steadily change our ideas of grammar, syntax, and vocabulary. With regard to it, RUOK?

34   Medicine is a favorite subject for discussions on the Internet now. New uses will offer a combination of speed and flexibility of response to an accident, disaster, or individual patients. The ability to incorporate broad bandwidth imaging and interaction will allow the practitioner to examine and diagnose the patient at a distance. Routine data gathering and monitoring of patients will be transmitted to the physician's database.

35   A wireless Internet will transform sightseeing, eliminating the need to carry heavy guidebooks. It will allow you to call up anything you want, with the right level of detail to satisfy your needs.

36   You will not need to know the name of a building since GPS, the Global Positioning Satellite system, will automatically take care of that. The Internet will facilitate getting around in strange cities, minimizing the possibility of getting lost with no ready way of calling for help.

Taking care of home

37   The Internet will be the core of the most important information-technology development in the home, the electronic home work-study center. It will bring together all of the information technologies

connected with the house and all of their functions: work at home, entertainment, recreation, and socialization.

38   A typical home will have seven or eight flat screens. The kitchen appliances will be connected to each other and networked to the Internet, allowing you to instruct them remotely from another room, your car, or your office. The ability to communicate internally with wireless will cost less than rewiring your house. Safety and security will cease to be concerns of the middle class and wealthy. The smart house will alert one to the presence of intruders, photograph them, and even capture them physically in many circumstances. The Internet will retain all the information it automatically sends to the police or fire department.

39   The Internet will allow you to participate remotely in celebrations, weddings, births, and funerals as you interact with other people through life-size wall screens. It will be the closest thing to being at the event, which may be 15 or 5,000 miles away.

40   The Internet will bring familiar forms of recreation into the home, but it will also lead to new types of entertainment and recreation. Socially, your contacts may be briefer but their numbers will be greater, and, on average, each will give satisfaction greater than you ever experienced before.

41   The boundless credible expectations of the Internet will enhance our li͏   i͏   ͏   e our work, free up our time, expand our contacts, ͏   ͏   ͏   **ter** ͏   ͏   isfaction in our activities.

Understanding the Content

Feel free to reread all or parts of the selection to answer the following questions.

1. On the technological side, what is the biggest thing affecting the Internet, according to Joseph Coates?

2. What is "one consequence of Internet-based purchasing," according to Coates?

3. What effect does Coates think the Internet will have on unions?

4. What effect did the events of September 11 have on oral communication?

5. How can the Internet be a factor in automobile safety, according to Coates?

6. According to Joseph Coates, how will the Internet affect homes?

Looking at Structure and Style

1. What is the thesis of this essay? State it in your own words.

2. What is the organizing pattern of paragraph 3?

3. What are the two organizing patterns used in paragraph 6?

4. What is the organizing pattern used in paragraph 13? What is this paragraph's relationship to paragraphs 10–12?

5. List the examples that the author uses to support his point that the Internet can be a factor in automobile safety.

6. Does the author use credible evidence to support his thesis? Explain.

Evaluating the Author's Viewpoints

1. What is the author's tone in this essay?

2. Does the author exhibit any kind of bias toward his subject in this essay?

3. What can you infer about how the author feels about the Internet and technology in general?

Pursuing Possible Essay Topics

Unless you have an idea for an essay based on what you have just read, wait until after you read the following essay, *The Information Revolution Will Not Be a Panacea,* for another view on the uses, purposes, and potential benefits of the Internet.

Preparing to Read

Take a minute or two to look over the following reading selection. Note the title and the author, read the first paragraph, and check the essay's length. Make certain you have the time now to read it carefully and to do the exercises that follow it. Then, in the spaces provided, answer the following questions.

1. What do you think the author will say about technology? _____

   _____

   _____

2. How closely do you think this author will agree with Joseph Coates, if at all?

   _____

   _____

Vocabulary

Good comprehension of what you are about to read depends upon your understanding of the words below. The number following each word refers to the paragraph where it is used.

eradicate (1) to get rid of

savants (2) learned persons or scholars

stave (2) to prevent

intrinsically (2) inherently; fundamentally

panacea (10) all-healing; a remedy

The Information Revolution Will Not Be a Panacea

Editors of *The Economist*

The Economist *is an authoritative weekly newspaper that reports on international and business news and opinion. All articles are written anonymously in collaboration with reporters and editors.*

1   "It is impossible that old prejudices and hostilities should longer exist, while such an instrument has been created for the exchange of thought between all the nations of the earth." Thus Victorian

enthusiasts, acclaiming the arrival in 1858 of the first transatlantic telegraph cable. People say that sort of thing about new technologies, even today. Biotechnology is said to be the cure for world hunger. The sequencing of the human genome will supposedly eradicate cancer and other diseases. The wildest optimism, though, has greeted the Internet. A whole industry of cybergurus has enthralled audiences (and made a fine living) with exuberant claims that the Internet will prevent wars, reduce pollution, and combat various forms of inequality. However, although the Internet is still young enough to inspire idealism, it has also been around long enough to test whether the prophets can be right.

2   Grandest of all the claims are those made by some of the savants at the Massachusetts Institute of Technology about the Internet's potential as a force for peace. One guru, Nicholas Negroponte, has declared that, thanks to the Internet, the children of the future "are not going to know what nationalism is." His colleague, Michael Dertouzos, has written that digital communications will bring "computer-aided peace" which "may help stave off future flare-ups of ethnic hatred and national break-ups." The idea is that improved communications will reduce misunderstandings and avert conflict. This is not new, alas, any more than were the claims for the peace-making possibilities of other new technologies. In the early years of the 20th century, aeroplanes were expected to end wars, by promoting international communication and (less credibly) by making armies obsolete, since they would be vulnerable to attack from the air. After the first world war had dispelled such notions, it was the turn of radio. "Nation shall speak peace unto nation," ran the fine motto of Britain's BBC World Service. Sadly, Rwanda's Radio Mille Collines disproved the idea that radio was an intrinsically pacific force once and for all.[1]

No Peace and Blue Skies

3   The mistake people make is to assume that wars are caused simply by the failure of different peoples to understand each other adequately. Indeed, even if that were true, the Internet can also be used to advocate conflict. Hate speech and intolerance flourish in its murkier corners, where governments...find it hard to intervene. Although the Internet undeniably fosters communication, it will not put an end to war. But might it reduce energy consumption and pollution? The Centre for Energy and Climate Solutions (CECS), a Washington think-tank, has advanced just such a case, based largely on energy consumption figures for 1997 and 1998. While the

---

[1]According to the United Nations, reports on the radio station helped incite the massacre of Rwanda's Tutsi rebels.

American economy grew by 9% over those two years, energy demand was almost unchanged—because, the CECS ventures, the Internet "can turn paper and CDs into electrons, and replace trucks with fiber-optic cable." No wonder one enthusiastic newspaper headline begged, "Shop online—save the earth."

4   Sadly, earth-saving is harder than that. Certainly, shopping online from home is far less polluting than driving to a shopping mall. Ordering groceries online, and having them delivered, means that, if the logistics are handled efficiently, one truck journey can replace dozens of families' separate car trips. Reading newspapers, magazines and other documents online is more efficient than printing and transporting them physically. Yet doing things online is more energy-efficient only if it genuinely displaces real-world activities. If people shop online as well as visiting the bricks-and-mortar store, the result is an overall increase in energy consumption. Thanks to the Internet, it is now easy for Europeans to order books and have them extravagantly air-freighted from America before they are available in Europe. And it is more efficient to read documents online only if doing so replaces, rather than adds to, the amount of printed [material].

5   Furthermore, as more and more offices and homes connect to the Internet, millions of PCs, printers, servers and other devices gobble significant quantities of energy. Home computers are becoming part of the fabric of everyday life, and are increasingly left switched on all the time. One controversial assessment concluded that fully 8% of electricity consumption in America is due to Internet-connected computers. The construction of vast "server farms"—warehouses full of computers and their attendant cooling systems—has contributed to the overloading of the electrical power network that has caused brown-outs in Silicon Valley.

Inequality Might Be Reduced

6   What about the belief that the Internet will reduce inequality? According to a study carried out by America's Department of Commerce, households with annual incomes above $75,000 are more than 20 times as likely to have Internet access as the poorest households. [Former president] Bill Clinton, struck by the "digital divide" between rich and poor, argue[d] that universal Internet access would help to reduce income inequality.

7   But, as the cost of using the Internet continues to fall (services offering free access are becoming the norm, and a basic PC can now be had for little more than a video recorder or a large television), the true reason for the digital divide between rich and poor will become apparent. The poor are not shunning the Internet because they cannot afford it: the problem is that they lack the skills to exploit it effectively. So it is difficult to see how connecting the poor to the Internet

will improve their finances. It would make more sense to aim for universal literacy than universal Internet access. Yet, even in the more ludicrous claims for the Internet, there may be germs of truth. This open network, so hard for governments to control, may indeed help to give more power to individual citizens and encourage democracies. As democratic governments rarely fight each other, that might promote peace. As for the environment, the Internet will allow many places of machinery to be monitored and tuned more precisely from afar. That will promote energy efficiency. Taxing or merely measuring pollution will be less expensive and so easier for governments to undertake.

8   Even inequality may, in some cases, be reduced thanks to the Internet. A computer programmer in Bangalore or Siberia can use the Internet to work for a software company in Seattle without leaving home, and can expect to be paid a wage that is closer to that of his virtual colleagues at the other end of the cable. The effect is not to reduce income inequality between people doing similar jobs in different countries, but to increase the inequality between information workers in poor countries and their poorest compatriots.

9   The Internet changes many things. It has had a dramatic impact on the world of business. Firms can now link their systems directly to those of their suppliers and partners, can do business online around the clock, and can learn more than ever about their customers. Economies may be more productive as a result. For individuals, e-mail has emerged as the most important new form of personal communication since the invention of the telephone.

The Limits of Technology

10   The extent to which the Internet will transform other fields of human endeavour, however, is less certain. Even when everyone on the planet has been connected to the Internet, there will still be wars, and pollution, and inequality. As new gizmos come and go, human nature seems to remain stubbornly unchanged; despite the claims of the techno-prophets, humanity cannot simply invent away its failings. The Internet is not the first technology to have been hailed as a panacea—and it will certainly not be the last.

Understanding the Content

Feel free to reread all or parts of the selection to answer the following questions.

1. What do "cybergurus" claim that the Internet can do, according to this article? Does the author agree? How can you tell?

2. What did Nicholas Negroponte claim regarding the Internet? What does his colleague, Michael Dertouzos, claim the Internet can do?

3. What effect does the Internet have on energy consumption and pollution, according to this selection?

4. What was former President Bill Clinton's argument regarding universal Internet access?

5. What changes has the Internet brought about, according to the author of this selection?

Looking at Structure and Style

1. Paraphrase the thesis of this essay.

2. Is credible evidence provided to support the essay's thesis? Explain your answer.

3. Why do you think the author begins this essay with a quote from "Victorian enthusiasts"? Is it effective, in your opinion? What does it tell you about how the author will feel about the Internet and technology, in general, if anything?

4. What are the "claims" made by cybergurus about the effects of the Internet? Does the author refute all of these claims? Does the author agree with any of them? Explain.

5. What is the author's purpose in including paragraph 7? What is its relationship to paragraph 6? To the entire essay?

Evaluating the Author's Viewpoints

1. What is the overall tone and attitude in this essay? How can you tell? Does the author exhibit any kind of bias toward the subject in this essay?

2. What can you infer about how the author feels about the Internet and technology in general? Compare the author's thoughts with the opinion of Coates in the previous essay.

3. Instead of making sure that the poor have Internet access, what would the author prefer? Why?

4. How will inequality be reduced thanks to the Internet? Do you agree or disagree with the author's assertion?

5. What changes does the author think the Internet will bring forth? Do you agree? Or do you think there are more changes that the author didn't list? Explain.

Pursuing Possible Essay Topics

1. Think about how, if at all, the Internet has changed your life. Write an essay discussing what changes have occurred since you started using the Internet.

2. How would your life be different without Internet access? Write an essay imagining life without online access.

3. With a classmate or in a small group, discuss which essay on the future of the Internet you agree with more. Summarize your notes into one cohesive essay.

4. What are the global benefits of the Internet? Write an essay discussing your viewpoint.

5. Do you think that there could be positive effects from universal Internet access, like former President Bill Clinton stated? If so, what are they? Write an essay.

6. Brainstorm or freewrite on one or more of the following:

   a. the Internet

   b. universal Internet access

   c. technology

   d. computer-aided peace

7. Pick your own topic related to media or technology and write an essay.

Student Essay

Read the following narrative essay written by a student. As you read, look for answers to these questions:

1. Does the essay fit the assignment to write on some aspect of the media?

2. Does the essay have a clear thesis and good support?

3. Does the essay follow the writing guidelines suggested in Chapter 2, "Viewpoints on Writing Essays"?

TV News: Journalism or Propaganda?

Jim Stone

1   Not all television news organizations report the news fairly or completely. They all may begin covering stories with the basic idea of truthfulness in reporting, but by air-time this has fallen by the wayside. All news organizations face pressures from many different angles. Each sponsor has its wishes, special interest groups have theirs, the network and local station executives have theirs, and finally, the censors and "old man time" limit what can be shown. These pressures, as well as manipulation on the part of government, can all act on a news story and, in many cases, slant it by the time we get it.

2   Here's how it typically works. A news crew, usually consisting of a reporter and a cameraman, is sent to the scene of an incident or press conference. Today's story is about a leaking toxic waste dump. A state spokesman is holding a press conference at the site of the dump. The conference is attended by most major newspapers, the major wire services (AP, UPI, etc.), and the local TV networks. The state spokesman presents the problem to the press in a prepared statement, and then our illustrious reporter faces the camera and paraphrases what the state spokesman just said. The crew then gets some camera shots of leaking chemical drums and proceeds to tour the neighborhood.

3   They are, of course, looking for "the man in the street" for a "salt of the earth" impression of this latest item of

gloom and doom. The first person being interviewed, someone who
wants the dump removed from his neighborhood anyway, begins
to see some fairly lucrative lawsuits on the horizon. When
asked to describe any recurrent or frequent health problems,
the interviewee rattles off a lengthy list including but not
limited to gout, ulcers, arthritis, hemorrhoids and many other
common ailments that he feels sure are caused by the leaking
dump next door. The news crew repeats this scene two or
three times with other disgruntled neighbors and gets almost
identical answers from each respondent. The news crew then
returns to the studio and proceeds to review the fruits of
their labors in the video editing room.

4   The editor then begins to "make" the story. This is where
the potential for propaganda comes in; the editor is the person
who bears the brunt of the pressures from special interest
groups. At this point he can downplay the story by stressing
the state's official assertion that they do not know the extent
of the hazard, while dropping the spokesman's later comment
that damage appears extensive. Or, at the request of another
interest group, such as an environmental one, the editor can
stress that damage is believed to be extensive and may even
be irreversible. He drops the spokesman's comment that damage
assessments cannot be made at this time. Or, the editor can
stress the cost of the cleanup in order to help the state
environmental protection agency secure a larger budget by the
use of public furor that will no doubt occur from an incident
of this sort. In this instance, he would probably tie in
footage of all the other leaking waste dumps around the state
as well as total cleanup costs. To add the human element, he
can put in some of the footage of the neighborhood people with
their assorted illnesses, or just the portion of the interview
in which the people express their shock and outrage over the
dump spill.

5   In most cases, if not all, the editor is trying to do us, the
viewer, a favor. He is creating a news story that is digestible
in the short time allotted for each news story. If time allows,

and the story is really important, the network can do an in-depth story which might include history, background, further ramifications, and future dump site plans. Most of us would not want to sit and sift through the daily deluge of news items. This would quickly become a full-time job and is best left to the professionals.

6   But in a few instances, the editor does the viewing public a disservice by slanting the story in order to influence public opinion. This can be done either through omission or through emphasis of key points, as is often done in political campaigns. The editor favoring a candidate can downplay or ignore negative items while stressing the good ones. In contrast, if the editor dislikes a candidate, he can emphasize the negative items and downplay the positive ones.

7   In today's political world, television plays a huge role in who will get elected. Most of us don't take the time to really deal with the issues. A *TV Guide* poll shows that most of us vote for the candidate who makes the most favorable impression on us. The politician knows this as well as news editors.

8   All of this leads to the conclusion that we still can't believe everything we see in print or on television. That old warning about buyer beware, caveat emptor, should be changed to include television news.

Reaction

In your journal or on a separate sheet of paper, write your reaction to the student essay. What would you tell the student about his essay? What do you like? What might improve the essay?

Viewpoints on Images

Though traveling together, everyone in the photo appears to be in his or her own world. Would you be doing the same if you sat in the empty seat? Would these people be relating to each other if they did not have their listening devices? Are iPods and MP3 players causing people to be alienated from each other and/or from society?

© Mary Altaffer/AP Images

On the Net

Many of the selections included in this chapter are critical of the media and technology. Research one of the following topics on the Web to find opposing views on each topic:

1. censorship

2. television

3. the Internet

Now that you have read opposing viewpoints on the same topics, decide whether you think the criticism contained in some of the selections in this chapter is justified.

CHAPTER

10 Viewpoints on Human Rights

Focus on What Is Meant By "Human Rights."

To help you focus on the subject of this chapter, take a few minutes to consider what you know regarding human rights. Prewrite on one or more of the following prompts, exploring your viewpoints on the subject(s):

1. when, if ever, is torture justified
2. when, if ever, should the death penalty be administered
3. what treatment should be given to prisoners suspected of committing terrorism
4. what rights should illegal immigrants have
5. what is meant by the term "human rights"

Someone once said that there are three sides to every questionable issue: your side, my side, and the "right" side. In truth, there may be many sides, depending upon the issue itself, making it difficult for any thinking person to make quick decisions.

According to psychologists, numerous studies show that the urge to conform to group thinking is too powerful for most people to resist. Unknowingly, we become conditioned to ways of thinking. This usually happens because we are molded at an early age by our parents, relatives, teachers, and friends. We tend to honor their value systems because we love them and trust their judgments. If our families vote Republican, we usually vote Republican. If our families go to a particular church, we tend to continue in that church. If our parents and church leaders speak out against abortion, we tend to accept such views as "right." Their beliefs become our beliefs without much questioning or thought on our part.

As we mature, our beliefs are also molded both directly and indirectly by our peers. What we wear, what we eat, what music we accept, even what media we enjoy become tied in with our desire to be accepted as part of a group. Even when we think we are acting as individuals by rejecting the ideas of one group, we are often just accepting the ideas of another. We become self-deceptive. Our thinking process can become overruled by others' opinions that we think are truly our own thoughtful reactions because we have heard them for so long. We can become biased and forget to weigh our opinions by looking at facts or reasoning that goes against our belief system. And even when we do try to see "facts," we often don't have the experience needed to evaluate the information. In such cases, it is better to suspend our decision on which side to take until we do some more investigating.

This chapter contains pro and con essays on three important topics: the use of torture, the treatment of prisoners suspected of terrorism, and capital punishment. All three topics can cause heated debate because of their political overtones and implications.

At this point you may or may not have a particular viewpoint of your own on one or more of these topics. Once you have finished the chapter readings, you will at least know more about the issues involved and will be better able to form an opinion. If you already have a viewpoint, try to suspend your opinions as you read the selections. Avoid letting your own biases cloud any opinions that are opposite to yours—not always an easy task. We sometimes have a tendency to think that our views are superior to another person's even though we may not have critically examined our own. Such tendencies limit our objectivity and keep us from learning from others.

As you read each selection in this unit, ask yourself these questions regarding the strengths and weaknesses of the arguments being made:

1. Is the **problem** being expressed too simplistically?

2. Does the author use mostly **facts** or mostly **opinions**?

3. Is the author trying to reach my **emotions** or my **mind?**

4. Are the judgments being made based on solid **reasoning** and **verifiable information?**

5. Is the **evidence** convincing and provable, or deceptive and distracting?

6. What **sources** are cited? Are they reliable?

7. Is the author an **authority** on the subject?

Use these questions to let go of your own feelings long enough to understand the author's position, especially if it is different from your own.

Even after reading the selections, you may discover you need more information than is provided here in order to take a stand of your own. That's a healthy sign that you are not being easily swayed. You will probably want to read more and discuss these subjects with others. That, of course, is why you are being asked to read these selections.

Hold your own opinions until you have read each pair of essays. See if they help you understand the issues any better. You will then be asked to write an essay on your viewpoints regarding each topic.

One final word: New information on these and other controversial issues continues to emerge. What you think today may not be what you think tomorrow. That's healthy, too, as long as you are truly making sound judgments and critically weighing the evidence. A changing mind is better than a closed one.

 ## Opposing Viewpoints on Torture

Ever since it was revealed through photographs of American soldiers committing torture at Abu Ghraib prison in Iraq, the question has been raised about the legality, morality, and usefulness of torture. The readings that follow offer two different viewpoints.

Preparing to Read

Take a minute or two to look over the following reading selection. Note the title and the author, read the first two paragraphs, and check the essay's length. Make certain you have the time now to read it carefully and to do the exercises that follow it. Then, in the spaces provided, answer the following questions.

1. What arguments do you think the author may use to support his position?

_____

_____

2. What is the author's tone in the opening paragraph? _____

_____

Vocabulary

Good comprehension of what you are about to read depends upon your understanding of the words below. The number following each word refers to the paragraph where it is used.

inducements (1) things that help bring about a desired action or result

signatory (5) bound by signed agreement

circumventions (6) acts of getting around restrictions

Justice
ALAN DERSHOWITZ

Alan Dershowitz, called one of the "most distinguished defenders of individual rights," and the "the best-known criminal lawyer in the world," is the author of 20 works of fiction and non-fiction, including six bestsellers. He rose to prominence defending such clients as O.J. Simpson, Michael Milken, Mike Tyson, Claus von Bulow, as well as indigent defendants.

1   What would you want the police to do if your child had been kidnapped and the police caught the kidnapper but did not find your child? They could threaten him, offer him inducements or try to trick him. But what if he mocked his interrogators and boasted that your

child would die of starvation within a few days. Would you want the police to administer non-lethal torture—say, a sterilized needle under the fingernails causing unbearable pain but no permanent damage—until the kidnapper led you to the child?

2   Germany recently confronted this situation, when the 11-year-old son of a prominent industrialist was kidnapped, and his kidnapper refused to disclose the child's location. Interrogators threatened to begin torturing him if he persisted in his silence, and one even threatened to have him "raped" by a predatory inmate. The kidnapper broke down before any torture was actually administered. The kidnapper admitted that he had murdered the child and led interrogators to the body. German legal experts are now debating whether the administration of non-lethal torture would have been appropriate—morally and legally—under those compelling circumstances.

3   When a similar case arose in the U.S. some 15 years ago, there was no debate. The kidnapper was tortured by police—they choked him and administered great pain—and he disclosed the location of the victim, who was found alive. The United States Court of Appeals for the 11th Circuit praised the police, characterizing them as "a group of concerned officers acting in a reasonable manner to obtain information they needed in order to protect another individual from bodily harm or death". The court justified the torture as having been "motivated by the immediate necessity to find the victim and save his life".

4   This brings us to the ticking-bomb terrorist case that we will eventually confront: the captured terrorist who knows where and when his fellow terrorists are planning to detonate a nuclear bomb in a crowded city. What should—what would—our government do in such a case? Based on our experiences with terrorists we've captured in the past, we would probably employ all forms of psychological pressure first. He would be threatened, offered a deal, deprived of sleep, isolated, blindfolded, questioned for hours on end, made to sit and stand in uncomfortable positions, and introduced to investigators from other countries known to use lethal torture. If these forms of intimidation failed to work, he might then be shipped to one of the countries to which we subcontract our torture. These countries include Egypt, the Philippines, Morocco, and especially Jordan because that kingdom is willing to torture not only terrorist suspects but also their relatives. Of course a torture victim might say anything to end his pain, so the interrogators must be certain they are obtaining the truth. They do this by continuing the torture until the subject actually leads them to the ticking-bomb or to the other terrorists. The information must be self-proving for the torture to stop, so as to discourage the subject from making things up.

5   These tactics can sometimes work quite effectively. In a 1995 case, Philippine authorities tortured a suspect for sixty-seven days until he led them to hard evidence of plans to assassinate the Pope and crash eleven commercial airliners into the Pacific Ocean. Torture does sometimes work and does sometimes save lives, but that doesn't mean that it is ever justified. Reasonable people can and do disagree about whether the infliction of non-lethal torture on an admitted terrorist who can help save lives is morally and legally acceptable. The Geneva Convention against torture currently prohibits all forms of physical and mental torture, but it is ignored by most countries, and even most democracies in extreme cases. The convention, to which we are a signatory, also prohibits subcontracting torture to other countries, but this too is often disregarded, even by the United States.

6   The shadowy circumventions of the letter and spirit of the law, on which we now rely, raise the question of whether it wouldn't be more honest to change the law so as to openly permit non-lethal torture in ticking bomb cases, if the President or a high ranking judge were prepared to certify, based on compelling evidence, that an emergency situation existed. This certification, which would be akin to a warrant issued for searches, would provide some degree of accountability for the choice of evils present by the ticking bomb torture dilemma. In a democracy, it is better to confront hard choices openly than to allow shadowy figures to make them secretly and with deniability whether it involves the fate of a single kidnapped child or an entire city.

Understanding the Content

Feel free to reread all or parts of the selection to answer the following questions.

1. Does the author believe that torture is sometimes morally and legally appropriate? Why or why not?

2. What was the end result of the torture case in the United States involving a kidnapper and the police? How did the United States Court of Appeals rule on this case?

3. To which countries does the United States "subcontract its torture"?

4. How do governments that use torture as a tactic insure that the torture victim is telling the truth?

5. What is the Geneva Convention and what does it say about torture? Is the Geneva Convention adhered to by most countries, according to Dershowitz?

Looking at Structure and Style

1. What is the thesis of this selection? Is it stated or implied? If stated, where?

2. Why do you think the author includes examples of successful non-lethal torture situations in this selection? Is it effective?

3. How well does Dershowitz support his thesis with facts? Is his argument persuasive? Explain.

4. Rewrite the topic sentence of paragraph 6 in your own words.

5. What is the purpose of paragraph 3, particularly in relation to paragraph 2?

Evaluating the Author's Viewpoints

1. Does Dershowitz display any bias in this essay, in your opinion? Explain.

2. Did you learn anything new from this essay? If so, has it changed your opinion on the subject of torture or human rights in general?

3. In your opinion, does Dershowitz put forth a persuasive argument regarding the torture of prisoners? If not, what could he have done to make his argument more persuasive?

4. Now that you have read the entire article, how would you answer Dershowitz's initial question: "What would you want the police to do if your child had been kidnapped and the police caught the kidnapper but did not find your child"?

5. Think about the other question that Dershowitz poses: "What should—or would—our government do" in the case of the ticking-bomb terrorist case? How would you answer that now?

Pursuing Possible Essay Topics

Unless you have an idea for an essay based on what you have just read, wait until after you read the following selection in this chapter and have studied the list of ideas at the end of that selection before developing an essay on the topic of torture.

Preparing to Read

Take a minute or two to look over the following reading selection. Note the title and the author, read the first two paragraphs, and check the essay's length. Make certain you have the time now to read it carefully and to do the exercises that follow it. Then, in the spaces provided, answer the following questions.

1. What does the title tell you about the author(s)'s viewpoint?

_____

_____

2. Do you think you will agree with the author(s)'s viewpoint? Why?

_____

_____

Vocabulary

Good comprehension of what you are about to read depends upon your understanding of the words below. The number following each word refers to the paragraph where it is used.

adversary (1) an opponent; an enemy

categorical (2) being without exception; uncompromising

genocide (2) the mass execution of a group of people from a national, ethnic, or religious group

squeamish (3) easily shocked; easily nauseated

tantamount (6) equivalent to

repugnant (21) revolting or disgusting

Is Torture Ever Justified?

EDITORS OF *THE ECONOMIST*

The Economist *is an authoritative weekly newspaper that reports on international business news and opinion. All articles are written anonymously in collaboration with reporters and editors.*

1   IN EVERY war, information is a weapon. In a "war against terrorism", where the adversary wears no uniform and hides among the civilian

population, information can matter even more. But does that mean that torture can sometimes be justified to extract information?

2   The answer in international law is categorical: no. As laid down in treaties such as the Geneva Conventions, the UN Convention against Torture and the International Covenant on Civil and Political Rights, the ban on torture or any cruel, inhuman or degrading treatment is absolute, even in times of war. Along with genocide, torture is the only crime that every state must punish, no matter who commits it or where. Defenders of this blanket prohibition offer arguments that range from the moral (torture degrades and corrupts the society that allows it) to the practical (people will say anything under torture so the information they provide is unreliable anyway).

3   The September 11th attacks have not driven any rich democracy to reverse itself and make torture legal. But they have encouraged the bending of definitions and the turning of blind eyes. There is a greater readiness among governments that would never practise torture themselves to use information which less squeamish states have obtained—through torture.

4   Start with definitions. Most civilised people squirm at the thought of putting suspected terrorists on the rack or pulling off toenails. What if that prisoner knew the whereabouts of a ticking bomb— maybe a biological, chemical or even nuclear one? Wouldn't a little sleep deprivation, sexual humiliation or even water-dunking be justified to save hundreds and perhaps thousands of lives? Whatever the law says, a lot of people seem to think so.

5   In a BBC survey of 27,000 people in 25 countries last October, more than one out of three people in nine of those countries, including America, considered a degree of torture acceptable if it saved lives. Opposition was highest in most European and English-speaking countries. Another poll in 2005 by the Pew Research Centre found that nearly half of all Americans thought the torture of suspected terrorists was sometimes justified.

6   Two Republican presidential hopefuls (in the 2008 primaries) Rudy Giuliani and Mitt Romney, support the "enhanced" interrogation of suspects in the event of an imminent attack. Dick Cheney, America's vice-president, recently suggested that "dunking" a terrorist in water to save lives was a "no-brainer". The ensuing uproar led him to backtrack, claiming that he was not, of course, referring to "water-boarding", or simulated drowning, a technique regarded as tantamount to torture and banned in the American army's own interrogation manual.

I'll Tickle You Into Submission

7   One objection to allowing moderate physical pressure is the difficulty of knowing where to draw the line. If stress positions and sleep

deprivation do not work, do you progress to branding with red-hot irons and beating to a pulp? And can you rely on interrogators to heed such distinctions? It is the danger of a slippery slope that makes opponents of torture insist on a total ban.

8   Israel is the only country in modern times to have openly allowed "moderate physical pressure" as a "last resort". Since interrogators used such methods anyway, it was argued, passing an explicit law would at least make it possible to set out some limits. But in 1999, citing the slippery-slope argument, Israel's Supreme Court ruled that torture could never be justified, even in the case of a ticking bomb. It went on to outlaw techniques such as sleep deprivation, exposure to extremes of hot and cold, prolonged stress positions, hooding and violent shaking.

9   In the 1970s Britain used similar techniques against suspected terrorists in Northern Ireland. These were banned in 1978 following a case brought by the Republic of Ireland to the European Court of Human Rights. Although not torture, such methods did amount to inhumane treatment, the court ruled. In 2002 the International Criminal Court for ex-Yugoslavia in The Hague decided that prolonged solitary confinement constituted torture. Such rulings did not prevent America from resorting to such harsh techniques when interrogating suspects in Afghanistan, Iraq and Guantánamo Bay, however. Former detainees in those places have spoken of severe beatings, water-boarding, excruciating stress positions, mock executions, sleep deprivation and much else besides.

10   Administration lawyers argued that since al-Qaeda and its Taliban allies were not a state party to the Geneva Conventions they were not covered by its ban on torture and other maltreatment. True, America had ratified (in 1988) the Convention against Torture, but that applied only to acts carried out on American soil, they said. And though America's own 1994 federal statute against torture did cover acts by Americans abroad, this applied only to full-blown torture, not lesser abuses.

11   In the notorious "torture memos" drawn up by the Department of Justice and the Pentagon in 2002 and 2003, the same lawyers sought to restrict the normal definition of torture—"severe pain or suffering"—to extreme acts equivalent to "serious physical injury, organ failure, or even death". Furthermore, as a wartime commander in chief whose main duty was to protect the American people, the president had the power to override both domestic and international law, they argued. After being leaked in 2004 most of these memos were "withdrawn", though not the one on the president's wartime powers.

12   Mr. Bush and his colleagues have always said that America neither authorises nor condones torture. "We don't do torture," the president

famously said. But Mr. Bush has been vaguer about the grey area between torture and more moderate pressure. Soon after suspected terrorists were first sent to Guantánamo in January 2002 he said that America's armed forces would treat the detainess "humanely" in a manner "consistent with the Geneva Conventions"—but only "to the extent appropriate and consistent with military necessity".

13   Not until the Supreme Court's ruling in Hamdan in 2006 did the administration accept that all detainees, wherever held, were protected by Common Article 3 of the Geneva Conventions, which bans all forms of cruel, inhuman or degrading treatment as well as torture. The 2005 Detainee Treatment Act, incorporating an amendment by Senator John McCain, already prohibited such treatment by American soldiers anywhere in the world. But it did not apply to the CIA.

Co-operating With Torturers

14   Yet it is the CIA that has been responsible for the "extraordinary rendition" of suspects to clandestine prisons in third countries for "enhanced" interrogation (whether by that country's agents or the CIA itself) amounting at times, many suspect, to torture. The programme's existence was not officially confirmed until Mr. Bush announced last year the transfer to Guantánamo of the last 14 "high-value" detainees then being held in so-called "black sites" around the world. Of some 100 suspected terrorists believed to have been "rendered" over the past six years, 39 remain unaccounted for, Human Rights Watch, a New York-based lobby, says.

15   In July this year [2007] Mr. Bush set out new broad guidelines for interrogations under a resumed CIA programme. He says the newly authorised techniques now comply fully with the Geneva Conventions' ban on "outrages upon personal dignity, in particular humiliating and degrading treatment" as well as torture. Even if true (which is hard to know because the details have not been disclosed), the programme itself with its enforced disappearances and black sites, which even the International Red Cross is not allowed to visit, violates basic tenets of international law.

16   Even if a country bans torture, how should it treat information that others have extracted this way? In 2004 Britain's Court of Appeal ruled that information acquired through torture was admissible as evidence in court. David Blunkett, then Britain's home secretary, welcomed the ruling. Although the government "unreservedly" condemned torture, he said, it would be "irresponsible not to take appropriate account of any information which could help protect national security and public safety." But the ruling was later overturned by the House of Lords.

17   A separate question is whether governments should use information extracted under torture by others for counter-terrorist purposes,

even if it is not admissible as evidence. Most probably agree with Mr. Blunkett that it would be irresponsible not to. But a case can be made that this is, in effect, condoning the use of torture by allies.

18   Britain has also run into trouble when trying to deport suspected foreign terrorists against whom it has not got enough evidence to secure a conviction in court. Under international law, a country must make sure that the person it wishes to expel is not in danger of being tortured or subjected to other abuse in the receiving country. In 2005 the UN's special rapporteur on torture criticised Britain for relying on "diplomatic assurances" that deportees would not be tortured. Charles Clarke, who had succeeded Mr. Blunkett as home secretary, retorted that the rights of the victims of the London Tube bombings that year mattered more than those of the perpetrators. The UN should "look at human rights in the round", he said, "rather than simply focusing all the time on the terrorist." Fine—except that no British court had convicted these suspects as terrorists.

19   To date, 144 countries have ratified the Convention against Torture. (The hold-outs include such usual suspects as Sudan, North Korea, Myanmar and Zimbabwe, but also India.) And yet, the UN's special rapporteur told the Security Council in June, torture remains widespread. Amnesty International noted cases of state-sponsored torture or other inhumane treatment in 102 of the 153 countries included in its 2007 report. The worst offenders were China, Egypt (both of which are parties to the convention), Myanmar and North Korea, along with several African countries. America's transgressions are trivial by comparison. The worry, argues Kenneth Roth, director of Human Rights Watch, is that when America breaks the rules it encourages others to do the same.

20   Why does torture endure? Part of the reason, argues Michael Ignatieff, a Canadian writer, may be that it is at times motivated not so much by a desire to extract vital information but by something baser, such as an urge to inflict pain, exact revenge, or even just for fun. That seems to have been part of the motivation of the Americans who abused prisoners in Abu Ghraib, for example. But torture may also endure because it sometimes works.

They'll Say Anything

21   Many critics of torture claim that it is ineffective as well as repugnant. Since people will say anything just to stop the pain, the information gleaned may not be reliable. On the other hand, if people do say anything under torture, you might expect some of what they say to be true and therefore—if those being tortured really are terrorists— useful to the authorities. Torture certainly helped induce Guy Fawkes to betray his co-conspirators after they had tried to blow up King James I and the British Parliament on November 5th 1605.

22   Asked recently about the CIA's use of enhanced interrogation in secret prisons, George Tenet, the CIA's director until 2004, replied that the agency's widely condemned rendition programme had saved lives, disrupted plots and provided "invaluable" information in the war against terrorism. Indeed, while denying the use of full-blown torture, he said that the programme on its own was "worth more than the FBI, the CIA and the National Security Agency put together have been able to tell us."

23   Mr Ignatieff, for his own part, sees no trumping argument on behalf of terrorists that makes their claims to human rights and dignity prevail over the security interests—and right to life—of the majority. Yet he continues to advocate a total ban. "We cannot torture, in other words, because of who we are," he says. He knows that many will disagree.

Understanding the Content

Feel free to reread all or parts of the selection to answer the following questions.

1. What does international law say about countries using torture to extract information from prisoners, according to this article? What laws do the authors cite to answer this question?

2. What percentage of people surveyed by the BBC thought it was acceptable to torture prisoners in order to save lives?

3. What is one objection to allowing moderate physical pressure in interrogation? Why does that objection arise when talking about moderate physical pressure? What is the one country that allows the practice of moderate physical pressure and why?

4. What was the content of the "torture memos" drawn up by the Department of Justice and the Pentagon in 2002 and 2003?

5. What did President Bush say about torture in general? Moderate pressure?

6. What is the 2005 Detainee Treatment Act? To what government agency did it not apply?

7. Which countries have not ratified the Convention against Torture? Has it had an affect on instances of torture being perpetrated?

Looking at Structure and Style

1. What is the thesis of this selection? Is it stated or implied? If stated, where?

2. What terms do(es) the author(s) define in this selection? Why? Are these definitions clear and are they necessary to your understanding of the article? Are they necessary to making this argument clearer to the reader? Explain.

3. The author(s) begin(s) paragraph 4 with the statement, "Start with definitions," but then true definitions of any terms aren't provided. What is being defined here in actuality? And what is the relationship of this paragraph and the definition it provides to the rest of the essay?

4. Do(es) the author(s) provide credible evidence to support the thesis?

5. Where in this selection do(es) the author(s) use comparison/contrast to show how countries think about torture, have used it in different circumstances, and have ruled on it in a legislative way? Is this effective in making the argument credible? Explain your thoughts.

6. What is the organizing pattern used in paragraph 21 of this selection?

7. The British spelling of some words is different from U. S. usage. What are some of those word differences used in the reading selection?

Evaluating the Author's Viewpoints

1. Do(es) the author(s) reveal any bias in this essay, in your opinion? Explain.

2. Did you learn anything new from this essay? If so, has it changed your opinion on the subject of torture or human rights in general?

3. In your opinion, do(es) the author(s) put forth a persuasive argument regarding the torture of prisoners? If not, what could have been done to make the argument more persuasive?

4. Do(es) the author(s) reveal any feelings about the Bush administration in this selection? The CIA? How can you tell?

5. Do you agree or disagree with the author(s) that the September 11th attacks have "encouraged the bending of definitions and the turning of blind eyes"?

6. Why do you think that some Americans "thought the torture of suspected terrorist was sometimes justified," when polled? Do you think that torture is sometimes justified? Why or why not?

Pursuing Possible Essay Topics

1. Go online and research the specifics of the Geneva Convention. Think about what you read in these two articles and what you researched on the Geneva Convention. Then, write an essay discussing your viewpoint on the torture of prisoners.

2. With a classmate or in a group, discuss these two articles. With which one do you, your classmate, or the group as a whole agree more? Or is it not that easy to determine? Write an essay discussing what you discussed with the other members of your class.

3. Do you think that one of the arguments presented in one of the two selections is more valid and more credible? Why? Write an essay discussing your viewpoint.

4. How do you think the United States has acted in terms of the interrogation of prisoners, as outlined in the two previous selections? Write an essay discussing your thoughts.

5. Brainstorm or freewrite on one or more of the following:
   a. Abu Ghraib
   b. torture
   c. moderate physical pressure
   d. terrorists
   e. human rights

6. Don't like these? Find your own topic related to torture and write about it.

 ## Opposing Viewpoints on Guantánamo Prisoner Treatment

After the attacks of 9/11, many persons suspected of being involved were captured and detained in a prison in Guantánamo Bay, Cuba. Many of the detainees were held without proof that they had been involved. Because the prison was a military facility, prisoners were not permitted due recourse of law. In time, prisoner abuse was charged and knowledge that some prisoners were shipped to foreign countries where they were tortured. Recently, efforts have been made to close the prison at "Gitmo" but as of this writing it is still in operation and holds several hundred prisoners.

Preparing to Read

Take a minute or two to look over the following reading selection. Note the title and the author, read the first paragraph, and check the essay's length. Make certain you have the time now to read it carefully and to do the exercises that follow it. Then, in the spaces provided, answer the following questions.

1. What arguments do you think the author may use to support his position?

   _____

   _____

2. What is the author's tone in the opening paragraph? _____

   _____

Vocabulary

Good comprehension of what you are about to read depends upon your understanding of the words below. The number following each word refers to the paragraph where it is used.

retrofitted (1) a modification of a product or structure

buffeted (2) struck against forcefully

amenities (2) material comforts

meting (9) distributing; giving out

excise (15) remove

consigned (16) gave over to the care of another; entrusted

arbitrary (17) determined by chance

cadence (19) the rhythmic flow, as in poetry

Verses of Suffering

Marc Falkoff

Marc Falkoff is an assistant professor at the Northern Illinois University College of Law and the attorney for 17 Guantánamo prisoners. The following article appeared in Amnesty International, recounting his interaction with the prisoners he is trying to defend.

1   I first met Adnan Farhan Abdul Latif soon after I filed a habeas corpus petition on his behalf in late 2004. We were sitting in an interview cell—really a retrofitted storage container—at Camp Echo in Guantánamo Bay, Cuba. Across the table, Latif sat with his arms crossed and his head down. The guards had removed his handcuffs, but when he shifted his weight his leg irons clanged and echoed in the bare room. The irons were chained to an eyebolt on the floor. Guards were stationed outside the door, and a video camera was visible in the corner.

2   Latif, a small, thin Yemeni man with a scraggly beard, had been in the prison for nearly three years. Upon his arrival in Cuba, he said, he was chained hand and foot while still in the black-out goggles and ear muffs he had been forced to wear for the flight. Soldiers kicked him, hit him, and dislocated his shoulder. Early on, interrogators questioned him with a gun to his head. Latif spent his first weeks at Camp X-Ray in an open-air cage, exposed to the tropical sun, without shade or shelter from the wind that buffered him with sand and pebbles. His only amenities were a bucket for water and another for urine and feces.

3   "This is an island of hell," he told me. Punishment for minor infractions of rules, such as squirreling away lunch food, included solitary confinement. No comfort items. No mattress. No pants.

4   "They take away your pants and leave you wearing only shorts. This is to prevent the brothers from praying. It would be immodest to pray uncovered. They do it to humiliate us," said Latif. Dressed in a pullover shirt and cotton pants dyed iconic Gitmo orange, he looked pale, weak and much older than his 28 years. He had been seeking medical treatment in Pakistan for a 1994 head injury when Pakistani forces detained him and turned him over to the United States for a $5,000 bounty. His health was deteriorating at Guantánamo.

5   Despairing of ever being released, Latif had sent a number of poems in his letters to me and other lawyers representing Guantánamo detainees. The Pentagon refuses to allow most of them to be made public, but it did clear "Hunger Strike Poem," which contains the lines:

They are artists of torture,
They are artists of pain and fatigue,
They are artists of insults
and humiliation.
Where is the world to save us
from torture?
Where is the world to save us
from the fire and sadness?
Where is the world to save
the hunger strikers?

6   The military won't let you read the rest of Latif's poetry.

7   *Poems from Guantánamo,* a collection of 22 poems written in the cages of Guantánamo, was published with great difficulty in August 2007. Six of the seventeen poets—all of whom, like the entire camp population, are Muslim—have been released to their home countries, but most, including Latif, are now in their sixth year of captivity in conditions harsher than "super maximum" security in U.S. prisons. They wrote their poems with little expectation of ever reaching an audience beyond a small circle of their fellow prisoners. My colleagues and I, all volunteer lawyers, first visited Guantánamo in November 2004 after receiving "secret" level security clearances from the FBI. We knew little about our prospective clients, due to the Bush administration's disinformation campaign that to this day includes the refrain that the prisoners "were picked up on battlefields fighting against our troops." (The reality, according to the military's own documents, is that only 8 percent of the prisoners are accused of being al-Qaeda, and only 5 percent were captured by U.S. forces on the battlefields of Afghanistan.)

8   What we learned from our clients on that trip was shocking. During the three years in which they had been held in total isolation, they had been subjected repeatedly to stress positions, sleep deprivation, blaring music, and extremes of heat and cold during endless interrogations. Female interrogators smeared simulated menstrual blood onto the chests of some detainees and sexually taunted them, fully aware of the insult they were meting out to devout Muslims. They were denied basic medical care. They were broken down and psychologically tyrannized, kept in extreme isolation, threatened with rendition, interrogated at gunpoint and told that their families would be harmed if they refused to talk. They were also frequently prevented from engaging in their daily prayers—one of the five pillars of Islam—and forced to witness U.S. soldiers intentionally mishandling the holy Koran.

9   "I've lost hope of being released," Latif told me on one visit. Three days before, he explained, he'd been visited by an "Immediate Reaction Force" team. A half-dozen soldiers in body armor, carrying shields and batons, had forcibly extracted him from his cell. His offense: stepping over a line, painted on the floor of his cell, while his lunch was being passed through the food slot of his door.

10   "Suddenly the riot police came," he recounted. "No one in the cellblock knew who for. They closed all the windows except mine. A female soldier came in with a big can of pepper spray. Eventually I figured out they were coming for me. She sprayed me. I couldn't breathe. I fell down. I put a mattress over my head. I thought I was dying. They opened the door. I was lying on the bed but they were kicking and hitting me with the shields. They put my head in the toilet. They put me on a stretcher and carried me away."

11   On my third trip to Guantánamo, Latif told me he had begun a hunger strike more than a month earlier. (The military calls it a "voluntary fast." Latif is currently in his sixth month of "fasting.") Twice a day, the guards immobilize Latif's head, strap his arms and legs to a special restraint chair, and force-feed him a liquid nutrient by inserting a tube up his nose and into his stomach—a clear violation of international standards. The feeding, Latif says, "is like having a dagger shoved down your throat."

12   At first, there was little we could do with any of this information. Anything our clients told us, military officials explained, represented a potential national security threat and therefore could not be revealed to the public until cleared by a Pentagon "Privilege Review Team." The review team initially used its power to suppress all evidence of abuse and mistreatment. Our notes, returned with a CLASSIFIED stamp, were deemed unsuitable for public release on the grounds that they revealed interrogation techniques that the military had a legitimate interest in keeping secret. Only threats of litigation forced the Pentagon to reconsider its classification decisions.

13   The Pentagon's reaction to the publication of *Poems from Guantánamo* has been predictable. Last June, in an article in the *Wall Street Journal,* Defense Department spokesman Cmdr. J. D. Gordon commented on the collection by saying, "While a few detainees at Guantánamo Bay have made efforts to author what they claim to be poetry, given the nature of their writings they have seemingly not done so for the sake of art. They have attempted to use this medium as merely another tool in their battle of ideas against Western democracies." Gordon had not, at the time, read the poems.

14   Perhaps the Pentagon's anxiety is justified, for the poems offer the world a glimpse of the profound psychic toll that Guantánamo has taken on the prisoners. They give voice to men whom the U.S. government has detained for more than five years without charge, trial or even the most basic protections of the Geneva Conventions. The prisoners remain entirely cut off from the world: military censors excise all references to current events from the occasional letters allowed from family members, and lawyers may not tell prisoners any personal or general news unless it "directly relates" to their cases. Indeed, dozens of prisoners have attempted suicide by hanging, by hoarding medicine and then overdosing, or by slashing their wrists. The military, in typically Orwellian fashion, has described these suicide attempts as incidents of "manipulative self-injurious behavior."

15   Many men at Guantánamo turned to writing poetry as a way to maintain their sanity, to memorialize their suffering and to preserve their humanity through acts of creation. The obstacles the prisoners have faced in composing their poems are profound. In the first year

of their detention, they were not allowed regular use of pen and paper. Undeterred, some drafted short poems on Styrofoam cups retrieved from lunch and dinner trays. Lacking writing instruments, they inscribed their words with pebbles or traced our letters with small dabs of toothpaste, then passed the "cup poems" from cell to cell. The cups were inevitably collected with the day's trash, the verses consigned to the bottom of a rubbish bin.

16   After about a year, the military granted the prisoners access to regular writing materials, and for the first time poems could be preserved. The first I saw was sent to me by Abdulsalam Ali Abdulrahman Al-Hela, a Yemeni businessman from Sana'a, who had written his verses in Arabic after extended periods in an isolation cell. The poem is a cry against the injustice of arbitrary detention and at the same time a hymn to the comforts of religions faith. Soon after reading it, I learned of a poem by Latif called "The Shout of Death." (Both of these poems remain classified.) After querying other lawyers, I realized that Guantánamo was filled with amateur poets.

17   Military officials at Guantánamo destroyed or confiscated many of the prisoners' poems before the authors could share them with their lawyers. In addition, the Pentagon refuses to allow most of the existing poems to be made public, asserting that poetry "presents a special risk" to national security due to its "content and format." The risk appears to be that the prisoners will try to smuggle coded messages out of the prison camp.

18   Still, the earliest of the poems we submitted for classification review were deemed unclassified, and it was only after the Pentagon learned that we were putting together a book of the poems that the hand of censorship came down. Hundreds of poems therefore remain suppressed by the military and will likely never be seen by the public. In addition, most of the *poems* that *have* been cleared are in English translation only, because the Pentagon believes that their original Arabic or Pashto versions represent an enhanced security risk. Because only linguists with secret-level security clearances are allowed to read our clients' communications (which are kept by court order in a secure facility in the Washington, D.C., area), it was impossible to invite experts to translate the poems for us. The translations included in the collection, therefore, cannot do justice to the subtlety and cadence of the originals.

19   Despite these and many other hurdles, 22 poems have now been published, and the voices of the prisoners in Guantánamo may now be heard. As the courts move sluggishly toward granting the prisoners fair and open hearings, and as politicians bicker about whether to extend the protections of the Geneva Conventions to the detainees, the prisoners' own words may now become part of the dialogue. Perhaps their poems will prick the conscience of a nation.

Is It True?

Osama Abu Kabir

Is it true that the grass grows again after rain?
Is it true that the flowers will rise up in the Spring?
Is it true that birds will migrate home again?
Is it true that the salmon swim back up their stream?

It is true. This is true. These are all miracles.
But is it true that one day we'll leave
Guantánamo Bay?
Is it true that one day we'll go back to our homes?
I sail in my dreams, I am dreaming of home.

To be with my children, each one part of me;
To be with my wife and the ones that I love;
To be with my parents,
my world's tenderest hearts.
I dream to be home, to be free from this cage.

But do you hear me, oh Judge, do you hear me at all?
We are innocent, here,
we've committed no crime.
Set me free, set us free, if anywhere still
Justice and compassion remain in this world!

Understanding the Content

Feel free to reread all or parts of the selection to answer the following questions.

1. Where did Marc Falkoff meet Latif? What were the circumstances surrounding their meeting?

2. What do the captors at the Guantánamo prison do to humiliate their prisoners?

3. What is the treatment of the prisoners at Guantánamo like, according to Marc Falkoff?

4. According to Falkoff, what is the purpose of the Pentagon's "Privilege Review Team"?

5. What has been the Pentagon's reaction to the publication of *Poems from Guantánamo?*

6. Why did the men imprisoned at "Gitmo" begin to write poetry, according to the author? What did military officials do with the poetry before the authors could share them with their lawyers?

Looking at Structure and Style

1. Rewrite the thesis of this selection in your own words.

2. Does Falkoff use credible evidence to support his thesis, in your opinion?

3. What is the purpose of the first two paragraphs of this selection? What is their relation to paragraph 16? To the rest of the essay?

4. What is the overall organizing pattern used in this selection?

5. Does Falkoff present a clear-cut argument in this essay? If so, what is it?

Evaluating the Author's Viewpoints

1. In your opinion, does Falkoff display any bias in this essay? Explain.

2. Did you learn anything new from this essay? Has this essay shed any light on the subject of the prison at Guantánamo Bay for you? What is your reaction to reading about the treatment of prisoners at this site?

3. Do you think that the poems written by the prisoners at Gitmo should have been published? Why or why not?

4. Do you think that the information the prisoners told their lawyers about the treatment they received "represented a potential national security threat," as the military claimed? Why or why not?

5. Do you think that what the prisoners wrote should be considered "poetry" or "art" or do you agree with the Defense Department spokesman that "they have attempted to use this medium as merely another tool in their battle of ideas against Western democracies"? Why or why not?

6. What can you infer about how Falkoff feels about the "military officials" that he describes and quotes in this selection? How can you tell?

Pursuing Possible Essay Topics

Unless you have an idea for an essay based on what you have just read, wait until after you read the following selection in this chapter and have studied the list of ideas at the end of that selection before developing an essay on the topic of Guantánamo prisoner treatment.

Preparing to Read

Take a minute or two to look over the following reading selection. Note the title and the author, read the first paragraph, and check the essay's length. Make certain you have the time now to read it carefully and to do the exercises that follow it. Then, in the spaces provided, answer the following questions.

1. What will this essay say about conditions at "Gitmo"? Will it contain different

   information than the previous essay? _____

   _____

2. What is the tone used in the opening paragraph? _____

   _____

Vocabulary

Good comprehension of what you are about to read depends upon your understanding of the words below. The number following each word refers to the paragraph where it is used.

communal (10) shared by a group of people

contingent (14) a representative group

transparency (16) completely open; visibility

ousted (19) removed by force; casted out

Pols: Gitmo Conditions Have Improved
Guantánamo Bay Naval Base, Cuba
Associated Press

The following news report filed by the Associated Press was reprinted in many newspapers and reported on television. This version is from FOXNEWS.com.

1   Progress has been made to improve conditions and protect detainees' rights at the U.S. prison for suspected terrorists, House Republicans and Democrats, including one who has advocated closing the facility, said Saturday.

2   The U.S. lawmakers witnessed interrogations, toured cell blocks and ate the same lunch given to detainees on the first congressional

visit to the prison for suspected terrorists since criticism of it intensified in the spring.

3   "The Guantanamo we saw today is not the Guantanamo we heard about a few years ago," said Rep. Ellen Tauscher, D-Calif.

4   Still, lawmakers from both parties agree more still must be done to ensure an adequate legal process is in place to handle detainee cases. In the meantime, said Rep. Joe Schwarz, R-Mich., "I think they're doing the best they can to define due process here."

5   Republicans and Democrats alike fear the prison at the U.S. Navy base in eastern Cuba is hurting the United States' image because of claims that interrogators have abused and tortured inmates. The White House and Pentagon say conditions are humane and detainees are well-treated.

6   Lawmakers wanted to see for themselves.

7   After getting a classified briefing from base commanders, the House delegation ate lunch with troops—the same meal of chicken with orange sauce, rice and okra that detainees were served. They then toured several of the barbed-wire camps where detainees are housed, viewing small cells, dusty recreation yards and common areas.

8   From behind one-way mirrors, lawmakers watched interrogators grilling three individual terror suspects. None of the interrogators touched detainees.

9   In one session, they questioned a man who defense officials said was a Saudi national and admitted Al Qaeda member who was picked up in Afghanistan and knew nine of the Sept. 11, 2001, hijackers. In another, a female interrogator took an unusual approach to wear down a detainee, reading a Harry Potter book aloud for hours. He turned his back and put his hands over his ears.

10   Bearded detainees in white frocks, flip-flops and skull caps quietly lingered nearby, although behind fences. At one communal camp for those given privileges because of good behavior, detainees played soccer.

11   Rep. Sheila Jackson Lee, D-Texas, is one of many Democrats who have called for an independent commission to investigate abuse allegations and said the facility should close. She stopped short of changing her position after the visit, but acknowledged, "What we've seen here is evidence that we've made progress."

12   The White House and Pentagon have defended their policies at the prison almost daily in recent weeks.

13   At a news conference last week, the president went so far as to invite journalists to visit the prison and see that the allegations were false. The Pentagon says about 400 news organizations have toured the prison since it opened.

14   A small press contingent joined House lawmakers on this week-end's trip. However, military escorts controlled how much journalists were able to see and hear. In an unclassified briefing, commanders stressed the "safe and humane custody and control of detainees" by troops.

15   On a tour of one camp occupied by detainees considered "high value" for providing intelligence, journalists saw no detainees but watched as troops passed meals through small cells on one block. Detainees were clearly upset at the sound of visitors, shouting non-English words and pounding on closed doors while journalists entered an interrogation room—empty except for a set of handcuffs, a folding chair, a small table and two padded office chairs.

16   Brig. Gen. Jay Hood, commander of the joint task force at Guantánamo Bay, said he's made transparency a priority. "It's probably my best, our best opportunity to set the record straight," he said.

17   Last week, human rights investigators for the United Nations urged the U.S. to allow them inside to inspect the facility. They cited "persistent and credible" reports of "serious allegations of torture, cruel, inhuman and degrading treatment of detainees" as well as arbitrary detentions and violations of rights.

18   In response, Vice President Dick Cheney told CNN on Thursday [2005] that the detainees are well treated, well fed and "living in the tropics."

19   The prison on the base in eastern Cuba opened in January 2002 to house foreigners believed to be linked to Al Qaeda or the ousted Taliban in Afghanistan. U.S. officials hoped to gather intelligence from the detainees after the U.S. invasion of Afghanistan in October 2001.

20   Bush declared the detainees "enemy combatants," affording them fewer rights than prisoners of war under the Geneva Conventions. Some detainees have been held for three years without being charged with any crimes.

Understanding the Content

Feel free to reread all or parts of the selection to answer the following questions.

1. What did U.S. lawmakers do at their visit to the Guantánamo Bay prison? What opinion did the group have after visiting the prison with regard to prisoner treatment?

2. What was the lawmakers' fear about the prison before they went there? Were their fears unfounded or proven? Or was it a little of both? Explain.

3. What role did Rep. Sheila Jackson Lee have in coordinating this visit? What was her conclusion after visiting the facility?

4. What did journalists see during their visit?

5. What did the human rights investigators for the United Nations say about "Gitmo"? What was Vice President Dick Cheney's response?

6. Why was the prison at Guantánamo Bay opened in January 2002?

Looking at Structure and Style

1. What is the thesis of this selection? Is it stated or implied? If stated, where?

2. This article is presented in 20 short paragraphs. Do any paragraphs need more explication? More detail? Or do the short paragraphs work as a whole to present the argument that "Gitmo conditions have improved"? Discuss your viewpoint.

3. Does this selection present enough credible evidence to support the contention that conditions have improved at the prison? List the evidence that the Associated Press uses to support this idea about the prison.

4. Is paragraph 20 an effective concluding paragraph, in your opinion? Why or why not? Write a conclusion which summarizes the information presented in this selection.

Evaluating the Author's Viewpoints

1. What is the tone of this essay?

2. Why do you think the author(s) of this essay repeatedly refer to both Democrats and Republicans? What is the purpose of including quotes from both political parties?

3. Compare and contrast the information that the White House disseminated regarding treatment of the prisoners with what the contingent who visited the site learned and what human rights investigators from the United Nations contended.

4. Think about this essay in relation to the previous one, "Verses of Suffering." Compare and contrast the images of Guantánamo Bay presented in each. How similar are they? How different?

5. How well does the author(s) describe the detainees? Compare and contrast this with the description of the prisoners in the previous selection.

Pursuing Possible Essay Topics

1. Which selection does a better job of characterizing the detainees or prisoners at Guantánamo Bay? Which does a better job of presenting an argument that

either condemns or defends the conditions at the prison? Why? Write an essay defending your position.

2. Do you think that the government was right or wrong in trying to delay—or prevent—the publication of the poetry by the prisoners at Guantánamo Bay? Why? Write an essay discussing your viewpoint.

3. Of the information presented in both selections, which are you more likely to believe and why? What went into your answer? Explain in writing.

 4. With a classmate or partner, discuss both selections and compare and contrast your opinion with that of your classmate(s). Write a brief synopsis of your discussion.

5. Do you think alleged terrorists should be given the same rights as any other prisoners in the United States? Why or why not? Write an essay discussing your viewpoint.

6. Brainstorm or freewrite on one or more of the following:

   a. prisoners' rights

   b. Guantánamo Bay

   c. harsh punishments

   d. terrorists

 ## Opposing Viewpoints on the Death Penalty

Capital punishment, the death penalty, is a contentious issue. Those in favor feel it helps deter crime, is less expensive than lifetime imprisonment, and is an appropriate justice for the crime committed. Those opposed to it argue that it does not deter crime, that some on "death row" are innocent of the crime, that it is prejudicial against the poor and blacks, and that it violates human rights. Most European countries, among others, have abolished the death penalty, but the United States government and 36 states still condone its use. The following selections offer different viewpoints on the subject.

Preparing to Read

Take a minute or two to look over the following reading selection. Note the title and author, read the first two paragraphs, and check the essay's length. Make certain you have the time now to read it carefully and to do the exercises that follow it. Then, in the spaces provided, answer the following questions.

1. What does the title tell you about the author's viewpoint? _____

   _____

2. What do you think you will learn about capital punishment from reading this

   selection? _____

   _____

3. Do you think you will agree with the author's viewpoint? Why? _____

   _____

Vocabulary

Good comprehension of what you are about to read depends upon your understanding of the words below. The number following each word refers to the paragraph where it is used.

clemency (1) mercy, leniency

constituencies (4) the voters represented by an elected official

heinous (4) dreadful, wicked

flagrant (6) obvious, conspicuous

sophistic (10) apparently sound but actually false

ambivalent (12) uncertain, mixed

paramount (15) primary, foremost, top of the list

Death and Justice

Edward I. Koch

Edward I. Koch—the mayor of New York City from 1977 to 1985—practiced as a lawyer until his involvement in politics. He has authored a book with William Rauch entitled Mayor.

1   Last December a man named Robert Lee Willie, who had been convicted of raping and murdering an 18-year-old woman, was executed in the Louisiana state prison. In a statement issued several minutes before his death, Mr. Willie said: "Killing people is wrong. . . . It makes no difference whether it's citizens, countries, or governments. Killing is wrong." Two weeks later in South Carolina, an admitted killer named Joseph Carl Shaw was put to death for murdering two teenagers. In an appeal to the governor for clemency, Mr. Shaw wrote: "Killing is wrong when I did it. Killing is wrong when you do it. I hope you have the courage and moral strength to stop the killing."

2   It is a curiosity of modern life that we find ourselves being lectured on morality by cold-blooded killers. Mr. Willie previously had been convicted of aggravated rape, aggravated kidnapping, and the murders of a Louisiana deputy and a man from Missouri. Mr. Shaw committed another murder a week before the two for which he was executed, and admitted mutilating the body of the 14-year-old girl he killed. I can't help wondering what prompted these murderers to speak out against killing as they entered the death-house door. Did their newfound reverence for life stem from the realization that they were about to lose their own?

3   Life is indeed precious, and I believe the death penalty helps to affirm this fact. Had the death penalty been a real possibility in the minds of these murderers, they might well have stayed their hand. They might have shown moral awareness before their victims died, and not after. Consider the tragic death of Rosa Velez, who happened to be home when a man named Luis Vera burglarized her apartment in Brooklyn. "Yeah, I shot her," Vera admitted. "She knew me, and I knew I wouldn't go to the chair."

4   During my 22 years in public service, I have heard the pros and cons of capital punishment expressed with special intensity. As a district leader, councilman, congressman, and mayor, I have represented constituencies generally thought of as liberal. Because I support the death penalty for heinous crimes of murder, I have sometimes been the subject of emotional and outraged attacks by voters who find my position reprehensible or worse. I have listened to their ideas. I have weighed their objections carefully. I still support the death penalty. The reasons I maintain my position can be best understood by examining the arguments most frequently heard in opposition.

5   (1) *The death penalty is "barbaric."* Sometimes opponents of capital punishment horrify with tales of lingering death on the gallows, of faulty electric chairs, or of agony in the gas chamber. Partly in response to such protests, several states such as North Carolina and Texas switched to execution by lethal injection. The condemned person is put to death painlessly, without ropes, voltage, bullets, or gas. Did this answer the objections of death penalty opponents? Of course

not. On June 22, 1984, *The New York Times* published an editorial that sarcastically attacked the new "hygienic" method of death by injection, and stated that "execution can never be made humane through science." So it's not the method that really troubles opponents. It's the death itself they consider barbaric.

6   Admittedly, capital punishment is not a pleasant topic. However, one does not have to like the death penalty in order to support it any more than one must like radical surgery, radiation, or chemotherapy in order to find necessary these attempts at curing cancer. Ultimately we may learn how to cure cancer with a simple pill. Unfortunately, that day has not yet arrived. Today we are faced with the choice of letting the cancer spread or trying to cure it with the methods available, methods that one day will almost certainly be considered barbaric. But to give up and do nothing would be far more barbaric and would certainly delay the discovery of an eventual cure. The analogy between cancer and murder is imperfect, because murder is not the "disease" we are trying to cure. The disease is injustice. We may not like the death penalty, but it must be available to punish crimes of cold-blooded murder, cases in which any other form of punishment would be inadequate and, therefore, unjust. If we create a society in which injustice is not tolerated, incidents of murder—the most flagrant form of injustice—will diminish.

7   (2) *No other major democracy uses the death penalty.* No other major democracy—in fact, few other countries of any description—is plagued by a murder rate such as that in the United States. Fewer and fewer Americans can remember the days when unlocked doors were the norm and murder was a rare and terrible offense. In America the murder rate climbed 122 percent between 1963 and 1980. During that same period, the murder rate in New York City increased by almost 400 percent, and the statistics are even worse in many other cities. A study at M.I.T. showed that based on 1970 homicide rates a person who lived in a large American city ran a greater risk of being murdered than an American soldier in World War II ran of being killed in combat. It is not surprising that the laws of each country differ according to differing conditions and traditions. If other countries had our murder problem, the cry for capital punishment would be just as loud as it is here. And I daresay that any other major democracy where 75 percent of the people supported the death penalty would soon enact it into law.

8   (3) *An innocent person might be executed by mistake.* Consider the work of Adam Bedau, one of the most implacable foes of capital punishment in this country. According to Mr. Bedau, it is "false sentimentality to argue that the death penalty should be abolished because of the abstract possibility that an innocent person might be executed." He cites a study of the 7,000 executions in this country from 1893 to 1971, and concludes that the record fails to show that such cases

occur. The main point, however, is this. If government functioned only when the possibility of error didn't exist, government wouldn't function at all. Human life deserves special protection, and one of the best ways to guarantee that protection is to assure that convicted murderers do not kill again. Only the death penalty can accomplish this end. In a recent case in New Jersey, a man named Richard Biegenwald was freed from prison after serving 18 years for murder; since his release he has been convicted of committing four murders. A prisoner named Lemuel Smith, while serving four life sentences for murder (plus two life sentences for kidnapping and robbery) in New York's Green Haven Prison, lured a woman corrections officer into the chaplain's office and strangled her. He then mutilated and dismembered her body. An additional life sentence for Smith is meaningless. Because New York has no death penalty statute, Smith has effectively been given a license to kill.

9   But the problem of multiple murder is not confined to the nation's penitentiaries. In 1981, 91 police officers were killed in the line of duty in this country. Seven percent of those arrested in the cases that have been solved had a previous arrest for murder. In New York City in 1976 and 1977, 85 persons arrested for homicide had a previous arrest for murder. Six of these individuals had two previous arrests for murder, and one had four previous murder arrests. During those two years the New York police were arresting for murder persons with a previous arrest for murder on the average of one every 8.5 days. This is not surprising when we learn that in 1975, for example, the median time served in Massachusetts for homicide was less than two-and-a-half years. In 1976 a study sponsored by the Twentieth Century Fund found that the average time served in the United States for first-degree murder is ten years. The median time served may be considerably lower.

10   (4) *Capital punishment cheapens the value of human life.* On the contrary, it can be easily demonstrated that the death penalty strengthens the value of human life. If the penalty for rape were lowered, clearly it would signal a lessened regard for the victims' suffering, humiliation, and personal integrity. It would cheapen their horrible experience, and expose them to an increased danger of recurrence. When we lower the penalty for murder, it signals a lessened regard for the value of the victim's life. Some critics of capital punishment, such as columnist Jimmy Breslin, have suggested that a life sentence is actually a harsher penalty for murder than death. This is sophistic nonsense. A few killers may decide not to appeal a death sentence, but the overwhelming majority make every effort to stay alive. It is by exacting the highest penalty for the taking of human life that we affirm the highest value of human life.

11   (5) *The death penalty is applied in a discriminatory manner.* This factor no longer seems to be the problem it once was. The appeals

process for a condemned prisoner is lengthy and painstaking. Every effort is made to see that the verdict and sentence were fairly arrived at. However, assertions of discrimination are not an argument for ending the death penalty but for extending it. It is not justice to exclude everyone from the penalty of the law if a few are found to be so favored. Justice requires that the law be applied equally to all.

12   (6) *Thou Shalt Not Kill.* The Bible is our greatest source of moral inspiration. Opponents of the death penalty frequently cite the sixth of the Ten Commandments in an attempt to prove that capital punishment is divinely proscribed. In the original Hebrew, however, the Sixth Commandment reads, "Thou Shalt Not Commit Murder," and the Torah specifies capital punishment for a variety of offenses. The biblical viewpoint has been upheld by philosophers throughout history. The greatest thinkers of the 19th century—Kant, Locke, Hobbes, Rousseau, Montesquieu, and Mill—agreed that natural law properly authorizes the sovereign to take life in order to vindicate justice. Only Jeremy Bentham was ambivalent. Washington, Jefferson, and Franklin endorsed it. Abraham Lincoln authorized executions for deserters in wartime. Alexis de Tocqueville, who expressed profound respect for American institutions, believed that the death penalty was indispensable to the support of social order. The United States Constitution, widely admired as one of the seminal achievements in the history of humanity, condemns cruel and inhuman punishment, but does not condemn capital punishment.

13   (7) *The death penalty is state-sanctioned murder.* This is the defense with which Messrs. Willie and Shaw hoped to soften the resolve of those who sentenced them to death. By saying in effect, "You're no better than I am," the murderer seeks to bring his accusers down to his own level. It is also a popular argument among opponents of capital punishment, but a transparently false one. Simply put, the state has rights that the private individual does not. In a democracy, those rights are given to the state by the electorate. The execution of a lawfully condemned killer is no more an act of murder than is legal imprisonment an act of kidnapping. If an individual forces a neighbor to pay him money under threat of punishment, it's called extortion. If the state does it, it's called taxation. Rights and responsibilities surrendered by the individual are what give the state its power to govern. This contract is the foundation of civilization itself.

14   Everyone wants his or her rights, and will defend them jealously. Not everyone, however, wants responsibilities, especially the painful responsibilities that come with law enforcement. Twenty-one years ago a woman named Kitty Genovese was assaulted and murdered on a street in New York. Dozens of neighbors heard her cries for help but did nothing to assist her. They didn't even call the police. In such a climate the criminal understandably grows bolder. In the presence of

moral cowardice, he lectures us on our supposed failings and tries to equate his crimes with our quest for justice.

15   The death of anyone—even a convicted killer—diminishes us all. But we are diminished even more by a justice system that fails to function. It is an illusion to let ourselves believe that doing away with capital punishment removes the murderer's deed from our conscience. The rights of society are paramount. When we protect guilty lives, we give up innocent lives in exchange. When opponents of capital punishment say to the state: "I will not let you kill in my name," they are also saying to murderers: "You can kill in your *own* name as long as I have an excuse for not getting involved."

16   It is hard to imagine anything worse than being murdered while neighbors do nothing. But something worse exists. When those same neighbors shrink back from justly punishing the murderer, the victim dies twice.

Understanding the Content

Feel free to reread all or parts of the selection to answer the following questions.

1. What argument *for* the death penalty does Koch give for each of the following arguments against?
   a. "The death penalty is 'barbaric'" (5).
   b. "No other major democracy uses the death penalty" (7).
   c. "An innocent person might be executed by mistake" (8).
   d. "Capital punishment cheapens the value of human life" (10).
   e. "The death penalty is applied in a discriminatory manner" (11).
   f. "Thou Shalt Not Kill" (12).

2. What do you learn about the author in the essay? Why does he tell you about himself?

3. Is Koch's argument based mostly on fact or on opinion? Explain.

4. What does Koch mean when he says, "the victim dies twice" (16) if the murderer isn't justly punished?

Looking at Structure and Style

1. Is the thesis stated or implied? If stated, where?

2. What is the point of quoting the two convicted murderers on death row in paragraph 1? Is this an effective technique? Explain.

3. Koch chooses to defend capital punishment by refuting what he says are the most prevalent arguments of those who oppose the death penalty. Is this a good method? Does it make him seem more knowledgeable on the subject? Explain.

4. What is the function of paragraph 4?

5. How well does the author use outside sources to reinforce his arguments? What are some of his sources?

Evaluating the Author's Viewpoints

1. Koch says, "If we create a society in which injustice is not tolerated, incidents of murder—the most flagrant form of injustice—will diminish" (6). Do you agree? Why or why not?

2. Do you agree with Koch's distinction between murder and capital punishment? Why or why not?

3. Do you agree with the analogies he draws in paragraph 13 about imprisonment versus kidnapping and taxation versus extortion (blackmail)? Are these good analogies? Explain.

4. How well does Koch conclude his essay? Is he convincing? Explain.

5. Look through the essay for the following:
   a. factual statements that support the author's thesis
   b. opinions or emotional appeals that support the thesis
   c. the most convincing argument for the thesis
   d. the weakest argument for the thesis

Pursuing Possible Essay Topics

Wait until you have read the following selection in this chapter and have studied the list of ideas at the end of that selection before developing an essay on capital punishment.

Preparing to Read

Take a minute or two to look over the following reading selection. Note the title and author, read the first two paragraphs, and check the length. Make certain you have the time now to read it carefully and to do the exercises that follow it. Then, in the spaces provided, answer the following questions.

1. Do you think the death penalty issue is a moral issue? _____

_____

2. What arguments do you think the author may use to support his position?

_____

_____

Vocabulary

Good comprehension of what you are about to read depends upon your understanding of the words below. The number following each word refers to the paragraph where it is used.

moratorium (1) a suspension of action

affronts (2) insults, offends

sentient (2) aware, conscious, having feeling

abhorrent (4) awful, detestable

de facto (4) actually, in fact, in reality

noncomplicity (6) noninvolvement

miscreants (7) delinquents, lawbreakers

modicum (13) little, small amount

restitution (15) compensation, reimbursement

Casting the First Stone

LLOYD STEFFEN

Lloyd Steffen is a Professor of Religious Studies and University Chaplain at Lehigh University in Pennsylvania. He contributes to professional and academic journals and writes a daily newspaper column for The Morning Call. *Among his latest books is* Executing Justice: The Moral Meaning of the Death Penalty. *The following selection appeared in* Christianity and Crisis.

1   Once again, America has made its peace with capital punishment. Since the moratorium on executions was lifted in 1975, courts and state legislatures have worked hard, and successfully, to reinstate the death penalty. Politically, the issue is no longer even interesting. As the 1988 presidential debates showed, what public debate exists around capital punishment is likely to be about its effectiveness as social policy, not with its status as a *moral* (or even legal) problem. And as social policy opinion polls tell us, America approves of the death penalty. Indeed, it seems to satisfy the American sense of justice and fair play. Given this context, it might seem futile even to ask whether capital punishment can still *be* a moral problem.

2   Yet even though opponents of capital punishment are in the minority today, they should not allow themselves to be placed on the defensive. A burden of moral proof in the debate over capital punishment still must be borne by those who support it. The death penalty must still be questioned as a moral act because it affronts the moral principle that the deliberate and premeditated taking of fully sentient human life is wrong. Therefore, it falls to those who support it to argue convincingly that killing convicted criminals is morally justifiable and not fundamentally destructive of the moral presumption against such killing.

3   Failure to debate the moral justifications for capital punishment could well lead to a situation where the practice of executing criminals is simply taken for granted. We may no longer demand a *particular* argument for capital punishment, one that is rationally compelling and able to withstand serious challenges; rather, we may come to assume that such an argument exists—somewhere. We could then justify the death penalty by the kind of moral "intuition" that concludes: "If it were really wrong we would not do it." At that point, capital punishment becomes a noncontroversial issue. . . .

The Innocence of the State

4   Once a society decides that it is useful to kill people—even people guilty of morally abhorrent acts—sanctity-of-life questions are no longer even arguable, since human life is de facto not sacred. Only those societies or states that have convinced themselves they can act as if they possessed absolute innocence can assume, in good conscience, the power to make premeditated killing a useful means to political and social ends. And, as history shows, when such states or societies acquire the power to decide which acts constitute crimes deserving death, the inevitable criterion is this: those acts that challenge the idea of absolute innocence.

5   Capital punishment is always potentially an instrument of social repression and political terrorism. As we have seen in China and Iran,

when the state claims the power to impose this punishment, it is not the notorious on whom death is most likely to be inflicted, but the nameless and obscure. Even though Americans who support the death penalty can express outrage over the executions that have occurred in these faraway places, the fact is that the 2000 condemned persons currently sitting on America's death rows are also nameless and obscure. The difference is that Americans can apparently justify killing those who disrupt our social order because our social order is "morally superior."

6   The myth of American innocence has suffered greatly in recent years. Yet it persists. Manifest destiny is still alive in the American consciousness. The myth of moral purity continues to affect how we who are not guilty separate ourselves from those who are; and those who are guilty continue to be predominantly poor, male, members of minority groups, now even those with mental disabilities. Are these people so painful a reminder of our national failure that we have deceived ourselves into thinking our innocence can be maintained if they are eliminated? Is capital punishment so popular today because it stands as a symbol of noncomplicity in antisocial acts? Does it serve the national will by perpetuating the illusion of American innocence, which is, after all, our ideological heritage?

7   My arguments, however, may seem to miss the point. Clearly the moral passion in support of the death penalty comes not from thinking about capital punishment in abstract ways, but as a just means of retribution for individual crimes perpetrated by individual miscreants on individual victims. Nonetheless, I want to interject a caution. While individual stories certainly activate the moral imagination, dangers always exist in allowing them to govern our thinking about issues that have profound social implications. Individual stories appeal to definite moral principles even if the principles themselves are not articulated, and when we appeal to them rather than to a formal moral argument, we beg questions regarding which principles should be invoked to help us decide that one story rather than another should govern behavior and guide action. Despite these problems, I can still imagine advocates of capital punishment defending their position simply by saying "What about Theodore Bundy?"

An Irrevocable Penalty

8   Bundy, who died in 1989 in Florida's electric chair, is as strong an anecdotal defense of capital punishment as we could find: A mass murderer who killed innocent women in several states, Bundy appeared to be a moral incorrigible, one who killed repeatedly and without inhibition, and who provided investigators with information about many of his unsolved crimes only because it was the last card he could play to postpone his execution. Seemingly incapable of remorse, Bundy was unquestionably guilty of the crimes for which

he had been convicted and many for which he hadn't. If anyone embodies the kind of moral monster who deserves the most severe punishment society can inflict, Ted Bundy did.

9   But if Ted Bundy's story "argues" for capital punishment, James Richardson's argues even more strongly against it.

10   In 1968, Richardson, a black Florida fruit picker, was tried and convicted of killing his seven children. Richardson allegedly had taken out insurance policies the night before the murder. While this established motive sufficient to convince a jury of his guilt, neither the defense attorney nor the prosecutor pointed out that the unpaid policies were not in effect when the children died. When Richardson's three cell mates were brought in to testify that he had confessed the crime to them, no one bothered to mention that the sheriff had promised the three reduced jail time for their testimony. The one surviving witness of the three has finally admitted that Richardson never made such a confession.

11   Richardson's lie detector results disappeared and were never disclosed, and the polygraph operator who administered another test to him in prison stated that he had "no involvement in the crime whatsoever."

12   Richardson's next-door neighbor actually poisoned the children while Richardson and his wife were working in the fields. Yet she was never called to testify. The authorities did not want the jury to know that her first husband had died mysteriously after eating a dinner she had prepared or that she had actually served four years in prison for killing her second husband. The woman, incidentally, after being admitted to a nursing home, confessed to staff there that she was the guilty party, but the staff, fearing loss of their jobs, did not report her confession to superiors. And the former assistant prosecutor in the town of Arcadia, where Richardson was tried, deliberately concealed over 900 pages of evidence that would have brought all of these facts to light. It took an actual theft to get these documents into the hands of *Miami Herald* reporters. Once there, the case was reopened, and after spending 21 years in prison for a crime he did not commit, James Richardson was released.

13   Richardson may not have been executed, but his is a story about capital punishment nonetheless. For he was sentenced to death, sat for four years on death row, and was even put through a harrowing "dry run" execution, complete with a shaving and a buckle-down in the chair. Richardson was not only a poor black man who received an inept defense. He was also an innocent man who was made a victim of lies, deceit, perjured testimony, false witnesses—and those who prosecuted him and knew of his innocence still demanded that he be executed. What the Richardson case points out is that the death penalty always holds the potential for interfering mightily with justice. In

the Richardson case, guilt lies with the accusers, and the irrevocable nature of the death penalty would have prevented Richardson from receiving even the modicum of justice he finally did receive. Despite being the result of a legal process, his death would have constituted an unjustified killing—an actual murder.

Justice and Social Murder

14   How is justice to be exacted when a murder is committed by all of society? Is guilt to attach only to the sheriff and prosecutor in the case? Would those two be appropriate targets for the death penalty today since they violated the moral prohibition against the taking of human life and sought deliberately and with premeditation to kill an innocent man—the crime for which we wish to impose death fairly and without caprice? That these events can occur leads to a question: Is killing a Theodore Bundy so necessary that we should accept the risk capital punishment poses to a James Richardson?

15   Supporters of capital punishment will say justice prevailed; Richardson did not die, and the case poses no challenge. I say, however, that Richardson's case is a fundamental challenge to capital punishment, since the only good thing to come out of the situation is the simple fact that he did not die. His innocence might have come to light even if he had been killed, so it is life, not just truth, that is at stake. Only the simple fact that Richardson is alive makes possible any hope for his seeking restitution from a system that at one point forsook justice and actually conspired to kill him.

No Moral Certainty

16   If Richardson had been executed and the truth found out, we might not even be asking whether it is morally permissible to continue a practice that by its very nature runs the risk of committing murder and depriving persons of any opportunity to redress injustice. Were Richardson dead, we would be facing social complicity in his death and probably looking for a way to justify his death in order to make it something other than murder. We would be defending ourselves with the very truths we refused to acknowledge to him: that our system of justice is fallible, that our knowledge and judgment can be swayed and distorted, that our moral certainty is neither pure nor absolute.

Understanding the Content

Feel free to reread all or parts of the selection to answer the following questions.

1. What is Steffen's basic argument against capital punishment?

2. When, according to Steffen, might capital punishment become a noncontroversial issue? Why does he want to put its supporters on the defensive and keep it an issue?

3. Why does Steffen take to task those supporters of the death penalty in this country who express outrage over executions that occur in other countries?

4. What caution does Steffen raise for those who feel the death penalty is just retribution for those who take another's life?

5. Who was Theodore Bundy? Who was James Richardson? What point does Steffen make with these two names? Why does Steffen feel that "Richardson's case is a fundamental challenge to capital punishment" (15)?

Looking at Structure and Style

1. What is Steffen's thesis? Is it stated or implied? If stated, where?

2. How well does Steffen support his thesis? Are his arguments reasonable and persuasive?

3. What is the function of paragraph 5? What does it have to do with Steffen's thesis?

4. What writing pattern is used in paragraph 12? Does it work well and provoke thought?

5. This essay was written in 1990. Is the content dated? Explain.

6. How well does Steffen anticipate the arguments of those with opposing views?

Evaluating the Author's Viewpoints

1. Steffen's claims that "Americans can apparently justify killing those who disrupt our social order because our social order is 'morally superior'" to that in "faraway places" (5). Is he right? Explain.

2. According to Steffen, "Once a society decides that it is useful to kill people—even people guilty of morally abhorrent acts—sanctity-of-life questions are no longer even arguable, since human life is de facto not sacred" (4). Do you agree? Why or why not?

3. Steffen sees the issue of the death penalty as a moral one. Do you agree? Explain.

4. Steffen asks, "How is justice to be exacted when a murder is committed by all of society?" (14). As a member of society, are you indirectly committing murder when someone is executed through the death penalty?

5. Which argument is better presented, Steffen's or Koch's? Explain your answer.

Pursuing Possible Essay Topics

1. Pick one of the essays on capital punishment and write an argument against the author's viewpoint. Show the fallacies (examples of false or incorrect reasoning) in the argument. Or, agree with one of the authors, but provide your own arguments. Use quotations from the essay to which you are reacting.

2. Write an essay that outlines your opinion of when the death penalty is and is not appropriate.

3. Between 1930 and 1977, 3,859 people were legally executed in the United States. Of this number a slight majority were African Americans, a proportion that is far above blacks' share of the population. Coretta Scott King, Martin Luther King, Jr.'s widow, and others have argued that there is racial discrimination when applying the death penalty. Do some research on the number of legal executions since 1977. Do current statistics imply racial discrimination?

4. In a 1986 Gallup poll, 70 percent of the people polled were in favor of the death penalty. Between 1977 and 1987, 37 states passed new death-penalty laws. Twenty years earlier, a slight majority opposed the death penalty. Should laws regarding the death penalty change based on popular opinion? Are most people well informed enough to make intelligent decisions on the subject? How important are emotions in making such a decision?

5. Brainstorm or freewrite on one or more of the following:

   a. death row

   b. degrees of murder

   c. death penalty as deterrent

   d. "an eye for an eye"

   e. punishment for crimes

   f. legal loopholes

6. If you don't like any of these ideas, write an essay on some other aspect of capital punishment.

Viewpoints on Images

Research the methods that the different states use for execution. Write an essay discussing the way executions are carried out in your state and your viewpoint on such methods.

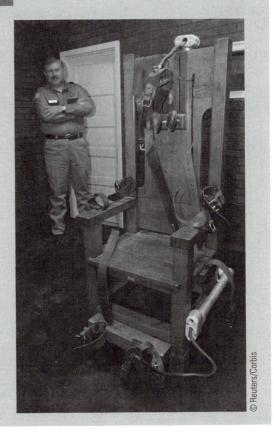

© Reuters/Corbis

On the Net

Choose one or more of the topics included in this chapter—torture, prisoner treatment at Guantánamo Bay, or capital punishment—and find two Web sites related to each. One Web site should be a "pro" Web site, the other a "con" Web site. Answer the following questions:

1. Do you think the sites are biased in their reporting on the issue (or issues) they are devoted to? Why or why not? How can you tell?

2. Which site does a better job of making an argument either for, or against, the topic it covers? Why?

Write a short essay describing which site you think is better organized and better supported—regardless of what you think about the opinion(s) held by the site's creator(s)—and how you think the other site could be better.

3. On the Internet, research the current state of the prisoners being held at Guantánamo Bay. What, if anything, has changed since the articles in *Viewpoints* were written? Write an essay on the current state of affairs for "Gitmo" prisoners.

Quoting and Documenting Sources

Quoting Sources

Quotations from other sources are basically used for one of three reasons:

1. they contain authoritative information or ideas that support or help explain your thesis,

2. they contain ideas you want to argue against or prove wrong, or

3. they are so well written that they make your point better than your own explanation could.

However, before you use any quotations, ask yourself what purpose they serve. Too many quotations can be confusing and distracting to a reader. Also, quotations should not be used as substitutes for your own writing.

There are several ways of quoting your source material. One way is to quote an entire sentence, such as:

> In her article "The State of American Values," Susanna McBee claims, "The recent *U.S. News & World Report* survey findings show that the questions of morality are troubling ordinary people."

Notice that the title and author of the quotation are provided before the quotation is given. Never use a quotation without providing a lead-in or context for it. Usually, verbs such as "says," "explains," "states," or "writes" are used to lead into a quotation. In this case, it is "claims." Notice, too, the placement of punctuation marks, especially the comma after "claims" and the closing quotation marks after the period.

Another way to quote sources is to incorporate part of a quotation into your own writing:

> In her article "The State of American Values," Susanna McBee claims that a recent survey conducted by *U.S. News & World Report* shows that "the questions of morality are troubling ordinary people."

Quotation marks are placed only around McBee's exact words. Because her words are used as part of the writer's sentence, the first word from McBee's quotation is not capitalized. Notice the way the quotation marks are placed at the beginning and end of the quotation being used.

At times, you may want to make an indirect quotation. Indirect quotations do not require the use of quotation marks because you are paraphrasing, that is, rewriting the information using your own words. Notice how the McBee quotation is paraphrased here:

> In her article "The State of American Values," Susanna McBee states that according to a recent survey conducted by *U.S. News & World Report,* the average person is bothered by what is and isn't moral.

When the exact wording of a quotation is not vital, it is better to paraphrase the quotation. However, be sure you do not change the meaning of the quotation or imply something that is not stated there. When paraphrasing, you must still provide the reader with the source of the information you paraphrase.

When direct quotations are more than five lines in length, don't use quotation marks. Instead, indent the quoted material ten spaces from the left and right margins and skip a line. This is called a **block quote,** and it shows that the quotation is not part of your own writing:

> In her article "The State of American Values," Susanna McBee con-
> cludes by stating:
>
> > Where individuals should be cautious, warn social scientists
> > and theologians, is in forcing their standards upon others.
> > In the words of Rev. McKinley Young of Big Bethel AME Church
> > of Atlanta: "When you find somebody waving all those flags
> > and banners, watch closely. Morality, if you're not careful,
> > carries a sense of self-righteousness. Whenever you pat
> > yourself on the back, it creates all kinds of cramps."

Here, quotation marks are not needed for the McBee quotation. But because McBee's quoted statement contains a quotation by someone else, those quotation marks must be included in the block quote. This is an example of a quotation within a quotation.

Try to avoid quotations within quotations that are shorter than five lines. They are awkward to follow. But if you do need to use them, here is the way:

> McBee concludes by saying, "In the words of Rev. McKinley Young of
> Big Bethel AME Church of Atlanta: 'Morality ... carries a sense of
> self-righteousness. Whenever you pat yourself on the back, it creates
> all kinds of cramps.'"

Notice the position of the first set of quotation marks (")—just before the beginning of the McBee quotation. Then, when McBee begins quoting Young's words, a single quotation mark (') is used. Because the entire quotation ends with a quote within a quote, a single quotation mark must be used to show the end of Young's words, followed by a double quotation mark to show the end of McBee's words. You can see why it's best to avoid this structure if possible.

Look in the example above at the use of what looks like three periods (. . .) between the words "Morality" and "carries." This is called an **ellipsis.** An ellipsis is used to indicate that part of the quotation has been left out. When part of a quote is not important to your point, you may use an ellipsis to shorten the quoted material. Be sure, however, that you haven't changed the meaning of the original quotation. Furthermore, always make certain that the remaining quoted material is a complete thought or sentence, as in the example.

Sometimes quoted material requires adding or clarifying information. Using square brackets within the quoted material allows you to insert information without changing the material you are quoting. In the following example, the writer quotes a passage with the pronoun "she," which refers to someone's name in a previous unquoted sentence. Brackets are used to insert the person's name.

The latest bone-density test scores revealed that she [Alice Cooper] had raised her percentage points by 11 percent.

Documenting Sources

Most English instructors require that you document your sources by following the guidelines of the Modern Language Association (MLA). The following examples show how to document most of the sources you would probably use. However, it is not complete, so you may want to consult the *MLA Handbook for Writers of Research Papers* for further information.

When you use quotations or paraphrase or summarize someone else's material, you must identify your sources. Documenting your sources lets your readers know that the information and ideas of others are not your own. It also lets readers know where more information on your subject can be found in case they choose to read your sources for themselves. You cite your sources in two places: in your paper after the quotation and at the end of your paper under the heading "Works Cited."

Citing Within the Paper

For example, here is how you would document the sources of the quotations mentioned earlier.

> In her article "The State of American Values," Susanna McBee claims, "The recent *U.S. News & World Report* survey findings show that the questions of morality are troubling ordinary people" (54).

The number in parentheses (54) refers to the page number in the McBee article where the quotation can be found. Since the author and article title are provided in the lead-in to the quote, only the page number is needed at the end. Readers can consult the "Works Cited" section at the end of your paper to learn where and when the article appeared. Notice that when the sentence ends with a quotation, the parentheses and page number go *after* the quotation marks and *before* the period.

When paraphrasing a quotation, use the following citation form:

> In her article "The State of American Values," Susanna McBee states that according to a recent survey conducted by *U.S. News & World Report*, the average person is bothered by what is and isn't moral (54).

Here the parentheses and page number go after the last word and before the period.

If the quote is not identified by author, the author's name should be included in the parentheses along with the page number. For example:

> A recent survey shows that the average person is bothered by what should be considered moral (McBee 54).

By including the author's name and page number, you let the reader know where to look in the "Works Cited" section for the complete documentation information.

Works Cited

All the sources used for writing the paper should be listed alphabetically by the author's last name in the "Works Cited" section. If no author's name appears on the work, then alphabetize it using the first letter of the first word of the title, unless it begins with an article (*a, an, the*). Here are the proper forms for the more basic sources. Note especially the punctuation and spacing.

Books by one author:

> Ford, Richard. *The Lay of the Land*. New York: Knopf, 2006.

A colon is used after the name of the city where the publisher is located, followed by the publisher's name. Book publishers' names can be shortened to conserve space. For instance, the full name of the publisher in the example above is Simon and Schuster. A comma is used before the date and a period after it. Book and magazine titles should be italicized; however, if you have no access to an italicized font, underline the title.

If two or more books by the same author are listed, you do not need to provide the name again. Use three hyphens instead. For example:

> ---. *Independence Day*. New York: Knopf, 2001.

Books by two to four authors:

Crowley, Sharon, and Debra Hawhee. *Ancient Rhetorics for Contemporary Students*. 3rd ed. New York: Pearson, 2004.

The same punctuation is used, but only the name of the first author listed on the book's title page is inverted. The authors' names are separated by a comma.

Books by more than four authors:

Savage, Alicia, et al. *Troubling Times for America*. Oxnard: Catalonia, 2007.

The Latin phrase *et al.*, which means "and others," can be used in place of all but the name of the first author listed on the book's title page. Notice its placement and the use of punctuation before and after. However, it is considered better form to list all of the contributing authors when possible.

Books that are edited:

King, Nancy M. P., Ronald P Strauss, and Larry R. Churchill, eds. *The Social Medicine Reader: Patients, Doctors, and Illness*. 2nd ed. Durham: Duke UP, 2005.

The citation is the same as for authored books except for the insertion of *ed.* to signify that the book was edited rather than authored by the person named. If there is more than one editor, follow the same form as for authors, inserting *eds.* after the last editor's name.

Magazine articles:

Carr, Nicholas. "Is Google Making Us Stupid?" *Atlantic*. Jul/Aug 2008: 56-63.

When citing magazine articles, use abbreviations for the month. The order of the listing is (1) author, (2) article title, (3) magazine title, (4) date, and (5) page number(s) of the article. Note carefully how and where the punctuation is used.

Newspaper articles:

Riccardi, Nicholas. "High Gas Prices Hobble Cities Nationwide." *Los Angeles Times*, 30 Jun, 2008: M2.

The citation is basically the same as that for a magazine article. The difference here is that you include the letter of the newspaper section with the page number ("M2" in the sample).

Scholarly journal articles:

Manson, Aaron. "A Theology of Illness: Franz Kafka's 'A Country Doctor'." *Literature and Medicine* 24:2 (2005): 297-314.

Citation for a scholarly journal article is similar to that for a magazine article except that the journal volume number (26 in the example) is given and the date (only the year in parentheses) is cited differently. Volume numbers for journals can usually be found on the cover or on the table of contents page.

Encyclopedia articles:

"Franz Kafka." *The Columbia Encyclopedia*. 2000 ed.

Since encyclopedias are written by many staff authors, no author can be cited. Begin with the title of the section you read, then the name of the encyclopedia and the date of the edition you used. No page numbers are needed. Notice the position of the punctuation marks.

Interviews that you conducted yourself:

Stone, James. Personal Interview. 9 Jan. 2008.

Lectures:

Barthelmess, Don. "History of Diving in the Channel Island." Santa Barbara City College. 8 May 2008.

If a lecture has no title, substitute the word *Lecture*.

Movies and videos:

The Borne Ultimatum. Dir. Paul Greengrass. Perf. Matt Damon. Universal, 2007.

The listing order is title, director, actors, distributor, and year the film was made.

Television news and shows:

"Countdown." Keith Olberman. MSNBC, New York. 30 Jun. 2008.

CD-ROMs (original printed source):

West, Cornel. "The Dilemma of the Black Intellectual." *Critical Quarterly*, 29 (1987): 39–52. *MLA International Biography*. CD-ROM. SilverPlatter. Feb. 1995.

The listing order for material that has a printed version is the same as that for the printed source with the addition of the database title (italic), the publication medium, the name of the vendor (if available), and the publication date of the database.

CD-ROMs (no printed source):

Reemy, Paul. "Company Disclosures," 13 October 1995. *Compact Disclosure*. CD-ROM. Disclosure Inc. 6 June 1996.

The listing order for material that has no printed source is the author's name (if provided), the title of the material (placed in quotation marks), the date of the material, then the database information as in the example for database material with a printed version (shown above).

CD-ROMs (nonperiodical publication):

Mozart: String Quartet in C Major. CD-ROM. Santa Monica: Voyager. 1991.

An article from an online journal or magazine:

Mooney, Christopher. "Who Is Responsible?" *Christian Science Monitor*, 6 July 1995: 9. Online. Dialog. 12 Jan. 1996.

The listing order includes what you would provide for a printed source, plus the medium (such as Online), the name of the computer service (such as Dialog, CompuServe, or America Online) or network (such as Internet), and the date of access.

Web sites:

```
Nuttall, Nick. "Environmental Post-Tsunami Reconstruction in Indo-
nesia." United Nations Environment Programme. 21 June 2005. United
Nations. 29 Aug. 2005. http://www.unep.org/Documents.Multilingual/
Default.asp.
```

The listing order is the author's name, the title of the work (placed in quotation marks), the title of the Web site (italic), the date of publication or latest update, the sponsoring organization, the date accessed, and the Web site address (in angle brackets).

A publication retrieved from an electronic database:

```
Storck, Thomas. "Censorship Can Be Beneficial." Opposing Viewpoints:
Censorship. San Diego: Greenhaven Press, 1997. Original from New York:
New Oxford Press, 1996. Online. Thomson/Gale Opposing Viewpoints Re-
source Center. 29 Aug. 2005. http://galenet.galegroup.com/servlet/OVRC.
```

Note the order of listing: Use the usual format for listing the book, journal, or newspaper article, then give the medium, the name of the service, the date accessed, and a brief Web site address (in angle brackets).

Acknowledgments

Alcorn, Randy. "The Species Called Homo-Simpsons," by Randy Alcorn, as found at Noozhawk. com, November 15, 2007. Reprinted with the permission of Noozhawk.com.

Alexie, Sherman. "Superman and Me," by Sherman Alexie, from *The Most Wonderful Books: Writers on the Pleasures of Reading*, by Michael Dorris and Emilie Buchwald (eds.) (Milkweed Editions, 1997), pp. 3–6 [ISBN: 10-1571312161]. Reprinted by permission of the author.

Al-Marayati, Laila. "It Could Happen Here," by Laila Al-Marayati, *Los Angeles Times*, May 18, 2003. Reprinted by permission.

Anonymous. "How Outsourcing Can Benefit Your Business," as found at Productivitytools .info, May 10, 2008.

Associated Press. "Gitmo Conditions Have Improved" Associated Press, June 27, 2005. Reprinted by permission.

Atkins, Ace. "Shut Up About My Truck," by Ace Atkins, *Outside Magazine*, September 2007. Reprinted by permission of International Creative Management, Inc. Copyright © 2007 by Ace Atkins. First appeared in *Outside Magazine*.

Bageant, Joseph. Excerpt from "The Ballad of Lynddie England," by Joseph Bageant, from *Deer Hunting with Jesus: Dispatches from America's Class War* (Crown Publishing Group, 2007), pp. 207–209, 217–220 [ISBN: 10-0307339378]. Copyright © 2007 by Joseph L. Bageant. Used by permission of Crown Publishers, a division of Random House, Inc.

Benne, Robert and Gerald McDermott. "Speaking Out: Why Gay Marriage Would be Harmful," by Robert Benne and Gerald McDermott, *Christianity Today*, February 1, 2004. Reprinted courtesy of the authors.

Blair, Gregory. "Who Cares If Gays Marry?" by Gregory Blair, as found at www.2writers .com. Reprinted by permission of the author.

Bowden, Mark. "Lessons of Abu Ghraib," by Mark Bowden, *The Atlantic Monthly*, July/ August 2004. Copyright © 2004 by Mark Bowden. Reprinted by the permission of Dunham Literary as agent for the author. Originally published in *The Atlantic Monthly*.

Bristow, Jennie. "Binge Drinking Is a Normal Impulse," by Jennie Bristow, from *At Issue: Alcohol Abuse*, Ronnie D. Lankford (ed.) (Greenhaven Press, 2007) [10: 0737711604]. Reprinted by permission of the author.

Coates, Joseph. "The Future of the Web," by Joseph Coates, *The World and I: The Magazine for Lifelong Learners*, April 2002. Reprinted by permission of *The World And I: The Magazine for Lifelong Learners*.

Cohen, Adam. "Televising Humiliation," by Adam Cohen, *International Herald Tribune*, March 12, 2008. From *The New York Times*, March 3, 2008. Copyright © 2008 The New York Times, Inc. All rights reserved. Used by permission and protected by the Copyright Laws of the United States. The printing, copying, redistribution, or retransmission of the Material without express written permissions prohibited.

Dershowitz, Alan M. "Justice," by Alan M. Dershowitz, *Penthouse*, March 4, 2003. Reprinted by permission.

Ehrenreich, Barbara. "Cultural Baggage," by Barbara Ehrenreich, from *The Snarling Citizen: Essays* (Farrar, Straus & Giroux, 1992). Copyright © 1992 by Barbara Ehrenreich. Reprinted by permission of Farrar, Starus and Giroux, LLC.

Falkoff, Mark. "Verses of Suffering," by Mark Falkoff, *Amnesty International*, Fall 2007, pp. 16–19. This article was first published by *Amnesty International* magazine, Fall 2007 (Vol. 33, No. 3), as found at www.amnestyusa.org/magazine. Reprinted by permission of the author.

Koch, Edward I. "Death and Justice" by Edward I. Koch, from *The New Republic*, April 15, 1985. Reprinted by permission of The New Republic. Copyright © 1985 The New Republic, Inc.

Kristof, Nicholas D. and Sheryle WuDunn. "Two Cheers for Sweatshops," by Nicholas D. Kristof and Sheryle WuDunn, *New York Times Magazine*, September 24, 2000. Copyright © 2000 The New York Times, Inc. All rights reserved. Used by permission and protected by the Copyright Laws of the United States. The printing, copying, redistribution, or retransmission of the Material without express written permissions prohibited.

Lancaster, Hal. "A Father's Character, Not His Success, Shapes Kids' Careers," by Hal Lancaster, *Wall Street Journal Online*, February 27, 1996. Copyright © 1996 by Dow Jones & Company, Inc. Reproduced with permission of Dow Jones & Company, Inc. in the format Textbook via Copyright Clearance Center.

Langan, Paul. "Zero," by Paul Langan, from *Making the Most of Your Life: Eight Motivational Stories and Essays* (Townsend Press, 2008), pp. 3–13 [ISBN: 10: 1591940907]. Reprinted by permission of Townsend Press.

Latif, Adnan Farhan Abdul. "Hunger Strike Poem," by Adnan Farhan Abdul Latif, from *Poems from Guantanamo*, as it appeared in Mark Falkoff, "Verses of Suffering" from *Amnesty International*, Fall 2007, pp. 16–19. Reprinted from *Poems from Guantanamo* by the University of Iowa Press.

Pitts, Leonard. "Your Kid's Going to Pay for Cheating—Eventually," by Leonard Pitts, *Miami Herald Online*, June 20, 2002, as found at www.miami.com/mld/miamiherald/living/columniss/leonard_pitts/3502990.../printstory.js. Copyright © 2002 by McClatchy Interactive. Reproduced with permission of McClatchy Interactive West in the format Textbook via Copyright Clearance Center.

Poniewozik, James, "Calling the C-Word the C-Word," by James Poniewozik, *Time Magazine Online*, June 18, 2002, as found at www.time.com/time/columnist/printout/0,8816,263504,00.html. Copyright © 2002 Time Inc. Reprinted by permission. Time is a registered trademark of Time Inc. All rights reserved.

Quindlen, Anna. "Our Tired, Our Poor, Our Kids," by Anna Quindlen, *Newsweek*, March 12, 2001, p. 80. Reprinted by permission of International Creative Management, Inc. Copyright © 2001 by Anna Quindlen. First appeared in *Newsweek*.

Quintanilla, Michael. "The Great Divide," by Michael Quintanilla *The Los Angeles Times*, November 17, 1995, p. E7. Reprinted by permission of *The Los Angeles Times*.

Rivers, Caryl. "The Issue Isn't Sex, It's Violence," by Caryl Rivers, *The Boston Globe*. Reprinted by permission of the author.

Roffman, Deborah M. "They'll Abstain If They're Given Good Reasons," by Deborah M. Roffman, *The Washington Post*, December 12, 2004, p. B.02. Reprinted by permission of the author.

Rothschild, Mathew. "Gagging Protesters by the Manual," by Matthew Rothschild, *The Progressive*, September 2007, p. 16. Reprinted by permission from *The Progressive*, 409 E. Main St., Madison, WI.

Russo, Francine. "Your Mirror Image?" by Francine Russo, *Time*, May 29, 2005, as found at www.time.com/time/connections/article/0,9171.1066899,00.html. Copyright © 2005 Time Inc. Reprinted by permission. Time is a registered trademark of Time Inc. All rights reserved.

Semour, Mary. "Call Me Crazy, But I Have to be Myself," by Mary Seymour, *Newsweek*, July 29, 2002. Copyright © 2002 Newsweek, Inc. All rights reserved. Used by permission.

Shellenbarger, Sue. "Boys Mow Lawns, Girls Wash Dishes," by Sue Shellenbarger, *The Wall Street Journal Online*, December 8, 2006. Copyright © 2006 by Dow Jones & Company,

Index